JULES
VERNE

JULES VERNE

The Definitive Biography

WILLIAM BUTCHER
Introduction by ARTHUR C. CLARKE

THUNDER'S MOUTH PRESS
NEW YORK

Jules Verne: The Definitive Biography

Copyright © 2006 by William Butcher

Foreward Copyright © 2006 by Arthur C. Clarke

Published by
Thunder's Mouth Press
An Imprint of Avalon Publishing Group, Inc.
245 West 17th Street, 11th floor
New York, NY 10011

AVALON
publishing group incorporated

First printing, May 2006

Library of Congress Cataloging-in-Publication Data is available.

ISBN-10: 1-56025-854-3
ISBN-13: 978-1-56025-854-4

9 8 7 6 5 4 3 2 1

Book design by Maria E. Torres and Maria Fernandez

Printed in the United States of America
Distributed by Publishers Group West

Contents

ACKNOWLEDGMENTS

Thomas McCormick, Agnès Marcetteau, Christian Robin, and Ian Thompson generously and constructively commented on the drafts of this book, which gained from Colette Gallois's help and would not have been possible without the love and support of Angel Lui.

I am especially grateful for the feedback and reactions of the two leading specialists: "The most documented, detailed, and accurate biography of Jules Verne," Count Piero Godnolo della Riva, creator of the legendary Verne Collection in Amiens; and "A fascinating portrait of a flesh-and-blood human being, warts and all," Volker Dehs, author of *Jules Verne* (2005).

This volume is dedicated to the memory of pioneers Raymond Ducrest de Villeneuve, Charles-Noël Martin, and Francois Raymond and to the far-flung camaraderie of devoted Verne scholars: Jean Chesneaux, Cécile Compère, Daniel Compère, Volker Dehs, Olivier Dumas, Arthur Evans, Agnès Marcetteau, Piero Gondolo della Riva, Jean-Michel Margot, Jean-Pierre Picot, Christian Robin, and Simone Vierne.

LIST OF FIGURES

The following five maps (adapted for the present publication) are reproduced with the kind permission of Ian Thompson and Mike Shand: The
Loire downstream from Nantes; Nantes; Central Scotland and the
southern Highlands; Le Crotoy region; and West of Scotland.

LIST OF ILLUSTRATIONS

LIST OF ABBREVIATIONS

ADF: Marguerite Allotte de la Fuÿe, *Jules Verne*

b.   born

BB: Jules Verne, *Backwards to Britain*

BSJV: *Bulletin de la Société Jules Verne*

CNM: Charles-Noël Martin, *La Vie et l'oeuvre de Jules Verne* (*The Life and Works of Jules Verne*)

Int.:   *Entretiens avec Jules Verne* (Interviews)

JD: Joëlle Dusseau, *Jules Verne*

JJV: Jean Jules-Verne, *Jules Verne*

JVEST: Jean-Michel Margot (ed.), *Jules Verne en son temps* (*Jules Verne in his Time*)

Lemire: Charles Lemire, *Jules Verne*

MCY: "Memories of Childhood and Youth"

OD: Olivier Dumas, *Voyage à travers Jules Verne* (*Journey through Jules Verne*)

Poems: *Poésies inédites* (*Unpublished Poems*)

PV: Philippe Valetoux, *Jules Verne: En mer et contre tous* (*Jules Verne: At Sea and at Odds*)

RD: Raymond Ducrest de Villeneuve's untitled biography

St. M.:   Document in Verne's hand listing his journeys on the *St. Michel II* and *III*

TI: *Théâtre inédit* (*Unpublished Plays*)

Unveiling Jules Verne,
a Century after his Death

JULES VERNE HAD ALREADY BEEN DEAD for a dozen years when I was born. Yet I feel strongly connected to him, and his works of science fiction had a major influence on my own career. He is among the top five people I wish I could have met in person.

Indeed, he and H. G. Wells are the two greatest names in science fiction—between them, they established it as a distinctive literary *genre*. Although Verne (1828–1905) and Wells (1866–1946) now seem to belong to different ages, their careers actually overlapped; Verne was still alive when Wells published his finest tales.

Verne lived through a period of such rapid invention and discovery. Major technological breakthroughs—including the telegraph, railway, electricity, and the telephone—happened during his lifetime. Many other possibilities, such as heavier-than-air craft and submarines, were being discussed speculatively. Large parts of the world, hitherto unchartered and unknown to the West, were explored and documented.

But instead of merely chronicling such developments, which would have engaged an ordinary writer for a lifetime, Verne wove them into works of fiction—creating vivid scenarios and stories that have enthralled generations of readers. A century after his death, he remains the most widely translated author in the world, a distinction unlikely to be surpassed in the near future.

At the same time, as this painstakingly researched new biography shows, Verne must rank as one of the most widely distorted, censored, and mistranslated authors of all time. Dr. William Butcher, a scholar whose mastery of French gave him rare insights, draws from hundreds of original manuscripts, archival material, and other evidence to reconstruct an authentic story of the life and work of Jules Verne.

It contrasts with the familiar image of Verne we have grown accustomed to.

For example, Butcher reveals how Verne's own publisher, Pierre-Jules Hetzel, excised large chunks of the author's original writing to suit some political and social interests. Equally disturbing is the fact that most books of Jules Verne available in English have been poor translations—and to make matters worse, generations of critics have debated and judged the merits and demits of the author without ever accessing the originals (either published French versions or the original manuscripts).

This book also reminds us how prolific and versatile Verne was: he wrote some 200 works, of which only a few can be categorized as science fiction. Many were adventure stories, traveler's tales or social commentary, even though we have to acknowledge that Verne is best known for what we now consider science fiction.

In an avid reader's mind, however, these genres blur easily. The only real question is whether it's a good story. I have always believed that the primary function of any story is to entertain—not to instruct or to preach. (Every writer should remember Sam Goldwyn's words: "If you've gotta message, use Western Union.") Promoting a particular scientific concept or technology or a utopian worldview should be the secondary aim of a science fiction story. This offers us a test to discern good fiction. The acid test of any story comes when you re-read it, preferably after a lapse of some years. If it's good, the second reading is as enjoyable as the first. If it's great, the second reading is more enjoyable. And if it's a masterpiece, *it will improve with every reading*. Needless to say, there are very few masterpieces—in or out of science fiction.

From the Earth to the Moon (1865) is one Verne story that I have found to have enduring entertainment value—even if some of its scientific premises were slightly dubious, especially the idea of shooting people to space from a mammoth cannon. It is difficult to say how seriously Verne took this idea, because so much of the story is face-tiously written. Probably he believed that if such a large gun could be built, it might be capable of sending a projectile to the moon, but it seems unlikely that he seriously imagined that any of the occupants would have survived the shock of takeoff.

However, in several other respects Verne demonstrated remarkable abilities of prescience. His chosen location for the cannon gun was not far from Cape Canaveral, Florida. He was the first to conceive the free return trajectory—the idea that it would be possible for a pro-jectile to go around the moon and then return to earth. Upon such return, Verne was again the first to suggest the use of water (oceans) as a medium for landing one's space ship in—the idea of splashdown. As I covered the Apollo moon landings for CBS television in the late 1960s and early 1970s, I couldn't help thinking over and over again how Verne had anticipated a good part of the overall scenario a cen-tury ahead of anyone else.[*]

Verne was a master in taking us on intriguing journeys to far cor-ners of our planet—and beyond. In *Jules Verne: The Definitive Biog-raphy*, William Butcher takes us on an equally interesting journey through the life of the author which has been hidden beneath layers of "fiction" and misconception. I am confident that this book will help set the record straight, while enhancing our understanding and appreciation of one of the greatest story-tellers of all time.

Arthur C. Clarke
Colombo, Sri Lanka
February 25, 2006

[*]For interesting discussions on many other ideas and inventions first imagined by science fic-tion writers, see the website Technovelgy, http://www.technovelgy.com/index.htm

INTRODUCTION

"JOOLSVURN" IS AN INVISIBLE MAN. The most translated writer in the world (*JVEST* 43) remains the opposite of a classic: a household name from Taipo to Tucson, but absent from the school curricula and histories of literature. The English-language encyclopedias peddle mistruths, and "his" truncated and illiterate messes, sold as "Complete and Unabridged" in America, are dysfunctional, howler-full monsters. Although his intelligence, technique, and general readability have created hypnotic page-turners, some booksellers seem unaware he actually wrote novels.

But why is this a problem? Why study the life of Jules Verne (1828–1905)? Quite simply, to understand his influence on the modern world, arguably as great as anyone's. Verne is the most read of all writers—nine times as much as the next Frenchman.[1] He invented a new literary genre, although not the one associated with his name. "Masterpiece" is the most frequent descriptor among his peers, the writers. The names he invented, Nemo and Fogg, dominated the box office in 2003, 2004, and 2005. But still their creator is ignored, his life a black box.

The crux of the matter lies in his reputation. In America and Britain there has been a total misunderstanding of Verne's work. He did not write for children; he did not produce science fiction; and he was not pro-technology. Evidence for each point will be hammered home throughout this volume.

Of his approximately 200 works, three are world famous. In *Journey to the Center of the Earth* (1864)[2] Professor Lidenbrock and Axel enter the crater of Snaefells in Iceland and head down through the successive strata of geological time. They discover a lost world containing the body of a white man, live sea-monsters, and a giant figure herding giant mastodons, before riding a volcanic eruption back up to the surface.

Twenty Thousand Leagues under the Seas (1869)—to give the correct English title—presents the enigmatic Captain Nemo through his obtuse prisoner, Dr. Aronnax. The two commune with the ruins of Atlantis, dive below the ice to discover the South Pole, fight off massed giant squid and Papuans, and plunge into the Maelstrom. But much of the interest comes from the anguish gripping the somber captain, and at the end a shocked Aronnax concludes that his aim in life is to go around sinking ships. (The published versions of the works will be summarized here; the manuscripts are very different.)

In *Around the World in Eighty Days* (1872), Fogg—stiff, repressed, British—bets the Reform he can circle the globe in the stipulated time. With an irrepressible Frenchman and an Indian beauty he traverses dense jungle, explores the Hong Kong of Jackie Chan's ancestors, shoots a few Sioux, and burns his boat for fuel—only to get back five minutes late. Realizing, however, that he has gained a day by traveling eastwards, he makes a triumphant entrance to his club.

Five other works written in the same decade are of similar interest. *Paris in the Twentieth Century* (1860–63) is set in 1960, complete with cars, faxes, pollution, and Americanization of the language and lifestyle, but without the capital city's culture and soul; the poet hero fails in both love and work and perishes from cold, hunger, and neglect. This anti-science fiction novel was unequivocally rejected by Verne's publisher, Hetzel; it was translated into English in 1996, when it became the most successful French novel ever in the United States.

The Adventures of Captain Hatteras (1864), with its poetic settings and riveting authenticity, features a Briton's quest for the North Pole. Setting off via Baffin Bay, Hatteras's expedition experiences hunger, frostbite, and disease. After various tragedies, the survivors discover an open Polar Sea and sail on. At the point where the meridians finally meet, there surges an island volcano in full eruption. The captain plunges into the crater to reach the absolute Pole, but his American rival drags him back. His failure drives Hatteras mad.

The good-humored *From the Earth to the Moon* (1865) describes preparations for a projectile launch from Florida, monitored from a giant telescope in the Rockies. However, the target is missed and the novel ends with the Americans lost in orbit around the moon.

"Edom" (date of composition unknown), a dazzling story opening in Baja California, features Atlantis and a twenty-first-century humanity, which slowly realizes it is just part of a recurrent cycle of destruction and rebirth: almost the only real science fiction signed by Verne.[3]

In *The Mysterious Island* (1874), five Northern balloonists escape the Civil War to land on a Pacific island. They proceed to colonize it while marveling at a series of providential events. Eventually they find a stranded *Nautilus* and a dying Nemo, renouncing his anarchistic activism for good deeds, piety, and nationalism, just before the island blows up.

Our understanding of Verne inevitably passes through generations of interpretations and cultural by-products. Unfortunately, the majority of works in English are doubly fakes, betrayals of censored works. Not one word of chapter 1, for instance, of the most popular English *Journey to the Center of the Earth* corresponds to the French original; and a majority of editions of *Twenty Thousand Leagues*[4] abridge the novel by one-fourth. Nor would the surviving sections pass muster in a tutorial. In English the hero visits the "disagreeable territories of Nebraska" or "jumps over" part of an island; reference is made to "prunes" or "Galilee"; and Napoléon dies broken-hearted in "St. Helen's," Lancashire. Verne himself wrote of "the Badlands," "blowing up," "plums," "Galileo," and "St. Helena" in the Atlantic![5] It is these invented, bowdlerized hack jobs that films and critical commentary have nearly always been based on. For further discussion of the problems with the English Verne, the reader is referred to the nine books I have published on the matter.[6]

In France Verne is the author generating the largest number of literary analyses, but in the United States and Britain he is not taken seriously, on the pretext that he is a science fiction writer. And yet this opinion seems manifestly absurd in view of such systematically low-tech or nontech works as *Five Weeks in a Balloon, Hatteras, Around the World*, and *The Mysterious Island*. The result is that for the English-speaking world most of Verne's authentic series of Extraordinary Journeys remain unknown, his life largely virgin territory.

Admittedly, 60 books and 3,000 articles have been written about his life. But I would claim that nearly everything remains to be done. Many biographical studies have been invented, derivative, or unduly biased by Verne's reputation.

My reservation about even the best of recent scholarship is ultimately methodological. Nearly all of it has appeared in French or German and addresses the intellectual history of Verne's writings but neglecting his everyday life. To understand the scope of the omission, consider the following list, almost Vernian in its length.

No biography has traced Verne's family tree back to the fifteenth century. No biography in English or French has analyzed his early environment or his finances. No English or French biography has identified his best friends or traced his path to kindergarten, to his grandmother's, or to church. No one has mentioned that his family was heavily involved in the slave trade. No one has listed his visits to the English-speaking countries. No one has listed the attic rooms he lived in.

No English or French biography has mentioned the most important source of information, a full-length treasure trove about the writer's early life by Raymond Ducrest, mostly brought up in Verne's home, of which only one copy survives.[7]

No biography has benefited from a unique, Borgesian collection of every article ever written on Verne, lovingly collected and cataloged over five decades by a Swiss American.[8]

No biographer to date has studied every work published by Verne.[9]

But this is still only half the story. Although *Jules Verne* will concentrate on the man himself, the writing cannot be ignored. Verne's repeated passing off and plagiarism started as private matters, but ended up in court. The many discoveries in recent years have reversed readings of the Extraordinary Journeys and overturned ideas about the writer's life.

One example is Verne's autobiographical works. While *A Floating City*, about his trip to New York, the Hudson, and Niagara, has been available since 1870, and "Memories of Childhood and Youth" since 1974, *Backwards to Britain* appeared only in 1992, and "Joyous Miseries of Three Travelers in Scandinavia" in 2003.

Other dramatic discoveries include the writer's correspondence with his family, laden with ejaculatory and scatological imagery and banned worldwide; 1,400 letters to the Hetzels, integrally published only in 2006; and many interviews with American and British journalists. (None of these volumes, I'm afraid, is available in English.)

Jules Verne provides the first analysis of these discoveries in English. Nevertheless, I would claim that this breakthrough pales in significance beside one astonishing fact: the novels summarized above do not in reality represent what was written. The texts hacked about by the English "translators" already betrayed the novelist, for the works devoured by hundreds of millions were twisted and corrupted by the French publisher.

Scholars have pored over every draft of quite minor literary pieces, but not those of the only universal Frenchman. Verne's manuscripts unfortunately remain about as accessible as the Chinese Politburo minutes, meaning that only a handful of sheets from the most famous works have been studied to date.

The good news is that I have obtained samizdat copies (becoming the first person to see the set since Verne). One focus here will therefore be the inception of the major works, how their plots and meanings evolved, or rather regressed, thanks to Hetzel. The apolitical, nonviolent, and desexed image of the Extraordinary Journeys is erroneous, as I shall show, draft by adulterated draft, comma by transmogrified comma. Previous studies of Verne have neglected this

[handwritten margin note: alas, true of all lit]

systematic censorship to their peril: they have invariably interpreted not what he wrote, but the expurgated, sometimes meaningless, versions that Hetzel published under his name.

In teasingly brief summary, then, we shall see how, originally, the United States attempted to muscle in on the North Pole, Hatteras dueled to the death with his American rival on an ice floe and committed suicide at the very Pole; how Nemo was a Polish noble revenging the Russian rape of his daughters; how Phileas Fogg's first faltering steps, backdated 14 years, were governed by anti-Semitism and the expressiveness of his lower body (this is the expurgated version!); how other famous works lost entire chapters, including a utopian underground city; how the dying Nemo remained free and defiant to the end; and how the futuristic aspects of "Edom" were not by Jules Verne.

[handwritten margin notes: # / worth- / less]

I do realize that these mostly exclusive revelations undermine both Verne's established image in the English-speaking countries and many previous critical studies of his works. General reaction may be much indignant denial. All I can do is repeat that the image is largely based on an illusion and that the works that have marked generations are not the ones the author wrote. The only intellectually honest course is to quote the authentic Verne—before he was savaged by the publisher, betrayed by the translators, ignored by the critics, and travestied by Disney.

In both this and the central focus of Verne's everyday life, my approach will accordingly be evidence-driven. At the risk of neglecting the metaphysics, ontology, and hermeneutics beloved of Continental scholars, my perspective will be modestly Anglo-Saxon, asking such resolutely untheoretical questions as when?, who?, what?, and how much?

I will thus be looking at the forgotten nitty-gritty of the novelist's life: his appearance, his schoolmates, the shape of his bedroom, what he ate for breakfast, who he slept with, who he fell out with or was sued by, the fibs he told, how he went to work, how he got on with his bosses, how much he made, what he did on his days off, what his sexual fantasies were, where he holidayed, what he read, and whether he was a good husband and father.

Two brief examples will illustrate my down-to-earth approach: whether Verne was homosexual; and why he was obsessed with all things Scottish. Bisexuality certainly occurs in Verne. His father's excessive severity, including the beatings; his timidity with strangers and yearning for reclusion; his relationship with probable homosexual Aristide Hignard at school, on both major foreign trips, and during collaboration on seven volumes; the double entendres to Hetzel about oral sex; the evidence of the series of Extraordinary Journeys, with an absence of desire for women and indeed of attractive women, but with much obscene ribaldry between the men; the probability that Verne fathered only one child—all implies that a homosexual streak permeated his character.

Verne had a noble Scottish ancestor, although no one has looked up his address. On his first real foreign trip, he describes waking up to a view of the volcanoes of Edinburgh Castle crag and Arthur's Seat; never having seen a mountain or lake before, "the terrible poetry of old Scotland" bowls him over. For the next 30 years, a litany of Walter Scott, glens, bens, and eruptions will flow from his amazed pen. But to date, no biographer has identified the Edinburgh lass he flirted with or the Western Isles, lochs, and mountains he swooned at, marking not only his three Scottish books but his entire life and works.

My mistrust of theory and generalization will impact on both the structure and emphasis of the argument. The crux of the matter is that what is true in 1840 may be false by 1900. The boisterous young provincial heading for the capital bears little resemblance to the conformist Amiens citizen at the peak of his fame. His underlying character may have stayed the same, for kindness and gentleness emerge from interview after interview even during the darkest years. But his behavior and views show little continuity. His attitudes toward Britain and America, for instance, veered from the adulatory to the libelous. At some stage in the 1870s, then, Verne's output and mood changed dramatically, whether because of his wife and family, his move from Paris, a crisis in the writing itself, his health, or the disastrous defeat by the Germans.

The dark decades did, nevertheless, contain enough drama to fill several volumes. Michel was judged insane by his father and imprisoned. Verne's favorite nephew shot him, crippling him for life. The numerous works published after Verne's death in 1905 puzzled many readers, for they contained radical political, philosophical, and scientific ideas, the reason being that Jules's son Michel wrote much of them.

It is clear, in sum, that the Verne phenomenon remains unknown in English. His reputation, even during his lifetime, already suffered, for his works could not express social, political, and religious views— if only because his characters were forbidden to visit France. Conundrum: Which writer never described his home country but set works in Russia, China, and America, only for each of them to be banned in its respective country?[10]

My central aim here will accordingly be to combine research on Verne's life with the evidence from the works, especially the all-important manuscripts. I will thus show what sort of man Jules was, how he achieved what he did, what went on inside his head, what really made him tick.

This book represents the sum of decades of living and dreaming Verne, dragging family and friends into "his" châteaus, over his mountains and down his rivers, and arguing his sexuality and politics over morning congee.

The result will amaze those who know Verne only by hearsay.

PROLOGUE

"I CAN'T STAND FUN any more. My character has changed beyond recognition, and I'll never get over what I've been through."[1]

On March 9, 1886, the man who would write these bitter words had had it all. His books had brought him global fame and fortune, he had two new grandchildren, and for the first time a science fiction story had appeared under his name.[2] *by the definition on p. 33 ?*

Yet within minutes his existence would be shattered. His nephew, perhaps the person he felt closest to, tried to kill him, crippling him for life and making him writhe in pain for years. A week after the attack, the friend died who had rescued him from poverty and made *Hatzel ?* possible all his masterpieces. A year later his mother passed away in turn, undoubtedly affected by the treacherous assault; but, heartbreakingly, he felt too ill to attend either funeral. To cap it all, his inspiration failed and his writing spiraled irreversibly downward.

The murder attempt did not come as a complete surprise, since everything had been in turmoil recently. His family's hereditary insanity had emerged repeatedly. He had again and again refused his son's crazy business schemes and paid off his womanizing debts. He had sold his beloved steam yacht to a Balkan prince.

The latter decision was certainly a mistake. Travel had obsessed him since earliest childhood. Travel transcended a post-Napoleonic, Prussianized France raging impotently at her dismemberment. Travel prevented the intrusions of his wife who did not read his books and had little idea why he wrote them. Travel created an ideal community of like-minded males living in closest intimacy. Travel had been, above all, his raison d'être ever since the first stunning bestsellers. His writing penetrated virgin territory, spiritually commingled with the globe's last unbesmirched realms; it avoided overt psychological analysis but revealed character through small-group interaction and exotic shared challenges. Giving it all up constituted personal and professional suicide.

By selling his dream machine, he severed his links with the wonder "out there"; he betrayed much of what he had written. His heroes' travels fed off his own wanderlust. By undertaking to travel only in dream, he took the dream out of travel. He abandoned Phileas Fogg desperately burning his boat, Captain Nemo defying the hurricanes, the teeming Polar Sea monsters, the killing underground dinosaurs, the South Pacific dream, the Atlanteans, the carefree space travel, the fresh Scottish lass, and the ravishing Indian beauty. He exchanged his yacht—the flesh of his flesh, his castle, and his last link to Brittany—for tax bills, club routine, and sandy deckchairs. Henceforth his perspective would be a smoky tunnel in an ugly industrial town and his wife's increasingly hamsterlike cheeks.

So the balding figure with the sagging left eye who had scoured the Union Club's periodicals that afternoon felt drained and stranded, half the man he'd once been. Perhaps he even helped bring on the tragic events, to provide a material pretext for his black despair, to slash some way out, any way out, of the failure of his life.

His mood was not good, in sum, as he turned right into Rue Charles Dubois at 5:15 that wintry Tuesday. He still had hale and hearty skin, crinkled around the warm, affectionate eyes. With his navy, almost ankle-length overcoat, circular, snow-white beard, peaked cap, and slightly bowed legs, he could pass for a captain still lusting for a sea-going breeze. The bare trees threatened slightly in the fading light, and the heavy houses betrayed the harmony of his half-classical, half-marine childhood dreams. How could he have swapped salt for soot, exoticism for comfort? Thriving as he did on adversity, had all the success removed some vital spark? He only knew the lethargy of his brain, its muddiness, its gravity. Where were the heady fantasies that used to come bucketing out? Now he had to plan everything, force himself a little, reorganize, and rehash a great deal.

At least his four-story house, with the spreading servants' quarters and airy reception room, displayed fanciful touches. But was the cobbled courtyard too barren, the circular tower too folly-like? Why didn't the gardener do something about the ivy strangling the trees? At least he'd get a warm reception from Follet, his jet-black spaniel, bounding out of her kennel, tail lolloping. So was it Honorine producing his dejection? She was certainly not the helpmeet he'd dreamed of in the early days.

He was following his neighbor Gustave Fréson, not even hailing him, and dejectedly opening the front gate, when he heard an explosion to his left.[3] A carnival was in full swing and he thought it just a firecracker. Had he subliminally noticed the stone doorframe spitting a fragment? In any case another blast came—and then a searing, bone-shattering pain as metal slammed into his ankle-length boot and crunched deep into his left shin. A cry came: "You bastard!" He bent to investigate the ankle. Even now, despite the unbearable pain, he maintained control. He shouted to Fréson, "Stop him!" and pointed to a young man only fifteen feet away. He loped agonizingly to the assassin, who was still shouting something.

With a heart-stopping shock, he recognized his favorite nephew!

His heart still beat madly as he observed Gaston's dusty shoes, disheveled hair, manic gleam, and shiny new revolver. He loved him. He treasured his seriousness, so unlike his son's frivolity and rashness. He had marveled at his high-powered job in Paris, due if truth be told to his own string-pulling.

A one-stripe policeman had appeared out of thin air. Gaston simply stood there like an automaton, arms hanging. The three men began to maneuver him into the courtyard, using reassuring body language. Only then did they enquire whether he might not wish to hand over the gun for safe keeping.

Verne's mind searched for reasons. With "the dreamy mouse," as he called him, he'd shared tempests and moments of tremendous happiness. Together they'd seen his adored Edinburgh and transcendental Western Isles, then, two years later, England, Holland, and Denmark.

He feverishly went over Gaston's nervous breakdown of several months ago, as well as his ravings about fighting duels to get his own back and giving the slip to the policeman following him everywhere. And above all he remembered their terrible arguments over the last few months. The nephew's motive had to be revenge for the "family affairs of such sensitivity that I am unable to divulge them," as Gaston told the chief of police that evening.

And then it was over. He forgot his responsibilities, his surroundings, everything, to concentrate on the volcanic pain erupting from his ankle. His whole being confronted the stellar sensation, sharp at the center and throbbing far up his leg. As he yielded to its invasion, his body pumped compensating fluid that made his other limbs glow with strength.

Afterward he forgot the sequence of events. Had Gaston fallen into the arms of Aunt Marie and his pretty cousin Suzanne? How long before Gaston was carted off to the central police station? Before the diagnosis that his wound wasn't serious? Before he sank gratefully into the oblivion of the first, botched, operation? Before he realized the bullet could never be extracted and that he was crippled for life?

In his few lucid moments between the ravings and fevers, the bleedings and infected suppurations, the ether and morphine, he considered the world's press, baying for news. He decided on maximum damage control.

The indictment was "attempted murder." Everyone knew Gaston had planned it carefully: escaping his aunt in Paris, buying a train ticket for Dover, but alighting at Amiens to pace up and down outside, with six seven-millimeter bullets throbbing in his weapon.

But what motive should be given? Most plausible seemed a refusal to protect Gaston from his enemies or give him money for England. The rest of the story read like a *crime passionnel*, with its unstable cocktail of resentment and rage, money and passion, illicit desires and unmentionable acts. Best to muddy the waters and lie if need be. He would invent a conversation between Gaston and himself before the shooting. He would cover up that the nephew had bought the gun that morning, that he had aimed between his stomach and his private parts, that he had shot to kill. He would cite absurd, contradictory motives supposedly given: to draw attention to his suitability for the French Academy or to send him to heaven.

So determined were the writer and his family to hush it all up that they silenced the papers, prevented all legal action, and needlessly confined Gaston Verne to a foreign asylum for the next 56 years.

So who was the victim? And what has he to do with us, from a different time, space, language, and culture?

Jules Verne, nineteenth-century French author, wrote about 200 works, the majority never published in English. It is those like *Journey to the Center of the Earth, From the Earth to the Moon,* and *Twenty Thousand Leagues* that make him such a fascinating, but opaque, figure. Their accumulated effect on humanity is immeasurable. Harry Potter, Frodo Baggins, or Hercule Poirot may at any moment outperform Phileas Fogg or Captain Nemo. Prince Hamlet or Don Quixote get longer entries in *Britannica*. But over time Verne has outsold Shakespeare and indeed everyone. No individual has spoken in his own voice, in signed works, to so many human beings.

If you mention these facts to literature teachers or encyclopedia editors, they reply with "children's writer," "poor style," "past-his-sell-by-date inventor," or, if East Coast–educated, "genre fiction." But they offer no information about the books or the man. The remarkable phenomenon, then, unfathomable once you start to think about it, is the extent to which the man who shaped our world has escaped notice. He hails from nowhere in particular, has no sound bite in the public consciousness, remains unrecognizable without his first name. He had a talent unparalleled among the 15 billion people who have lived for writing universally appealing stories—and for concealing his own fame.

If we look at his hundreds of portraits, thousands of letters, scores of interviews, handful of autobiographical pieces, Verne shows a strong character, a distinctive mode of behavior, a unique way of life. Like all geniuses, he both inhabited his time and transcended it. Unlike many of his compatriots, he was not straightaway identifiable as French. Like many writers, he channeled much of his personality back into his books. Unlike most famous men, he kept himself to himself.

The cover-up of the murder attempt, then, epitomized Verne's efforts to hide his private persona from posterity. This book will destroy his efforts.

To fully understand the ins and outs of the tragic affair that so categorically ruined the life of a unique writer, and for a brief moment illuminated the man inside, we need to go back to the beginning. Only by systematically "gathering truth from facts" (Deng Xiao-Ping), can we understand the insouciant boy and the tragic man he fathered.

CHAPTER 1

Island Adrift:
1828–35

IN 1826, FRANCE was a constitutional monarchy. After the Napoleonic escapades, economic stability and artistic creativity were helping the cultural center of the world to find her feet again.

Nantes could be considered the Berwick or Berlin of Brittany: the French invasion had left this capital stranded from its cultural hinterland, with only islands of Breton speakers remaining. The city had an important middle class: conventional, complacent, and closed to outsiders, trying hard to ignore the rural discharge and exotic whiffs all around. Memories were fading of the *Boudeuse* and the *Méduse*, respectively the ships of the first French circumnavigation and horrifying acts of live cannibalism. Nantes still occupied the apex of the triangular trade—importing tropical raw materials, exporting trinkets, and moving slaves sideways—that, from this city alone, had dumped a half-million Africans in the West Indies and Indian Ocean. But with Haitian independence in 1804 and silt in the Loire, the triangle seemed increasingly wobbly. Many of the vessels were now square-sailed barges trans-shipping the tobacco and raw sugar up from Paimboeuf. For the moment, though, the prohibition of "black ebony," as the merciless slavers called their stock in trade, had merely increased Nantes's monopoly and hence prices.

It was this colorful setting, built on a trade already abhorrent to an enlightened few, that Jules Verne saw when he first opened his eyes. He also breathed in an illustrious family heritage.

"Verne" means alder tree, as in the family coat of arms. The first recorded ancestor was one Vital Verne, a sixteenth-century shoemaker in the Massif Central (see Figure 1).

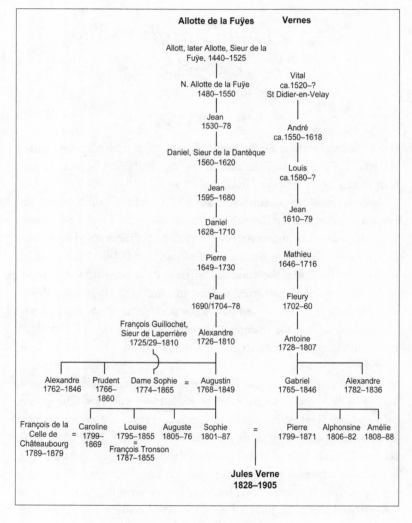

Figure 1: Jules Verne's family tree

His ultimate forebears may have been either Italian or from Le Vernet, in Thélis la Combe commune, a little downstream from La Versanne.[1] Starting with Vital's son, the descendants were invariably lawyers, although another branch founded the famous Banque Vernes. After an eighteenth-century Antoine, senior legal advisor, came a Jean-Gabriel, seigneur of Cormantin and Uxelles, and his cousin Gabriel, magistrate in Provins, south of Paris.

Gabriel's third child, Pierre Verne, spent a few months as an advocate in Paris, then settled in Nantes to join his long-established uncle. In late 1826 this half-Parisian bought, on credit, into Monsieur Paqueteau's practice on 2 Quai Jean Bart (JJV 2). Looking out onto Feydeau Island, the building stood at the corner where the Loire absorbed the Erdre, which François I called "the most beautiful river in France."[2] Despite the virtual closed shop operated by the local legal establishment, Pierre aimed to build the best law practice in Nantes. His social background and literary taste helped, and he had the gravitas. He began to expand the practice's client list into the lucrative marine business, including slave traders.

In an oil painting, Monsieur Verne appears unexceptional beside a small rolltop desk, with perfect order presiding over his paper cutter and blotter. Later photographs reveal that the lawyer is tall and ascetic and likes to spread his arms proprietorially. Longish light brown hair and a devotion to paperback fiction mitigate his balding pate, grim face, and thin lips.

Pierre's grandson described him as "highly intelligent, pleasant, and witty, a passionate music lover, the life and soul of our family get-togethers" (JJV 2). His great-grandson remembered "a good and charming man under a slightly severe appearance . . . A respected legal expert, an erudite scholar, and a fine spiritual poet, he liked to discuss science and recent discoveries" (JJV 2). He was remarkably liberal and open-minded in some ways, and Jules dubbed him "a veritable saint."[3]

But saints are impossible to live with. Pierre was also a strict Jansenist, a stickler for detail, and a puritan who despised the poets' lifestyles (JJV 2–3). Although endowed with great charisma and talent, generosity and tolerance were not Pierre's fortes.

According to the family tradition, one fine day the lawyer was walking under the cropped elms of La Petite Hollande, the triangular garden at the tip of Feydeau Island (see Figure 2).

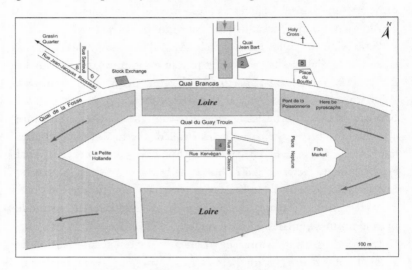

Figure 2: Feydeau Island

In front of him spread a sandy bathing beach, blue-sailed fishing boats, and the oceangoing port. But a slim, vivacious woman captured his attention instead, with green eyes, reddish-gold hair, and the demure look of the better classes. After the vision had vanished, he reportedly learned that Sophie Allotte de la Fuÿe was twenty-five years old but still not married (ADF 8).[4] (We are forced here to follow the often unreliable family biographer; all references including "ADF" should put us on our guard.) The two were introduced and duly fell in love, the only surviving tidbit being that Sophie joked she was good at making cakes and jam. Pierre wrote in his best handwriting, asking for her hand (ADF 75), and they married on February 17, 1827.

Was it urgent? In any case, the wedding took place without most of
Pierre's family, five days away in Provins (ADF 10).

Sophie, without profession, came from Morlaix and was gentle,
gay, and superimaginative. Following an intensively Breton education, she took Catholic devotion to extremes (JJV 3). Whether one *vague*
was considered Breton by "real" locals resembled being a genuine Scot ?
or Hong Konger, the hardliners using a mix of ill-defined criteria like
blood, birth, and upbringing to exclude the outsiders. Like Gaelic or
Cantonese, the language was of little currency but central to the
myth. Morlaix itself was synonymous with the tragic French-speaking ?
Acadians, brutally sent "home" from British North America before
being dispersed to Louisiana.

Sophie's father, Augustin (b. 1768), ran the indirect taxation
system in Nantes but had previously been manager of Huelgoat
Forge; the family went back, via Sophie's slave-trading grandfather
and military and naval ancestors, to a Daniel Allotte, Sieur de la Fuÿe.
Both families in fact overflowed with nobles, including seigneurs de ?
Montbel, Chignet de Champrenard, de la Perrière, de la Dantèque,
and du Sapt, as well as many humble *de*'s that at least indicated an
aspiration towards nobility. Pierre was himself an *écuyer* (member of
the gentry), his arms emblazoned on a seal passed down since time
immemorial (RD 2). All the relatives led prosperous existences: the
four parents were to live to an average of 86.

In an oil painting symmetrical to Pierre's, again painted by her
artist brother-in-law, Sophie appears thoughtful beside a keyboard,
hands at awkward angles and dress scraping as she leans forward. But
in another, ten years later, a country lass wears a simple shawl, straggly
hair, and an expression mixing sadness, kindliness, and wryness. Her
one surviving letter shows affection and naivety, together with mountains of religiosity.

Despite his family's extensive landholdings, Pierre claimed to be
badly off and moved in with the bride's parents. Augustin and Dame
Sophie Allotte de la Fuÿe (b. 1774) rented the fourth floor of 4 Rue

de Clisson for FF 200 a month (about $600 in modern-day values). With four main rooms plus a study and attic above, the apartment was finely furnished, boasting arched doors and elaborate parquet (ADF 10). On the walls hung stern portraits of Sophie's grandfathers, a Feydeau shipowner and a mariner who had braved the Arctic (ADF 11). However, Augustin signally failed to live up to their scrutiny, for his mother had died bearing him, his business ventures kept failing, and he was always away gambling and womanizing. A few months later he moved out for good.[5]

No. 4 stood on the corner of Rue Kervégan, the broad avenue bisecting Feydeau, built by the great slave traders, no doubt including Augustin's father. It was not a natural island, and is no longer one, surrounded as it is by expressways; but it was then *the* place to live, a boat-shaped haven at the heart of town. A charming gouache by J. M. W. Turner, done that same year, shows the classical terraces of Quai Duguay-Trouin, bonneted pumpkin sellers, and remarkably junk-like boats nestling on a too-broad Loire. The island's checkered history showed in the visible subsidence and the street names: Jean Bart and René Duguay-Trouin were buccaneers, Clisson an Anglo-French turncoat.

At noon on 8 February 1828, Jules-Gabriel saw the light of day. It seems typical of Pierre that his son should emerge in the earliest month allowed by society. A mere three hours later, the birth certificate was signed. Accompanying Pierre to the registry office was François Tronson (1787–1855), Sophie's brother-in-law and magistrate, neighbor, and family friend.[6] This was the family's first Julius/Jules (the names are the same in French), called after the Roman emperor, a fourth-century Breton martyr, and a pope with three children. The boy was also named for grandfather Gabriel and the Archangel of that name.

Although wet nurses were normal, the infant was probably breast-fed.[7] Baptism did seem urgent, for a third of babies were lost and Jules would have risked limbo without it. Indeed Jules's probable cradle mate, Léontine, born to the Tronsons two months after, was to die at the age of one; her sister, Céline, had also been lost in 1823. Pierre had excellent church connections, and a quickie baptism was conducted the following day with special permission from the bishop. To calm the baby's crying, Pierre probably used the unconventional method of reading out long passages from contemporary literary works.[8] Sophie sang songs over the cradle, fed her baby on demand, planted kisses, and often stayed watching him all night.[9]

The official christening provides an opportunity to meet the relatives. To allow Pierre's family to travel in better weather, it takes place on May Day, in the nearby Holy Cross Church, with an ornate façade but rather a dumpy behind. Built into a column near the door opens a giant seashell, large enough to bathe a baby. Gabriel and Dame Sophie are the godparents; Pierre's pretty sisters, Alphonsine and Amélie, also attend, barely out of their teens, but already interchangeably old-maidish (ADF 9).

For the banquet, although really it should be the debauched Augustin, Dame Sophie's second brother-in-law presides at the top table. This bachelor and eccentric is Jules's great-uncle, but everyone calls him Uncle Prudent. A former shipowner, buccaneer, and triangular trader, he has retired to gentleman-farming in the village of Brains, where he has just become mayor. Despite his age, he often walks all the way to Nantes (ADF 10).

During a lull, one of the beautiful Provins maiden aunts turns to her brother:

"This child has your eyes, but your wife's nose and mouth. He will be a poet like you and manipulative and kind-hearted like Sophie . . ."

"My son will be a lawyer like me, and I'm counting on his domain being a prosperous practice."

Pierre has in fact cut into an important oration by Prudent about the Scottish origins of the family. Prior to discreetly slipping away, therefore, we should hear the good uncle out:

"Before becoming shipowners here, the Allottes lived for seven generations at Loudun, in Poitou, in a manor house smaller than my press-house, but whose *tourelle* [turret] dovecote exercised a right of *fuye* [feudal right] over the neighboring fields. Hence our name . . . As for the name Allotte, it comes to us from a certain Allotted, a Scottish archer, who . . ."

"Here he goes again," interrupts Pierre. "Uncle Prudent's getting started about the legend of Louis XI's archer and his Scottish domain" (ADF 11).

On the face of it, this story of British ancestry might indeed seem mere hearsay, as the lawyer here alleges and biographers have often assumed. Before she died, however, Verne's great-niece Marie-Thérèse Lassée provided further tantalizing snippets:

> In 1462, N. Allott, a Scot who had come to France with Louis XI's Scottish Guard, rendered service to the King, who ennobled him and gave him the "droit de fuye," the right to have a dovecote, at that time a royal privilege. He built the Château de la Fuÿe near Loudun, and became Allotte, Seigneur de La Fuÿe.[10]

The Scottish Archers of Louis XI, king from 1461 to 1483, are well documented, the hundred members being from the best pedigrees. A *fuie* (*fuye* in the Poitou region) means a small dovecote, usually on pillars, in other words a *tourelle*. The name Allott is unknown in France, Allotte in English. Daniel Allotte's grandson, Paul, lived in Martaizé, six miles south of Loudun. The "Ancestors" file in the Centre International Jules Verne in Amiens contains an anonymous family tree. Amazingly, it begins "Allott, Sieur de la Fuÿe, 1440–1525" and "N. Allotte de la Fuÿe, 1480–1550." Although it contains no further information, the dates must come from family documents. In sum, the Caledonian ancestry does seem probable.[11]

Fortunately an unsuspected but incontrovertible keystone survives. The Château de la Fuÿe, the home of the proto-Allotte de la Fuÿe, is still standing, on the southwestern outskirts of Loudun. Curiously, no biographer has thought of looking for it in the phone book. The surprise on locating the legendary building could not be greater than at discovering Captain Nemo to be a pensioner in a seaside boardinghouse.

In yellow freestone, with 600 feet of façade, castellation, moat, and drawbridge, the château, built in about 1465, boasts three internal towers for pigeons, plus two external *fuies*. The owner, Monsieur Jacques Lallemand, has confirmed that the property belonged to the Allotte de la Fuÿes, as indicated by the coats of arms ("Gules with golden crescent") formerly in the stonework.[12]

The evidence, in sum, for the existence of N. Allott, Scoto-French noble, and hence of British forefathers, is compelling. Even if we do not believe in "blood," the Scottish ancestry mixing in with the Breton surely conditioned the Allottes' attitude to the British. Given the love-hate relationship between the two nations, an Allotte could never be just another French citizen. From the beginning, Jules carried a great weight of tradition on his infant shoulders.

After less than a year, the Verne family moved to 2 Quai Jean Bart. If Pierre was seeking peace from his mother-in-law, he made a mistake, since his home and office were now one and the same (JJV 2). What was more, the new dwelling stood across a narrow channel from Dame Sophie's, meaning she could peer inside. However, to drop in she had to make a wide detour.

As administrator of the Catholic charity that owned the building, François Tronson no doubt arranged the rental. Sophie's brother-in-law was the son of yet another triangular sea captain, "punctual and methodical" (RD 9) and a convinced Legitimist (supporter of Charles X): he went so far as to resign as magistrate in protest at the 1830 Revolution that removed the king from the throne. From 1819 to the mid-1820s, François and Louise Tronson had lived at 14 Rue Kervégan, 20 feet from Jules's birthplace.

As the first floor flooded every few years, 2 Quai Jean Bart had been converted to shops, rather lowering the tone (ADF 8). Above rose a mezzanine, two high-ceilinged stories with six windows apiece, then mansarded maids' rooms. Colorful wall hangings, tropical-wood furniture, and Chinese porcelain adorned the interior. The house was terraced in Louis XVI style, corresponding to Georgian style. Like Jules's birthplace, it had internal shutters and an unsafe-looking wrought-iron balcony on each window. And no. 2 again stood on a corner, but now with a spectacular view over the Erdre, Feydeau, and the Loire.

Despite the five-story grandeur, the Vernes had only the thousand-square-foot middle floor, barely twice an Edinburgh living room, to accommodate an increasingly busy office and six people. As if to compensate, the block appears in an 1828 gouache by Turner—and in the jazzed-up version, retitled "Nantes from Feydeau Island" (1830). The river scene has now been Italianately remixed, with blue and red awnings on the gondolas, curlicues on the mansions, and Mediterranean fishing smacks invitingly lined up before Jules's windows. The pumpkins have been airbrushed out and the medieval Bouffay Tower behind Quai Jean Bart appealingly rounded off. The chiaroscuro irresistibly draws the eye from the left-hand focus, at the shady Verne residence, over a dusky arched bridge, to the obscure block at the right-hand focus, the boy's birthplace on Feydeau. Turner's eye for the ley-lines hidden in age-old thoroughfares uncannily coincides with the family's taste for dominant views.

On June 25, 1829, Pierre-Paul Verne was born, named after his father and the last Allotte to live on the de la Fuÿe domain. Jules lost his mother's attention but acquired a virtual twin, only 16 months younger. Paul and he would become very close; even the difference in size fading as they grew up.

Jules was a slender, handsome child, with curly reddish-golden hair, large blue eyes, and a broad nose. His main weakness was a love for venturing out onto the perilous balconies.

By modern standards, his early years were uncomfortable. The apartment had a toilet with a disposal tube but no flush mechanism or toilet-paper, and no bathroom or hot tap. In the kitchen, the only reliably warm room, with its Aga stove and tempting smells, the two young live-in maids gave Jules a window on the earthy traditions of the Breton countryside. One was called Mathurine, who later married a pork butcher from Chantenay, Monsieur Pâris (ADF 100). An affectionate pre-Proustian portrait, superstitious and humorously wary, lives on in the opening chapters of *Journey to the Center of the Earth*, whose manuscript hints at goings-on with her employer.

While checking what Mathurine was up to, Sophie had the leisure to play the piano, con brio; read books, so long as she avoided atheists and free-thinkers; or simply dream of her boys' futures: terrible womanizers like her father, desiccated lawyers like the rest of the family, or incurable romantics like herself?

Jules's first memory dated from July 29–30, 1830, when he heard strange crackling noises coming down the Erdre. His parents explained to him, with worried looks, that rough men were fighting with guns. The windows remained tightly shut despite the heat, and he had to sit quietly. When he later recounted "I can still hear the rifle shots . . . [as] the population fought the royalist troops" (MCY), he was surely echoing long-gone voices. His parents made it sound as though the people were the troublemakers on the liberal barricades in Place Graslin, when 16 men died.

Since the living room took much of the apartment, the bedrooms lurked at the back. Jules's room must have looked out onto the side street, Rue du Vieil Hôpital, poky but countrified, with the view to the right blocked by a bend, and that to the left offering a narrow vision of the Erdre and the houses on the far bank. He may also have had a window on the back courtyard, really just an air shaft, where you had to crane your neck to see the least scrap of sky.

His early environment was incredibly rich. Even before he stepped out, his senses were assailed by coffee, cocoa, sugar, indigo, and mangoes, by ship repairs, seamen's arguments, mewing seagulls, and clip-clopping carriages. From the living room he could clearly see the houses on Feydeau, the mascarons above each window, stonily pupilless but winged to catch the sea breeze: faces transfigured by some unseen horror, angelic breeze-puffers, jovial mustachioed buccaneers.

Quayside ships literally overshadowed the front door, with dock-yard cranes behind. Jules could watch each tide bringing in the sardine boats, brigs, or huge, leaning Cape Horners, salt water when the moon lent her help, and, once in a blue moon, a lost porpoise. If the west wind dropped and the Loire was high, skill was needed to luff into the Erdre, meaning that Jules learned about nautical operations at an early age.

The dark raison d'être of most of the vessels would have been hidden from the child. The city continued to run about half the French trade in human beings. Admittedly, the commerce in slaves, although not the keeping, had been banned in 1827. But with her tradition for flouting far-off regulations, Nantes simply resorted to flags of convenience and brig conversions outside French waters. As her stranglehold increased, the port armed hundreds of slave ships in the 1820s, with 1830 representing a peak. In 1835, more than 80 Nantes captains continued the triangular trade.

Jules's own family took part, although they concealed the fact. Family biographer Marguerite de la Fuÿe drops hints about the family's "muscadin" behavior: foppish, Royalist, and tropically decadent. Pierre had arrived on the recommendation of Alexandre Verne (1782–1836), who married into the Bernier family, active in the slave trade (JJV 2). Uncle Alexandre, a former quartermaster, was himself some sort of businessman, like Sophie's father; Eugène (b. 1792) and his half-brother Gustave Allotte (b. 1801/02), Sophie's cousins a hundred yards up the Erdre, were shipowners, like most of the family friends and Dame Sophie's maternal grandfather.[13] Her paternal grandfather was a close associate of François Guillet de la Brosse, militia chief in the French colony of Santo Domingo (Haiti). The Allottes were related to René-Auguste Chateaubriand, father of the famous writer, René, and career captain of pirate slaving ships, crewed largely from Nantes. Uncle Prudent's savings, some of which would be bequeathed to Jules, must have come from buccaneering and slave trading.[14]

The real money in town came from the slave trade, and a whole web of cross-links entangles Verne's extended family into the nexus of Feydeau Island, (noble) descent, reactionary politics, fervent Catholicism, shipowning, plantation management, and illicit tropical commerce. Some of the kindly relatives bouncing the infant on their knees had to be slave traders, with hundreds of deaths and thousands of ruined lives on their consciences.

Sophie worried about the dampness. At the first spring sun, she would walk her boy under the mature magnolias of Quai de la Fosse, which manages to look positively Neapolitan in Turner's 1828 oil of it. Jules's great-niece biographer throws in that the trees were "planted by the shipowners of Santo Domingo in memory of their houses, wrecked by the blacks" (ADF 14), another hint at dark doings in the family.

The quayside had walls higher than Jules's head, with tempting gaps and slippery steps down to the sewage-laden water, his mother's nightmare. But the boy's attention was especially captured by a man who hired boats for a franc a day. True, the boats had water sloshing around everywhere, but one of them, he noticed, had three masts, just like the real luggers (MCY). Jules, already a keen boat-spotter, was able to tell a gunwale from a poop, a schooner from a man-of-war.

Beside the Stock Exchange, within spitting distance of La Petite Hollande, Sophie and Jules would pass shops selling brown coconuts, pink seashells, and green pineapples. Nearer home, the bird shop on Quai Brancas displayed monkeys, parakeets, and canaries. On summer nights their gibberings and screeches echoed through the Verne apartment (ADF 14).

If they ever tired of watching the rivers' forced couplings, Jules and Paul played hide-and-seek in Dame Sophie's attic, among their great-grandfather's telescopes, sextants, and dusty correspondence. Their grandmother would tell stories of her father's naval feats against the British in the Seven Years' War.

To walk to Dame Sophie's Jules crossed the Pont de la Poissonnerie. By luck, Turner again acts as guide. He zooms in beside the dark-sided bridge of 1830 to swivel left and pan out for a stunning Goya-like gouache of a muddy humpback thick with quarreling fish-wives. If Jules found it too noisy, he could head past the crawling shellfish, cod, and tuna of the Fish Market on Feydeau's stern, another Turner subject. He could then turn into Rue Kervégan, nego-tiating further pockets of loose change and baskets of shining seaweed crying "Fresh fish!," "Fine mussels!," "Live crab!" If he doubled back instead to Quai Dugay-Trouin, more wives would be boozily picnicking on the water's edge, calling out to passersby. But at least he could pre-tend to be studying the fish-shop-cum-swimming-establishment moored alongside, also drawn by the busy artist.

Along the shore docked tiny smacks from Atlantic port Le Croisic, selling fresh fish and shellfish and besieged by mewing seagulls. According to the family, Jules would dream of sailing off to sea and bringing back miraculous catches. What seems certain is that sixty years later, he was still yearning for the river scene and the forbidden sensual escape it offered:

> Ships lined the wharves two or three deep . . . In my imagina-tion, I climbed their shrouds, I scrambled to their topmast tables, I gripped the knobs of their masts. How I longed to cross the trembling boards from the quayside and tread their decks! (MCY).

The boy's surroundings showed surprising reversals. The rivers below his window regularly flowed upstream, choosing different moments to do so. Often the quays would flood, with horse-drawn vehicles and household punts braving the waves. In March the Loire would bring down fields of brown ice, and on the incoming tide Jules's island of birth would glide back out to sea, delighting and wor-rying him. In his mind, the normal categories became blurred by all these upheavals and inversions. The Indies, not too far downstream, belonged to both America and Asia. "The Isles" were in both river and ocean, lay both east and west. If terra firma could mysteriously yield to the foot, an island drift like a boat, a boat feel like both a man and a woman, the river could be salty. Feydeau leaned at drunken angles and when the Erdre one day ran dry under the boy's window, little more was needed to set off his imagination. Natural and artificial, trees and masts, water and land, up and downstream, alive and dead irremediably melded in his mind. All his life he would suffer from left–right and east–west disorder, category confusion, and unquenchable pansexuality.

The family worshipped at Holy Cross, trying to steer Jules away from his sweet and toy shop, Au Rat Goutteux (The Gouty Rat).[15] Although Pierre would read James Fenimore Cooper to Jules,[16] with his *Last of the Mohicans* and Franco-British rivalry, in general he neglected his son. Sophie followed his example of strict discipline, while encouraging Jules to invent new games.

The parents would invite friends in to drink Uncle Prudent's homegrown Gros-Plant wine, including lawyer turned priest Monsignor Alloue, the aristocratic W. Arnous-Rivière, the ever-polite shipowner Monsieur Bourcard, and Monsieur Jean-Baptiste Coquebert, army paymaster-general and relative of Chateaubriand—reactionary defenders of the establishment one and all. Table talk would include Charles X's dissolution of the Chamber of Deputies, his subsequent abdication, and the accession of Louis-Philippe. It might range from the ongoing conquest of Algeria, via Morse's new telegraph, to the measles and whooping cough all the children seemed to be catching. Given Pierre's interests, the first passenger railway would have been discussed, as well as Walter Scott's death and the plans for street-lighting.

François Tronson, Charles Musseau, Alfred Guillon, and Pierre Verne recited their own poetry, sang their own songs, performed their own playlets, and played literary guessing games.[17] Pierre's compositions contained emphatic religious messages and witty allusions to those present. Jules and Paul, watching from the wings, laughed at the serious lawyer's antics, but wondered why the poems and plays bore so little relation to real life.

At 8 Rue Jean-Jacques Rousseau, fifty yards from Quai Brancas, Jules often visited his childless uncle and aunt, François and Caroline de la Celle de Châteaubourg. An accomplished miniaturist and a tobacco warehouse owner, Uncle Châteaubourg was not only the son of Charles-Joseph de la Celle de Châteaubourg (living in Place Graslin and also a miniaturist, who had painted Napoléon and Josephine), but also the nephew of Pauline or Bénigne de Chateaubriand, the writer's sister.[18] Uncle Châteaubourg would often tell Jules heroic stories of the New World, especially of his great-uncle's encounters with French trappers, Iroquois warriors, and bison swimming the Father of Waters. According to Uncle, Chateaubriand had gone to America to find the Northwest Passage to the Pacific before the British (ADF 15). (We now know that the writer invented many of his adventures while sailing home, not even getting as far as the Mississippi.)

A final item in Jules's early environment seems less edifying. Pierre's religious fervor led him to self-mortification: to reinforce his wavering faith he would probably fast or even physically punish himself. This masochistic flagellation, recorded by Jules's grandson, was applied with a scourge.[19] To perform it satisfactorily, to ensure that the thongs did the necessary damage, often required deft wrist-action and persistence. Although flogging was normal for ascetics or criminals, to do it oneself surely constituted a neurotic disorder and an appeal for help.

Jules perhaps heard muffled groans and moans. Did he possibly wander in one day to find his father in flagrante delicto? Did Mathurine the maid venture to show him lines of blood and pus on crumpled hair shirts? The boy could have no understanding of the sins Pierre punished himself for, whether committed by himself, with prostitutes, or with the maids, but his father's self-inflicted tortures may have marked him deeply.

Pierre also reputedly beat or starved his son, undoubtedly normal in that class and time. However, the father's transition from the unnatural self-mutilation to the searing pain he inflicted on his son, whatever he might have done, may have created terrible doubts about its justice. Even a small boy could wonder whether the brilliant but twisted psyche constituted a fair judge and jury. In any case, the paternal violence caused certain harm and may have led to the timidity that blighted Jules's whole life.

CHAPTER 2

Chantenay Castaway: 1836–39

AT THE TENDER AGE OF SIX, the boy was sent away to boarding school.[1] Mme Sambin's upper-class *pension* stood at 5 Place du Bouffay, where a public guillotine had operated a generation or so before.[2] It stood beside Turner's ruined medieval prison tower, less than a hundred yards from Jules's home, and—some compensation—near the sceptr'd isle, beside the splendid mansion that backdropped the quarreling fishwives.

Mme Sambin was the abandoned spouse of an Indies-bound naval officer. "Sambin must have left his wife in the middle of the honeymoon," reported one of her flock; "30 years later he still hadn't sent news."[3] The schoolmistress often assured her pupils that he had foundered on a desert island and would return, Crusoe-like, with man Friday and a green parrot on his shoulder (ADF 16–17). Did the child appreciate the human tragedy, the nature of male wanderlust? More probably, he believed every word, coming to equate tropical shipwreck with happiness. (The myth of ultramarine bathing and squeaky white sand hadn't yet been invented.) Verne's works would often refer to Lady Franklin, who lost her husband but never gave up hope, sending expedition after expedition in search of him. The heroine of *Mistress Branican* (1891) heads out herself, and finds her husband after 14 years.

Despite elderly Mme Sambin's gentleness, she had to whip a little
to maintain discipline. Another punishment involved the culprit
kneeling with donkey ears in the middle of the class. Rewards
included being promoted from the shared benches of the *hoi polloi* to
raised individual seats or hearing tales from Sinbad the Sailor or the
Revolution. Her students debated whether her name meant "without
bath" or "100 baths."[4] Mme Sambin's teaching consisted mostly of
traditional values, plus a few games. Even at kindergarten level,
schools took their job seriously, with much religious instruction. But
Jules reserved much of his energy for the playground. Classmates
recalled the eight-year-old as "fair-haired and slender . . . throwing
himself into every game and physical activity . . . his hair blowing,
energetically exercising on stilts or the bars."[5]

An invaluable record of Verne's family life survives, never published and existing in a single copy, authored by Jules's nephew Raymond Ducrest de Villeneuve (1858–1930). According to this
biographer, Jules and Paul attended school together, learning to read
and write there, although Paul was a year behind. In most schools, the
children learned different styles of writing, including italics and broad
Gothic, the schoolmistress going around sharpening the quills to fit
the exercise. All his life, Jules exhibited a remarkable facility at
switching from bold upright, to typographical joined-on copperplate
with curlicued capitals and parallel descenders, to minute italic
scrawl, later the bane of researchers' eyes.

In the summer, Nantes became a dusty and oppressive place. Even
Jules's playground on Quai Jean Bart seemed less pleasant, for the
Erdre had been diverted. The dry trench resounded with picks and
shouts from the construction of the Nantes–Brest Canal, eventually
completed in 1836. A slender compensation for all the brouhaha and
disruption was that no. 2 acquired the only gas lamps in the area. The
Vernes escaped the town for entire summers to Uncle Prudent's, at
no. 8 La Guerche, a hamlet adjoining the village of Brains, ten miles
southwest of Nantes.[6]

The journey started from the Pont de la Poissonnerie on an

"unexplodable" steamboat, so called, Verne remarks dryly, "because it exploded a little less than the others" (MCY). But it came as a relief to leave the busy town center and feel the cool water underfoot. Brains was a real country village, with only a shop and a forge. From the church, a private avenue led grandly through the high-walled estate, around a rather pondlike lake, and up to Prudent's manor house. The property boasted a library, a vegetable garden, and an orchard. On the right stretched the wooded hills of Le Plessis-Cellier, featuring Uncle Châteaubourg's ancestral château, complete with drawbridge. A stream known as the Ruisseau de la Sauvagerie linked the two uncles.[7] Also close by lived Paul and Juste Lucas-Championnière, old family friends, and distant relatives, prominent in Nantes society.

Prudent's elegant manor suspiciously resembled three cottages run together. A single maid, often replaced, lived in, plus a score of servants and farm workers in the outbuildings. Prudent loved dogs, giving them unusual names like Nina or Raton, which Verne would put to good use in his fiction.

Jules and Paul adored Uncle Prudent, approaching seventy but still hale and hearty, because he had traveled to South America and told wonderful tales about his exotic adventures. With his bachelor freedom, pirate past, mayoral authority, great conviviality, private wines, and rich domain, he provided an important role model for the boys, especially compared with the flogger father.

Besides, the Tronson cousins, who lived very near Uncle Châteaubourg's in Nantes,[8] often stayed at Uncle Prudent's: five boys and two girls, Caroline and Marie. Whereas the elder was "lively and gay," the younger had a pretty face and was "full of common sense . . . thoughtful, kind, and sensible."[9] The nine children would play snakes and ladders with Prudent, run with sticks and hoops, or explore the countryside, paradisiacal with its heavy vines, lush meadows, and treacherous marshes.

But already Jules dreamt of an elsewhere, of the Isles, Indies, and Americas just around the bend. In his memory of these bucolic idylls, he employed the same metaphors melding land and ocean, quick and dead, stasis and motion, as for Feydeau weighing anchor:

> Since we were unable to sail the sea, my brother and I used to navigate the heart of the countryside, across meadows and woods. Not having a mast to climb, we would spend whole days in the treetops. We competed for the highest lookout. We chatted, read, hatched plans to travel, while the branches, shaken by the wind, simulated pitching and rolling.[10]

Jules in fact wrote down his travel plans, which constitute his earliest known writings. He also composed "invocations, some even in verse, that will never be published but opened out there, rocked by the breeze through the branches, like fruit or flowers."[11] The religious upbringing clearly conditioned these delicate entreaties which, given their poetic form, may have been either magic spells or pleas for help with his efforts to delight cousins Caroline and Marie.

But the endless summers had to eventually come to a stop. Only too soon, it was back to the dusty city and the sludgy inkwells.

In understanding Jules's early years, there is a huge problem: the absence of firsthand accounts. Various documents must have informed the three family biographers, but nothing has been divulged. Even Mme Sambin's pupils signally failed to come forward with reminiscences of the most successful writer in the world. Did he have any friends? Pets? Did he like fish? Did he sleep with Paul? A total blank.

All the same, the first luster determines character, as the Jesuits famously opined. Jules's seven-year-old personality emerged clearly.

First, his family exhibited a surprising stability. No deaths, no long-distance removals, no exotic holidays, no upsetting job changes, no further squalling babies, for some reason.

Second, torturing himself with his sensuality and guilt, Pierre the flagellator seems less of a positive influence than the six Allotte uncles living close by. Although lawyer François Tronson lacked charisma, he did faithfully attend the family get-togethers and could bask in the reflection of the pretty girls he had engendered. Uncle Prudent and the two Uncles Châteaubourg, with their devotion to the arts, independence of mind, and talk of exhilarating foreign parts, formed fascinating figures. Collectively and individually, they molded Jules's character.

Many other influences stood out: Mathurine the maid, spoiling the boys as she stirred the *bourguignon* and dreamed of a husband; the excitement of watching maneuvering ocean vessels, with clove and nutmeg wafting in; the treacherous undertow of the Erdre–Loire confluence competing with the Atlantic influx; the perilous gargoyles, crooked caryatids, and louche aristocratic air of Feydeau mixing with the noisy street life; the memories of pirates, rebels, and slaves on every corner; the tastes in music, painting, and literature that the upper-class family had the leisure to indulge; the family names commemorating an aristocratic dovecote and a precocious tree partial to river banks; the four grandparents living to ripe old ages; and the glorious ancestors, whether infinite ramifications of seriously successful lawyers or rich owners sending killing fleets off to Africa's shores.

But the biggest influence, surely, came from a nobleman from an impossibly remote time and space. The romance of Scotland dominated the contemporary imagination with its adventure on savage mountains and lakes, but the forebear had sailed the sea and far away, defended King Louis XI, built himself a castle, and bequeathed his fiery hair-color and temperament.

It proved all too much for a sensitive child. The pressure from towering ancestors, shady businessmen, separated grandparents, spinster aunts, and frustrated schoolmistress combined with Pierre's beatings to make the boy shy to the point of neurosis. His communing with nature, his thirst for exoticism, his poetry, his longings for faraway places, his love of heights—all constituted signs of the expectations thrust onto him by disappointed adults. Jules reportedly loved only three things in life: freedom, music, and the sea.[12] Not a person in view! In his marine-scented but landlocked childhood, school and family forced him to hide his affections deep and to be masochistically evasive in speaking, if not writing, his yearnings.

"The sea! Well neither I, nor my brother, who became a sailor a few years later, knew it yet," he remarks flatly sixty years on (MCY). How many lost paradises can be read in that calm regret!

Sometimes, though, Jules overcame his timidity. At the age of eight his family took him to Paris and probably to Provins, sleeping overnight in the brougham August 14, 1850. (Given the very large number of references to Verne's letters, an abbreviated system is adopted here, consisting simply of the date of composition. "50" of course means 1850; all such letters until chapter 10 are to his parents unless indicated otherwise; where part of the date is in italics, this means that information has been interpolated.)[13]

One fine day Jules ventured fearfully onto a three-master moored at the Quai de la Fosse, while the watchman was "on duty in a nearby tavern" (MCY). Ecstatically leaning over the open hatches, the boy sensually breathed in the tarry spices. He delighted in the marine bouquets of the interior and dreamed of making the cabin his home. Finally he dared to turn the wheel, in his imagination ocean bound on a good wind. In his naive rapture, he failed to understand the acrid smell from the unwashed human cargo of the trade triangle's middle leg.

Jules's earliest known document, a letter to Aunt Caroline Châteaubourg, revealed a loving home environment:

I'd like you to come and see us . . . and then can you bring the small telegraphs you promised as paul will also have one paul loves you with all his heart I'm writing this letter because paul doesn't know how to write he's only just started and I've been at boarding school over a year now and how is Uncle.

[Great-]Auntie Verne arrived from La Rochelle . . . not long ago before her brother wrote in his letter a terrible piece of news that her husband [Alexandre] had died my grandma Mummy

Auntie Tronson . . . know our two cousins henri and edmond
are at high school in canbon [Cambon?] they don't know . . .
My dear aunt and uncle I kiss you both with all my heart.[14]

This charming, period-less missive, addressed from Lorient,[15]
eighty miles from Nantes, showed the impact of a middle-class education, using the aunts' surnames and self-consciously displaying concern for others, especially Paul. Jules's pride shone at being able to
write; but the letter hardly shows a precocious interest for advanced
technology, for the "telegraphs" must be toy semaphores.

At this time Uncle Châteaubourg painted two unnamed brothers
posing on a verdant path of his Plessis-Cellier domain. One handsome reddish-blond boy, in waistcoat, English "redingote," raised
collar, and tie, holds a hoop and stick, with the other's hand resting
proprietorially on his shoulder. Despite the gorgeous colors, the portrait appears stilted. Somehow the boys do not come across as human
beings, because of their self-conscious representation of adult values.
The painting has invariably been described as showing Jules and Paul,
but probably in fact depicts Henri and Edmond.[16]

The Tronson children represented Jules's only cousins in Brittany.
Hilaire was four years younger, which left as playmates only Henri,
Edmond, and Caroline, respectively four, three, and two years older,
and Marie, two years younger. The children surely bathed together in
the hot weather, following the new British fashion for communing
with nature, giving the eight-year-old the perfect opportunity to satisfy his curiosity about girls' bodies, so different from his own.

Jules's letter and the stylized portrait gain poignancy from a disaster that struck his playmates that same year. On October 18, 1836,
Henri and Edmond went duck hunting on the marshy Isles of
Mauves-sur-Loire, ten miles east of Nantes.[17] One got into difficulty,
disappearing under the water. The other tried to save him—and perished as well.[18] The scene of the homecoming of the two brothers
stretched out in their drenched pallor can only be imagined, like the
breaking of the news to Jules, a stranger to death.

The loss of the eldest children, the third and fourth in succession, must have shocked and horrified the whole family: the Tronson boy conceived a year later was morbidly called Henri-Edmond. Ducks would later play a prominent role in Verne's works, with hunting producing strong emotions, usually negative. His feelings about the surviving Tronsons, simultaneously friends and cousins, surely mixed inexplicable warmness and an ineffably tragic note.

With his practice prospering, Pierre rented a house in the hamlet of Chantenay, beside Nantes, in about 1837.[19] The proximity of the Châteaubourgs was the obvious reason for the delightful location chosen, facing south over the Loire. For the next decade, the family would spend most of Easter to November in the countryside, heavy with flowers and fruit, surrounded by lush fields and groves. Tempting valleys cut the slopes; smiling paths ran sheltered by tall beeches, severe poplars, and gnarled oaks; old farmhouses nestled in the folds of the land. The very name sang magic—the place Jules liked best in the world. Chantenay marked the boy forever:

> From my tiny bedroom, I could see the river unwinding for two or three leagues, through the meadows it flooded every winter. In the summer . . . strips of fine yellow sand emerged, a whole archipelago of shifting islands! Ships could hardly thread their way through the narrow passes . . . The need to sail would not leave me (MCY).

Every detail of the house would imprint itself in Jules's mind. On arrival from the church square, a large brown double gate gave access through the gravel yard to a century-old detached residence. Along the façade ran flowerbeds and hydrangea, laurel, and prickwood bushes, with a large fig tree on the left. Although the yard lacked grandeur, the shade of the two lime trees on the right felt welcoming in the summer heat.[20]

A red-tiled vestibule, with four little sideboards in the corners, led through a large glass door and down to the garden via a double perron. On the far left was the parents' room, lit from both sides and with a full-sized bathroom with its own steps. Next came the dining room, with a large hearth, where the family spent most of the time, the living room, and two bedrooms—the (male and female) servants were consigned to the attics. In the basement, with direct access to the garden, were the pantry, kitchen, linen room, wood store, huge billiards room, fruit store, and cellars running far under the yard.

The family used the upper story of a wing to the left of the yard, but let the lower one to their former maid. Now called Mme Mathurine Pâris, she ran the pork butcher's shop looking conveniently out onto the church square.

One of Jules's bedroom windows overlooked the side lane, and he had his own corridor leading into the courtyard. His other window opened on a magnificent panorama above the small fruit tree: the entrance to the port, where "the yellowish Loire majestically broadened," Mabon Island School for Cabin-Boys, the wooded slopes of Bouguenais, the monastery of Les Couëts, and the sunken pastures of "the island-village of Trentemoult, whose inhabitants . . . marry only among themselves" (*BB* iv). The ever-present Loire provided a moving tapestry of barges, yachts, and clippers.

Below stretched two terraced gardens. Bunches of grapes wound graciously down the balustrades of the steps, and begonias and wisteria ran under the windows and up the wall, with tendrils dropping down to the billiards and linen rooms. In front of the perron hung baskets of zinnias, petunias, and geraniums.

Through the top garden, laid out in English style, ran a broad straight path where the family liked to sit after meals, bordered by newly-planted magnolias. An avenue of mature lime trees, severely pollarded, ran along the terraced wall overlooking the bottom garden, culminating in a bower that formed a perfect trysting-place, with its complete privacy and intimacy.

Jules would run down another stone perron to the lower garden, laid out in geometrical French style as eight fruit and vegetable squares. Along the south-facing terrace wall grew strawberry bushes and peach, plum, apricot, cherry, pear, and apple trees, producing almost too much fruit; at the bottom of the garden ran another avenue of cut lime trees. The environment was perfect for two growing boys, healthy in the sun and fresh air and able to make as much noise as they wanted while being discreetly watched over.

Pierre's attitude mixed affection and severity, loving epithets of "*choux*" (darlings) and "You're late!" his telescope fixed on the clock of Les Couëts. The boys came home from school to questions about their marks, with much witty repartee, sometimes a little scathing.

Family fun and games centered on Jules. The boys had long billiards sessions; in the evening the family would read out loud or play snakes and ladders (ADF 21). If the stars come out, Jules and Paul would ask Pierre to show them faraway worlds with telescopes, which they imagined they were going to inhabit, at least according to Ducrest (RD 29). Pierre's explanations judiciously mixed references to the Creator of All Things and the Greek myths.

Sunday church was obligatory, as the priest was a good friend of Pierre's. But as compensation, local merchants set up in front of the church to sell Jules and Paul barley-sugar pipes and other local candies (RD 73).

The inseparable brothers would occasionally come back from school on foot, under the limes and beeches of the brothel-laden Quai de la Fosse. The unloading of boats fascinated them, and they would chat with the sailors, building up a library of memories (RD 27–28).

Usually, though, they took a horse-drawn omnibus, sharing the two rows of seats with all walks of life. Nicknamed White Ladies after a Walter Scott heroine, their bodywork, four horses, and drivers' uniforms shone white. A hidden music box driven by the wheels endlessly played music by François Boieldieu, with no on-off switch. Leaving from Place de la Bourse, around the corner from Uncle Châteaubourg's, Jules and Paul would get off at the Warehouse stop, threading their way through the kegs of rum, bales of coffee, sacks for the Rice Mill, and sticky rubber-tree-leaf gunny bags for the molasses refinery. Their path led above the quarries of Les Salorges, teeming with the descendants of the Nantes Revolutionaries who had drowned hundreds of opponents in 1793: "They coupled only among themselves and feared neither man nor God, spawning a degenerate race of terrifying appearance" (ADF 27). Stories circulated that they were not really human, making the boys rush past (RD 20).

The Towpath led Jules and Paul past the Pannetons', with huge exotic cedars, and the Chéguillaumes', with a pretty daughter called Ninette. Other neighbors the family would visit included old Desgraviers, who knew conjuring tricks. Armand Desgraviers was, in Jules's sarcastic words, a "genius who doesn't know it" (June 15, 1856); but there was another attractive girl, Angèle, two years older than Jules. The Langlois also had children of the same age, though the father seemed rather intimidating, fitting his building of the forges of Basse-Indre, two miles downstream.

In the middle of the bucolic groves and idyllic orchards clanked and roared the government machine factory at Indret. Despite the terrifying cacophony, oil, and dirt, something in the equipment fascinated Jules. Every so often he made a special trip to see how work on the ships was progressing (*Int.* 88). People even talked of building a *Leviathan*, a ninety-cannon warship. How could a machine work on its own? All those pistons and levers moved with worrying but exhilarating regularity. Jules never liked the precision stuff, the dry paper-bound intellectualizing. But he loved the power and movement, the simulacrum of life—with, lurking underneath, a fear that autonomous, animate machines were dangerously trespassing on the divine.

Uncle and Aunt Châteaubourg lived close by the Vernes, with a huge estate for the children to play in. Often cousins Caroline, Marie, and Hilaire would come out to Chantenay for parties and excursions. Jules's favorite walk followed the river banks, through the blossoming meadows to the pastures of Roche-Maurice, a mile downstream, or La Musse and the valleys of Saint-Herblain. Sometimes they even did the five miles to the Couëron ferry, admiring the magnificent view from the slopes opposite Indret (*BB* iv), and hence ending up at Uncle

Prudent's. The Tronsons would also often visit Chantenay for the evening, for "music, parlor games, rhyming couplets, charades, and impromptu verse" (RD 29). Occasionally the Vernes made the trip to the Tronsons' own country house on the River Sèvre (RD 21).

Jules always regretted leaving the Eden-like countryside. Each September, the dreaded moment when he would swap paradise for school drudgery loomed closer and closer. But even back in grimy Nantes, the excitement continued, because of the "pyroscaphs," long-funneled passenger paddle-steamers heading up and down the Loire. Downtown was an active seaport: tall ships brought whiffs of Canton, Batavia, or the South Seas into Jules's bedroom.

As if to emulate the Cape Horners and whalers, the two brothers taught themselves to sail. "Sometimes I was captain, sometimes . . . Paul. But Paul was the better" (*Int.* 87):

> At the end of Quai de la Fosse stood a boat-hire at a franc a day. It seemed a lot to us, risky too, for the boats . . . leaked everywhere. First we hired a one-master, but the second had two, and the third three, just like the real coastal luggers (MCY).

Cooper had instilled only the theory of tacking, luffing, and sailing close to the wind:

> The atrocious helm changes . . . the shame of veering into the wind when the swell ruffled the broad Loire basin between Trentemoult and our Chantenay! . . . We would leave with the ebb and head downwind, which helped us come back on the flood-tide . . . Our crude, disgraceful vessel sailed past Haute-Indre, then between the charming shores of Basse-Indre and Indret. And struggling from bank to bank, what lustful looks we would cast on the pretty yachts skipping over the water! (MCY).

Jules and Paul went as far afield as the Erdre and Sèvre, north and south of Nantes. If you knew what you were doing, you could sail all the way to the Tronsons', though you had to be a dab hand to get around the corner of Jean Bart without getting out and pulling.

Their home stretch hummed with sights and sounds:

> On the fine meadows, submerged and fertilized each year, horses grazed freely after the haymaking and the wandering cattle produced long lowing sounds . . . The echo brought in a cacophony: the sea salts coarsely calling between the ships, the regular chants of the mariners hoisting heavy burdens, the boatmen lewdly catcalling over or striking up in unison the bawdy shanties of "The Couëron Sailor."
>
> From every angle loomed up verdant isles, dappled with flocks of aquatic birds and dotted with ruminants reclining under the willows.[21]

With her dead nephews gazing naively out at her, Sophie lay in bed and worried herself sick about the boys' escapades.[22]

By October 3, 1837, the first day of term, Jules and Paul had become boarders at St. Stanislas School.[23] From fifth grade in this junior boys' school, or rather seminary, Jules's future was mapped out: after seventh or eighth grade, he would proceed to St. Donatien Junior Seminary. Designed mostly for priests, taught by priests, fewer than half of St. Stanislas's 122 inmates were Nantais, some hailing from the French Caribbean or New Orleans, born Frenchmen but now Americans. The pupils from the diaspora surely told exotic tales of their homelands.

The view was fantastic. On a hill outside Nantes, with gardens down to the Erdre and vineyards all around, the Louis XV mansion faced south. It had two tacked-on wings, a three-story arcaded building running westward, and a square tower at the southern tip.[24]

Lay headmaster Pierre Litoust had lost his position as judge for refusing to swear loyalty to Louis-Philippe's progressive government. With an open and cheerful, almost family-like atmosphere, standards were reputedly good.[25]

There were two terms, with prize days in May and late August. Each year, especially at the beginning, Jules won a few second-rank prizes in singing, geography, Greek, or Latin, making him a goodish student, while Paul got prizes in spelling and grammar.[26] In any case Jules disapproved of working too hard: "hard-working students invariably become blockheads as adolescents and fools as adults" (March 14, 1853).

A schoolmate retained vivid memories of: "a bubbling schoolboy, out of breath as he sprinted with his hoop across the broad terrace . . . a dissipated youngster, showing more enthusiasm for play than work; but under this exuberance witty repartees already germinated. You knew that this green fruit, scarcely budded from its flower, would later ripen" (*JVEST* 64).

Did St. Stanislas leave any trace? The traditional education left little room for science or math; the Greek made virtually no mark on Jules, apart from an interest in mythology. Although never mastering Latin, he retained ever after a conviction of its usefulness and a predilection for obscene French-Latin puns. But his favorite subject was geography, and here a humble sixth prize would evolve into a guiding passion and world fame. Teachers should never despair, even if their charges seem to learn the wrong things.

About a year after his first nautical exploits, Jules luffed off alone in a one-master, although unable to swim properly (23 May 78 from Hetzel). Sailing into the wind, he got into difficulty near Binet Island or Binet Mound (see Figure 3):

> Five miles down from Chantenay, a plank broke and the water poured in . . . The skiff sank like a stone, so I . . . threw myself onto an islet with dense reeds and tall waving plumes.
>   . . . I was Daniel Defoe's hero. Already I planned to make a wattle hut, a hooked line from reed and thorns, a fire by rubbing sticks, just like a savage. I wouldn't make signals, as . . .

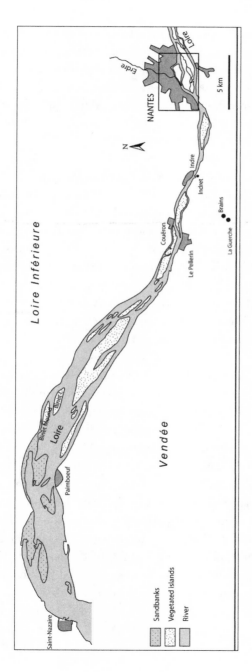

Figure 3: The Loire downstream from Nantes

I'd be saved too soon! . . . In the end, I knew solitary need and
suffering on a desert island. My stomach cried out . . .

It only lasted a few hours and as soon as the tide went out,
I just had to cross ankle-deep to . . . "the mainland" . . . And
so I went calmly home and ate family dinner, rather than the
Crusoe-esque one I had dreamed of: raw shellfish, a slice of
peccary, and manioc-flour bread! (MCY).

Ignoring his cousins' death, taken over by Johann David Wyss's
The Swiss Family Robinson (1812) and Daniel Defoe's *Robinson
Crusoe* (1719), Jules sought an idealized life as a castaway, but one
already ironically passé. He precociously realized that even paradise
was sullied with rainbows. Those born too late to pioneer desert
islands could only self-consciously recreate the towering ancestors'
adventures. The genre was already a bit frayed at the edges.

Biographer Marguerite Allotte de la Fuÿe famously claimed that,
at either 11 or 13 to 14, Jules ran away to sea. In the great-niece-by-
marriage's words, at six one summer morning

Jules slipped out of the house . . . and had still not come back
by half past twelve! . . . Colonel de Goyon, living in the nearby
château of L'Abbaye, galloped off to tell Pierre Verne. Suddenly a sailor from the Grenouillère crossing came to say that
while at the L'Homme-qui-Porte-Trois-Malices Inn, run by
Jean-Marie Cabidoulin, he had seen Monsieur Jules and two
cabin boys in a small boat accosting the ocean-going *Coralie*.
This three-master, belonging to shipowner Le Cour-Grand-
maison, had that morning weighed anchor for the Indies,
although due in at Paimboeuf that evening. Fortunately there
was the pyroscaph! Reaching Paimboeuf by six, Pierre Verne
collected his son, who had somehow embarked by buying out
a cabin-boy's engagement, and had regretted it ever since
Indret.

What hysterical desire to bring back a coral choker for capricious Caroline had suddenly taken hold of him?

Given a good talking to, thrashed, and reduced to bread and water, Jules had to vow to renounce imaginings of the Indies and limit his wanderings . . . "Henceforth I will travel only in dream," he swore to his mother.[27]

The story seems too good to be true, especially as Cabidoulin is not an authentic surname. Nonetheless, many of the details do bear scrutiny. The three-master *Coralie*, owned by the firm of Le Cour Grand-Maison, has been confirmed. The epic horseman was Charles-Marie-Auguste de Goyon (1802–70), owner of a property 200 yards away and later general. The other two family biographers support much of the story, because . . . their relatives told them.[28] However, Ducrest considers many of the details inaccurate and states in particular that the adventure happened to Paul, not Jules. Also, the intention was to descend the Loire without going further than the inland hamlet of Paimboeuf.

The ultimate source for the anecdote may simply be an article still out there. One trustworthy witness who claimed to know Jules "very well" reported that his aim on this occasion was "to locate Captain Sambin and bring him back to his wife."[29] According to another article, Verne told the author in 1861 that at the age of eleven he took a small boat and tried to catch up with the *Octavie*, en route for the Indies.[30] Yet another states that the events took place on July 15, 1839.[31]

Whether it was Jules or Paul, coral or the castaway, the East or West Indies or Paimboeuf, something must have happened. As deep as you dig into Jules's psyche, you discover a yearning for escape and transcendence, sullied by a nagging doubt that reality may not live up to his imagination, a realization that "they" will follow you to the ends of the earth, that the whole world has been mapped out. His prepubescent dream, repeated over the next seventy years, of creating an unknown island paradise, of being a "king without subjects" (*Five Weeks* i), was precociously pregnant with world-weary wisdom.

CHAPTER 3

Schoolboy Writer:
1840–46

IN 1837, AFTER AN EIGHT-YEAR GAP, Jules acquired a sister and the following day acted as stand-in godfather for her baptism in Holy Cross. Sophie felt delighted to finally have a daughter, although her husband (whom she called "Verne") was always getting doo-doo on his knees.[1] Anna was soon followed by Mathilde (1839) and Marie (1842), whom Jules again held over the baptismal font.[2] Anna, Jules's favorite, would be brunette and bright, learning to sight-read piano music. Punning Mathilde would be blonde and graceful, looking like Jules, with her "Greek chin, smiling and witty mouth." Marie, with a magnificent red hair, would become elegant and witty, "a charming little imp with a rebellious air," laughing and dancing all day long.[3]

By 1840, Pierre had made his practice the busiest in town (JJV 4). To have more room, the family moved, renting for the moment but later buying; Pierre also bought Chantenay only in 1849 (as shown by the land deeds). The new apartment, again on a corner, was really two put together, with entrances at both 6 Rue Jean-Jacques Rousseau and 2 Rue Santeuil. Jules usually gave Santeuil or Jean-Jacques as the address, so that the dangerous freethinker's name would not scorch his lips.

At the bottom of the street stood a bookshop and publisher, famous for reactionary politics and tempting charts and maps; further up was another, run by the literary Monselets. Directly across the street lived

General Viscount Cambronne, reputed for his defiance at Waterloo ("*Merde!*"), and about whom Jules was to write a naive poem, all gung-ho and derring-do. Uncle and Aunt Châteaubourg were neighbors, in fact on the same intersection, at 8 Rue Jean-Jacques, or thirty feet from Jules's window. Their two fourth-story façades met at an acute angle, rounded off by a gracefully curving window. From the Verne living room, it looked too thin to live in, although it was a palatial 2,000 square feet once one got inside. The three Allotte families were therefore living cheek by jowl,[4] seeing each other at least once a day. Jules spent much of his time shouting across the street: "come over for dinner tomorrow" or "have you got any brown sugar?" He had few contacts outside the family and the handful of family friends (RD 9).

Just visible up Jean-Jacques stood the magnificent Place Graslin, with a brand new theater. At the end of Rue du Chêne, the continuation of Santeuil, Jules contemplated the changing seasons in the gardens. At the bottom of Jean-Jacques flowed a stretch of river, including the beloved La Petite Hollande and the busy commerce on the Loire. The tallest ships in fact swayed over the downstream housetops (JJV 4) to the hammering and sawing from the nearby shipyards.

The move had one important consequence for Pierre. The parish now became Saint-Nicolas; the family priest, and friend, a Félix Fournier. Very popular locally, a newly promoted conservative open to social change, he planned to knock down crumbling Saint-Nicolas Church, dark and medieval, and build a shiny new Gothic creation in its place, with a spire soaring 270 feet toward the heavens. Pierre Verne gave generously and would soon become Secretary of the Rebuilding Committee (JD 37) (see Figure 4).

On entering the Vernes' proud new third-floor apartment, one discovered an imposing, eight-room palace, with two live-in maids, probably as cook and chambermaid. From the entrance hall, a tiled corridor on the right led to Pierre's law cabinet. Other doors opened into the parents' and boys' bedrooms, circular living room, dining room, and sisters' rooms.[5]

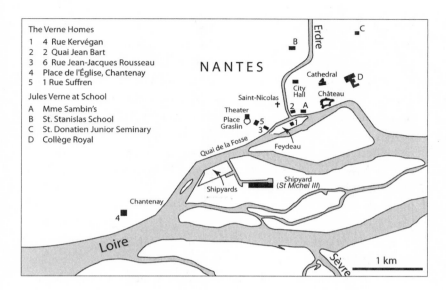

Figure 4: Nantes, showing Jules's successive homes and schools

After dinner everyone would gather around the hearth in the parents' room. Conversation revolved around the family's doings, events in Nantes, and the children's reading and schoolwork. Pierre's great memory and erudition, his alter egos as man of letters and man of science, lent interest to all he said. Jules began to find a human being under the ascetic martinet.

On the mantelpiece of Pierre's study stood a bronze clock, two Empire vases, and two Empire candlesticks. Three work tables filled the center, for files and business correspondence, law treatises and reviews, and his in-tray. Jules and Paul not only studied and read there, but chatted for hours, making it the room they spent most time in.[6]

Beside the courtyard window stood a side table with a large telescope. To the left of the window, the fireplace wall ran towards the front of the building, with a superb Louis XVI desk bearing an "electric machine, [with] footstools with glass feet and Leyden jars," as well as "microscopes and jars containing animals and chemicals."[7]

Bookshelves covered three walls: law tomes, with precious old editions of Roman law; complete illustrated classical poets and historians; rows of ancient and modern history; French, Latin, Greek, Italian, and English authors, often in the original, including Charles Dickens, well-known from 1837; journals and voyages and discoveries, including Classical geographies; and a special shelf containing magazines for young people. Jules probably focused on the last two sections.

He read keenly, books forming his main entertainment. Early on he may have read *The Adventures of Baron Münchhausen* (1793) (*Int.* 232); but his favorite remained Wyss: "of all the books of my childhood, the one I loved most was *Swiss Family Robinson*. How many years I spent on their island! How passionately I joined in their discoveries! How jealous I was of their destiny!" (MCY).

He read mostly desert island tales: "The Robinsons were the books of my childhood, and I still retain an indelible memory of . . . Mme Mallès de Beaulieu's *Twelve-Year-Old Crusoe* [1818] and Mme de Mirval's *Robinson of the Desert Sands* [1837]."[8] He also appreciated Alexander Selkirk, Crusoe's real-life model; Louis Desnoyers's *Adventures of Robert-Robert*; Ernest Fouinet's *Crusoe of the Ice* (1835); and Catherine de Woillez's *The Misses Robinson* (1835).[9] Later came Captain Frederick Marryat's *The Wreck of the Pacific* (1836) and *Masterman Ready* (1840) and Cooper's *The Crater* (1847).

Jules's family subscribed to the *Journal des enfants*, *Magasin pittoresque*, and *Musée des familles* (founded in 1819, 1832, and 1833) (RD 17). All three magazines contained lavish illustrations, with an emphasis on education and popularization.

That year of 1840 proved exciting, as Jules saw the sea for the first time. For this landmark occasion Paul and he traveled grandly by steamboat:

One day, my brother and I finally get permission to travel on *Pyroscaph No. 2*. What joy, we're over the moon! . . .
We leave behind the ports of call to right and left, Couëron, Le Pellerin, Paimboeuf. The pyroscaph cuts across the broad

estuary. We see Saint-Nazaire, its embryonic pier, its old church with the leaning slate tower, and the village, just a few houses and cottages . . .

A few leaps are enough to rush . . . over the seaweedy rocks, palm some sea-water, and taste it.

"But it isn't salty," I say going pale.

"Not a trace!"

"We've been had!" I exclaim in deepest despair.

What idiots! The tide was out, and we had simply gathered Loire water from a rock pool! When the sea came back in, we found it salty beyond our wildest dreams (MCY).

That same 1840, the "ambitious Robinson" (MCY) and Paul switched school again, to the St. Donatien Junior Seminary (Petit Séminaire Saint-Donatien). Of good reputation, it was on Rue Saint-Clément, again in the countryside, nearly a mile northeast of Jean-Jacques. Directly across the street sprawled one of the best girls' schools, the Convent of the Adoration.

Generally only state *lycées* could prepare for the baccalaureate examination, but some junior seminaries, including St. Donatien, enjoyed a special authorization. The school was "principally intended to receive young people preparing for the ecclesiastical condition."[10] Parents like Pierre, unhappy with the freethinking of the state-run Collège Royal, could choose this devout establishment.

In his unfinished novel *A Priest in 1839* (ca.1846), Verne gave a description of a new seminarian's life at "Rue Saint-Clément." The seminary seemed a relatively "good place to board," for "alongside a murderer, the common thief becomes an angel." The inmate wore

too broad square shoes . . . and a too narrow waistcoat buttoned hermetically to the neck (obviating the need for a white shirt) . . . The tie had originally served another purpose . . . [The uniform] was black mixed with dark gray and a subtle reddish-brown tint, an indeterminate color normally found only on junior undertakers (xxi).

The headmaster, "tall, thin, and dry, of a hard appearance," described his establishment: "The ecclesiastical students pay just half, but the lay ones double, so as to make up the loss." Worship was mandatory: "By overwhelming [the boys] with prayers, Masses, sermons, catechisms, Vespers, and Benedictions, we end up forcing a few religious ideas into their heads" (xxi).

Pierre or Sophie would visit at least once a week and the boys were sometimes allowed out. Twelve-year-old Jules was now in eighth grade. He did lots of Latin versification and poetry, including learning parts of Virgil and the *New Testament* by heart, his sole distinction being a seventh place for recitation from memory in tenth grade; to judge from *Paris in the Twentieth Century* (i), he hated prize days anyway. Paul started in seventh grade, proving more successful.

Jules's twenty-six classmates often behaved unpleasantly, like Cain. The teaching failed: "The other institutions which buried young proselytes in the caverns of pedantry totally lacked competence . . . among several ciphers one had to choose the least worthless" (xxi).

Verne's story "The Marriage of Monsieur Anselme des Tilleuls" (ca.1855) has a hero with unruly blond hair, who in 1842 dreams of "palpitating virginal bodices," taught by a grotesque Latin teacher, confirmed bachelor Naso Paraclet. The novel *Hector Servadac* (1877) lampooned an egotistical physics master, tormented by a noisy and cheeky student who gets "500 lines for tomorrow" for sabotaging experiments (II i). It has been claimed that Brutus Villeroi (1794–1874), who in 1832 built and tested one of the very first submarines at the mouth of the Loire, taught Verne mathematics or design in 1840 or 1842,[11] but no evidence has ever emerged.

Jules was perhaps right to doubt the value of his education, for his first surviving letter to Pierre contains nearly a dozen spelling mistakes:

I was very sorry to learn you had fallen ill and were obliged to

stay in bed . . . From last week on nobody came to see us . . .
Mum told us leeches had been applied and maybe would have
to be put on again, which upsets me . . . Your son who loves
you with all his heart.

Jules Verne—Junior Seminary (May 30, 1840?, in CNM
22–23).

What may have added to Jules's frustration was knowing that play-
mate Caroline, her virginal fourteen-year-old bodice now bur-
geoning, lived, breathed, slept, and bathed only twenty feet away,
behind bars in the inaccessible convent. In August 1839, the two
families had stayed at Uncle Prudent's, roaming the countryside
together.[12] Did his cousin help Jules with his homework, her long
blonde hair brushing his hand? Did he sometimes carry her books
home, trying not to look at her body too often?

After Jules's first prose and verse travel dreams and "invocations," he
produced more compositions from about 1840, to please his family
this time: "It was all poetry then . . . a 'compliment' [I composed for
my father's birthday] was thought very good" (*Int.* 87).

A fascinating poem by Pierre (1842) provides our first eye-witness
description of Jules:

J   Jewel-like Loire where softly slide
U   Undulating waters cradling a smack
L   Leagues from men, already in the beyond   *acrostics*
E   Elevating boys on its dreamy ride
J   Salt sea bound
    On its calm waters frolic children
    In their smack already midshipmen
P   Pyroscaphs and dinghies advance
A   Amongst the billows they dance
U   United in a great heaving romance
V   Leans and sways a dense woodland.[13]

This revelation of 2005 shows the father's great poetic talent, love
for the two brothers, and, more important, their predilection, at thirteen and fourteen, for navigation and dreams of becoming naval officers.[14] The acrostic form resoundingly confirms the message, for the
first letters read "J U L E S . . . P A U L."

An even more important composition reads:

> Puff! Puff! says the steam engine
> In deafening commotion
> The child openmouthed with admiration
> Lives full hours of contentment
> Tomorrow, tonight, in a few rhymes
> He will narrate the sea, the far climes
> The parting boats he will paint
> Yonder, far from time, from any habitant
> He will say, mother do not lament
> Your young Jules shall be a savant
> More than a boat-captain.[15]

In this first-hand contemporary description, whose juvenile language
implies an original composition going back many years, "the child"
gapes at a fixed steam engine, necessarily at Indret, and writes poetry of
an autobiographical and romantic bent. Jules prefers isolation and
escape from present-day society, despite Sophie's apprehension. He may
already be planning a writing career, certainly an intellectual profession
involving research, possibly as a scientist, lawyer, or teacher. But the sea,
always the sea, will remain the heart of his universe.

Jules wrote his first surviving letter to Sophie from boarding school:

> I learned from Father yesterday that you were relatively well; I
> know that it is quite natural for you to be tired now. I long to
> see you, but don't bother to come and see me, my dear
> Mother, it's too far . . . Paul has a bad cold. As for me, the clogs

you sent won't stay on because the straps . . . are too narrow
. . . Now dear Mother I forgot to ask Father to send me a set-
square . . . Please also ask him to send me the romance
"Farewell my Beautiful Ship" . . . because my class teacher . . .
asked me to get it for him.

   . . . God be with you.

Your son who loves you dearly, Jules Verne.[16]

The style is formal but fluent, signing with both names and not
even mentioning the birth of Jules's sister, a week before; but child-
ishly direct about school life. His teacher clearly liked him; but his
parents no longer visited.

A week later Jules wrote Sophie a poem:

Rush, my child, into the arms of your mother;
Suffering and weariness, torment and pain,
To give you life she accepted every sacrifice . . .
If, despite every care and tenderness,
You voice some complaint, she hastens to your side,
Presents you her breast, feeds you abundantly
With that nourishment God plans for small children;
Then she kisses you and in a quiet, gentle voice
Sings her child sweet little songs
Her voice waning while the little one slumbers . . .
How much caring for her son in his first year;
Then without cease she nurtures his mind,
Inculcates virtue, guides, molds.
That is what your bountiful mother did;
Prove to her, my child, your gratitude.[17]

The attempt reads well, poetic but not too much so, although
communicating little apart from maternal and filial tenderness and
the implication that the birth in question proved difficult. The bared
breast comes as a shock, for a child who can rush up seems too old to

suckle. Indeed the ambiguity between present and past, newborn and toddler, second and third person, normal intimacy and sexual baring of generous breast, culminates in the surprising realization, given Marie's birth a fortnight before, that the child is male.

Jules's other compositions at this time included a prayer, word games, anagrams, epigrams, parodies, and a poem, "The Return," dedicated to Pierre.

In 1843, Jules attended the Collège Royal, but now living at home.[18] Despite Pierre's hatred of the school's "Voltaireanism," the move may have been to increase the brothers' chances at the baccalaureate, help Paul's naval career, or circumvent the religious and boarding restrictions of St. Donatien.[19]

By 1844, Jules had only reached eleventh grade. So he must have been ill for a year or, more probably, repeated tenth or eleventh grade, meaning he may easily have failed the first part of the baccalaureate.

The school, again on a hill, had been restored and energized by a new headmaster a few years before, growing to 620 students. Because it was half a mile from the center, he arranged a special student price of five centimes on the omnibuses.[20]

Jules's teachers included Plihon for English, Lemonnier and Deladérère for math, and the forty-one-year-old Pierre Sivanne for "arts and rhetoric": a schoolmate presented him as "a fellow who fortunately didn't torture anybody or know anything . . . He taught [his students] almost nothing."[21] Others may have been Auguste Damien, who taught tenth grade, described as stupid and cruel enough to make his charges cry, and Eugène Talbot for Classical literature: a great fan of Hugo's *Orientales*, "gracious and brilliant . . . loving aphorisms . . . inventing puns and epigrams about his pupils."[22]

The adolescent did not exert himself excessively. The school's *Centennial Yearbook* (1908) boasted of its many celebrated alumni, like Georges Clemenceau and General Georges Boulanger, but snubbed the most famous one: "His successes were few and far between and did not presage [his] future." The disappointed, understated innuendo surely avenged the authors' long-gone reports from frustrated schoolmaster savants. And the judgment seems harsh in the light of Jules's seventh place for French speaking in eleventh grade and eighth for translation into Latin the following year; he may have also got a reasonable place in geography.[23]

On July 29, 1846, young Verne took his baccalaureate in arts in Rennes, getting the overall grade of Fairly Good (*Assez Bien*). His individual results varied: Latin and Mathematics, Good (*Bien*); Greek and Philosophy, Fairly Good; Composition, French, History and Geography, and Physics and Chemistry, Pass (*P.*). It is not clear how much English, if any, Jules did—vanishingly little to judge from his subsequent competence. The irony, of course, remains that the educational authorities failed to detect his world-beating ability at French and geography.

With his baccalaureate under his belt, and Chantenay and extended family stretching before him, Jules Verne, eighteen, was a free agent.

"My brother Paul was . . . my dearest friend . . . from the first day that I can remember" (*Int.* 87). Little information survives of any friends outside Jules's relatives until his late teens. However, according to Ducrest (34), Jules and Paul

had been friends with several boys in Nantes since the Collège Royal and boarding schools and whom they kept faithful friendship with over the long years that followed: . . . Genevois, Hignard, Bonamy, Serpette, G. Schwob, a whole constellation of young people, intelligent, enthusiastic, and of varied taste, some musicians, others poets, artists, or writers. They met often, as they had done near the *lycée* entrance, constituting the Nonboarders Club [*Club des externes*]. All were ambitious.

The secret seven dated back, then, to at least the age of eleven. Other friends of Verne's in the Nonboarders Club included Émile Couëtoux du Tertre from Blain and probably Stéphane Halgan, later politician and writer. The Club met "in old Bodin's bookshop" on the Place du Pilori, just around the corner from Holy Cross, quarter of a mile from the school.[24]

Like Jules, Ernest Genevois,[25] Édouard Bonamy, and Halgan were born in 1828, the first three destined to become lawyers; shipowner's son Bonamy lived in Rue de Clisson, beside Jules's birthplace. Unlike Verne, Genevois, Bonamy, and Halgan won top prizes at the Collège Royal.[26] In contrast, future journalist and editor Georges Schwob, if he did indeed live in Nantes,[27] was a surprising six years older; as was Aristide Hignard, son of the chief medical officer at the Hôtel Dieu Hospital, living in Jean-Jacques, later a composer, and reportedly homosexual (Maudhuy 112): "gentle, witty, a little nonchalant, slightly slow, legs a bit short for him to be a great walker, but very artistic" ("Joyous Miseries").

Other good friends were Charles Maisonneuve, also born in 1828 and later a banker and lawyer, and Émile Lorois, born in 1831, the son of the Prefect of Morbihan and later lawyer, government engineer, and deputy of Morbihan himself. Other twelfth grade classmates included Victor Marcé, a brilliant student of the same age,[28] later Verne's physician, and David Pitfold, six months senior, probably a friend from St. Donatien days.[29] Of British ancestry but born in Guadeloupe, he was a pious boarder, winning top prize for religious knowledge.

Among others Verne knew at the Collège Royal may have been Ernest Boulanger, who died as a volunteer in the American Civil War, plus "Jules Vallez, Chassin, Poupart-Davyl, Paul Chauves, Étiennez, Dubigeon," all at least three years his junior.[30] Poupart-Davyl would later be his printer;[31] the other Jules V. (1832–85), adopting the spelling Vallès, would also become a famous writer, with *The Child* still read widely today.

One final school friend was Paul Perret, two years Verne's junior and initially closer to Paul, but with whom Jules was soon to share accommodation. Later a theater critic and author of guide books and fifty novels, including erotica, he was regularly invited to Chantenay in 1847, with one or two friends. The group "would practice firing pistols during the holidays . . . it would continue until a terrified servant came and begged us to stop, because the little girls cowered in absolute terror, crying hot tears," whereupon they would retreat into Jules's private wing on the corner.[32]

As Verne's boyhood draws to a close, a witty letter sent from Uncle Prudent's depicts a fitting Indian summer. Present were the Tronson family and, in an over-casual reference, the smart and energetic, blond, Germanic-sounding Nanou Gruast (or Gruau?). The young man started by admitting that, although he had forgotten to pack his shirt, stockings, and nightcap and arrived soaked to the bone, he could not bear to leave "this place of pleasures":

> My uncle spends his nights in his wine presses and his days grape-picking; Grandpa was shaved in Le Pellerin today; Aunt Tronson puts into practice the culinary theory she took lessons in long ago and surprises us with unbuttered beans and charred gruel. Her young ladies have also livened up and choose their games, playing the wallflower or mangling stockings; Hilaire distinguishes himself by his ever-increasing grime, Henri remains a charming small monkey.
>
> That's the personnel of La Guerche, ah! I was forgetting golden-haired Nanou Gruast, whose actions are proportional to her wit.
>
> We go for walks, we work, I am the too-patient teacher of a willful pupil who shows me that everything is not as rosy in the teaching profession as formerly appeared. We visit the picturesque surroundings and the charming environs of La Guerche, leaving now a stocking on a path, climbing stiles, mounting gates, crossing muddy brooks, and floundering in swamps which are not too dry (September 15, 1845, in CNM 25–26).

Of significance is the mention of games of "wallflower or mangling stockings" by Caroline, nineteen, and Marie, fifteen; Jules's sessions as an apprentice teacher, presumably of Marie and now Hilaire, thirteen; and the implication that the various parents rarely cooked their own meals. Fascinating is the discreet eroticism of much of the passage, heightened by the presence of three attractive girls. The long walks, natural beauty, girls' enlivenment, obsession with stockings, ascending of obstacles, probable baring of much flesh in the mud, the incomplete comparison ("now . . ."), and the climax of removing a stocking on a secluded path—Caroline's, Marie's, or Nanou's?—everything shows that, whether or not anything actually happened, Jules lived in a pastoral paroxysm, all quivering with suppressed sensuality in this place of physical pleasures.

Jules's character had now come more into focus. While the young man's soul still proved elusive, his behavior traits shone out loud and clear. The young man appeared "attractive, albeit always badly dressed, but with a fine profile and magical eyes; his reddish-blond locks of hair, naturally wavy or curly, always dropped over his brow" (ADF 25).

From his father, a "legal eagle with the soul of a classical poet," he inherited a "love of travel, discovery, and exploration stories."[33] From his mother he got an "Allotte imagination," with a sly sense of humor: his jokes, delivered with imperturbable seriousness, misled some and, when too smutty or close to the bone, shocked many (RD 30).

Verne always presented himself as pure Breton, meaning stubborn, faithful in friendship, clannish, and slightly mystical. Energetic but with a melancholy, even depressive, side, he retained equanimity even in tragedy. His characters will often be externally cold and impassive but volcanic inside, stoical in the face of adversity but manic-obsessive. Very sensitive, Jules hid his sentimental Celtic side under a disconcerting frankness or even brusqueness.

All his jokes hid inner tension, as did the idea of running away from home. A romantic, both in his literary taste and in his love of nature and the intangible, he lived for the water, whether Loire boating, his belated encounter with the sea, the wider horizons of ocean navigation, or dreams of becoming a sea-captain. One heartfelt cry sums up his longings: "I cannot see a vessel put to sea, whether warship or fishing smack, without my entire being sailing off with her."[34] His romance- and adventure-based writings already reflected a dichotomy: sentimentally positivist, effeminately rugged, and poetically scurrilous.

What really counted for him? The answer was deceptively simple: machinery, the river, and poetry: "This Indret factory, or excursions on the Loire, and my scribbling of verses were the three delights and occupations of my youth" (*Int.* 88).

All three centered on Chantenay, his dream and his reality, his home from home, his paradise on earth. The strength of Verne's later writing came from his early combination of security and freedom, land and water, solitude and crowds, and family and near-incestuous urges.

evidence for the "near incestuous urges"?

CHAPTER 4

What Use Are Girls?: 1846–48

ON HIS LONG COUNTRY WALKS, alone with birdsong and babbling
brooks, contemplating the Loire, coolly following its private destiny
down to the ocean, Jules surely wondered about his life so far and
where it could be going. The rich countryside around structured so
much of his life. Since he didn't own a boat, the river pointed tanta-
lizingly to exotic destinations just around the next bend but also
formed a barrier. In Nantes, bridges abounded but the far bank still
represented terra incognita. In Chantenay, his domain ranged similarly far and wide but seldom southward.

His thoughts came closer home. Paul had appeared a little cool
lately. His brother seemed more like Father, stronger on technical
details like mathematics and spelling: the poor boy tried hard to cul-
tivate his imaginative side, but lacked some inner sense. He couldn't
put his finger on it, could it be something to do with Mother's crazy
fantasies? Was it really Breton, or did French people have it too? It felt
nice having a brother so close in age—and luckily Paul usually recognized who was the older. But what should they do about girls? Often
they liked the same one; did the girls do it on purpose? Paul planned
to be a captain and travel to the ends of the earth. So easy for him! As
long as he could remember, Father had dropped heavy-handed hints
about *his* father and his father's father, cloistered in law offices all day

with rogues and crooks and dusty files. Lawyers had no money worries, but, try as he might, he couldn't see himself sitting at an ancient rolltop desk, supervising spotty clerks, and maintaining black was white. In any case he wanted to leave Nantes, for two good reasons. Firstly people were so conservative, they hated even the mildest of jokes: so pompous, as if they had batons up their derrières, who did they think they were? And secondly their daughters . . . He'd never been bold enough to pick up working girls. Even if he did, where could he take them? Nantes was such a small town, people knew everything. As for girls of his own class—to sound like Father—the rules beat the *Napoleonic Code* for inflexibility and caveats. His friends boasted what they had gotten away with, and with whom, and how many times, but he didn't quite know whether to believe them. Every time he fell for a girl, which was happening increasingly often, she seemed to stop talking like a human being. It was obviously a trick to make you so desperate you'd propose—after which you stood some chance of getting under those frilly petticoats. But it never worked out as he dreamed. Even pouring out his romantic poetry just produced blushes, giggles, and frenetic fan-beating.

His only hope lay in Paris, where things were different, as he knew from glimpses. People spoke freely, they went to cafés—sometimes they lived in sin and had breakfast together. The artistic set seemed to spend its whole time doing exactly what he wanted to.

As Jules checked the westerly horizon for signs of cooler weather, he realized how attached he was to this neck of the woods. He knew every shortcut, every branch, every cartwheel track. He had calculated every combination to get back home by a different route, while avoiding the neighbors' domains, where you had to stop and chat.

At least his schooldays had come to a close. He hated some of the lessons and wondered how the teachers could spend year after year spouting such inanities. Boarding school had been much worse, though. No escape for months at a time, no secrets, every hour catered for so as to stop idle hands and evil thoughts. And all that religious babble! Even if you believed every last word in the Bible, all that empty ceremony, all that off-key platitudinous chanting! How could any boys become trainee priests? Did they really want to shut themselves off from the world before even trying it, or did their parents decide for them? Of course no need to worry about the next meal. And plenty of like-minded fellows, no need to look far for a companion, if you liked that sort of thing.

All his thoughts seemed to keep focusing on the future, but girls, profession, and location kept getting entangled. Maybe it was best to eliminate certain possibilities, starting with Nantes, in order to get away from all his failures. But luckily there was no need to decide just yet, since he could do a bit of law—it couldn't do any harm—and see where he got to. No doubt it would all come out in the wash.

From puberty, Jules had thought about his cousin Caroline, quiescent periods alternating with great passion. Was it real love, or just a combination of lust, availability, and the invigorating country air? In any case he ecstatically breathed in the "perfume she exhaled" (*Poems* 14). Slightly older, precocious, and flirtatious, she made the most of her generous body, smooth skin, and doe-like eyes, reportedly accepting the Chantenay flowers he had pushed through the visitors' grill at the Convent of the Adoration (ADF 24).

They not only ventured onto the path of romance, but also into joint literary endeavors. Jules, Paul, Caroline, and Marie had apparently often begun composing collaborative works of a romantic nature, but either not finished them or not kept the results (RD 30). The two brothers had also written verses dedicated explicitly to the two sisters; Jules, at least, reportedly declaimed his to Caroline with great feeling, although irony kept raising its cleft head (RD 30–31).

These early phases probably culminated in some sort of childish betrothal, subject to parental consent. Some biographers have cast doubt on the depth of this juvenile passion, but the documentary evidence seems strong. The *Poems*, published in 1989, record the stations of Jules's cross. In a poem dedicated by name to Caroline, Jules at long last declares his love. The "little girl" blushes and smiles: "you are kind; you need to seek my parents' permission" (*Poems* 14). The second stage occurs in the play *Broken Straws* (1850):

> In my missal I keep the poor violets
> He gathered beside the path
> And bore to his lips while taking my hand.
> In my schoolbooks I concealed them
> To accompany my solitude with their gay perfume.

The same piece refers to the convent girl's dreams of "eternal love," leading to blissful domestic scenes with her "husband . . . the adorable cousin who gave her the flowers." In the culminating stage:

> But the supreme moment
> Drew near very tardily
> Finally arrives the great day
> Already nudging the bank,
> The boat of love;
> The girl climbs in . . .
> He detaches the rope . . .
> Sail, sail off forever! (*Poems* 15).

All these literary elements probably reflect a reality: Caroline accepted love tokens from her Jules and held hands with him on a country idyll, dreaming of married bliss. But did they realize how impossible it all was? Marriages between first cousins were permitted but, as in most countries, frowned upon. Nevertheless, the four parents were brought in, and Caroline's father opined that neither possessed the maturity needed to found a home.[1] Jules's father simply thought of her breathtaking magnetism: "Ah, God! How beautiful she was."[2]

In about 1845, the young beauty came out at balls given by the mothers of her Chantenay friend Angèle Desgraviers and Nantes friend Herminie Grossetière. Dancing in white chiffon with a pink belt, she captivated scores of suitors. Was it here that Jules made hesitant declarations, as Marguerite suggests? In any case, Caroline did not take them seriously (ADF 24).

All the previous promises counted for naught; Verne's unhappiness came close to breaking his heart. Caroline left a deep mark because she was Jules's first love and because of his passionate nature. The blow to his pride felt all the greater when Caroline preferred another cousin called Jean Cormier, then got betrothed to a man 19 years her senior, whom she soon married. On the day of the wedding, Jules was still dedicating an anguished poem to her.[3]

Although Jules had eventually to accept that he could not avoid his cousin for the rest of his life, traces of his anguish would be transferred to her brother Hilaire, whom he never liked. The traces would perhaps still smolder on forty years later, for the lovers of *Family without a Name* perish, their love unconsummated, down Niagara Falls, in a burning boat called . . . the *Caroline*. In *Claudius Bombarnac* (1892), Caroline Caterna is "still a pretty blonde with blue eyes, but a deteriorating complexion" and poor taste in clothes (iii).

Probably on the rebound, Verne fell for Caroline's friend Angèle, the same age as her and whom he had seen growing up at Chantenay. "With a gait full of nobility and distinguished diction," witty but lacking in poise,[4] she had a strong character, sometimes defying her family's wishes. Despite his passion for her, Angèle in turn got engaged and married, a few months after Caroline. Did it make things worse for poor Jules that her doctor husband had a pseudo-aristocratic handle to his name and that her new parents-in-law were also Chantenay neighbors?

To get over Caroline and Angèle, Verne "tried distractions of all sorts," apparently involving whole nights out (ADF 26, RD 39). At that time a continuum ran from actresses, through working-class girls on the side, courtesans, and mistresses, to brothels with coarse ladies painting themselves on doorsteps; the most convenient ones lay at the top of Jean-Jacques and all along the Quai de la Fosse. Given the indignation with which Ducrest greets Marguerite's innuendo (RD 39), the young man possibly did sample the wares.

Now free of the *lycée* shackles, Verne had to decide what to do with the rest of his life. He is reported to have thought briefly of teaching.[5] One factor in deciding his future was his frustrated passion for Caroline, whose engagement must have been announced in fall 1846. He confessed his bitterness to friend Aristide Hignard, already studying music at the Paris Conservatory, whereupon his friend urged him to come to the capital to forget his misery (ADF 25).

But in his father's game plan, Jules would take over his thriving law practice. The Vernes had been lawyers for three generations, as Pierre often repeated, after all Jules was the oldest son and dowries would be needed for the three girls. The father insisted Jules stay in Nantes until springtime, and meanwhile begin law study. Jules reluctantly agreed, although supposedly indicating his refusal ever to follow a legal career (ADF 25, cf. RD 35—"supposedly," because Marguerite often massages the chronology to achieve greater dramatic effect). Since there was no law faculty, or indeed university, in Nantes, Pierre tutored Jules, using the standard textbooks (JJV 10).

So that autumn Jules studied at home, getting practical experience with his father's back-office clerks. His friends at this stage remained Ernest Genevois, Émile Couëtoux du Tertre, Charles Maisonneuve, and Édouard Bonamy. In December the student wrote the mayor a rather dry letter requesting permission to take books out of the city library—presumably literary as well as legal ones—as his "studies and occupation" prevented consultation at the normal hours (December 30, 1847, in CNM 32). The library was near Saint-Nicolas, so he could watch as the Gothic monster rose slowly from the ruins of the medieval masterpiece, thrusting out here an ambitious flying buttress, there a bulging rump, here a tempting belvedere, there spurting gargoyles, rudely angled and bulging at just the right place.

From about 1845, Verne produced a large literary output. His cultured home environment provided one stimulus, but his biggest literary inspiration was Victor Hugo, and the Nonboarders Club also had a great influence on him (RD 34):

It was on the corner of the table of old Bodin's bookshop that Verne wrote a tragedy whose name has not survived. He took it to the manager of the Riquiqui puppet theater on Sauvetout Bridge . . . but was refused. Even worse, when Jules solemnly read his tragedy to Caroline in Uncle Prudent's press-house . . . she listened coldly and his male cousins catcalled. Their opinion was that rather than the elegiac, he should stick to caustic, bawdy, Rabelaisian farces. Only Marie Tronson understood. The author thanked her in a sonnet [referring to her] caresses (ADF 22).

In line with his cousins' advice (at least according to Marguerite), Jules wrote a frivolous vaudeville, hidden from his father but secretly circulated—and praised—in the local Cagnotte Literary Club (ADF 27).

His first surviving completed play, revised in May and June of 1847, is the fascinating five-act *Alexander VI*, about the hypocrisy of organized religion. This tragedy may have backhandedly commemorated his great-uncle Alexandre Allotte, who had died the year before. The play depicts the sadistic reign of terror launched by the medieval Pope and his illegitimate son Cesare Borgia: Alexander forces his papal attentions on a girl called Rosa while his grasping son assassinates cardinals. With scenes of murder, rape, and incest, the play possessed a cruel precision and considerable tragic presence.

The young man may have already completed short stories and humorous verses (RD 34). One strand of his imagination was a highly developed social observation, mocking the pompous or the rigid. At this period he wrote three chapters and a synopsis of a novel, "Jedediah Jamet," where the covetous hero pursues from Tours to Holland and the Rocky Mountains an inheritance from an uncle, prosperous businessman and soldier in the War of Independence. He nearly finished *A Priest in 1839*, a turgid, Hugo-esque horror-cum-love story set in a Nantes church, featuring a Jules Deguay from Nantes, a lawyer, and an evil defrocked priest called Pierre.

In 1847–48, Verne also composed a large number of poems,

consciously imitating his father (*Int.* 100). The subject and form varied: one with a dedication in Greek characters, borrowed from Victor Hugo, one from Byron, one for Anna's First Communion, one about fifteenth-century St. Peter's Cathedral in Nantes, and even an obscene one about the gallows, "where so many hideous people famed for their criminal depravity / Finished their lives ithyphallic to honor public morality." One doggerel employed vulgar slang: "I began as a bigshot, / Even quite a toff; / But it didn't give me the hots, / So grabbing my fill I f . . . ed off" (*Poems* 132; 162; 79; 109).

A surprising number focused on politics, like the diatribes against Louis-Philippe's progressive government or the attempts of the pretentious Duchess of Berry to restore the monarchy (1832). One general theme was government abuse, viewed from a near-anarchist perspective: an allegory of Corruption being literally conceived by Power; the Praslin Affair, where an adulterous peer massacred his wife; or the scandal-laden "Brigand" Cabinet (1840–47) and its dramatic downfall (*Poems* 40; 49; 42). The most interesting was a "Song of the Barricades," in favor of the overthrow of the monarchy (*Poems* 125).

When Jules mentioned he might try to make a career out of writing, Pierre blew his top (RD 34).

In spring 1847, Jules wanted to join Paul, embarking as cadet officer on the merchant ship *Régulus* for a few weeks of coastal trading. Paul had longed to sail to distant parts for as long as he could remember, and had finally begun to satisfy his dream, perhaps with help from Uncle Châteaubourg. However, Pierre refused Jules permission.

He studied all that winter, but his mind was not really on it—in fact he was a "somber agitated lunatic" (ADF 25). As the year turned, his family began to plan Caroline's wedding, sewing gowns, booking venues, arguing guest-lists, meeting family. By providential luck, Jules had an engagement of his own: his first-year law exams, conveniently distant in Paris.

This is the first record of his having traveled alone. Even with his family, the only long-distance trip, apart from Provins, was to stay with one Mme Mispreuve, when Jules broke his chamber pot, and Pierre saved the day by smuggling in a replacement in his hatbox (August 5, 1848).

At the beginning of April Jules steamed up the Loire as far as Tours on a pyroscaph. After lunch he caught a stagecoach, then the new Orléans railroad (JD 56), to stay in Paris under the wing of Great-Aunt Rosalie Charruel, 69, sister of his grandfather Gabriel Verne who had died the year before.

She lived at 2 Rue Thérèse, near the National Library. Jules hated the experience, later describing his great-aunt as "moderately stupid" and her apartment as "a shaft without air or wine."[6]

After his exams and a fortnight in the capital, he did his own packing for once. It had been decided he would stay with Pierre's newly-widowed mother and the cooing spinster sisters, in Provins, a small town 50 miles south-east of Paris, known for its medicinal roses. Despite the rickety carriage, he enjoyed a delightful journey through the Brie countryside and valley of the babbling Voulzie, "which a giant could drink in one gulp."[7] He probably filled the time in Provins by writing historical tragedies.

Back in Chantenay at the beginning of May, he worked fitfully at his plays and second-year law books. But without the company of Caroline or Paul, he was bad-tempered, moody, silent (ADF 26). The family circle that had meant so much to him now seemed restricting, as he longed for wider horizons. Even listening to virtuoso Anna at the piano, or singing and acting sketches with the family, could no longer console him (JJV 11).

He wrote dejected letters to Hignard and Genevois, and upset his mother with his frequent disappearances. She sent him to society balls, but he said not a word to the girls. Mme Louise Macé de la Barbelais declared him boring as mud and not sociable at all (ADF 26–27).

He did have some admirers, though, for one flattering portrait read:

Although rather wild and quite mad he had an extraordinary fascination. Not very tall, but extremely slim with strong

shoulders; an eccentric manner so you didn't know what he'd
say next except it would be witty, perhaps disconcertingly so
. . . Then profound silences. An unforgettable look, wonderful
teeth, and a shock of hair like a flame. Sometimes he affected
a bohemian style of dress, sometimes he posed as an exquisite
dandy.[8]

That same year, Jules fell for the love of his life, one who would
break his heart and whom he would never forget.

Her name was Herminie Arnault-Grossetière. She was four
months older than Jules, the daughter of landed proprietors—a step
above the student son of a commercial lawyer with not quite enough
blue blood. Blonde, blue-eyed, slim, delicate, and beautiful, but with
a haughty expression and "not very witty" (June 15, 1856), she was
apparently a talented musician (JJV 167). Another friend of Caroline's, she too had danced at the balls where the flighty cousin had displayed her maidenly allures.

Did the young man's infatuations for Caroline, Angèle, and Herminie overlap? Certainly, although his active attempts to court
Herminie were concentrated in the second half of this decidedly
fatal 1847.

In nearly 30 poems Jules poured out his entreaties, often explicitly
naming the girl. One, undoubtedly of April, the same month as the
Carolinian dedication, announced that he wept for lack of her smile,
the first letters, using his father's literary device, reading "H E R M I
N I E." Voyeuristic eroticism creeps into the elegy of the girl who goes
to sleep "leaving her dress to float open to the winds" (*Poems* 30). One
inebriated poem implies a favorable response, declaiming:

Never had a heart, a beloved heart
Said "I love you!"
So, day of happiness, day of peace in the heavens,
Day of drunken intoxication,

That tender phrase placed on my blessed brow
That tender caress! (*Poems* 14).

However, another is headed "Oh, if only it were true!" (*Poems* 31). Jules also lost no. 3. He apparently blamed it on the gossip of a sixty-four-year-old "Mme C. . . ," C. not being her initial, but the swear word, as he did for f. . . His 2,000-word diatribe attacked the looks, intelligence, and politics of that "Jesuitess . . . the most perfect incarnation of the devil on earth":

Let it be graven on her tomb
Here lies a stupid woman
Wicked, corrupting, eccentric bigot
Base, lying, ugly
Tight and foul (*Poems* 94).

Clearly, she had said something about him. It may all have been connected with his practical jokes, which had produced stories that had gotten back to his parents (RD 35).

Whatever brought on the heartbreaking rupture, Herminie got engaged, like the others, in early 1848; and married one Armand-Joseph-Auguste-Marie Terrien de la Haye in Nantes on July 19. Probably the noble owner of a manor at La Chauvellière, Armand was well over twice her age, in line with the previous pattern.

Jules felt angry beyond measure, and never reconciled himself to the situation, tormenting himself with it for decades. As the mismatched couple consummated their vows, he was still absolutely obsessed with her, although doing his best to conceal it: "Good heavens, I was forgetting: there's something else I can't get out of my mind . . . What's happening about the wedding . . . ? I'd be glad to know exactly what the situation is" (July 21, 1848).

The exam period again providentially coincided with the wedding season. But as if Jules's heart were not broken enough, a revolution broke out while he was planning his journey. It did quiet down, but just when he should have been packing, it flared up again.

In February 1848 Louis-Philippe had been forced to abdicate, inaugurating the Second Republic, with a moderate parliament elected for the first time by universal male suffrage. At these elections, Verne distributed voting slips in Nantes in favor of the provisional government.[9]

However, the left-wing elements who had introduced democracy objected to the results, provoking demonstrations and riots, which culminated on June 23 in the Insurrection of Paris. In response, a brutal repression began, under General Eugène Cavaignac. Several thousand workers died, together with two generals, Monsignor Affre, Archbishop of Paris, and more officers than in the entire Napoleonic Wars.[10]

A fortnight after the fall of the last bastion at Faubourg Saint-Antoine on 26 June, Pierre judged it increasingly urgent to pack Jules off, despite his mother's resistance, provided he promised not to get into fights (ADF 27).

Great-Aunt Charruel had fled to her country residence, so Jules was due to stay with his cousin Henri Garcet. Thirteen years older, Garcet was Pierre's nephew, a mathematics teacher at the Latin Quarter Lycée Henri IV, one of the best high schools in France. Once in Paris, however, Jules lived alone, at least from July 11, arranging his own food, room, and even laundry (July 17, 1848).

One of his first things he did was wander around Paris, studying the damage. He supported the center-right student movement based in Rue de Poitiers, in the Seventh Arrondissement,[11] as well as Adolphe Thiers's "quiet moderation" (July 21, 1848). Thiers opposed the 1848 Republic, campaigning for a constitutional monarchy and emphasizing law and order; but he supported Prince Louis-Napoléon in the presidential elections. Verne's position, in sum, was moderate conservative. The same year, he wrote a long essay entitled "Is There a Moral Obligation for France to Intervene in the Affairs of Poland?" in which he answered his own question with an impassioned no.

The 14th of July passed without major disturbance, although Paris remained messy:

> I visited the various points of [Right-Bank] Rues Saint-Jacques, Saint-Martin, and Saint-Antoine, Le Petit-Pont, and La Belle-Jardinière, seeing houses riddled with bullets and traversed by cannonballs. You can follow the track of the balls along the streets as they broke and swiped [*sic*] balconies, signs, cornices on their passage: a terrible sight (July 17, 1848).

He went to the Chamber of Deputies, thanks to a card from Monsieur Braheix, a deputy and a lawyer from Nantes. Debate centered on the arbitrary arrest of a prominent journalist and playwright, Émile de Girardin. Poet-politician Alphonse de Lamartine attended, together with General Cavaignac, Girardin himself, and several other renowned politicians and writers, including Verne's great hero, Hugo: "to see him properly I knocked down a lady and tore the lorgnettes from a total stranger's hands" (August 5, 1848).

During this time, Jules's social contacts were his parents' friends. He dined at Mme Arnous's, a shipowner's wife, and, several times, with Henri and Eugénie Garcet, taking along ex-Nonboarder Charles Maisonneuve, now a financier (July 21, 1848).

Amid the political and social effervescence, Verne was revising intensively for four subjects: Criminal Instruction, Penal Code, Procedure, and Civil Code. But he still worried about the orals, in the heart of the Latin Quarter:

> The examiners . . . must have great fun looking for all the most difficult and unexpected questions to throw in your face and then say, I covered it in my lectures (July 21, 1848).

> I fear I'm going to be in the odorous position of Sancho's laxatives when he removed the strap from the top of his breeches

and an unusual perfume came to tickle Don Quixote de la Manche's olfactory nerve! Fortunately there are toilets on Place Saint-Sulpice! (July 30, 1848).

Eleven days after Herminie's fatal wedding day, Jules's heart over-flowed, and he wrote his mother a delirious, surrealistic letter-cum-short story. The literary inspirations included E. T. A. Hoffmann, Victor Hugo, Gérard de Nerval, and the whole Romantic movement:

Alas, dear mother, life is not all roses, and fellows who build shining castles in Spain don't find them even in their own land . . .

Consommatum [*sic*] *est*, like St. Louis's, please excuse the Latin, and the anapestico / o / o / o / o / oc of Aeschylus would seem appropriate in the circumstances.

Besides, Morpheus opened the ivory gates for me one night and a fateful dream came to beat its bat-wings with curved nails over my leaden eyelids! . . .

Two young spouses were preparing to tie an altar knot capable of resisting the sharpest divorce blade. Both were good-looking and, as Jean-Jacques says, their bodies made to lodge their souls! The bride wore white, symbolizing her fiancé's naive soul; the groom, black, an allusion to the color of her soul! . . .

And outside a man, with holes in his elbows, a black goatee . . . a florid complexion, and legs finely worked and machine-finished, was sharpening his teeth on the doorknocker . . .

The bride felt cold to the touch and . . . a strange idea of old loves may have shivered through her . . .

As the bridal chamber opened to admit the trembling couple, heavenly joys flooded their hearts while . . . a sulfurous and bitter smoke filled the joyless, darkened rooms . . .

I shall console myself by killing the big cat on the first occasion . . .

My heart needed to overflow! That funereal ceremony

needed to be couched on paper so that one day I could say: *Exegi monumentum* [I have built a monument] (July 30, 1848).

Was Jules drunk or drugged ("Morpheus")? He had been out for a society dinner that evening, and appreciated his wine, although the conclusion is perfectly lucid. In any case, he fully revealed his frustration, jealousy, and bitterness, inaugurating a comparison between marriage and funerals for the next sixty years. At least one modern literary critic would base part of his distinguished career on little more than an interpretation of this letter.[12] Many of the details admittedly do remain unclear: were the holes in the man or his jacket, and was it a self-portrait?

As if regretting the outpouring, which marked the ending of his childhood, Jules would henceforth be less open with his parents. His letters to his father, especially, became little more than mere material enumerations, useful for understand his life in Paris but not the workings of his soul.

After taking his oral examinations on August 3, Jules had his baccalaureate in law. That same evening he left for another few days in Provins, packing his meager possessions in a hatbox. He spent much of the summer writing or planning tragedies and going for long solitary walks around Chantenay, now entirely bereft of charm for him. In September Paul came back for a few days, with fascinating stories of Martinique, Réunion, and Pondicherry, eager to practice four-handed piano again with his brother.

Having gotten some of his feelings about Herminie out of his system, Jules found that more kept flooding back in. For long months after, he wrote vengeful sonnets forecasting her unhappiness. Then he went through them and crosshatched her name in the dedications. In the end he had about sixty poems, the majority implicitly or explicitly about Herminie, which he carefully copied into a notebook bought at the bottom of Rue Jean-Jacques. He then kept the notebook until his death, like a final regret, although it is not clear how he prevented his wife from stumbling across it.

Some poems expostulate and threaten: "*Catinetta mia* [my

enchained], I tell you, be careful!" (*Poems* 169). Some recount the seduction of the young bride: "At the dark rendezvous . . . / She has to leave aunt, parents, sister, husband! . . . / She must betray them all; I'm on tenterhooks" (*Poems* 31). One or two others speculate on the consequences: "A noble gentleman with his lucre / Robbed that girl from my honest love! . . . / He caresses sons he thinks are his / Fashioned by sweet union in a joint account" (*Poems* 167).

Thirteen years later, when asked to inscribe an album for a friend, he copied out one of the Herminie sonnets.[13]

As the summer turned to autumn, Jules still seethed with resentment and anger at both Caroline and Herminie. He hated their hypocrisy, their self-interest, their betrayal of the ideal of love. In part of his mind he was convinced Herminie still loved him, but had been forced to marry a man old enough to be her father.

His fury extended to the whole of Nantes, for they were all fools and philistines, unable to judge his true worth:

Of knowledge a people incapable
Always filthy about it
A few thousand empty brains
Incorrigibly stupid . . .
The fairer sex anything but,
An inept clergy, a stupid prefect,
No fountains: this is Nantes!!!

The objects of his rage included himself, for wasting his love on such unworthy objects. This would be the only extended fit of blazing anger in his life. Later, when he became depressed, indignant, upset, he invariably kept an icy, almost British, calm.

The whole twelve months remained blighted for him. Perhaps inevitably, it was decided (by whom is not entirely clear) to distance him from the disgusting activities of the six newlyweds. This time, it would be a definitive rupture from his social circle, without possible return to the place of his frustrations and humiliations. On future visits to Nantes, he would see only his family and a few friends who had returned (RD 36). For the rest of his life he would remain in proud exile.

Sophie worried about the continuing Revolution and the thousands of deaths in the past few weeks. Against that could be used the argument that ex-Nonboarder Édouard Bonamy was already reading law in Paris (JD 57). Exactly the same age, Bonamy showed little sign of independent thought. His dull conventionality may have convinced her.

Later Jules invariably insisted he was pushed, "sent" by his father.[14] However, it must also have been his own idea, supported by Paul, to increase his exam chances by attending law lectures in Paris, from which the questions were often taken.

His grandmother, mother, and sisters did his packing (ADF 28). Just before leaving the student sent one last half-self-pitying, half-pompous shot across Herminie's bows: "Fine, I'm leaving, because they didn't want me, but men and women will see what wood that poor young man called Jules Verne was made of."[15]

He was perhaps better out of it, after all. The gutters ran with the blood of half a million Africans torn from their homes, tortured, and worked to death. From the failure in love of the "poor young man" would spring one of the greatest imaginations of the century.

CHAPTER 5

Law Student in the Literary Salons: 1848–51

AT 9 P.M. ON FRIDAY, November 10, 1848, the snowy Place Graslin witnessed a humdrum scene which would change the course of French literature. Verne and Bonamy climbed excitedly into the stagecoach (ADF 31). As it pulled away, their tearful mothers no doubt told them to tuck in their scarves; their gruff fathers, to write the moment they arrived.

The boys were dying to reach Paris to join the street party for the Second Republic. The star was that dangerous romantic poet, Lamartine; but at least Monsignor Sibour, Archbishop of Paris—replacing poor martyred Affre—would be sanctifying things with a solemn Te Deum (ADF 31).

At the railhead in Tours, Verne and Bonamy tried to slither aboard a National Guard train. "But where are your uniforms, my young men?" "In our luggage." "And your mayor's authorization?" The two quietly slipped away again. They finally steamed in on the Sunday, just in time to see candles mockingly smoking across the garbage-strewn Place de la Concorde (ADF 32).

The two trudged through the sludge and up many a dark, dank stair, doubting that they could live in such windowless eighth-floor closets. At last they found 24 Rue de l'Ancienne Comédie, on about the sixth floor (November 27, 1848). This bookshop-lined street in the Sixth Arrondissement, home to Louis XIV's Comédie-Française, led from the glorious Luxembourg Gardens down to the eternal Seine. At the throbbing heart of the Latin Quarter, steeped in 2,000 years of history, the building looked out on the Place de l'Odéon, scene of the battles of young romanticism. Opposite stood Café Procope, perhaps the oldest in the world, where Lt. Bonaparte had left his hat as deposit and where Diderot, Franklin, Voltaire, and Robespierre had set the world to rights.

An address to die for, one dripping with literary destiny. Sprinting up and down the flights, Jules couldn't believe his luck. The images of Herminie became slightly less hallucinatory.

The landlady, one Mme Martin—instantly nicknamed Lamartine—brought up fresh milk and bread, washed the dishes, and slopped out the chamber pots (February 22, 1849; November 22, 1848). Verne paid 30 centimes per garment to an out-of-town washerwoman. He soon told his mother that his shirts "no longer ha[d] a front nor indeed a behind" even if people might not notice (October 14, 1852). He owned only two pairs of socks and had no bathing facilities. Fortunately the temperature stayed below zero.

Although the idea of cooking on his wood stove apparently never crossed Verne's mind, he did manage to make himself a breakfast of coffee and two rolls, to keep him going until dinner (November 21, 1848). He was careful to dilute Seine drinking water (November 27, 1848) and claimed to walk two miles to a one-franc tavern on the Right Bank. "I eat beefsteaks as hard as Uncle Prudent's soles after trekking to La Guerche," he supposedly wrote; "the meat filling me must have pulled many a Paris bus" (ADF 52).

For him, body and spirit were one: "I've virtually no literature, producing nervous cramps whenever I pass a bookshop" (December 6, 1848). He indulged in a fine complete Shakespeare, devouring him on a boulevard bench, then lived three days on dried Chantenay plums to pay for the indulgence (ADF 34).

He paid about FF 80 ($240 in modern values) a month for food, FF 30 for rent, FF 10 for wood and oil, and FF 4 for linen (December

6, 1848). Jules's letters emphasized his expenses, but with some of the details airbrushed out, on the pretext of arithmetical incompetence. His father picked up the tab for "misc.," into which Jules slipped law-books, travel, and 100 stamps a month.

To twist the knife, the young poet revealed: "as I've been poorly, the doctor's ordered more food" (December 12, 1848). He told gut-churning stories of intestinal eruptions and enema-provoked explosions, uncontrolled vomiting, and dire emergencies in public toilets (November 21, 1848). Imagining he had cholera, he still managed brave jokes about all the two-way rectal traffic.

The heart-rending tales of freezing, starving, and bodily flows produced the desired effect. Tender-hearted Sophie secretly sent money, plus trunkloads of sheets, shirts, socks, lime-blossom tea, figs, and the jam that had first enraptured Pierre (ADF 33). Eventually even Pierre's stony heart melted and—after double-checking his son's fig-ures—the allowance rose to FF 125, then to the giddy sum of FF 150, three times more than an unskilled worker (Mar. 51).

What did Verne do for sex? In response to his mother's concern, Verne said he loved bachelorhood: "I can think of no happier state for a man" (March 9, 1850). Much later, in comments on the Latin Quarter lifestyle, he described himself as "a man about town (boule-vardier)" and emphasized the easy conquests and working-class kept women ("grisettes") (Int. 129; 89). We don't know whether he nudged or winked as he did so.

Then came a shock: "I've stopped taking the pills and haven't used the prick ointment!" Although the vulgar term must have flabber-gasted his father, Dr. Dumas's book does read "pommade Chibré," probably meaning penile cream. Jules wrote with astounding frank-ness about intimate health problems; and soon after, his father did blow up about something.

We can only conjecture what the ailment was, and how he caught it.

Of Verne's schoolmates, Ernest Genevois, was also studying law in the capital, and Charles Maisonneuve already worked in finance.

Maisonneuve and Hignard possibly lived on the same landing as Verne and Bonamy.[1] Nearly all of his other Paris friends consisted of Nantes schoolfellows, six or seven years older and still unmarried, now studying music. Although Verne felt close to Victor Massé (later a famous composer)—"an excellent friend and a good comrade," about whom he would soon publish an article—Hignard's name came up most. Thanks to Aristide, Verne joined a musical set in pianist and composer Adrien Talexy's salon, on Right-Bank Rue Louis le Grand.

In a different category were his parents' friends, invariably upper crust and interconnected. He was successively wined and dined by Bonamy's father, the Garnier family, Paul Championnière (former neighbor of Prudent's), and Messrs Braheix and Prévôt, whose "oldest daughter is very pretty" [April 2, 1849]. Jules continued to resent Great-Aunt Charruel, as she forgot his New Year present and "ordered" a poem from him "about a china pooch she's giving to some girl."[2] Refined Mme Arnous-Rivière, wife of the Verne soirée regular, lived in the center: Verne picked up his luggage there and often went back (ADF 34). Still keeping an eye on him was Henri Garcet.

More importantly, Uncles François de Châteaubourg and Auguste Allotte unexpectedly arrived shortly after Jules, declaring themselves "unmarried husbands" for the duration (November 27, 1848). They invited the delighted youth to a Meyerbeer comic opera perhaps starring Jenny Lind, who, however, attracted Verne's scorn for making " 18 million francs," although a "poor singer" [August 22, 1852].

Châteaubourg, above all, took Jules into society, starting with Madame Jomini's political salon. Verne marveled at everything the ladies knew, or at least could talk about, but felt tongue-tied and provincial, and did not return (ADF 34). But he loved Joséphine de Barère's literary salon, in nearby Rue Ferme des Mathurins. Joséphine was a youngish bluestocking, a seasoned traveler, and an excellent caterer.[3]

All the dinner invitations and resulting opera tickets, including one where he spotted President-elect Napoléon Bonaparte, caused just one problem. Verne and Bonamy owned only one outfit between the two of them. They took it in turns to go out, making a great joke of their penury (ADF 34).

With his literary culture, good looks, sensibility, and breeding, the ugly duckling blossomed. Shining in his new freedom, Verne soon met the oh-so-young Count de Coral, editor of the *Liberté*. The Count promised to introduce him to Victor Hugo and the whole Romantic set (December 6, 1848).

Verne was over the moon. In one part of his mind, though, he remained calculating, for it was still his ambition to meet the literary insiders. He wanted his writings to be read and instantly recognized for their real worth. But thousands of young men had the same dream, and he knew the odds against him. Reaching such heady heights after less than one month, he decided to keep his powder dry.

People thought him wonderful, he reported, because he always agreed with fools: "Twenty years old, twenty years old! One day I'll get even with them!" (December 29, 1848).

Two authorities report that Verne did meet Hugo at this time.[4] But in any case his mind soon turned to other matters, for at Joséphine's he was introduced to Chevalier Casimir d'Arpentigny, the famous palm-reader (*JVEST* 45). Although distinctly uninterested in chiromancy, Verne made a good impression, and was quickly invited into his salon (ADF 35).

The Chevalier was on excellent terms with Alexandre Dumas, *père* (1802–70) and *fils* (1824–95) (*JVEST* 217). Decades later, Dumas *fils* still defended the "misunderstood, unknown science" of palmistry and d'Arpentigny, its "founder." Dumas had found instant stardom with his novel *La Dame aux camélias* only months before. With his planned stage adaptation *Camille*, and soon Verdi's operatic version *La Traviata*, as well as his flood of popular plays, he would shortly become France's leading dramatist.

Going beyond his wildest dreams, the fresh-faced provincial met Dumas *fils* at the beginning of January 1849. With only four years between them, the two hit it off from the beginning:

the friend to whom I owe the deepest debt of gratitude and affection is Alexandre Dumas the younger . . . We became chums almost at once. He was the first to encourage me. I may say that he was my first protector . . . He introduced me to his father; he worked with me in collaboration (*Int.* 90)

By February 8, Verne could casually tell his father that he and Dumas *fils* were close, as was "old Dumas who I see occasionally."

Dumas *père* had been one of the most famous men in the world since *The Three Musketeers* (1844) and *The Count of Monte Cristo* (1844–46). When Verne met him, he had just become manager of the Historic Theater and was about to reopen it with much ado. His own lavish *Youth of the Musketeers* premiered to huge fanfare on February 10th (or 17th). Jules Verne was the guest of honor: "I sat in [Dumas's]stage-box, what a privilege! . . . Old Dumas was incredible about his play. He couldn't help telling us what was about to happen. I saw a lot of well-known people who came into the box" (February 22, 1849).

Verne was not exaggerating, for that evening he met drama critic Jules Janin, novelist Théophile Gautier, and Girardin, whom he had seen at the Assembly. He must have been perpetually rubbing his eyes.

Dumas *père* spent much time at Monte Cristo, his two-year-old oriental-romantic-baroque castle in Saint-Germain en Laye, near Paris. With exotic servants, lakes, grottoes, and a complete menagerie, the parties lasted entire months. Verne was soon sitting in the celebrated gardens, working on a play with Dumas *fils*.

He couldn't conceive greater happiness. Instead of solitary scribbling, he shared a give and take where all his ideas bubbling up were heeded and even treated seriously. At the same time, he found it humbling when the expert unerringly homed in on his weak exchanges and penned witty new dialogues almost as quickly as he could read them.

Verne devoured Dumas *père*'s over-rich concoctions, but wondered about their origin, "without name in or on any tongue (ADF 35)." One of his interviewers later added:

> Between two serial installments, Dumas *père* would descend to the kitchen to whip up his magical mayonnaises. Although silver was lacking—not greatly surprising those present—the champagne bubbled, the women were pretty, and nobody complained about having to share a glass with the girl beside him (*Int.* 135).

Monte Cristo had in fact gone bust in January 1848, with the furniture sold off in May, followed by the castle itself in May 1849. No wonder the guests sat outside and the cutlery seemed so sparse.

Did Verne marvel at the distance covered in four months? A lovelorn adolescent with no immediately visible talent had met the only person to review his novels seriously for the next forty years, plus one of the globe's most influential people, and collaborated on an equal footing with the new world star. So dizzying was the ascent that Verne surely again swore to himself not to blow his chances by showing his true colors. He had learned how unfair people could be. He had often gotten so near a desired goal, only to unerringly say the wrong thing in the wrong place. He just had to hope that Paris literary society would be freer than Nantes, a little more accommodating of anyone who thought differently.

In 1848–49, Verne was voraciously reading the romantics, especially Dumas, Alfred de Vigny, Alfred de Musset, Goethe, and Friedrich Schiller. But his greatest love remained the granddaddy of them all: "I was greatly under the influence of Victor Hugo, indeed, very excited by reading and re-reading his works. At that time I could have recited by heart whole pages of *Notre Dame de Paris* [*The Hunchback of Notre Dame*] (*Int.* 89).

From the start in Paris he thought only of money, enemas—and a literary career. His studies at the world-famous Law Faculty opposite

Garcet's *lycée*, like his father before him, hardly registered. When his father predictably blew up, Verne beat around the bush. On November 21, he had written that a law career would give him the means to *also* lead a life of letters, but three weeks later that he much preferred verse to . . . politics: "I couldn't care less about ministers, President, and Chamber while one poet remains in France to steal our hearts away." Although he planned to do a degree in French literature (December 17, 1848), his interest in the matter remained, he emphasized, purely academic: "it's fantastic . . . to be in close touch with literature, to sense the direction it's going . . . there are seminal studies to do on the present period, and on the genre to come" (December 12, 1848).

Verne somehow forgot to mention that he was a full-time author himself, composing a prodigious three or four volumes a year. Three main outlets were available at the time: poetry, the novel, and drama. But the greatest of these was playwriting, the genre to come and the one Verne thought himself best at.

His first plays, on which he had been hard at work since 1846, imitated Hugo's. In one five-act tragedy, *The Gunpowder Plot*, Guy Fawkes plans to blow up the Protestant monarchy. Another verse tragedy of heartrending intensity, *A Drama under Louis XV*, abounds with torrid love scenes, with much rape and murder, but could not be completed because of official censorship (January 26, 1851).

Whether because of the world's failure to recognize his talent, an improvement in his mood, or a change in public taste, Verne's writing evolved. He penned a long series of vaudevilles, full of farcical quid-pro-quos, bedroom scenes, and risqué jokes, with corrosive satires of the bourgeois thrown in for free: the one-act *Sea Outing*, an 1820 skit about French smuggling and the Scottish aristocracy, full of "grog"; *Rabelais's Quarter-Hour*, with a jilted girl taking revenge; *Sometimes You Need Someone Smaller*, about rivalry in love; the two-act "Don Galaor," where true love conquers all; and the three-act "The Savants," supposedly based on learned neighbors of Uncle Prudent's, Messrs Championnière (ADF 42).

His libretti for comic operas included the one-act *The Grouse*, in synopsis form only, where a woman dreads marrying a fifty-year-old, and two-act *Abdullah*, about an Arab visiting Versailles and risking the death penalty for love of a Frenchwoman. *Abdullah* was probably revised by Georges Schwob in 1849 (Lemire 7).

By 1850–51, Verne had completed a score of plays, often containing brilliant comic shafts and striking one-liners. While most still make interesting reading, none had yet found a home. His nightmares surely swam with misplaced manuscripts and brutally casual rejection slips.

While still on the high of his carefree social life and literary creation, Verne quoted Goethe's "Nothing is illusion that makes us happy" (December 12, 1848). He also—perhaps a mistake—sent his father a verse composition boldly uniting sex and politics: "the Republic is just a whore / Quite shameless / Top people, and even further up / She accosted to run her store / And paid for their pimping services!" (*Poems* 160). He may have let it drop that although one of his plays might finally be staged, his degree would not be finished until at least August . . . (January 24, 1849).

The father's reaction was devastating. A long, aggressive reply declared that consorting with dissolute artists was Not a Good Thing. Pierre's outraged missive consisted mostly of moralistic diktats and below-the-belt blows. Jules responded robustly that: he had always tried not to appear eccentric, at least in his own eyes; you shouldn't believe all the tittle-tattle you heard; he *had* read his mother's letters and *was* sending news home; if his letters often seemed incomprehensible, his thoughts were much clearer; the word "salon" probably frightened his father more than the reality; pleasure and happiness shouldn't be confused; he *had* worked hard for his exams; perhaps he did look down ever so slightly on the provinces, for the girls were so much prettier in Paris; and although "I always said I'd be a lawyer," a writer was "the finest position any man can have in this world . . . although we haven't quite got to that stage" (January 24, 1849). The surface Jules tried Jesuitically to mollify, but the underlying Verne remained entirely subversive. He knew where he was going.

Verne thought *The Gunpowder Plot* and *A Drama under Louis XV* best suited the Historic Theater. But Bonamy preferred *Broken Straws* and so, early in 1849, Verne submitted all three. Dumas *père* reportedly rejected the tragedies, but found the comedy promising (ADF 37).

It must have been an early draft, since the Monte Cristo collaboration involved this same *Broken Straws*. Although Dumas *fils* did not list it among his collaborative works, Verne later affirmed: "Dumas *fils* gave me the subject, as far as I remember"; "together we wrote a play together called [*Broken Straws*]."[5] He dedicated it to Dumas *fils*, who, he told his father, had "saved" it (June 28, 1850). In return, the student almost certainly ghost-wrote books for his busy senior, although we can only guess which.[6] On the basis of their work together, in both directions, Dumas *fils* later wrote that Verne shared with his prolific father "imagination, verve, good humor, invention, health, clarity, and that virtue looked down on by the impotent: fecundity."[7]

In the completed *Broken Straws*, the aged Count d'Esbard, jealous of his teenage wife, locks her up. They play the game of "Broken Straws," where the first to accept something from the other loses. The Count bursts into the wife's room, the lover hides in the wardrobe, and the husband demands the key—so losing the game. Among the bedroom scenes, Verne worked in mocking references to the pumped-up self-importance of Nantes's most prominent figures.

Verne probably submitted the revamped play in person, since Dumas *père* regularly invited him to his home (March 9, 1850). In any case, the upshot again exceeded what could reasonably have been dreamed of.

Broken Straws opened at the Historic Theater on June 12, 1850, the first performance of a play by Verne. It ran for fourteen full nights, with all of Verne's friends coming along to laugh at the right places, helping with the reviews. The FF 15 ($45 in modern values) profit even covered his expenses, and Adrien Talexy threw one of his famous parties to fete the new dramatist. As icing on the cake, the play opened at the Graslin Theater five months later; all Jules had to do was brave the notables' angry protests. Local critics reportedly considered it "truly a work of art," but the plot "so risky that only the author's grace and wit rendered [it] acceptable" and the moral "desperate news for any husband over 50" (ADF 40).

The waking dream continued with publication of the play, arranged by Dumas *fils* and bankrolled by Charles Maisonneuve.[8] Telling his father of his first time in print, Verne cautioned that the play might seem a little risqué: "I've never claimed a mother could take her daughter to it, I'm not responsible for educating French virgins." All his friends wanted copies, but he thought they could buy them in the bookshop.

During all the excitement, events had continued apace. In March 1849 Verne had drawn a lottery number that meant he avoided conscription. In response to his father's complaint, Verne said he detested the military (March 12, 1849).

That same month Bonamy left Paris, receiving a valedictory sonnet, and Verne happily moved to a new room on the third floor (March 12, 1849). His whole day was now spent within four walls, broken only by dinners and invitations. But the creative opportunities surely outweighed the occasional depression and doubts about his future. He admitted to feeling lonely when he made a visit abroad without his brother, presumably to Belgium, Switzerland, or Germany (November 16, 1849).

In any spare moments, Verne studied ("crashingly boring but not difficult") (December 6, 1848). After writing a dissertation in Latin he ended up with a total of two "passes" and two "distinctions." In August 1849 he mentioned to his father, rather cruelly, that the paper work had been ready for ages and that to become a lawyer he now just needed to take the oath.

The first surviving portrait of Verne dates from this time. A striking stereoscopic photograph shows a man with smooth skin and warm, intelligent eyes (*BSJV* 150:10). He boasts a wispy moustache, a roman nose from his Mediterranean ancestors, long fairish hair from his Scottish ones, and a Romantic pose that proclaims his new profession to the whole world.

Did his law studies help his writing? Stendhal claimed to read two or three pages of the *Napoleonic Code* every day to find the right tone for his writing. If culture is what remains when you've forgotten the rest, Verne seems to have merely stripped the stylistic veneer off his legal studies, for the precision of his language sometimes seems decidedly statute-like. In any case the law degree served mostly as a stepping-stone to escape his father's shadow, to avoid what he had seen at breakfast every day, to deny provinciality and religiosity. And yet Jules was sufficiently cautious, or willing to please his father, to finish it.

At this stage, he felt he stood on the brink of . . . well, he wasn't quite sure, but knew it would change his life. He was doing what every young man dreams of: finding himself and exposing himself to wider horizons.

Parrying his uncomprehending father, alternately fighting and giving in to his sensual urges, combining work and play, slipping from adolescence into precocious fame, Verne's character was complex. He himself felt clear about only three things, his incompatibility with the legal profession, his literary star, and his instinct for subversion: "Don't believe I'm having fun all the time here, for fate keeps me tied to Paris. I may become a good writer, but only a poor lawyer as I invariably see the comic or artistic side of things, missing their precise reality" (January 26, 1851).

Although his unconventionality, comic invention, and belief in a manifest literary destiny had failed him in Nantes, they seemed to possess some value in the capital. But he had no idea just how hard it would get.

At the beginning of 1851 Verne met the famous Jacques Arago (1799–1855), thanks to Evariste Colombel, mayor of Nantes and family friend [April or May 1851]. Although almost blind, Arago had taken part in the 1849 Colorado gold rush and visited the Antarctic, South Seas, and the stratosphere. Among his dozens of books, *Journey Around the World* (1840) appeared on every bookshelf. His brother General Jean Arago had fought for Mexican independence under Santa *a.* Anna and scientist brother François Arago was a household name. Jacques Arago immediately took Jules under his wing, with the two becoming firm friends. He took him on errands around town, told him tales of adventure, and invited him home (14 Rue Mazagran), to meet the throngs of travel writers, geographers, and scientists hobnobbing there. The two even embarked on writing a play together (June 29, 1851). ✓

For one July weekend that year, although "harassed and ill," Verne could not resist taking the new train to Dunkirk to see his Uncle and Aunt Auguste Allotte. Even if the trip to the "pretty little seaport, very Dutch" with friend Pitre Gouté took his last five-franc piece, he was able to write, with great satisfaction: "I have seen the North Sea" (July 29, 1851). From a well-to-do family, Gouté, "slightly pernickety" but "faithful in friendship," composed music with Hignard.[9] Given his lifelong obsession with travel, it seems significant that Verne's first known destination lay due north, in an Arctic whaling port in a scarcely Gallic region: traditionally Flemish-speaking, the "flat country" had been French for only twenty years.

By that same 1851, Verne had written two further short stories, "The First Ships of the Mexican Navy" and "A Balloon Journey." Verne read both to Arago and submitted them to the director of the *Musée des familles*, an upscale literary and encyclopedic *Reader's Digest*, modeled on British magazines. An eight-page weekly, with a pronounced religious emphasis, it covered "manners and customs, history, nature studies . . . trade, industry, mechanics, astronomy, travel, geography, and cities," with a massive circulation of 300,000.[10] Fellow Breton, Collège Royal alumnus, and family acquaintance Pierre Chevalier had written several books on the Quai de la Fosse and Nantes (OD 61). Within a fortnight he accepted both stories. However, he forgot to consult about an important change to the title: as the twenty-three-year-old writer pointed out, "The First Ships . . . : South America" should have been "North America" (July 29, 1851).

Verne's first published prose work already bears his trademark exotic setting and information overload: "On October 18, 1825, ship of the line *Asia* and eight-gun brig *Constanzia* lay off Aguijan,[11] one ✱

of the Marianas." Having got rid of the captain, a mutinous lieutenant plans to sell the *Asia* to the Mexican Revolutionaries. Surviving an avalanche, he climbs Popocatepetl, but two loyal sailors cut a bridge he is crossing, and virtue and the Spanish colonial government finally triumph. The dramatic descriptions and nautical terminology blend well with the geography, history, and inspired dialogue. But shocking racial and bestial obsessions lurk, with names for each combination of "miscegenation" between Spanish, Indians, and Blacks, or the offspring "of a coyote and a mulatto [or] . . . a coyote and an Indian woman" (iv).

In "A Balloon Journey," an innovative craft is launched, but a crazy stowaway takes control of the narrative, recounting a long history of aerial navigation; after a long struggle the madman falls to his death. The story, with five fine engravings, was quasi-plagiarized;[12] and shows the influence of Verne's English reading. Chevalier mislabeled "The First Ships" a "Historical Study," despite all the dialogue, and "A Balloon Journey," an "article."

The stories made little impact, and Verne underplayed their significance: "First Ships" was "just a simple adventure . . . in Cooper's manner" (March 1851). Although asking his father to resubscribe to the *Musée*, Verne got upset when rumors of fantastic payment circulated in Nantes, saying money was hardly the incentive; only much later did he actually admit the stories were unpaid (June 29, 1851; December 2, 1852 *Int.* 136).

In fact these early essays, only with hindsight "the first indication of the line of novel that I was destined to follow" (*Int.* 90), did not divert Verne from his chosen path. The breakthrough of *Broken Straws* had spurred him on, aided by sibling rivalry, for Paul had put on a mime play in Martinique, capturing the hearts of the languorous young beauties (ADF 50). The older brother switched to higher gear and began to churn out three plays a year.

People meeting Verne for the first time often had an inaccurate impression, for timidity and taciturnity hid his virtues. But certain characteristics were beginning to emerge: a sardonic wit when relaxed or aroused; a preference for male companionship, combined with a strong sensuality; a homosexual leaning, that would become more pronounced in later years; a remarkable capacity for sustained work and abundant output; an ambition for his plays to reach a wide audience; and an energetic temperament allowing him to face adversity and convert crisis into opportunity.

He would never totally become Parisian, if by that we mean smoothness and superficial cosmopolitanism. However, he could already pass for an adopted Parisian, with his vivacity, culture, and freedom from convention. Honoré de Balzac pointed out that we all belong to the generation of our twenties. In 1848 a movement ran like wildfire across Europe, liberating attitudes and lifestyles, akin to 1968 for a later generation. Verne indeed shared the aspirations of the whole Romantic age, the yearning for individuality, creativity, freedom, something beyond our ken. His late-Romantic, or early-modern, generation lived in the Latin Quarter village at a magical moment before that community disappeared. The new ideas had freed society from the weight of the past, but gas and steam had not yet besmirched Europe with their relentless search for productivity and their mechanization of human relationships. Verne was very much a man of 1848.

CHAPTER 6.

Plays and Poverty: 1851–54

LIKE MOST WRITERS, Verne attached great importance to his surroundings. Possibly in late 1850 he lived on the Right Bank, in Rue Louis le Grand, along from Talexy's salon, perhaps on a first floor. He lived with fellow gunman Paul Perret,[1] also theoretically studying law while actually pursuing literature. Perret had an untamed imagination, often erotic in bent. At one stage the flat mates were in danger of being dragged off to the police station on charges of breaking their courtyard windows.[2] It is not known whether their advanced legal knowledge helped them on this occasion.

In about February 1851, Verne moved into a furnished room in a hotel. He complained about his bohemian neighbors, in uproar day and night, "exactly like a public square, making me perpetually chase my ideas" (ADF 43). On Jules's request, Pierre reluctantly agreed to bankroll first his board and lodging, then a real apartment (March 1851).

Friend Aristide Hignard lived on the top floor of 18 Boulevard Bonne Nouvelle, at the intersection with Rue Mazagran, fifty yards from Arago's place. The boulevard area, housing most of Paris's theaters, had been created by Georges-Eugène Haussmann, as he cut broad swathes through the medieval quarters of the Right Bank. The eighth floor planed majestically "at the brain" of the block, 120 stairs up from a tobacconist's.[3] Since accommodation was available across the corridor from Hignard's, Verne moved in, on April 9. He delightedly reigned over "a light and airy room in which I can put my ideas in order" (ADF 46), facing due south. By student standards, it was a palace, with windows on four sides, two main rooms plus an entrance cubby-hole, en-suite bathroom and kitchen, a stove, washbasin, and chest of drawers in one room, a marble chimney in the other, and a sofa for entertaining visitors. Verne proudly positioned his large work desk and modest bookshelves in the dining room.

Aunt Garcet helped buy linen and a mattress and sew his curtains.[4] He appreciated his mother's food parcels, with fruit from Chantenay, but even more the money she secretly sent him.[5] Contemplating Paris as from the top of the Pyramids (April 1853), Verne felt like a Napoleonic conqueror. He found room for a FF 25 pre-Revolutionary piano.[6] On either side of the chimney hung Mathilde and Anna, as he put it, facing a wrecked fishing smack in Uncle Châteaubourg's best storm-tossed style.[7]

It was not all sitting in front of a blank sheet of paper. Verne and a whole circle of friends would crowd into Hignard's rooms, musicians Massé and Talexy to work (Lemire 14), Maisonneuve and Félix Duquesnel (1832–1915) to play. Musical performances turned into baccarat sessions, the stakes escalating astronomically from 50 centimes. The young crowd would leave late, "after the curfew had sounded, slamming the door, lighting a few wax friction matches, and gaily singing poetry as they descended."[8]

Henceforth, Verne would use "we" to describe his activities, not needing to mention Hignard. Crossing the corridor one evening to write together, Jules forgot to lock his own door. When he returned, his gold watch had disappeared. The two young men went to the police, who licked their pencils and enquired whether it was an "escapement watch." "Not half!" Verne is said to have exclaimed, departing with roars of laughter.[9]

When Prince-President Bonaparte seized absolute power as the self-proclaimed Emperor Napoléon III, Verne excitedly wrote of the fighting: "the shops have all shut. Barricades are going up everywhere: people are being arrested and dragged along by their hair"; "there were fierce battles at the bottom of the street, houses destroyed by cannons!"[10]

The discussions about Jules's future dragged on for more than half a decade. He took several unambitious jobs, starting with no. 5 supernumerary clerk in Monsieur Gamard's law office at FF 50 per month, but soon abandoned it in disgust at the exploitation. He tried working in a bank, but soon switched to private law tuition. Pierre was not amused, especially when he realized Jules had sold some of the things bought for Ancienne Comédie; the lessons soon stopped (March 1851). Jules approached Monsieur Vernes [sic], the Protestant banker, on the pretext of a search for shared ancestors, although a job may have been uppermost in his mind (January 17, 1852).

In the end Pierre sent an ultimatum: Jules must either come back to Nantes for two years' legal apprenticeship or work as a lawyer in Paris. His son responded: "a job in a law practice means 7:30 in the morning till nine at night . . . literature above all as that's all I can do well . . . If I practiced both . . . one . . . would win out, and . . . the bar'd have a low life expectancy," (March 1851).

He accepted, however, to work seven or eight hours a day for lawyer Paul Championnière (1798–1851) (March 1851). Championnière had trained and practiced with Pierre back in 1825; he was distantly related to the Allottes by marriage; and he and his brother had supposedly been lampooned in Verne's "The Savants" (ADF 42). However, before Jules could check in, Monsieur Championnière caught cholera and died, shocking the would-be lawyer: "He was the first person I knew in the prime of life who's left us!" (April 7, 1851). After this bolt from the heavens, Jules Verne, Esq., abandoned the idea of any sort of work as "a litigious, quibbling hurler" (May 6, 1853). While continuing to sign "lawyer," notably at his own and his sisters' marriages, he was now committed to making it as a writer—or bust.[11]

In January 1852 Pierre made one last attempt, offering Jules his entire legal practice, worth about FF 120,000 (September 7, 1856). "Anyone else would be crazy not to jump at your offer . . . I know what I am, I understand what I may one day become . . . [The] practice . . . would just wither away" (mid-October 1851). Two years later, Pierre finally gave in, sold his hard-won practice, and retired.

From about 1852 Verne began to visit the library "very often" (31 May 52). His reading at this time included Samuel Richardson, especially *Clarissa* (1748); Balzac, in bed every evening; and two textbooks by his cousin Garcet, *New Lessons in Cosmography* (1853) and *Elements of Mechanics* (1856).[12] The intellectual stimulation may have been one factor behind his slow evolution from drama to historico-geographical prose.

With Monte Cristo closed down, Dumas *fils* invited Verne several times to his home, north of the Tuileries, to eat his celebrated flambé omelets, and perhaps to work.[13] Dumas was about to announce ambitious plans for a series of novels following the Wandering Jew down through the centuries, although completing only the 700-page *Isaac Laquédem* (1852–53). Verne is meant to have talked of his own research and plans for a similarly multi-volume epic (RD 43). This "novel of science" would supposedly be a vast fresco, "a viaduct with a hundred arches thrown from yesterday's romanticism to tomorrow's symbolism, a simultaneously realistic and lyric work of art" (ADF 44). In this version of events, Dumas keenly supported the idea, resulting in some of Verne's early short stories. However, these three-quarters-of-a-century-old recollections of Verne as planning a "novel of science" and as a remarkably precocious precursor of symbolism are almost certainly distorted by his false reputation for anticipation— although Dumas certainly proposed some major form of collaboration, which Verne accepted [April 29, 1853].

Verne soon published a third historical story in the *Musée*, "Martin Paz" (1852). Staying with Arago for a few months was a talented Peruvian artist called Ignace Merino, founder of the Lima Academy of Fine Arts. He had brought over with him a documentary album: not only did Verne's locale and inspiration come from Merino's watercolors, but several of them accompanied his text, meaning the tale was probably written to order (ADF 49). When "Martin Paz" came out, the author was "Jules Vernes": perhaps just an unfortunate slip, but an identical error occurred the following year, before being "corrected" to "Charles Verne" the year after (Lottman 38). To lose *one* wife might be careless, but to mislay an author three times . . .

In the presentation preceding it, the story resembled Cooper's *The Spy* (1821) and *The Pioneers* (1823); it had "history, races, customs, landscapes, styles of dress . . . poignant scenes, wild tableaux, and outlandish characters." With its geographical insight and impossible love between an Indian and a Spanish woman, "Martin Paz" remains readable today. Despite its disturbing anti-Semitism ("The Jew Everywhere a Jew" who "descended from the Judas that delivered his master for 30 pieces of silver"), it revealed two of Verne's strengths: his tight narrative and dramatic scenes drawn from an inner eye. "Most people like it and just couldn't wait for the ending," he modestly wrote; in fact critical reaction was good.[14]

Pleased by Verne's efforts, Chevalier ordered "a very long article on *Lucia* [*di Lammermoor*]" (March 22, 1852), Donizetti's opera (1835), based on Walter Scott's *The Bride of Lammermoor* (1819). The importance of the command was not only that Verne added a music-criticism cord to his bow, but that the location was Edinburgh and the rest of Scotland, for Verne was soon to start a three-book series in the same locale.[15]

That same year the *Musée* published Chevalier and Verne's comedy *Castles in California*. Literary collaboration was probably the reason the new author stayed two days with his editor in Marly.[16] The play, full of mangled proverbs, shows a disillusioned '49er returning from newly-American California to his conventional middle-class home, an allusion to Arago's adventure. The publisher continued his autocratic ways: for *Castles* "what was highly annoying was that the engravings were done in advance: I had to write a text which fitted around them and add totally unnecessary characters" [July 1852].

Perhaps Verne refused his father's FF 120,000 offer because a more interesting one was in the works. At twenty three, he started his first real job, as secretary of the Théâtre Lyrique, under director Edmond Seveste (January 17, 1852). The Lyric, on the Boulevard du Temple, was the new name of the Historic Theater, of *Broken Straws* fame, built by Dumas *père* in 1847 but gone bust twice in the meantime. The position may have been thanks to Dumas's string-pulling, for Verne met Seveste through him (JD 101). The director, however, died in February, surely making Verne think he hexed his bosses. His brother Jules Seveste took over.

Verne's aim seems to have been greater visibility, by getting to know the leading authors, composers, and critics; he was indeed to meet Scribe and Auber.[17] But despite running the theater virtually single-handedly, his humble job-title meant he got little credit. Although he was paid FF 100 a month (January 17, 1852) for the first few months—compared to diva Marie Cabel's 6,000—Jules Séveste cut this to nothing, promising in return to stage one Verne play each year; the secretary also made a few carriage trips at FF 2 per hour.[18] Verne later vehemently denied he had ever been paid (December 2, 1852). So upset were his parents by his new position that he "forgot" to tell them that he had returned to it, presumably after the summer break.[19]

The secretary's work started at midday and filled his evenings (December 2, 1852). He huddled in a dark, draughty little office on Rue Vieille du Temple, not far from his apartment and on the edge of the medieval Marais, picturesquely dank and crumbling. But he had the run of the magnificent building, with its elliptical auditorium, 2,000 seats in five tiers, enormous stage, and plush red and gold hangings (JJV 21).

Verne spent much of his time on posters, décors, complimentary tickets, contacts with critics, and settling arguments between the temperamental Cabel and her companions and singing partner (ADF

65). According to one contemporary account, he felt cold one day and borrowed a sumptuous fake-ermine cloak from the wardrobe-master. The actors and actresses delightedly watched Jules mincing about in a superb parody of the diva. When she discovered, Cabel was not amused.[20]

Verne got on well with his boss, with genuine mutual affection. But the theater's activities were savaged by the critics ("childish"— *Revue des deux mondes*, cited by ADF 67): although Seveste bore the brunt, the secretary was equally responsible.

After two years Verne was hoping to do something at the Odéon or Gymnase in the summer (May 17, 1854). To tell the truth he felt decidedly fed up with "that tiresome Lyric" (April 19, 1854), prob-ably because it took so much time. He tried to resign—but Séveste refused to let him go.

In June 1854, however, Seveste caught cholera in turn and died a few hours later. The hex was working overtime, compelling Verne away from any stable position. "I was very fond of him but . . . at last I'm free of the theater" [July 1, 1854]. Legally free, perhaps, but moral pressure made him stay on another fourteen months (*BSJV* 143:14), and even then, he was not released without a struggle. The interim director—who beat Jacques Offenbach to the position— "offered to make me theater director . . . with a share in the profits . . . I refused; I want to be free and prove what I have done."[21] Under Jules's hand, the theater had lost about FF 500 a day, about the same as his successors.[22] At the age of nearly twenty-eight, permanently broke but believing he just needed to capitalize on his previous efforts, Verne renounced the directorship.

Verne's double-or-quits renunciation of such a prestigious and powerful position seems distinctly rash. He may have regretted it over the next eight years.

With the initial self-confidence gained from the Lyric, Verne founded a weekly dining club called The Eleven Bachelors ("Les Onze sans femme"), sworn to never admit a woman and initially drawn mostly from Talexy's musical set. The Bachelors met at Vachette's, 30 Boulevard Poissonnière, nearly next door to Verne's, or in a private dining-room at the distinguished restaurant Brébant.[23]

Verne would play practical jokes, perform in a mini-orchestra conducted by Hignard, read out the rude parts of his letters, or recite his love poetry, possibly including a scurrilous poem sometimes attributed to him, "Lamentations of a Fanny Hair." This text runs the whole gamut of obscenity, with descriptions of urine, menstruation, crabs, cunnilingus, and venereal disease, and the passage of schoolboys, Academicians, and decrepit old men—not bedtime reading.

All eleven were struggling young musicians, writers, or painters, mostly conservative in politics. We have already met four: pianist Talexy himself, schoolmates David Pitfold and Ernest Boulanger, and rowdy serenader Charles de Béchenec, soon to work for the Lyric. The six others would make a mark in their chosen fields: comic opera virtuoso Charles Delioux, as a famous composer; art student Stop, as caricaturist on the satirical magazine the *Charivari*; Eugène Verconsin, as author of one-act comedies for salons and casinos; career civil servant Ernest L'Épine, as author of comedies with Alphonse Daudet; Henri Caspers, as author and comic librettist; and witty Parisian Philippe Gille, who had exhibited at the Salon in 1851–52, as literary editor of the *Figaro*.[24]

Others dropped in from time to time, including such familiar figures as Hignard, Massé, Maisonneuve, and Lorois. Talexy regular young Léo Delibes would become a composer; Charles Bertall, an illustrator and photographer; Henri Larochelle, director of the Porte-Saint-Martin Theater; "Bazille" (presumably François Bazin), composer for Labiche's comic operas; teenager Raymond Fournier-Sarlovèze, soldier and politician; Félix Duquesnel, stockbroker and director of the Châtelet Theater; Pierre Véron, librettist and editor of the *Charivari*; Philoxène Boyer, publicist and author; Count Henri d'Ideville, writer, diplomat, and publicist; Gustave Nadaud, author of songs later performed by Georges Brassens; and Hippolyte de Villemessant, director of the *Figaro*. By some trick of fate, all of

Verne's misogynous companions, although mostly unknown then, would a generation later form a roll-call of the good and great.

However, Verne's closest friends formed a tight-knit Nantais group: Genevois, Lorois, a Charles Liton, and Pitre Gouté, with whom he had traveled to Dunkirk [end of March 1855].

When two good friends died, Verne was shocked. He wrote a long letter in praise of author Jules Lorin, although, or because, he had been living in sin with a married woman; Lorin had dedicated a romantic poem, "Beside the Lake," to Paul Verne. The death from consumption of ex-Nonboarder and Bachelor David Pitfold also greatly upset him (March 14, 1853).

From his mid-twenties, Verne felt left on the shelf and lonely in Paris, where at first he had seemed so gloriously free. His provincial dream of taking the capital by storm had not worked out; and as time went on, his poverty became increasingly hard to bear. His social, sexual, and financial problems emerged in a series of letters begging his mother to find him a mate, any mate: "Marry me off, any wife you choose. I'll take her eyes shut and purse open"; "Find me a hunch-backed woman with private means . . . Jules Verne who, the devil take it, longs to marry a rich young woman"; "I don't see why in Paris society I couldn't dig up a rich young woman who's made a mistake, or might be ready to do so—and Bob's your uncle."[25] He indulged in much greater crudeness with Genevois, invariably connecting sex and diarrhea, money and love: "the bosom is important, I will admit . . . but I prefer [my wife] to have only one breast and an extra farm in Beauce, a single buttock, and huge pastures in Normandy."[26]

Verne's parents still hoped to marry their eldest son in Nantes. When his mother thought she had found the perfect match—who may be the same as the "pretty little Creole face" Paul was pining after—Verne feigned horror at her origin and temperament, but exulted at her 15,000 a year private income: "a Creole! But that's mar-rying Vesuvius and Etna! How many Pompeiis and Herculaneums our lavas would cover . . . all the same I authorize the young . . . woman to officially request my hand."27 He confirmed his desire, "provided my Creole agrees to come and live in Paris."28

Another might-have-been was a Louise François, whose parents were friends of the Tronsons. For ages and ages Jules fantasized about one girl, undoubtedly her: "Tell me about Mlle . . . What's-her-Name . . . She . . . has the privilege of being the only thing I've thought about for several months" (November 5, 1855). Soon afterwards Louise got engaged to a fellow property owner.

Then came Laurence Janmar, the fifth in Jules's serious hopefuls and again driving him mad. A notable's daughter with private means herself, probably still boarding at a Nantes convent while her parents were in Paris, Laurence possessed strikingly beauty, with alluring eyes of velvety darkness, a pale complexion, and a fine, supple, sinuous body; with an English-style deportment, she was reputed fickle and capricious.29

To avoid upsetting Seveste, Jules requested his father to write about urgent family business (JJV 25). He went home for a week or two at the turn of 1853–54, the main purpose being to pursue Laurence at a fancy-dress and masked ball given by Count Eugène Janvier de la Motte, precocious chief justice at the county court. Although the Count later attracted a reputation for consorting with actresses and working-class girls, this particular occasion seemed highly respectable.

Verne went in the tight-fitting eighteenth-century dandy costume once worn by womanizing Uncle Augustin Allotte. Proper dandies wore a ridiculously short jacket, top hat, and whitish midcalf breeches. Flimsy dancing slippers and skintight stockings highlighted the soft, tight covering of every genital crack and bulge—no modest codpieces in France. Laurence came as a Spanish gypsy, flaunting her lithe body, impossibly slender waist, irresistible eyes, and rich brown ankles, despite a recent papal ban on such displays as likely to engender uncontrollable lust. Also present were her close friend, Ninette Chéguillaume, and a certain Charles Duverger.

In the middle of the ball, the dancing stopped for Jules and two friends to perform a one-act comedy of his composition, making the girls fix their eyes on the young author.[30] Jules and Laurence were getting on well when he overheard her whisper to Ninette that her whalebone corset was killing her ribs. His repartee was the pun "Oh, why can't I have a 'costal' whale of a time?"—perhaps too daring for Nantes. Someone intervened, although Laurence's eyes continued to speak volumes to Jules over Duverger's shoulders (ADF 62).

After the ball Pierre reportedly approached Laurence's family with a view to marriage, but without success. All the while, in Jules's own words, Laurence had had "two irons in the fire at the same time, [making] a poor young man like Jules Verne die of love" (April 19, 1854). Inevitably, the bewitcher soon got engaged. As the betrothal continued, Jules was still achingly yearning for her, consoling himself the marriage hadn't been consummated yet.[31] The wedding took place in August.

No. 6 came soon after. In April 1854, Verne traveled to Mortagne, a market town southwest of Paris, ostensibly to repair his health. The trip was his mother's idea, to meet "Erménégilde" (a boy's name!), daughter of Count Fernand de Bouillé, family friend and extreme reactionary (ADF 63). In Jules's description of the visit, we must, as so often, strip off the humorous exaggeration to find a mostly sincere message beneath:

It's the perfect moment to marry me off, dearest mother . . . serve me up as succulently conjugal . . . cry me as your ware ("Try my fine son") and put me in the hands of some nice young lady with plenty of money. If necessary, I'll move to Mortagne . . . As for the daughter, she's neither pretty nor ugly, stupid nor intelligent, amusing nor disagreeable, and gives me a son or daughter every nine months as regular as clockwork . . . Don't think I'm joking: I love country life, I adore domesticity, I worship children . . . if you agree to lend a hand, I swear you'll be a grandmother by the end of the year (April 7, 1854).

No. 7 was another raven-haired beauty, Héloïse David from Chantenay, older but still rather "naïve and guileless" (June 15, 1856). Turning up one day at the Lyric with her father in tow, she asked for complimentary tickets. Feigning wariness at her short fuse and blatant sensuality, Jules reportedly denied all interest: "heavens above, what has Mlle Héloïse come to the capital for? A husband? Could it be me? That girl is temperamental to the eyeballs. I wouldn't be the one to get her going for all the tea in China!" (ADF 59). He duly fell in love with and paid court to Mlle David (December 14, 1854), who shortly after got betrothed to a white-haired quinquagenarian.

No. 8 was Chantenaysian Ninette Chéguillaume. Following the portentous ball, Paul had become enamored of this friend of Laurence and of sister Anna, eight years his junior, and very well off. Pierre received a discreet overture from her cotton-merchant father—who seemed in fact to prefer the older brother! Jules declared himself only too keen to pursue the matter, and sent choice Lyric tickets to "the father of young Ninette (his young Ninette!)."[32] Verne may even have been interested in another Mlle Chéguillaume, as he seemed strangely upset by the very existence of Ninette's brother-in-law (June 21, 1855).

Ninette's flightiness was to prove even more damaging than Laurence's, for a year later Chéguillaume reactivated his plan to marry off his daughter. After all the usual procedures had been gone through, the formal engagement of Paul and Ninette was announced with appropriate pomp. The only condition was that Paul had to resign his naval commission. When he did so and returned in May 1857, his bride-to-be had changed her mind—leaving poor Paul with no wife and no career (JJV 48).

No. 9, with Sophie as perpetual go-between, was a long shot called Pauline(?)[33] Méry, "as brilliant a match as Ninette," apparently on the rebound, but worth a go on an all-or-nothing basis: "drive to her family . . . and ask for the young lady's hand on my behalf. They'll immediately ring for a servant, who'll show you to the door" [November 1855].

As Jules dispiritedly exclaimed, "all the girls I honor with my munificence marry soon after!" (December 14, 1854). Every single bit of skirt he glimpsed, such as Eloïde and Pauline Bourgoin at Uncle Prudent's, left "many regrets and little hope!"[34] Just the first league, without mentioning the quickly extinguished flames, read impressively, as the years tolled out the successive blows to Verne's hopes: Caroline, 1847; Angèle, 1848; Herminie, 1848; Louise, 1853; Laurence, 1854; "Erménégilde," 1854; Héloïse, 1854; Ninette, 1855; Pauline, 1855. Nine serious attempts, nine degrading rebuffs.

Jules clearly felt frustrated at his repeated failures, especially as by 28 no liaison whatsoever with a girl was recorded. He cynically considered that girls at balls dreamed of many simultaneous suitors (April 17, 1853). In the same vein, marriage, joyless sex, and adultery melded, as he wrote ribaldly to Genevois:

> you're now about to get married . . . it is a great b. . . You will certainly get a stomach . . . can you then rest on top for 12 consecutive hours . . . or is the wife able to remain on top for a set amount of time? . . . You'll be beaten by your wife . . . In case . . . I was forced to play . . . the role of a consoler I beg you to choose her brunette and well endowed.

> The lover of a married woman saves on a servant and two maids.[35]

After all his heartbreaking disappointments, Jules would systematically associate, in both his life and works, nuptials and last rites, virginal white and mourning black, loss of maidenhood and loss of life. As just one example, when his doctor and friend Victor Marcé got hitched: "I went to Saint-Germain des Prés for the interment. I must admit I was singularly moved when the funeral procession arrived" (April 17, 1856).

One contemporary solution was to pay for sex. Verne wrote as a fine connoisseur to Genevois about the brothels of the boulevard area:

> You also seem to believe I don't make any conquests!

Ungrateful wretch! Have you forgotten the best houses of the Rue d'Amboise or Rue Montyon where I'm received like the family darling (what am I saying), the spoilt child of the family! Am I not loved for myself, when I have the chance to waste a few score francs there.[36]

In other words, Verne regularly visited at least two brothels, conveniently around the corner from Boulevard Poissonnière.

The names were immediately familiar to any Parisian. Since at least the eighteenth century, such establishments had represented discretion and "decency . . . actresses, dancers, and courtesans of the first order." All-in-one packages of dinner and accommodation were available in Amboise; and a certain Mme Blondy kept a house on Boulevard Bonne Nouvelle for a wide range of purses, with "girls and women, French and foreign, reasonable and over the hill."[37] What was more, the second floor of the seventeenth-century mansion at 8 Rue d'Amboise was a well-known brothel inhabited by Toulouse-Lautrec from about 1893, where he painted 16 of his most celebrated works. In that year indeed he produced the fur-coated, redheaded *Madame de Gortzikoff,* the elegant poster silhouette of *Le Divan japonais,* and the cancanning *Jane Avril.* It seems unlikely Jules watched the same Venetian blond putting back her bun as in Toulouse-Lautrec's mature *Femme de maison refaisant son chignon.* But we can dream that he contemplated the same garish wallpaper, imprinted the same double bed as in *Dans le lit,* or gazed postcoitally through the same double windows as the *Femme à sa fenêtre.*

Despite the release afforded by commercial sex, Verne's urges seem to have been blocked so long as to be displaced from their normal locus, his only clear interest in the erogenous zones implying an infantile regression and ambiguous sexuality: "I saw His Highness the Prince Imperial, and his wet nurse, very pretty; I would have loved to have changed places—with the wet nurse I mean" [June 27, 1856].

In a preliminary stage of perversion, he planned, in unmistakably vulgar terms, the defilement of Great-Aunt Charruel: "we'll have to take her by assault . . . seize her demilunes . . . fire the cannon on the day of the capitulation." When playing a piano whose color and discordance approached hers, he continued, "I sometimes even imagine I'm touching the excellent aunt, a woman who is hardly touched any more; the comparison particularly disgusts me when I play down there."[38] The crudeness, in a letter to his mother, betrayed the depths of his sexual disturbance.

Procreation, which most of the belles engaged in within a year of captivating his enraptured gaze, may also have been tarred with the same brush. Certainly, when he reluctantly agreed to meet Caroline, he made a characteristic dig about her numerous children: "I'll be as nice as my peculiar character permits . . . it seems [she]'s slightly less pregnant than usual" (May 6, 1853).

Trawling fashionable salons for a mate got him little further (RD 50). But often the light is darkest near the end of the tunnel. As his bachelor friends dwindled—"One more down!"; "only [Paul and me] left"—he announced plans to leave "for Amiens, as my friend [Auguste] Lelarge is marrying Mlle Aimée de Viane. I'll be away for two days."[39]

CHAPTER 7

Tribulations of a Frenchman in France: 1854–57

IN 1854, VERNE PUBLISHED a fourth story in the *Musée des familles.* The Hoffmannesque and Poe-esque "Master Zacharius: The Clock-maker who Lost his Soul" brilliantly prefigured many of his later themes. In medieval Geneva, Zacharius attempts to "discover the workings of the union of body and soul" and hence achieve both per-petual movement and eternal life. The search involves "Our Lady of Sex" (iv) (presumably a close relative of Ste Colette the Hip-Swayer ("Jedediah Jamet"). But instead, his immortal soul is lost to a clock-devil—to whom desperate Zacharius asks his daughter to give her body—and all his clocks go wrong, with fatal results. However, his death does lay the foundations of modern civilization. The tale thus centrally debates the nature of time, vitalism, reductionism, and the ✗ origins of modernity.

Pleased with the success of "Zacharius," Chevalier commanded a new piece in "two volumes" (May 17, 1854). As Verne possibly started some of his novels in the late 1850s, the volumes conceivably formed a book, but more probably "Winter amid the Ice," about a search for a lost ship. At the end of the fishing season Dunkirk skipper Louis Cornbutte is to marry first cousin and foster sister Marie, 20, "with a few drops of Dutch blood" (an echo of Verne's first cousin Marie, with drops of Scottish blood, virtually part of his

household). But Cornbutte falls overboard near the Norwegian Maelstrom. His father refuses to give up and sails off in search, with his
adopted daughter as a stowaway. After a wintering off Greenland and
a mutiny led by a sailor lusting after Marie, Cornbutte is discovered
safe and sound on the ice pack, although his father dies of exhaustion.

The story, with obvious links to Verne's 1851 trip, came out in April
and May 1855, possibly with half the text cut [April 29, 1853]. A preliminary note emphasized its authenticity and exhaustive research.
Interestingly, "Winter amid the Ice" was the only one of Verne's first 40
published prose pieces to depict France, however briefly. Even more
than in "Zacharius," the mature storyteller's themes surfaced here, especially the geographical quest under extreme conditions and the love for
the polar regions, the last virgin areas on the globe.

Verne wrote at least three other stories in the 1850s, but could not
find a publisher for them. All exhibited greater freedom of expression,
playfulness, imagination, or range of genre than the published tales.
Chevalier may have ordered but refused some of them, for he again
invited the writing jobber to stay in the country, as he "had a task to
finish for him" (September 10, 1856).

In "Pierre-Jean" a man escapes from Toulon penal colony, with
Verne mostly taking the side of the downtrodden convicts. "San
Carlos" features smugglers on the Franco-Spanish border. The customs boats pursue a vessel "of bizarre construction": when surrounded, the eponymous hero "opens a valve in the bottom, and
escapes by sinking to a depth of ten fathoms." The submarine, one of
"those mysterious vessels that are kept submerged at a constant depth
by means of forward and rear sections filled with air," prefigures the
Nautilus, especially as both captains are Spanish-based[1] outlaw heroes
who love tax-free cigars and volcanoes.

"The Marriage of Monsieur Anselme des Tilleuls," based on a historical figure, is an astonishing vaudeville in prose satirizing the aristocracy, Latin teachers, and betrothals, full of scatological puns and
erotic double-entendres. At the hero's successive marriage proposals,
"the eldest sister fell into a faint, the second a nervous breakdown, the

third a swoon, the fourth head over heels, and the fifth from her high horse": "had he had a tail it would not have been up in the air."

"The Siege of Rome," where the French rescue the Pope from Garibaldi's wicked revolutionaries (1849), at least in Verne's version, reads like a Gothic novel, with broken love, another evil priest, dark tunnels, oubliettes, and an unhappy young man whose kidnapped wife goes mad.

On March 8, 1855, Verne moved back into a hotel, possibly at 47 Rue des Martyrs.[2] On the 15th he switched with a sigh of relief to the sixth floor of 18 Boulevard Poissonnière, near the stock exchange. To move the 200 yards from Bonne Nouvelle he rhymingly begged FF 60 from his father, signing "Penniless Jules Verne."

The health problems he experienced on arriving in Paris worsened the longer he stayed there. Some were probably psychosomatic, especially his "cruel insomnia," which sometimes stopped him sleeping altogether, until, strangely, he started taking fencing lessons (end of December 1855). But many of his worries had a genuine foundation. The cholera that swept across Europe in spring 1849 had carried off two of his bosses. At one stage he seriously thought he had caught it himself (April 2, 1849). As protection, Jules carried his grandmother's rabbit skin on his stomach day and night.

Among his manifold symptoms, "stomach" and face were the most frequent. His "colic," meaning violent cramps in the intestines, occurred "all the time," blamed on Sophie's genetic inheritance: "what a nasty stomach Mother gave me there."[3] He also suffered from both chronic diarrhea and constipation, the sum effect being a lasting yellow complexion. Dr. Victor Marcé eventually analyzed a slight "prolaxus," Verne's joke for "prolapsus," meaning "my behind does not close properly" or part of the rectum dropping.

Treatment for the various disorders involved fasting, daily centaury (a sort of gentian), herbal verbena tea, self-administered ether, and repeated purges—"I detest castor oil."[4] Some were laxative and some "constrictive": "charcoal and bismuth subnitrate" or mysterious "potions," the alchemistic term showing Verne's mistrust of medicine's scientific pretensions.[5] But the most frequent remedy was syringed enemas. Part of the problem may simply have been his diet: for breakfast "a piece of well-cooked cold veal and a cup of chocolate"; "I only eat stale bread . . . in such weather you need to eat meat, vegetables being bad for digestion."[6]

He often came close to a nervous breakdown: "four days ago I had a terrible migraine with a fit of nerves"; "I went to visit a friend of Alphonse [Garcet, his cousin], a medical student, almost a doctor; and I fainted at his place!"[7]

The other chronic illness began as atrocious headaches and earache, but quickly deteriorated into a form of facial neuralgia, involving both a painful nerve and a paralysis which closed his left eye and twisted his mouth. Dr. Marcé admitted he had little idea what was going on, and the malady blighted Verne's whole life. Major attacks occurred in 1851, 1855, 1858, and 1864. In the approximately fifty photographs taken from the 1850s to 1905, Jules's left eye always appears smaller and dimmer, the lid drooping obliquely in sympathy, even though many were taken at an angle to hide the defect.

The ferocity of Verne's humor again betrays his anguish: "provided I do not open my mouth, close my eyes, sniff, or wrinkle my forehead, nobody notices anything"; "one half of my face is alive, the other dead . . . On one side I've the profile of an intelligent man . . . on the other an idiot."[8]

"Electric discharges" provided temporary relief: "my face has got its majestic lines back, it's gay on both sides, I can frown as I wish" (November 10, 1851). Marcé's main other treatment involved blistering agents and strychnine frictions—with often the poison seeping through the punctured skin! Because of the frictions "I've cut my entire beard . . . I horribly resemble Mathilde; I've her fine smile on her Greek chin, her smiling and witty mouth; I am pretty, pretty, pretty"; it also led to him hardly leaving his apartment for 18 days [February 1855].

The lethal combinations proved effective up to a point: "The vesicant [blistering agent] worked with the electricity for the top of my face, but the bottom doesn't yet meet general satisfaction" [February 1855]. He rebuffed his mother's suggestion of "cauterization": "I'd rather see my mouth above my nose!" [February 1855].

Underneath lay the worry that signs were emerging of the madness that regularly descended on both sides of the family. But what Marcé never suspected was an inflammation of the middle ear, due to his cold room and office, and easily curable today.

Sometimes the two maladies joined forces and adumbrated a whole league of brothers. Verne suffered from bilious attacks combined with atrocious headaches, earache, fevers, and "sensibility." At twenty-five he already felt old. With a few grey hairs, he had become "wrinkled like the Roman countryside after the siege trenches [of Napoléon III], with crow's feet on my temples . . . [like a] grandfather" [April 1853].

Were his medical problems the reason he underwent hypnosis? He enthusiastically wrote about a "mesmerizer" called Alexis who gave public performances. He attended at least twice, reporting that Alexis told him "miraculous" things about his siblings, including the name and location of Paul's ship (June 28, 1850).

In Verne's mind excess and illness went hand in hand, so renunciation led to better health. He did not shrink from sharing his crude conclusions, with one vulgar letter about his father's intestinal explosions in a closed carriage. Another purportedly describing a real visit, with a 600-word scatological story, full of "mountains of manure," "family outings" on ponds of animal urine, detonations of wind, and sexual analogies between cows and women.[9] The distant descendants of one particularly vulgar image would be Fogg's mutism and Nemo's misanthropy:

> I long to become a hermit like Alceste or mute like a Trappist . . . Having pondered for ages how to express perfect silence, the sculptor imagined a man with one finger in his mouth, the other in his behind . . . it was convenient for his model, because if tired of having a finger in his mouth, he could change hands (November 15, 1852).

The scatological and sexual wove intricate webs together, in a long series of genital and rectal similes, some for Genevois and some for his mother:

> I am strongly attached to him . . . he's lost the habit of enlarging me by sticking his fingers into my depths . . . I am perhaps a little long, but . . . your distinguished son shows me off on every occasion . . . my secretions are not too abundant.

> One of my childhood stories that has always stuck in my mind is an intimate story of Monsieur Mazieux who according to his better half went underneath himself! . . . my rectum's tending to escape outside and consequently not contain hermetically the charming things it's meant to conceal . . . serious disadvantages could ensue for a man destined to go out in society and not underneath himself . . . as the time for the enema is approaching, the decoction steaming, the rhatany [astringent root extract] boiling, the hose stretching out, the nozzle standing up, the flexible tube extending, I need to close my mouth and open my . . . [the ellipsis is Verne's].

> I'm normally loose in the bowels, which proves I've a character naturally weak like colic and easy like diarrhea . . . Recently I forcefully administered myself an enema; my behind has been discovered not to close well; it lets wind out and draft-excluders are going to be applied to it. I hug yours for you.

> He did not see a soft hollow growing on his member / Which grew a league long / To be haggled over by the market trollops.[10]

What are we to make of such rude, "anal-expulsive" missives? It is not even clear to what extent Verne suffered from genuine organic ailments or imagined much of his sickness. But the net effect was surely troubling: hardly a healthy body in a healthy mind, and a sign of troubles to come.

Throughout these years Verne stayed in contact with his parents through hundreds of letters. One constant remained his lack of funds, with repeated loans from cousin Henri and an unspecified uncle, secretly reimbursed by his mother [beginning of 1853]. He sent his shirts and stockings home for repair, but still looked as unkempt as "a lyric poet"; his underpants had "neither back nor front nor legs nor buttons" (December 14, 1854; November 29, 1856).

He may have gone home for the funeral of his grandfather Augustin Allotte in October 1849. He came back to Paris from a mysterious "little excursion" in much better form (January 22, 1851). Later that year he probably stayed with his parents at the seaside resort of Pornic, indulging in the strange English fashion of bathing in the icy Atlantic [summer 1851]. Although his father presumably visited once or twice, Jules only occasionally went to Chantenay (for instance, probably in June 1853); he also made a few shorter trips, including Provins [mid-October 1851].

In August 1853 he escaped Paris for three days to greet Paul, back from monitoring Emperor Soulouque's bloodthirsty activities in Haiti (ADF 58). A celebratory lunch was organized at Uncle Prudent's: Verne composed rhyming quatrains, hidden under the napkins, for seventeen of the eighteen guests, including himself. Hilaire was punished for being Caroline's brother by getting only two lines; Sophie's nose was "astonishing," Paul, unhappy in love. That evening he organized fun and games on La Guerche's grand avenue.[11]

Verne's main efforts continued to be devoted to play- and operetta-writing.[12] Following *Broken Straws* (performed and published in 1850), both pieces performed over the following seven years were at the Lyric, in return for his secretaryship, although three ought logically to have been accepted: one-act comic operas *Blind Man's Bluff*

(1852; 1853) and *The Knights of the Daffodil* (1853; 1855).[13] Both
were coauthored with professional librettist Michel Carré, constantly
in demand by composers and vaudevillians: Verne had met him, nine
years his senior, through Hignard (JJV 19), who wrote the music for
both pieces.

In *Blind Man's Bluff*, three students play hide-and-seek with three
flower girls among the primulas. "Each part had to be specially
adapted for the actor to play it" (May 4, 1853). The operetta met
considerable success, with 43 performances, several further runs, and
more than a dozen positive reviews, including Berlioz's.[14] "Your
'never' is already in the pluperfect," Verne triumphantly told his
father (August 22, 1852).

Jules himself preferred *The Knights of the Daffodil*, where "both
music and lyrics are tremendously gay". The Knights are a young and
facetious group who use flowers in their buttonholes as a mark of
recognition. They overrun an inn to seduce the innkeeper's wife and
abduct his daughter. Simplice, in love with the girl but timid, finds in
drink the courage to defend her and the two get married. This
operetta brought Verne FF 180 ($540) and a negative and a positive
review ("sparkling with wit and gaiety").[15]

A huge number of his plays remained unpublished and unper-
formed at this period. Verne had completed about fourteen
between 1850 and 1856. The heroine of *The Guimard* (1850) split
painter David from his love. *Who Laughs Dines* (1850), about the
rivalry in love between a bourgeois and a poor, witty poet, full of
puns and comic misunderstandings, caused "Dumas *fils* and
Alexander Dumas to split their sides" (Jan. 51). It ended with a
brave poem "To the public": "The play we have had the delight /
Of doing was not penned by a great knight, / Nor a poet or play
maker, / But a poor devotee of the romantic genre, / Untempted by
the lure of royalties."

Five-act drama *The Tower of Montlhéry* (1852), about a crusader's
wife kidnapped by a lord and wrongfully killed by her jealous husband, was coauthored with Charles Wallut, whom Verne called "my

best friend."[16] A far from experienced playwright, Wallut became director of the *Musée des familles* after the death of Chevalier in 1863.

Verne took pride in *Mona Lisa* (1851–55) which preoccupied him for many years: it depicted Leonardo painting Mona for her husband, the smile indicating tenderness mixed with pity for the man naive enough to prefer art to women. The one-act comedy *War on Tyrants* (1854), about a wife wrongly accused of adultery, may have been cowritten with Dumas *fils* (May 17, 1854). Another one-act comedy, *Beside the Adour* (1855), about a wife fleeing her husband, seems to have enchanted Dumas, who "does not see a word to change; he's so pleased with it that he took it to the director of the Gymnase this evening" [end of 54?], who, however, did not produce it.

The five-act verse comedy *Happy for One Day* (1855–56) was a serious and well-constructed play, benefiting from Pierre's detailed comments. Financier Montbrun plans to short the market and grab the proceeds by marrying his client's daughter. As young Breton Pierre seems likely to win the girl instead, Montbrun challenges him to a duel, but is unexpectedly killed. The comedy, which turns to tragedy in the last act, attacks Parisian vanity and greed, high society, and the theatergoers' and critics' indifference.

The year 1856, when Verne seemed to have been in Paris for a lifetime—in fact eight years—constitutes a good place to take stock of what he had achieved and what sort of man he had become.

At the age of twenty-eight, he felt depressed at the mess of his sexual and professional life. He was about the only Bachelor still standing firm on the sinking island of misogyny. Although he had experienced deep infatuations with heartbreaking frequency, he had never really been in love. Male–female relations in his works accordingly swung from satirical attacks and physical assaults to a total absence.

Five of his eight short stories had been published, perhaps the least interesting ones. All touched on the difficulty of getting things going, like Verne's own life. Under his own steam he had hardly initiated anything, for even his six pieces in the *Musée* ultimately stemmed from his parents' *guanxi*; and in any case had abruptly halted, for he would publish no more while Chevalier was still alive.

Of his approximately twenty-six plays only three had been performed, albeit with some success. After a decade of continuous effort and a third of a million words, he was making well under FF 100 a month but needed 500 to live.[17] He was effectively unemployed and remained humiliatingly dependent on his father, who still edited his manuscripts and corrected his letters for style and taste.

And yet he did not give up. When a theater friend, noticing his restlessness, told him he was not made for Paris and bohemian life, Verne simply ignored the comment.[18] Once, only once, had he contemplated crawling back to Nantes with his tail hanging loose between his legs.

The problem was that his goal lay hidden below the horizon. With hindsight, nearly all of the themes and structures of Verne's novels could already be made out, but the missing link still proved elusive: perhaps simply an outlet for his talents. He had the two main qualities: a verbal brilliance and ability to conjure up people, situations, and events; and a capacity for hard work, every one of the three thousand days of professional purgatory. He even had intimations of the revolution to come: "I'm studying more than I'm working, for I'm glimpsing new systems" (April 19, 1854). "New systems": the philosophical term provides a hint at his ambitious ways of thinking, his wish to jump out of his present skin.

He had already tried out different genres, styles, subjects—anything to get out of the cycle of composition, rejection, and shoving the curling manuscripts back into the overflowing drawers. He could only grit his teeth and give it his best, while suspecting that something was escaping him, that by changing just one variable, he could get his fingernails into the overhanging ladder, some ammunition to throw in the face of doubters. If fate could have shown her brown ankles just once, a glimpse of the route north to the Promised Land, he could have enjoyed life more, expanded his geographical and stylistic horizons, perhaps even written better. Instead destiny had led him up the garden path, but not behind the bike-shed: a few minor successes had given him just enough impetus to continue. Verne himself surely played with the probabilities. One in a couple of hundred provincial wannabes made it, but less than one in a thousand fifty-year-olds.

Would he have succeeded more quickly if he had been prepared to compromise? He bitterly attacked playwright Alfred de Musset's unprincipled act of joining the "old fossils" of the "funereal dome" of the French Academy (May 31, 1852). On his slender operatic fame, he was apparently approached by an editor of the prestigious *Revue des deux mondes*, who wanted his support for an Academy prize—but refused (ADF 49).

For the moment, however, alone in his room, his life formed a black hole: "my isolation really weighs on me; my heart is a despairing vacuum and to be frank, I long to get married . . . but as long as I stay a supernumerary applicant for literature, parents will be right to turn their backs on me" [June 27, 1856].

What sort of man was this supernumerary in love, literature, and friendship? Although favoring the Romantic school over the Classical, he was mostly an unreconstructed independent: "I'm afraid the only [school] I belong to is my own."[19] He was not a religious or political animal. On the one recorded occasion he went to church, he lambasted the sermon (May 31, 1852). A notable absence from his concerns was the Crimean War (1853–56), perhaps the most important event of the decade. In fact he had clear antimilitaristic and anarchistic tendencies: he condemned the army's "annihilation of 400,000 French intelligences" and exulted at the destruction of property: "I watched the magnificent fire of the Manutention [Government Stores] . . . It was the most glorious sight I've ever seen; I'm even sorry it didn't burn down two or three more buildings."[20]

While reasonably good at many school subjects, and more intelligent than his teachers realized, his strength lay not at the scientific/mathematical end of the spectrum but at the artistic or literary-linguistic one. A good pianist, he on occasion composed music and would display great musical passion throughout his life. He indeed claimed he could have turned professional had he wanted (*Int.* 89).

Although he thought himself easygoing, he already displayed the writer's obsessive characteristics. His thought processes were subjective and intuitive, and he sometimes indulged in specious logic and rhetorical subterfuge. In money matters, even when caught in fibs, he simply blustered, insulting the intelligence of his long-suffering father. Similarly, when accused of mocking religion, he hypocritically denied having done so. Even if we thought, debatably, that the French educational system encouraged allusion and periphrasis, all writers need clarity of thought, at least for internal usage. Genevois, according to Pierre, considered Verne "frivolous, capricious, superficial"; his mother, "that she would greatly pity my wife."[21]

On the rational–emotional scale he veered off the chart at both ends, showing the limitations of psychometrics for exceptional beings. On the introverted–extroverted scale, he was consistently shy and protective of his feelings, especially in comparison to the usual Gallic extraversion. His stoicism governed, however, only his conscious mind, for underneath boiled a cauldron of emotion, sexual in origin but going back to his early childhood. He was both anxious about chimera and genuinely ill without knowing the cause, hypochondriac and more perspicacious than his doctor.

What sustained him was this independence of thought, this freedom from any school, this intimate conviction that he knew best about his own life and that only he was able to separate the wheat of artistic truth from the chaff of public opinion. He wrote not only because it might be useful, but instinctively, as an extension of his personality, as he breathed. Nevertheless, at this stage he had rarely reached the concision and cohesion of the highest levels of writing. If the profession had been invented, he might have become an inspirational, but ultimately unsuccessful academic, failing to steer his unbridled imagination between the shoals of scholastic convention and the reefs of explicit didacticism.

But in part of his mind, he must have realized that light vaudevilles wasted his talent. In a novel written soon after, Verne made sly fun of his own efforts by having his hero work on a comedy called "Do Your

Pants Up."[22] Perhaps in his heart of hearts he realized he could never make a living out of it.

The solution to his writing impasse, as so often, would come from a combination of hard work and a new angle on an old question.

The wedding Verne had gone to "for two days" did not turn out quite like that; indeed it would revolutionize his life. He acted as best man (*garçon d'honneur*) for the groom, lawyer Auguste Lelarge (b. 1827), a college friend who was already cousin Henri's brother-in-law. After a week, despite the glacial hotel room, Verne had still not torn himself away: "the family's gracious pleas made me stay . . . among kisses, handshakes, embraces, and tears of joy and pleasure" [May 24, 1856].

He liked the bride's family: "a very nice young widow, the bride's sister . . . and a young man of my age, a jobber in Amiens . . . really the nicest boy on earth. The de Viane father is a retired soldier, better than most warriors, and the mother has inordinate wit." He finally revealed the reason for his happiness: "I do think I'm in love with the young twenty-six-year-old widow! Oh, why has she got two children! I'm out of luck—I always run into some sort of impossibility!" [May 24, 1856].

By her younger sister's marriage, Honorine-Anna-Hebée Morel, née de Viane, had become a distant relation of Jules's, twice over.[23] A widow for ten months, elegant and well-endowed, she had a good complexion, amused eyes, a clear laugh, and an attractive light soprano voice. Honorine was graceful, lively, witty, reasonably educated, and attractive to men. But her feminine charm remained mostly on the surface (RD 51–54) and she was, to judge from her letters, insensitive to good writing. About five foot two, with a long nose and narrow eyes, she had already lost her youthful bloom.[24]

She's fairly pretty . . . her lips a little too pinched for upheavals ever to get there—emotional ones I mean, because I like to believe she occasionally throws up, just like everyone. I say emotionally, because I don't think she's very kind: I've had proof (June 15, 1856).

Verne was talking about the bride, but much of the description applied to Honorine herself. The best man in fact showed more interest in brother Ferdinand de Viane (1828–70), for with no attempt at transition he detailed his status as qualified lawyer and his employment as "stockjobber [*remisier*], intermediary between the shareholders and stockbrokers . . . With no risk, he often makes 50,000 commission a year." Then the cut to the chase: he himself could do the same thing in Paris and make 1,800 a month, "no risk whatsoever"—you just had to wait for the shares to go up [May 26, 1856]. In less than a week, Verne had decided to throw in his lot with Honorine and high finance, not necessarily in that order.

His father supposed it a mere passing fancy, but over the following months Jules did not blink. He emphasized the financial benefits, and then moved on to the clinch: Auguste Lelarge had bought a fortieth share in a Paris stockbroker's for 50,000 and made 600 a month. By an amazing coincidence, this same sum, already a subliminal echo of a previous amount, constituted Jules's expectation from his parents on their decease.[25] His father bounded at the implications.

Even Verne's putative allies doubted his ability. The young widow and Lelarge both reportedly pleaded with him "to seek a lucrative situation outside the stock exchange," just about anywhere, for instance in the administration, especially the Telegraph Department.[26] Jobber de Viane himself remained skeptical at Jules's commitment and refused five times to employ him in Amiens.

To all his father's objections the would-be financial wizard had fluent answers. He had already admitted that a jobber was just a "salesman" and that he might give up literature for a year. He bandied profits around of "easily 10 or 15 percent" on "our" investment and showed off his immense knowledge of the stock market.[27] To show his commitment, he went to stay with the Lelarges in Château Thierry, 50 miles south of Paris.[28]

Having exhausted logic, Verne's summing up for the jury employed was pure emotion: he felt "very upset by [his father's] reply"; "I need to be happy, nothing more or less."[29] Worn down by all the special pleading, the jury chairman finally agreed to put up the magical FF 50,000 ($150,000).

In the interim Honorine had hardly had a look in, although Verne presumably contacted her through an intermediary to confirm she might be interested. Once Pierre had performed due diligence on the family, gentry from Périgord and therefore acceptable, the two sides could get down to brass tacks. Outside lawyers appeared redun- *cliché* dant, given that Jules, Pierre, and de Viane had been in the trade themselves. First Monsieur Verne formally requested the girl's hand, producing an equally stiff acceptance from Monsieur de Viane.[30] Jules and Honorine were now officially engaged.

Having secured his home ground, Jules sallied forth with a brief but respectful letter to "Mme Honorine Morel" on about November 12.[31] Then came a very polite missive to her elder brother, agreeing that since little could be done to employ him in Amiens until married and so suggesting they should "celebrate the wedding earlier."[32] But all Verne's maneuvering came to naught, as he never did secure a job in Amiens, and was left with just the early wedding as consolation prize.

In late November the date was duly fixed for mid-January, to fit with the ball season in Nantes, the needs of Honorine's two daughters, and the conventions about mourning. The wedding would take place in the midway house of Paris.[33]

Jules pondered about presents: "silverware doesn't seem right . . . it would look like a gift to myself" (November 22, 1856). For Honorine, he decided to spend FF 250—so borrowed 500 from his father and in the end gave her a "pretty gold and jasper key-chain."[34] Since the fiancée already had plenty of dresses, cashmeres, earrings, and diamonds, Verne thought she should simply remount her diamonds if she wanted any more pretty things [December 3, 1856]. "Honorine is very sensible and doesn't really want to cover her shoulders with

Tibetan fleeces," he announced confidently (December 7, 1856). In return Honorine's family sent Sophie some lace, which she hated. Jules got a top-of-the-range gold watch from Mme de Viane and, from "my fiancée, a very beautiful chain!!!" (December 17, 1856). Was he upset at the symbolism of the golden ties that bind or at the tactless repetition of his own present?

All Jules's advocacy now switched to creative accounting. Of the 50,000, 10 or 20 had somehow got lost on the way, "bringing it back down to exactly 30,000" [mid-December 1856]. The remainder was to work triple overtime: as an advance on his inheritance, as his marriage settlement, and to provide a jobbing future.

According to the age-old custom, a wedding contract was necessary. On January 8, 1857, the binding document was signed in Château Thierry, by Jules, Pierre, Honorine, her father, and her first husband's mother.[35] While the couple's future acquisitions would be in common, their individual finances would remain separate.[36]

Jules had not a centime in cash to his name. His net worth amounted to "clothing, linen, furniture, book collection, piano, and watch," total 3,000, his new timepiece accounting for most of it; his scores of curling manuscripts didn't get a mention. Honorine brought 6,000 worth of clothing, jewelry, and furniture,[37] plus an alluring 75,000 in cash, shares, and bonds. Of the 81,000, however, the two daughters expected 32, bringing it back to 49, or 46,000 after her trousseau.[38] All the same, the pleasing near-symmetry with Jules's original contribution was deceptive. Honorine already enjoyed 50,000 (the leitmotif sum, decidedly, of the whole affair) from her first marriage, although first clawed back by her parents, then recycled as her second dowry, and in any case partly held in trust for her children; whereas Jules's money anticipated the death of one of his parents. Destroying the carefully engineered balance, in fact, Honorine enjoyed additional expectations, as Jules gleefully emphasized: 60,000 from her parents and at least 80,000 from an uncle, amounting to a sum of "nearly 200,000" [end of November 1856].

As final preparations for the marriage made in a golden heaven,

Jules traveled to what he called the "very dear city" of Amiens (*cher* meaning "dear" in both senses), to stay with Honorine's "rich uncle" and marvel at the week-long foot of snow [November 22, 1856]. Previously he had said "not to get married is the only way not to be cuckolded."[39] But now he dedicated "Our Star" to "Mlle Honorine de Viane," where a "discreet . . . solitary . . . and modest" heavenly body reminds lovers of the time they "were happy . . . without realizing" and will act as a bond while they are parted.[40] He glimpsed married bliss at the end of his long bachelor tunnel; he planned to finally become "the happiest of men!" (November 29, 1856).

CHAPTER 8

Married, with Portfolio: 1857–59

THE ONLY EXTANT OPINION from Honorine on anything before the wedding occurs in an appendix to Verne's letter, complaining "Monsieur Jules" did not leave room for her to write anything else, "which is not very nice" (December 17, 1856). Jules's persistent linkage of affairs of the heart and the purse worked both ways: he seemed sincere in his love, while at the same time financially interested. With hindsight, and knowing Verne's habit of slipping in telling details, many features of the wedding did augur badly for the future. Most of the fine points indeed told against an Abelard-like devotion: the presents, the involvement of the late husband's family, the date, the location, the guest list, the length and importance of the ceremony, the groom's apparel, the origin of the poem Verne recited, the honeymoon, and the living arrangements afterwards—all in fact constituted rather sinister portents.

For the moment, Verne referred obscurely to "the Morel family" (December 29, 1856), as if including, Banquo-like, the ghost of the first husband, but also to "Mlle de Viane" when he meant "M. de Viane" (November 29, 1856). In his classic funeral–wedding, or more likely criminal, conflation he talked about the "perpetration of my marriage" (December 7, 1856).

Verne's parents probably traveled up to Paris just before Christmas Day. They then joined Jules in Amiens and reluctantly lodged with the de Vianes for a few days. When Pierre and Sophie retreated to Provins, Jules stayed on to move Honorine's things, carrying them up to his bachelor flat himself.[1] On about January 7, the de Viane and Verne families came together in a Paris hotel, normal etiquette being for the bride to be present but not the groom (December 17, 1856). At some stage, perhaps after the wedding, a Verne family council made financial decisions.

From the beginning Verne insisted on a quiet affair, eliminating almost everyone: "the fewer madmen there are, the more we'll laugh" (December 7, 1856). All eight grandparents were absent; "Aunt and Uncle Châteaubourg have been invited on condition they refuse"; sister Marie did not come ("there's not much room for her"), nor brother Paul (December 7, 1856). Amiens thought he was getting married in Nantes and Parisian Aunt Charruel, in Amiens.[2] Honorine's only sister skipped the great day on the pretext of pregnancy, although less than five months gone [mid-December 1856]. The future couple's daughters also kicked their heels.

The wedding would cost the Verne side less than 5,000, including presents and setting up in Paris (November 22, 1856). Originally Jules planned the church ceremony to take place on the inauspicious 13th, with the registry office the day before (December 17, 1856); but in the event both were polished off in rapid succession, allowing no time for minds to change.

And so it came to be that on Wednesday, January 10, 1857, a dozen people gathered in the registry office on Place des Petits Pères, not far from Jules's flat. With comforting near-medieval houses all around, the groom signed, for once, his full name, "Jules-Gabriel Verne."

The church Saint-Eugène squatted nearby, in Rue Sainte-Cécile— in fact on an extension of the street housing Verne's favorite brothel, whose windows were clearly visible. Only a year old, the church indiscriminately mixed styles but without creating any of its own. On the groom's side sat Jules's parents, Mathilde, Anna, Mme and Monsieur Henri Garcet, and Hignard, with the latter two as witnesses; on the bride's, only her parents, plus brother Ferdinand de Viane and brother-in-law Auguste Lelarge as witnesses. In other words, Verne had only one friend present, and Honorine none, with no best man recorded: a total of thirteen people. While the priest was blessing the couple, did Verne's mind wander salaciously along to his previous "conquests"? In any case, it was elsewhere:

> I was the groom, and I had a white suit and black gloves! I didn't know where I was, and I handed out money to everyone: Town Hall clerks, beadle, sacristan, errand boy. Someone shouted for the bridegroom. That meant me! Thank heavens only a dozen people were watching the spectacle![3]

Having wanted everything as "furtive" as possible, Verne succeeded, for his father described it as a slapdash affair.[4]

Verne had arranged "a simple meal at any old chain restaurant" (mid-December 17, 1856). Aristide provided the music to accompany Jules's seven-verse poem for Honorine: "Of fine words filled with bombast / What need is there / And truly how far away the heart / Lies from such long phrases . . . I love ye quite simply." Behind the sincere emotion, however, lay the fact that Verne did not write the poem for Honorine, but originally dedicated it to musician and collaborator Alfred Dufresne.[5] At dessert Pierre responded with a few lines welcoming his "fourth daughter" into the family, but also indelicately referring to the asymmetrical financial arrangements: "I knew full well that for my retirement / [Jules] would bring back the surrender / Of some prosperous plunder."[6] Although plenty of laughter rang out, the lunch finished quickly (JJV 45). As Verne had wanted, it all amounted to "no sort of ceremony, no sort of celebration"; Pierre confessed that he and Sophie disliked its bohemian style.[7] They may or may not have gone "to a show afterwards" (December 7, 1856). And, after a few short hours, that was that. No honeymoon was taken.

However, despite his horror of ceremony, and despite all his wisecracking, Jules had freely chosen Honorine—unless of course it was the other way round. Behind all the tomfoolery, and even if other motives abounded, he may have been happy after the wedding (RD 55). Both he and his wife appeared at this stage to have been sincere in their love for each other and their desire to make a life together.

A week after the wedding, the two went to see P. J. Delbarre, photographer to Her Imperial Highness Princess Mathilde: the resulting snap apparently showed an attractive young woman and a man with an Olympian air, thick curling hair, and a magnetic gaze (ADF 79). Nevertheless, a photo of the same year showed Verne's mouth entirely hidden by whiskers, baggy eyes, a receding hairline, and a faraway look (ADF 48–49). Jules is meant to have taken Honorine to the Louvre to see the Venus de Milo, telling her she was only woman she ever should feel jealous of—and then headed for Provins, where they duetted in the aunts' drawing room (ADF 79), but somehow the great-niece's story feels false here.

Only too soon it was back to reality. For the first three months, Valentine, four, Suzanne, two, and the maid stayed with the family in Amiens, meaning the couple had no domestic help [mid-December 56]. By some miracle room was found in Verne's studio apartment for Honorine's sofa, eight ornate chairs, and bronze mantelpiece ornaments (ADF 77). At the end of April Verne's new daughters joined the household and the family moved into more comfortable lodgings at Rue Saint-Martin, closer to the river (JJV 46).

The grandparents refused to let Verne adopt Valentine and Suzanne, so their surname remained Morel.[8] Jules never in fact considered Valentine and Suzanne entirely his own: "my wife has three children and I have one" (Lemire 41). In any case, he equated happy couples with those without children.[9] Nevertheless, the girls did call him "Father" and Sophie "Grandma."[10]

In 1858 the family moved again, to 54 Rue du Faubourg Montmartre, in the Ninth, a historic avenue close to the previous apartments.[11] That same year, or possibly before, they moved to an upper floor on Boulevard Montmartre, probably no. 18.[12] Their favorite bread shop was just around the corner, in Passage des Panoramas, and their cake shop in Rue Vivienne (*BB* ii). In the first half of 1861 the family moved once more, to 45 on the tree-lined Boulevard de Magenta; and then in mid-1862 to 18 Passage Saulnier,[13] directly above the workshop of Dumas *fils*'s engraver and beside Offenbach's home.

Each time Verne moved their furniture and meager possessions himself and covered "his" four walls with maps.[14] The reason for the many moves may have been short-term leases or dissatisfaction at cramped and noisy conditions, but hardly increasing prosperity. Generally, this period was one of discouragement for the writer, troubled by screaming children in a small space, making work difficult (RD 59). With the father's money presumably stopped, the family must have lived off Verne's literary and financial efforts and the income and/or capital of Honorine's FF 46,000, surely invested by her brother.[15] The main purse-strings, in other words, remained under the wife's control.

Honorine finally acquired her diamond earrings, provoking a "she's mad" about the exorbitant FF 350 price—even though they were probably just the prenuptial gems remounted [March 1857]. She spent much time cooking sophisticated meals that Jules hardly appreciated. Mme Verne didn't really understand what he said, or why he spent so long reading and writing, and so kept disturbing his work. Fortunately her wit was as quick as his, still making him laugh out loud (JJV 47).

Over these years Verne's life was not that different from before. Brother Paul, now a free man, came to stay, as did Uncles Châteaubourg and Allotte. The couple offered lots of entertainment, with card games and musical evenings (CNM 112). Jules's friends still came around every Thursday evening; however, Honorine was irritated by the ex-Bachelors' weekly dinners to which she was not invited.[16]

Jules and Honorine enjoyed outings with his and her friends (RD 56). In July 1859, they had a long country weekend at the Lelarges' in Château Thierry. Despite the hot weather, the couple had great fun with Valentine, already six, Hignard, Delioux, and Lorois; and Jules was highly impressed by Reims Cathedral (July 15, 1859). No doubt the family visited both sets of in-laws at least once a year.

One August, probably in 1860 or 1861, the family traveled to Amiens.[17] Against his better judgment, Jules was persuaded to go hunting on the plains of Picardy. In the remarkable description he published in 1882, Verne caustically depicts his seven or eight huntsman companions, all terrible liars and oblivious to the horror of blood sport. In March 1862, however, while Jules went to Amiens for three days, Honorine stayed on, presumably with the children, leaving him alone in Paris for a month.

Verne still occasionally went to salons, such as the Count of Osmond's. He figured among the 50 guests, "the cream of the Paris literary world of 1861," invited to a sumptuous reception at the house of the celebrated singers, the Lionnet brothers. It was that same evening that Bachelors Pierre Véron and Ernest L'Épine introduced Alphonse Daudet, freshly arrived in Paris (ADF 111). As in Hugo's case, in sum, the two soon-to-be-famous writers crossed paths, but left no record of the occasion.

Even before his wedding, Jules had read about the stock exchange in books, including, strangely, his cousin's *Elements of Mechanics*, hot off the presses (September 5, 1856). He had also attended the Paris stock exchange for an apprenticeship with Ferdinand de Viane's associate Giblain, taking lessons, studying the market, and observing operations (September 5, 1856, September 7, 1856). He was unable to take his new persona seriously: "Yesterday evening I lost a wonderful opportunity to run off to Brussels with Honorine, and set myself up in magnificent style. I was carrying 500,000 in bonds in my briefcase and 95,000 in cash . . . However, I decided to be patient."[18] No doubt because of his bad attitude and writing skills, as Hong Kongers crudely say, Giblain refused to renew his "temporary apprenticeship" as "correspondence writer." De Viane then declined to employ Verne directly in his own business, because he was a relative. He would not even allow him to live in Amiens and somehow pick up the ropes, perhaps as an unpaid supernumerary. Jules's fourth attempt at employment, as we saw, was to rush headlong into marriage, so that he could somehow work for "Monsieur Ferdinand," as he respectfully called him, although of exactly the same age.[19] All the while, Jules was telling his father, insincerely, that he didn't really want to work in Amiens (November 22, 1856). De Viane accepted the former proposal, but again refused the latter. To mollify his future brother-in-law, he finally promised he could work for his partner Fauvel, due to set up in Paris in December; but this idea also came to naught.[20]

In the end the 50,000 or 30,000 from Jules's parents was probably used to buy a share in the firm of Eggly, located at 72 Rue de Provence, in the Ninth, a street Balzac and Charles Baudelaire had lived on. Non-boarder Maisonneuve was already working in a sister establishment, and reportedly showed Verne around his new employer. Eggly was a well-established stockbroker of great integrity, later to become one of the best and richest in Paris.[21] However, jobbers were normally employees rather than partners in such companies; and Verne later said his "dreams of wealth . . . led me into one or two speculations at the Bourse" (*Int.* 90), meaning he was risking his own money. It is not impossible, therefore, that he diverted the nuptial windfall from its promised destination as buying into the partnership and into his own private investments.

In his new life he would get up at five, put his trousers over his nightshirt with Honorine's belt to hold them up, and swallow a cup of coffee. Then he would read and write until ten, lock away his man-uscripts, sit down to breakfast, put on proper clothes, and head for the office. After a couple of hours at Eggly's, he would proceed to the stock exchange, in the Bourse quarter, to work from one to three.[22]

As a jobber, he acted as liaison between the clients and the "outside brokers," the only ones authorized to execute and who kept 70 percent of the commission [May 26, 1856]. More specifically, "the work con-sists of building up clients and receiving their orders for buying and selling shares," work simplified by his shadowy status and lack of both "official title" and "offices or complicated accounts to maintain" [May 26, 1857]. "Every day I write a summary of the stock exchange," presumably for his clients [March 1857]. The work, requiring little more than "absolute accuracy," was, in a word, "boring" [July 1871].

In reality, Verne never built up a thriving clientele, a proportion of his investments being for his father and Uncle and Aunt Châteaubourg. Despite a rising index and Maisonneuve's support, he never reached approached the fantastic levels he promised his father. One colleague was meant to have said that he "succeeded better with his witty expressions than with his business."[23]

More than lucre, the attraction of the exchange was as a sort of gentlemen's club. One good jobber friend of Verne's was future impresario Félix Duquesnel. Later rude to Flaubert and employer of an unknown called Sarah Bernhardt, he had "a sweet philosophy and a charming optimism. He found everything logical and natural, and so rarely complained or criticized."[24]

Verne rapidly found himself ringleader of a legendary group, which used to indulge in tremendous fun and games to the right of the pillars of the Colonnade.[25]

Around a predominantly Nantes or Breton core, with many former Nonboarders and Bachelors, nearly all destined to achieve success in the theater or literature, there clustered any number of associates, drifting in and out with the seasons. Many Colonnaders were already Jules's chums, like Maisonneuve, Hignard, Wallut, Delioux, Lorois, and Gille, as well as Raymond Fournier-Sarlovèze and Charles de Béchenec, honorary Bachelors and Poissonnière landing serenaders. Relatively new friends were: William Busnach, later Verne's coauthor, Ernest-Aimé Feydeau, new star novelist and father of the playwright, and Zabbah, staffer on the *Charivari*. Count Frédéric de Cardailhac, codirector of the Vaudeville Theater, had put on Dumas's *Camille* and would soon stage Verne's *Eleven-Day Siege*. On the fringes, as visitors to the exchange, there revolved Dumas *fils*, librettist Alphonse Royer, journalist and writer Xavier Aubryet, Frédéric Gaillardet, playwright and collaborator of Dumas *père*, and Hector Malot, future novelist and Verne's reviewer. In still more distant orbit were the famous caricaturist Cham and Joubert, founder of the Banque de Paris.

While nominally working, Maisonneuve and Verne spent most of their time messing around.[26] They disrespectfully called those of maturer years "the Forebears": Feydeau would fling some mocking quip as he rushed past, with Verne giving as good as he got.[27] Between the brief bouts of work, the Colonnader friends would exchange ideas for plays.

* * *

In Verne's letters of this period we begin to see an interaction with his literary endeavors. He quotes from "Zacharius"; he admits to using padding as a writing strategy; in one exercise in style all ten paragraphs begin "I." In another, he lengthily thanks his mother for her present, although not knowing whether to hang it on his watch chain or polish the floor—then finally admits he has not in fact received it.[28]

Although Jules still thought he could live only in Paris, he had lost his confidence in his star, and even in his own literary judgment: "I'm scared and discouraged and I no longer dare to try a new subject: I'm no longer able to tell good from bad ideas in the theater."[29] Failures stretched out in his imagination as far as 1863: "I'm frightened . . . when I think that at 35 I may be scarcely more advanced than I am now" (July 4, 1856). All he had left was his grim determination for he had burned all his bridges: "literature is an art with which I am identified and which I will never give up" (May 29, 1856).

In 1857, he got a much-needed boost from publishing seven of his poems in Aristide Hignard's collection of *Rimes et mélodies*. While one had an oriental setting, most harked back to Romantic pastoralism. In the volume, Herminie creeping out of her husband's bed for a tryst with young Jules cohabited easily with Honorine's pale "Our Star" and recycled sincerity of "quite simply" as if the intervening years had not happened.

That same year Verne branched out into art criticism. He derived awareness of contemporary production from his cultivated family: with his uncle and great-uncle having been in the trade and with a highly developed visual imagination, he could claim to some expertise in the field of the plastic arts. With no apparent effort he published eight long review articles of the 1857 Salon, an amazing total of 32,000 words. Given their scope and unity of theme, we should undoubtedly consider the articles collectively to be a book. *The Salon of 1857* thus constitutes Verne's first completed prose endeavor of any length. Its existence, and his art-criticism expertise, has never been realized, and is exclusive to the present study.[30]

The writing reads cogently and fluently, exhibiting great knowledge of the art world. The Universal Exposition of Fine Arts, known informally as the Salon, was a particularly Parisian institution with few barriers to exhibiting; as result of the variable standards, established artists often declined to participate. The illustrious predecessor, Baudelaire, had pointed the way, with art-criticism essays and reviews collected as the two volumes of *Les Salons* (1845–46). Verne's book appeared as individual articles in the *Revue des beaux-arts: Tribune des artistes* (1850–61), under director Félix Pigeory, architect and author of regional guides. This fine-arts periodical was notorious both for its reactionary politics and for giving prominence to reviews of comic opera, presumably the ex-secretary's method of entry to its hallowed pages.

Verne's opening piece "Preliminary Article," is perhaps the most interesting, since it summarizes the whole exhibition, although many of the painters cited have of course left little trace today. He very much favored the Breton and Nantes artists amongst those exhibiting. The so-called "First Article" covers the works of 20 artists, including paintings of Frenchmen and Highlanders fighting side by side in the Crimea by neoclassical Horace Vernet (1789–1863), grandson of the famous Joseph Vernet. The "Second" covers Jean-Baptiste Corot, Jean-François Millet, and Gustave Courbet; and the "Third," Maurice Sand, not only author of *Six Thousand Leagues at Full Steam*, but cat painter and the son of George Sand. The "Fifth" piece lambastes Gustave Doré—who was never subsequently to illustrate a Verne work, as if in revenge. The "Sixth" gives an honorable mention to Merino, Verne's Peruvian inspirer and illustrator.

Many individual analyses emphasize the subtle colors of Brittany, with particular attention paid to Charles Leroux's paintings of the River Erdre and Théodore Rousseau's touching portrayal of a fragile skiff threatened by a storm on the lower Loire. But interesting insights into artistic creation also emerge, adding up to a revealing manifesto by Verne: the two-way interchange between literary and pictorial representations; the human meaning embodied in landscapes; the exoticism of the Orient or Eskimo kayaks and the dreams thereby enegendered; the importance of energy and simplicity of expression in artistic endeavor.

Finally, an independent 600-word piece in the same volume, "Portraits of Artists . . . XVIII,"[31] analyzes Victor Massé, good early friend, Bachelor, and rowdy serenader. If we wished to speculate, Massé may have set up the series of articles in the first place, with the publicity Verne's way of thanking him.

In the light of Verne's later career and friends, many of the people involved with the Salon of 1857 seem significant. Famous photographer and publicist Nadar was a member of the influential and controversial jury which screened would-be exhibitors, and also wrote a book in 1858 about the 1857 Salon. Verne must therefore have at least bumped into him at this stage; and Nadar must have known Verne's own volume on the subject. A further tantalizing link, to whom Verne gives many column-inches, is Ernest Meissonier, friend and portraitist of publisher Hetzel.

In 1858, the writing success continued. One-act operetta *Mr. Chimpanzee* (1857), by Verne, Carré, and Hignard, carried the fashionably anti-Darwinian message that to marry was to make a monkey of yourself. It opened at the Bouffes Parisiens in 1858, staged and directed by the famous Offenbach, whom Verne possibly met at this time.[32] However, positive reviews were few and far between. With Carré and Hignard again, modest one-act operetta *Inn of the Ardennes* was staged at the Lyric Theater (1860) of unhappy memory, now being run by Bachelor and Colonnader Philippe Gille; it was also published the same year. Light and punning three-act comedy *Eleven-Day Siege*, written with Charles Wallut and Victorien Sardou—and possibly Dumas, as one journalist claimed (*Int.* 90)—mocked newlyweds' adultery and marriage as social climbing. It was staged 21 times at the Vaudeville and published in 1861, making FF 715, of which Verne got a quarter.[33] After 15 years of trying, it represented his first opening night outside the Lyric (ex-Historic Theater).

Throughout this period Verne asked for feedback from Genevois, his father, the mayor of Nantes, even his doctor, but often felt disappointed by the results. As his plays got better, he continued to hope for a big break: about one attempt, he said that "if it fails you have to believe the devil and fatality have been meddling" [June 27, 1856]—whereupon it did bomb.

While on the outing at Château Thierry, Hignard had mentioned an offer by his brother Alfred, in the shipping business: a free trip to Britain on a cargo vessel, at which Jules leaped without hesitation (July 15, 1859).

He already knew Scotland from his reading, having devoured much of Walter Scott, especially *The Antiquary*, *Rob Roy*, *The Heart of Midlothian*, and *Ivanhoe*. As further preparation, he considered that adding to his five or six words of unintelligible English less important than rereading his Dickens, especially *Nicholas Nickleby* and *The Pickwick Papers*. He also studied Francis Wey's *The British at Home* and Louis Enault's *England, Scotland, and Ireland*, with its engravings by Gavarni, who had helped illustrate his own *Castles in California*; and destroyed Victor-Adolphe Malte-Brun's map of Scotland with the "frenetic points of his compass" (*BB* i) in a transparently sexual metaphor.

Verne obtained a passport after much bureaucratic hemming and hawing (*BB* ii). On July 28, 1859, he left Paris on the new overnight train, leaving his wife and daughters in Amiens, and joined Hignard in Nantes.[34] The two learned, however, that the ship was to sail from Bordeaux instead. They waited two days for the regular steamer down the coast, filling the time by mocking the new Palace of Justice, with the hypocritical steps on the façade leading merely to the cul-de-sac of "a statue of justice in an advanced state of pregnancy" (*BB* iii).

Then, beside himself with excitement at the idea of visiting his ancestral homeland, Verne descended the Loire with Hignard, passing Trentemoult, admiring Chantenay's "sharp spire thrusting into the evening mists," and inhaling the "tarry exhalations" of the Indret steam-engine factory.[35] When their steamer first scraped and then ran aground near Le Pellerin, to be stranded overnight, Jules exulted, remembering his own shipwreck on these shores 20 years previously.

In Bordeaux the two stayed at the Hôtel de Nantes, fascinated by the singing southern accents. But they eventually had to wait 17 days for the ship. They visited the town and Bay of Arcachon, learned how to drink Château d'Yquem, and passed the time as best they could.

Verne's first ever sea journey (see Figure 5), on the *Hamburg* on August 23, made him inordinately happy; he got up each night to contemplate the starlit ocean for hours on end, dreaming of Chateaubriand. (*BB* xii)

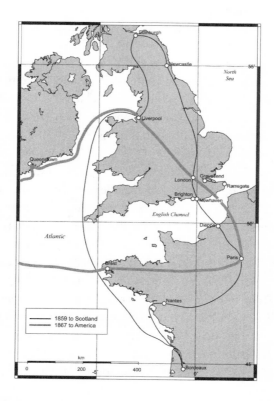

Figure 5: Great Britain, showing the journeys to Scotland in 1859 and America in 1867

For his first recorded steps on foreign soil, Verne landed in Liverpool, to shocking social conditions, including blatant prostitution. One of the girls, barely in her teens, made a very crude suggestion which Verne did not dare repeat. After a virtuoso tour of Liverpool docks and a punch-up in a dockside pub, he and Hignard made a beeline for Scotland.

On the morning of the 27th, after a night in Lambré's Hotel at 18 Princes Street, the two wake up to a view of ten-story medieval houses and the volcanic Edinburgh Castle crag and "mountain" of Arthur's Seat (*BB* xix). From this point on, the architecture, history, literature, food, and ale amaze and delight him. The "utter misery" of the fetid slums and stepless stairs of the "dark, dank, horrid" closes; the splendidly pretentious banks; the pretty fishing village of Newhaven; the cleverly counterweighted windows; the exotic botanical gardens; the royal "pleasure château"; the magnificent New Town; and the glorious avenue up the Queen's Park, due to Scott's "writing a few lines" in a novel (*BB* xx). The Classical and marine view from the top of Arthur's Seat form a sublime vision; henceforth nearly all his volcanoes will seem strangely Scottish.

Comic relief is provided by an open omnibus outing to the fine beach of Portobello. Bathing huts paradoxically combine with nude bathing and our two heroes resolve to conform, in spite, or because of, all the "pretty young misses" on shore. But at the vital moment, having briefly plunged into the "bitter swell," they emerge shamefully from the sea backwards, their proud manhoods facing out to sea.

The two visit a William Bain, a distant relative of Hignard's, at 6 Inverleith Row, impressed by the Victorian solidity of the architecture. To Verne's glee, Bain has an enchanting 17-year-old daughter, "Amelia," who can speak perfect French.[36] He falls under her spell as she plays Highland tunes on the piano and royally informs and entertains the two, taking them to the Botanical Gardens and Warriston cemetery and writing out an itinerary which . . . involves their leaving Edinburgh forthwith.

They accordingly sail up the Firth of Forth (see Figure 6), heading

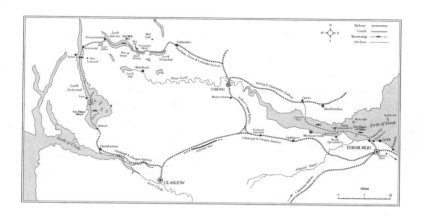

Figure 6: Central Scotland and the southern Highlands, showing the 1859 journey

for a splendid "château" called Inzievar House in Fife, to be greeted by a William Smith, a Catholic priest they had met at the Bains'. Verne admires the stables and heated and irrigated greenhouses. Covering considerable ground, he and Hignard fly through Stirling, Bannockburn, Glasgow (not appreciated), Balloch, Loch Lomond by boat, Luss, the mountain road to Loch Katrine by carriage, Loch Arklet, Ben Lomond, and Callander.

They marvel at a people full of "abnegation and devotion" and a landscape "whose sublime beauty defies the imagination," which *is* history, with its "savage, melancholy, and plaintive" meaning and its "sublime beauties."[37] They even see the Aurora Borealis and Queen Victoria's train with Highland guard, all shaggy sporrans and knobbly knees. For Verne each loch, hill, and island is straight out of *The Heart of Midlothian* or *Rob Roy*, each burgher an Antiquary, each peasant a Fergus or a Macgregor.

Verne's northern urge is abruptly curtailed. After glimpses of Linlithgow Castle, the Pentland Hills, and the Water of Leith, the two suffer an infernal overnight journey besieged by lager louts (September 3). After a glimpse of Newcastle's mines, a whirlwind tour of London, involving Mme Tussaud's, a last memory of Scotland in a performance of *Macbeth*, the Blackwall Tunnel, and the *Great Eastern*. And then brokenheartedly home again.

Although spending less than a fortnight in Britain (August 26–September 6), Verne's entire life would be deeply marked by the experience, especially Edinburgh and the Highlands. It formed, after all, his first real trip outside northern France, his first sea voyage, his first contact with foreigners, his first mountains and lakes, and his first unspoilt terrain. To get inside his head, you need to stroll along the Royal Mile, sail the lochs, and climb Ben Lomond, following Verne's route inch by inch.

Verne's journey was recorded in his lightly fictionalized *Backwards to Britain*, his third book. Narrated by a recently married jobber, 30, with a musician as "closest friend," the manuscript lay moldering, perhaps giving off the faintest whiff of heather and whiskey, until 1989. It was then published and hailed as keenly observed travel writing and an inescapable document for understanding the young author. Its importance lies in being one of his rare uncensored books, with juvenile passion leaping from every page, full of humorous exaggeration about the sea, hunger, antimilitarism, Scottish music, Edinburgh lasses, weather-beaten priests, naval architecture, romantic ruins, and landscapes deliciously devoid of any human presence.

The volume above all gives body to the travel urge which will be the alpha and omega of Verne's writing and life. A travelogue crossed with a literary creation, it forms another artistic manifesto, where the whole future series of Extraordinary Journeys can be made out like an inverted mirage. For several decades, a litany of desolate moors, lochs, and volcanoes will flow from his pen: the haunting music; the science–literature link, for Scott's and Watt's statues are interchangeable; the "sinuosities" of Loch Lomond, hiding-place for untold mysteries; mingled masts and trees, homage to Pierre's poetic gift and early sign of the mechanics–biology equivalence that haunts Verne; and the dream of the north, the seed for the lines-on-a-map generation of the greatest masterpieces.

CHAPTER 9

Destiny Draws up her Skirts: 1860–63

IN ABOUT 1860, VERNE WROTE a draft of his first completed novel, the bleakly pessimistic *Paris in the Twentieth Century*. At 32 he was in despair: like the hero, he had met repeated failures in his writing career and felt misunderstood.

In 1960, orphan Michel Dufrénoy is attending prize day at the 186,000-student Instructional Credit Union, but is booed as an out-of-date Latinist. A Breton poet living in an Americanized Paris, he knows, and mostly detests, electric lifts and lighting, horseless carriages and the Metro, machines to make calculations, transmit stock prices, and facsimiles sent around the world. The air is polluted, the French language anglicized, art and music all but abolished, Balzac, Hugo, and Lamartine replaced by Paul de Kock (*sic*).

Through his favorite uncle, Michel meets Lucy and conducts her around Paris. At his bank job in Rue Drouot, around the corner from Eggly's, he works on the Great Ledger, under the sympathetic Quinsonnas, a closet composer. However, the musician spills ink on the Ledger during an argument with Michel, resulting in their joint sacking. The young poet finds a job in the Comedy Department of a government play writing and censoring factory, but hates it. His verse is rejected by every publisher; he loses his flat; and he ends up starving. His last franc spent on flowers for Lucy, he realizes she has moved, with no forwarding address. Michel wanders aimlessly across

Paris, finishing up among the great writers' snowy graves at Père Lachaise, where he drifts into unconsciousness.

Paris in the Twentieth Century is a typical first novel. Autobiographical and lacking in narrative drive, the main interest comes from the vivid descriptions of the historic neighborhoods where the author studied, worked, and wrote, the houses he lived and loved in, the shops and theaters he knew by heart. While missing the elegiac heights of *The Adventures of Captain Hatteras* or *Journey to the Center of the Earth* and with little sense of an ending, the work remains a fascinating picture of mid-nineteenth-century life.

Any reading is colored by our knowledge of subsequent development, allowing us to admire Verne's prescient attacks on scientific dehumanization and marvel at how many of his "predictions" miss the mark. The sweet-sour anticipation-retrospection of the publishing phenomenon of the 1990s lays bare the Paris of 1860 and the process of historical change. The superficial journalistic analyses must not be allowed to obscure Verne's uncanny insight in this past-in-the-future work, anti-scientific and eminently human and social.

In 1861, Verne visited Germany, Sweden, Norway, and Denmark with Hignard and Lorois, spending five weeks away. He thus missed the birth of his only son Michel, despite an instruction to his wife to delay the event, at least according to Marguerite. The sole surviving chapter of the account, the humorous and high-spirited "Joyous Miseries of Three Travelers in Scandinavia," appeared only in 2003.

In this important piece, Verne conceived of the northern countries as remote and compelling, as fulfilling a long-suppressed thirst for escape from urban France, as compensation for the exoticism he had missed: "These were my savages of Oceania, my Greenland Eskimos, Switzerland on a grander scale." All these "adventures, discoveries . . . explorations," such magical words, "made me ill; a nostalgia for foreign countries took over my life. To leave France . . . where I no longer lived, no longer slept, hardly breathed, was an absolute must." The urge strangely echoed that produced by the Loire below his bedroom window.

Fascinating in the light of his soon-to-start career is his indication of sources, the most complete account extant of his "ten years of constant reading" and therefore of his intellectual development in Paris. Verne scanned the 66 volumes of the *Univers pittoresque* magazine and took out a subscription to *Tour du monde*, "falling head over heals for Doré's and . . . Riou's engravings." He liked Frenchmen Jules-Sébastien-César Dumont D'Urville and Dumas and Britons James Cook, James Ross, and John Richardson. He loved *Norway* (1857) by Louis Énault, who had guided him around Scotland. He adored Ossian, legendary third-century Gaelic warrior, whose poetry, modernized and perhaps largely invented by James Macpherson, helped make Scotland a major focus of the Romantic movement.

Verne, Hignard, and Lorois bought rum, tobacco, pistols, walking sticks, matching FF 25 mackintoshes, and FF 210 tickets to Stockholm.[1] Leaving from Gare du Nord on Tuesday, July 2,[2] they crossed southern Belgium and passed through Cologne and Hanover (see Figure 7).

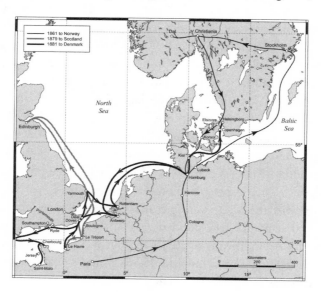

Figure 7: Northern Europe, showing the journeys to Norway in 1861, Scotland in 1879, and Denmark in 1881.

The three spent about two days in Hamburg, staying in the Zum Cronprinzen Hotel on Jungfernstieg: Verne enjoyed the evening panorama from the tower of St. Michael's Church but hated the architecture of the theater.[3]

At Lubeck they embarked on the steamship *Svea* for Verne's third open-sea voyage, again sending him into ecstasy. In Stockholm, with the "most educated and courteous population" in Europe,[4] Verne realized he had lost his FF 2,000 Rothschild Bank money draft and spent whole days visiting every bank to cancel it. Only in the last one, as he finished explaining his plight yet again, did the draft drop out of his guidebook (*JVEST* 44–45). Then the three "traveled from Stockholm to Christiania [Oslo] by canal, mounting ninety-seven locks, an extraordinary voyage of three days and three nights in a steamer" (*Int.* 94).

After Christiania's "white-stone and redbrick houses," set in a superb amphitheater of mountains and fjord,[5] civilization came to an abrupt halt as the three headed for the wild Telemark region. Having sailed to Drammen and traveled overland to Hokksund, they made a nine-hour journey by horse-drawn sleigh along a narrow fir-lined track. From the dirty and expensive tavern in the small hamlet of Tinoset, they jolted on an unsprung two-wheeled post-horse cart, their trunks and bags hanging perilously off the back. Then by the tiny steamboat *Rjukan* over stormy Lake Tinn to Mael, and by cart along a narrow track skirting precipices to the tiny hamlet of Dal.[6] At some stage they also rode on horseback.

"Fresh and smiling" Dal enchanted them, with its babbling brook and handful of houses painted "budding green, pale pink, and . . . blood-red." Their roofs grew wild flowers and grass, harvested each autumn, with the whole scene picturesquely softened by "damp green mists."[7] Telemark, Verne decided, was "the most charming place in the world."[8] The friends stayed at the inn in Dal, where Verne felt shocked at the grammar mistake Hignard made in the register and the menu was just black bread and fish tails.

The three friends traveled ten miles up the spectacular valley of the River Maan to see the 900-foot Rjukan Falls, five times as high as

Niagara and the most famous in Europe. To fully indulge his senses, Verne edged over a projecting ledge, fearfully but happily deafened by the thundering roar and soaked by the thick spray.

Only too soon it was time to return. From Tinoset, the trio took a longer and easier route back via Bamble, rejoining their outward route at Kongsberg.[9] They crossed the Baltic from Helsingborg in Sweden, admiring Kronoberg Castle and the Karnan Tower on the way. At Elsinore in Denmark they were longing to see Hamlet's castle, but felt disappointed it had been knocked down and rebuilt.[10] Verne was expecting a letter from Honorine; it arrived belatedly, causing him to rush home alone, paying a FF 300 supplement (PV 46). Hignard stayed on, still seeking the prince's ghost so as to write an opera of the same name.[11]

In southwest Copenhagen, presumably while waiting for a railroad connection, Verne may have climbed a church spire on the Island of Amager. A spiral staircase enlaced the monument, "protected only by a thin rail, with the steps getting ever narrower, apparently climbing up to infinity." The spectacular, vertiginous vista was ample reward, however: "The Sound unwound to the Point of Elsinore, speckled with a few white sails exactly like seagulls' wings, as to the east the coast of Sweden rolled through the mist."[12]

The normal onwards route was by train to Korsor and boat to Kiel, "like a nest amid a trellis of branches,"[13] in the part of Denmark Germany would seize three years later. Verne presumably then took the train to Altona, on the outskirts of Hamburg, past a backdrop of thistles and lonely storks. Altona was where the passionate love scenes of *Journey to the Center of the Earth* would take place, unfortunately chopped at manuscript stage. The solitary traveler got back home on August 8.[14]

Having spent the princely sum of FF 3,500, Verne was impressed by the Scandinavian equality of citizens, civism, and participation in public affairs. While musician Hignard was responsible for noting the Nordic melodies and lawyer Lorois the accounts, playwright Verne kept a splendid leather-bound notebook, with a brass clasp and pencil holder. In it he produced remarkable sketches of the castles, boats, and curious windowless dwellings he saw.[15] But until the city of Amiens changes its current black-box policy, with no information whatsoever divulged about documents acquired with public money, we can only guess at the details of Verne's journey.

The trip further transformed the youngish man. By blending the Norwegian spray into the Scotch mist he had preciously bottled in his innermost recesses, Verne found his voice: a potent mix of geographical research, visual imagination, and humorously self-mocking exaggeration, shaken together but not stirred. "Joyous Miseries" indeed proposes a delightfully terse manifesto for the next 60 books: "to see things on your travels that don't exist." Henceforth an irresistible urge would draw him:

> to the hyperboreal regions, like the magnetic needle to the north . . . I love cold lands by temperament. [As] Énault says: "As you head north, you constantly get higher; but so uniformly and imperceptibly that you only realize the height you've gotten to by looking at the rise in the barometer and the drop in the thermometer."

Verne equates altitude with both latitude and the deliciously cold temperature, three borrowed scales measuring out his Nordic obsession. Énault's three-way metaphor lies at the heart of Verne's universality.

Because he traveled by public transport, lacked money, and was stimulated by Hignard—to whom the Extraordinary Voyages therefore owe an enormous debt—the author participated fully in Scottish and Norwegian life. Both these proud nations, not yet states, suffered under a more comfortable half-brother fated by geography to regulate their commerce with the rest of the world. Verne's superficially unmetaphysical worldview, his fascination for what people ate, drank, traded, sang, traveled on, wore, or spent, was more than satisfied. He blended into the social landscape of the two countries whose character so closely resembled his own: prickly, independent, egalitarian, and hard-working. The man who embarked on the Scottish epics was not the same as the one who returned from the Norwegian one.

Verne came back home to find a five-day-old son—and, no doubt, Honorine brandishing a huge rolling-pin. Certainly his absence, whatever the justification in terms of changing the literary landscape, constituted a poor start to fatherhood and a sign of selfishness as a husband, at a time when childbirth involved considerable danger to the mother.

Having made the official declaration of birth (CNM 120), Verne found a name for the child, apparently without much help from Honorine. He had first used Michel for the hero of *A Priest in 1839*, noting facetiously in the margin "*St. Michel*, patron saint of bakers because of the '*miches*' [buttocks; crusts]"; the name would be used again in the moon novels and *Strogoff*, as well as three successive boats. From the beginning Michel proved a difficult child, but Verne did worry about his son and try to care for him (JJV 54).

After his marriage, Verne continued to return regularly to Nantes and Chantenay, following the tradition of abandoning Paris over the stifling summer. He must have attended the weddings of Anna (1858), Paul (1859), Mathilde (1860), and Marie (1861) and the funerals of Uncle Prudent (1860) and his grandmothers (1861, 1865). Did Honorine go with him and did she remark pointedly that the rest of the family started strings of offspring within weeks of their weddings?

Probably in the summer of 1860 Verne attended a family gathering at Provins. Two charming photos showed Jules, all smiles, playing the fool behind Honorine's back, as well as 14 of his relatives, including his daughters Valentine and Suzanne. The contrast seems striking between his dowdy wife and his sisters, eyes so identical to Verne's they appear stuck on, radiant with inner calm and beauty, and lips glowing with sensuous health.

Using contemporary documents, an identikit portrait of Verne can be assembled by stages:

a handsome man with a flaxen beard and a kind but serious expression, a little cold-seeming.

His face seemed a little long, with a firm chin, fine and mocking lips, witty nose, expressive nostrils, and abundant curly chestnut-brown hair, matching his pointed beard; his blue eyes, with a very clear expression, sparkled with mischief.[16]

A quicksilver expression hid an underlying Breton obstinacy, producing a strange cocktail of passion, sensibility, and aloofness, perhaps stemming from his indifference as to what people thought of him:

He frightened [us nephews and nieces], although behind all the jokes we saw the goodness and affection.

a warm heart and an alert mind behind a cold appearance, reluctant to open up to the first comer.

He conveyed a vague impression of involuntary mistrust . . . "I'm a provincial Parisian or a Parisian provincial, whichever you prefer!"
An agreeable companion, as playful as a cat, a charming and entertaining talker; but a joker and banterer, skeptical about everything.

A mixture of . . . dryness and sweetness, he resembles cooling steel, which bends for some and stands stiff for others . . . but what really makes him seem curt and abrupt is his voice, at once effervescent and haughty, combined with his speed at repartee.[17]

Novelist Ivan Turgenev claimed to be "profoundly disappointed" by his "tedious and very silent" behavior;[18] Only three people had unalloyed praise: "hard-working and good-looking, intelligent and witty," "the most upright of men, the simplest, the most unassuming," "the best of fellows."[19]

Probably in the first half of 1862 Verne wrote a fourth book, about balloons this time. According to a mysterious disappearing letter reported by Marguerite, the idea had germinated by February of that year: "In my own balloon, I don't plan to go for a duck—or a turkey for that matter, as it would just be taken for a ride."[20] At the end of May Honorine reportedly wrote to Sophie that the book was nearing completion (ADF 90). Once it was finished she was meant to have exclaimed "Thank heavens his balloon is over and done with!" (JJV 54).

Prior to July 1862, perhaps over a period of years, Verne's prose manuscript or manuscripts were apparently rejected by a number of publishers.[21] It is not impossible that the *Revue des deux mondes* accepted the balloon story, but without payment, an offer Verne refused.[22] One day he supposedly threw his books onto the fire, from which they were hastily rescued by his wife (ADF 90). He was meant to have felt very discouraged, saying that if he wrote a play for a director, the director changed; if he thought of a good title, three days later he would see it on the billboards; if he penned an article, another came out on the same subject (ADF 90).

Perhaps to escape Michel's cries, Verne joined the Circle of the Scientific Press, probably in the fall of 1861.[23] The Circle, founded in 1857 by Figuier and two other journalists, promoted serious scientific journalism, even if this meant criticizing the establishment, including the powerful Academy of Sciences. Its interests ranged far and wide: electric valves, magnetism, mesmerism, guano, undersea cables, arts criticism, and philosophy. Holding weekly meetings, it published pamphlets as well as the *Presse scientifique des deux mondes*, the periodical's editor being chemistry teacher Jean-Augustin Barral (1819–84).[24] In 1850, Barral had survived a dangerous escapade, with doctor and politician Alexandre Bixio (1808–62), when their balloon burst at 17,000 feet and fell to earth in less than five minutes.

It was probably at the Circle that Verne remet Nadar,[25] caricaturist, writer, founder of reviews, and photographer of Baudelaire, George Sand, and Gioacchino Rossini. Nadar had perhaps come to play cards at Verne's apartment in the 1850s (Lemire 11); as authors of competing books about the 1857 Salon, they had surely bumped into each other. As their friendship blossomed, they no doubt discovered their shared passion for balloons and bounced fashionable flying ideas off each other.[26]

In late summer 1862, Verne contacted publisher Jules Hetzel, transforming his writing fortunes.

From an Alsatian family, Pierre-Jules Hetzel (1814–86) had a long aristocratic face, penetrating gaze, and swept-back romantic hair. Republican chief of cabinet under two ministers of foreign affairs, poet Lamartine and brave balloonist Bixio, he had been wounded on the June 1848 barricades, before working as General Cavaillac's secretary, then heading into political exile in Brussels (1851–59). A friend of Baudelaire's, he had published Stendhal, Hugo, Sand, and Dumas and imposed his corrections on Turgenev and Balzac (JD 159–62). A good talent spotter, he brought out an unknown called Émile Zola two years later. His publishing house, founded in 1843, produced affordable editions of literary authors as well as books for young people—many under his own signature. Hetzel often "borrowed" texts from abroad and fraudulently published them as his own creations.

The circumstances of the fateful encounter are unclear, since the earliest accounts came decades after and are strong on generalities but weak on details. Verne reportedly met the publisher through an intermediary:[27] possibly Nadar or Dumas *père* or *fils*. But most probable was fellow Breton Alfred de Bréhat (b. 1826), who wrote books for boys about the British Empire and entered Hetzel's stable in 1861, although Verne could have met Bréhat himself through Nadar or the Dumas.[28]

Given that both his previous finished volumes were nonfiction, Verne's balloon book perhaps comprised a collection of documentary articles on aeronautics and Africa, with the invented adventures of

Dr. Fergusson forming merely one episode.[29] The initial submission was probably by mail; but Verne also went to see Hetzel twice.[30] At least one meeting very probably took place in the publisher's office at 18 Rue Jacob; the other supposedly occurred with Hetzel in bed, either ill or late to rise.[31] Hetzel perhaps refused the first submission, liking the idea of Africa but not the form of the work.[32]

A fortnight later Verne was meant to have gone back to hear something like, I deeply regret that, despite the great merits of this work, I am unable . . . In this version, Verne snatched up the manuscript, about to storm out, when Hetzel called him back with words to the effect: but you have all the characteristics of a great storyteller.[33] The great publisher apparently underscored passages, concluding with, Link them up, structure it as a whole, make a real novel, and bring it back as soon as possible. Verne "rolled up" his manuscript, bowed, and withdrew—over the moon this time.[34] A mere fortnight later (rather implausibly, for a rewrite would have taken longer), the author reportedly brought back a completed novel and outlined an ambitious program encyclopedically surveying the entire cosmos (ADF 93). Either on the spot or a week later, Hetzel promised "immediate" publication, "printing [it] the same month."[35] However, since no document has ever emerged, it remains perfectly possible that the biographers invented the whole story. With the benefit of 20–20 hindsight vision, the publisher would claim fourteen years later that "from the beginnings of this writer . . . I was sure of the future of his work" (*BSJV* 144:12). It may be true but if so, he forgot to tell the writer himself.

The novel giving meaning to Verne's thirty-five years of existence and twenty years of writing had an innovative theme. Fergusson plans to map out central Africa and explore the upper Nile. On a grant from the Royal Geographical Society, he builds a balloon, which employs the frightening combination of naked flame and double hydrogen envelope to rise and descend and so catch the westerlies. Setting off from Zanzibar with servant Joe and friend Kennedy, he confirms that Lake Victoria is part of the river system. After hostile cannibals, fierce storms, grasshopper plagues, terrible thirst, and a burst envelope, the trio finally discovers the source of the Nile—where Arab legends had placed it (and beside the real-life one, discovered soon after). As the craft carries on, Fergusson jumps out to save weight, lands in Lake Chad, and is rescued from marauding Arab horsemen. Verne uses a desert scene, derived from Pascal and one of his most moving, to portray the anguish of the individual lost in empty space. In the climactic scene, the stranded balloon is surrounded by "Talibas" rebels. The three men build a fire, take off using the hot air, and jettison the basket to make one final leap to a French outpost in Senegal.

While not as polished as later works, *Five Weeks* does show great variety and pace. It has good characterization, with Fergusson, Joe, and Kennedy as scientist leader, handyman servant, and note-taker sidekick. Like early Tintin, the work appears unsophisticated (and racist), but remains a highly readable story. With its high adventure in desolate places, it is quintessential Verne.

Among possible sources were a balloon built by Verne's salon host and illustrator, Gavarni, as described by Chevalier in the *Musée* (1857), including the method of rising and descending.[36] Using the trade winds may have come from military engineer Captain Meusnier's paper to the Academy of Sciences.[37] Verne was also influenced by Richard Burton's exploration from Zanzibar to Lake Tanganyika from 1857 on and David Livingstone's search for the origin of the Nile starting from 1855.

But the main source was Verne's love of geography and exploration:

> I wrote *Five Weeks in a Balloon*, not as a story about ballooning, but as a story about Africa. I always was greatly interested in geography and travel . . . there was no means of taking my travellers through Africa otherwise than in a balloon . . . at the time I wrote the novel . . . I had no faith in the possibility of ever steering balloons . . . / "Then you had no scientific studies to go upon?" / "None whatever."

My love for maps and the great explorers stories led me to my composing . . . my long series of geographical stories.[38]

Both quotes, thirty years on, showed Verne's dismissal of the tissue of lies growing around him, formed of an insidious progression from travel, through transport technology already a century old, to science, futuristic invention, anticipation, and science fiction. To his increasing irritation, people ignorant of his actual books embroidered his publisher's half-truths and ultimately produced the absurd situation where the novelist would be thrust, screaming and kicking, into a genre invented long after his death. To summarize his own words as baldly as possible, Verne did not like balloons, considering them either too low-tech or too high-tech; he had no scientific knowledge; and most of his novels, including the best-known ones, contained no science beyond clocks, sails, volcanoes, hollow-earth monsters, and hot air. He was not a science fiction writer.

The first extant document about *Five Weeks* is the contract, signed on October 23,1862, and referring to a "work" called "Journey in the Air" by "Jules Vernes [*sic*]."[39] It stipulated 25 centimes per small-format copy at FF 3, a print run of 2,000, an advance of FF 500 ($1,500), and 5 percent on any illustrated editions (at FF 4 or 7). This fixed 8 $\frac{1}{2}$ percent on the paperback edition seems reasonable, although far from generous—modern contracts offer 12 $\frac{1}{2}$ percent for big reprints. Hetzel appeared far from bowled over at this stage, making no plans for serial publication or any further works. Then as now, the overwhelming majority of new books sank without trace, the serial pulping paid for by the occasional success that surprised everyone.

But in any case, Verne felt delighted, already hung his financial future on this tiny FF 500, and planned to leave the stock exchange. Or at least he did according to a friend with implausibly perfect forty-three-year recall: "My children, I think I'm going to leave you . . . I'm getting married, on my route I've met the richest of partners, Monsieur Hetzel . . . I'll be doing novels while you're still buying options. I have an idea who's going to make the most."[40]

Even after the successful meeting, Hetzel imposed changes on the novel, including having Joe jump out in Fergusson's place and cutting an episode involving the saving of the servant.[41] Verne's preferred title was dumped in favor of *Five Weeks in a Balloon*.

In December 1862, Verne composed three successive blurbs, important for understanding his intention. A small part of them is cited here, on an exclusive basis, with the Lake Chad episode different from that of the published version:

> En route [Fergusson] is lucky enough to save a French missionary about to be martyred by barbaric tribes; having a dreadful fall over Lake Chad, he cheats death only through the devotion of one of his companions / . . . This book, destined to have an immense success in Britain, will surely interest French readers, and we recommend it strongly to our readers.[42]

Following publication on January 31, 1863, four favorable reviews appeared: "amusing and vigorous," "fascinating and captivating, cheerful and moving," "[it] will have a huge impact and become a classic of its kind," "success has already been achieved."[43] One review even included the novel among authentic expeditions, causing at least one reader to request Fergusson's address.[44]

With a single reprint of one thousand copies the same year, bringing in an additional FF 250, the book had disappointing sales[45]—and, despite the nationality of its characters and the hopeful draft blurb, it failed to come out in English. (Over Verne's lifetime, however, *Five Weeks* proved the classic slow burner, selling second best among all his books, with an estimated one-third of a million copies in French alone.[46]) The author was thus wise to hang on to his day job; but could have some hope of living off his writing if he could write seven or eight further books. Hetzel indeed said: "my child, do not dissipate your efforts on other work; you have renewed a genre of writing that seemed exhausted. Take the path chance has shown you. And provided you do not get lost in shortcuts you will find fame and fortune."[47] In other words, the canny publisher wanted to have first refusal on any subsequent efforts, just in case the book did belatedly succeed.

Verne may have been lucky with his first book, or perhaps skillful, to get in ahead of a craze that would sweep across France. To make money for his campaign for real aircraft, Nadar planned to build a hot-air balloon, the *Géant*. In July 1863, the photographer with an eye for nation-wide publicity founded the Heavier-than-Air Society.[48] Verne was one of the very first members, happy to find again Barral from the Scientific Press and attending most of the weekly meetings. The novelist became the questor in January 1864 (JD 165), helping to enroll in the society a long roll-call of the famous, including Dumas *père* and *fils*, Girardin, Hugo, Offenbach, Sand, Maxime du Camp, Colonnade hanger-on Malot, and Edmond About, author of another book about the seminal 1857 Salon.

On October 4, 1863, the FF 200,000, 6,000-cubic-meter *Géant*, almost as high as Notre Dame, took off before two hundred thousand spectators, carrying picnic hampers, champagne, and thirteen passengers, including Nadar himself and Bachelor Villemessant. In two, not entirely trustworthy, accounts, Verne was due to join the flight, but made his excuses minutes before the launch.[49] A new flight on October 18, with eight passengers, was carried away on a storm and crashed in Holland, seriously wounding several of the balloonists (JD 165).

In December 1863, Verne published in the *Musée* an article called "About the *Géant*" eulogizing the aerostat, paradoxically enough as he mistrusted balloons. The piece ended with the famous quotation: "Let's go then for the helicopter, and adopt Nadar's motto: Everything that is possible will be done." Although Verne's book had been out for eleven months, both the article and Nadar's flights gave a boost to sales, according to the grandson (JJV 58). If that was true, however, the book must have been doing catastrophically, for sales over the whole of 1864 still only amounted to 1,000, even more disappointing than the first year.[50]

All in all, the year had been a better one for Verne, converted at the desperately unprecocious age of thirty-five from virtual unknown to man of letters. In *Castles in California*, the maid had produced an epigrammatically obscure pearl, "Better skate than lemon." It fitted Verne's tardy, but still infinitely modest, breakthrough.

CHAPTER 10

Golden Years: 1863–66

VERNE'S LIFE LOOKED UP. In 1863, after only a few months, the family moved from Passage Saulnier to the leafy, well-healed area of Auteuil (September 10, 1863). (Henceforth, all letters cited, using the minimalist system explained in chapter 2, will be to Hetzel unless indicated otherwise.) No. 39 Rue La Fontaine lay well within the modern 16th Arrondissement in Paris, not far from the future Eiffel Tower; it is now an upscale Chinese restaurant. It is unclear how the Vernes financed such a move, for Jules had earned only FF 750 from *Five Weeks* by the end of 1863, barely enough to pay the deposit, let alone a few months' rent.

Verne spent 1863–64 in a whirlwind of activity. In Wallut's *Musée* he brought out an article about Edgar Allan Poe and a historical novella "The Count of Chanteleine," a rather conventional story about the Wars of the Vendée (1793–96), where Breton peasants rise up against the French Revolution. He also contributed to a second collection of songs with Hignard, including "Memories of Scotland" and "The Tankadère." Finally, he wrote 200,000 words for Hetzel. All the while, he was continuing with his day job.

While Verne did his utmost to please Hetzel, the efforts were never reciprocated, for the publisher never took his star writer seriously. The editor and the novelist, each with decades of experience of the publishing business, both had agendas for collaboration, but so radically different as to mean the abandonment of many of Verne's most cherished dreams. Some of the discussions took place over steaks at Hetzel's regular table in the Caron café; on the corner of Rue Jacob and Rue des Saints Pères, unchanged for a generation and rather dark, it catered for writers and professors (September 12, 1864).

For his part, Verne observed the contemporary corruption of the intellect and commercialization of literature: "In our time Hugo would declaim his *Orientals* while cavorting on circus horses and Lamartine would plug his harmonies hanging upside down from a trapeze."[1] He no doubt wished to discreetly profit from the opportunities thereby opened up, but above all longed, ambitiously enough, to transform society by the force of his writing. His central aim was to denounce the social ills: he "conceived vast enterprises, aspired to the triumphs of Balzac, and dreamed of shaking modern society to its very foundations by the audacity and cruelty of his depictions."[2]

With this aim, Verne submitted his social satire of contemporary France, *Paris in the Twentieth Century.* However, Hetzel categorically refused the novel, writing that he found nothing good in it: "frankly nothing . . . a disaster . . . almost as if by a child . . . a failure . . . a painful thing, so dead . . . inferior on nearly every line . . . mediocre . . . no real originality . . . no wit," and so on, for 500 words of literary assassination [end of 63 or beginning of 64]. And yet the novel must have had something, for it later became the most successful French novel ever in the United States.[3]

Verne must also have tried to interest Hetzel in *Backwards to Britain*,[4] but again failed to place it, despite the book's strength. Another submission was the novella "The Count of Chanteleine," which went to proof stage before rejection (January 5, 1879). One final work not produced by Hetzel was the short story "The Blockade Runners." It was published in the *Musée* instead in 1865, a fine tale set in Civil War Charleston and Glasgow, with ships, love, and a certain amount of sympathy for both Northern and Southern causes.[5]

It was to be Verne's last independent venture. Henceforth, all his output had to pass muster with Hetzel, who rejected many of Verne's best ideas, especially those involving the slightest hint of sex, violence, or politics. Bestiality and shaking society to its foundations were both out. The reason the publisher so categorically rejected many of Verne's finest efforts seem to have little to do with their literary value, and more with his commercially inspired decision to concentrate on a partly juvenile audience. He thus precluded all contemporary reality or social commentary including—surprising as it may seem—any depiction of France. Verne would be stuck in the limiting genre of young people's writing about foreign parts for the rest of his life.

In 1863–64, Verne wrote *The Adventures of Captain Hatteras* (1865), a compulsive page-turner and disturbing mood-changer that takes the obsessed captain of the title ever further north through the Arctic. The 130,000-word double-decker was one of Verne's most personal novels, with the poetic descriptions of the icy wastes and gripping authenticity reflecting his newfound self-confidence. The North Pole, where the meridians and oceans met, was a magical spot for a writer obsessed with physical space and its natural and artificial structures, allowing him to give full rein to his creative imagination.

Richard Shandon receives a mysterious letter asking him to construct a reinforced ship in Liverpool, purchase six years of supplies, and assemble a highly paid crew for an unknown destination. As the ship heads off for Melville Bay, only a "dog-captain" has appeared. At 78°N, things are becoming chilly and the men restless—when a crewman reveals himself as John Hatteras. The captain is determined to use his steam engine to plant the Union Jack on the North Pole. With Dr. Clawbonny, who has Dickensian optimism, curiosity, and commonsense, he sets out over the icy wastes in search of fuel. The two rescue Altamont, sole survivor of an American expedition, but when they return, the crew has mutinied. Hatteras and his companions remain without food or resources at the coldest point on earth.

The five remaining men, with Hatteras's faithful dog Duke, build an icehouse for the winter. When Altamont insists on calling the land

New America, an argument breaks out, for Hatteras suspects him of designs on the Pole. However, Altamont saves Hatteras from musk oxen and the two make up. They trek north to a warmer zone, with paradisiacal frolicking animals and monsters in the open sea. From a factual bedrock, based on extensive research, the novel has gradually entered a state of high excitement, bathing in an unreal atmosphere of late Romanticism, Poe, and Cooper.

At the very Pole stands a volcano in full eruption. Wishing to reach 90°N, Hatteras climbs up through the lava as if hypnotized, and throws himself into the glowing abyss—only to be caught by Altamont, magically at his side. The captain's failure to reach his goal sends him mad and he finishes up in a Liverpool lunatic asylum.

Three French books are by far Verne's most important sources: *Journeys in the Ice . . . Extracts from the Reports of Sir John Ross, Parry . . . McClure* by Amateur Hervé and Ferdinand Lanoye (eds.) (1854), St. Stanislas schoolmate Lucien Dubois's *The Pole and the Equator* (1863), and Lanoye's *The Polar Sea* (1864). Verne borrows throughout from Hervé and Lanoye, indeed copying about eight pages word for word, mistakes included, making this the lengthiest plagiarism identified in his works.[6]

So riveting were the novel's descriptions that early reviewers again wondered if the book might be authentic. Real-life explorers said that it gave one of the most accurate pictures of Arctic life ever.[7] Sand called it "captivating"; Gautier, "excellent"; Zola, "a great imagination and very keen intelligence"; and Julien Gracq, "a masterpiece."[8] Playwright Eugène Ionesco claimed "all my texts were written, directly or allusively, to celebrate [Hatteras's] discovery of the North Pole."[9] Modern critics have similarly considered it "masterly" and "perhaps [Verne's] greatest masterpiece."[10]

However, the dazzling story is not authentic, not what Verne wrote. The true story, which I discovered in 2005, is to be found in the manuscript.[11] A chapter entitled "John Bull and Jonathan" (II xxi) opens with Altamont raising the Stars and Stripes. When Hatteras cuts it down, the American attacks him and the two men decide on a duel to the death to determine whether the new continent will be American or British. Landing on an ice floe, the two start fighting with knives (II xxii). The floe gradually sinks, but the battle continues as the water covers their knees, and then their heads. An emotional scene follows their rescue, with Clawbonny pouring his heart out in reproaches and humanistic sentiment.

With the Briton and American still at loggerheads, the expedition reaches 89°N. The manuscript closes with an outstanding commemoration of Hatteras's true destiny:

Hatteras was waving [the Union Jack] with one hand, and with the other pointing at the Pole of the celestial globe, directly overhead.

All of a sudden, he disappeared. A terrible cry from his companions must have sounded as far as the mountain peak; a quarter of a minute, a century passed, and then the unfortunate man could be seen launched by the explosion of the volcano to an immense height, his flag distended by the breath from the crater.

Then he fell back down into the volcano, whereupon Duke, faithful to the death, threw himself in so as to share his tomb . . .

And, of the memories of the Arctic expedition, the most indelible was that of a Mount Hatteras smoking on the horizon, the tomb of a British captain standing at the North Pole of the globe.

The excision of the duel, with its dramatic consequences for Anglo-American rivalry, seems to be the longest deleted section in the Extraordinary Journeys. Verne must have felt death in his heart when the publisher sacrificed the dramatic episodes and the core of his plot, ones brilliantly reflecting contemporary geopolitical reality. The real Hatteras sacrificed himself to achieve his lifelong goal—and yet nobody suspected it for well over a century. That Verne was able to make a career in spite of Hetzel's censoring of his most cherished passages speaks wonders for his forbearance.

In *Journey to the Center of the Earth* (1864), Professor Lidenbrock, "an old geologist, very gruff and unpleasant" (*BSJV* 135:46), discovers a runic ciphered document containing the claim of twelfth-century Arne Saknussemm to have reached the center of the earth via the crater of Snaefells in Iceland. Dragging his nephew Axel away from his fiancée and hiring stoical Icelander Hans, Lidenbrock finds the extinct volcano and travel downs through the geological strata of the past. Deep underground, the three men discover a lost world containing a large sea, with plants, fish, and dinosaurs, some very much alive. After trying to cross the sea, they find a path down again, marked with Saknussemm's runic initials but now blocked. They attempt to blow it up, while sheltering on a wooden raft, but instead carry part of the sea down with them into the bowels of the earth. Implausibly riding up on a volcanic eruption, they are finally thrown out on the slopes of Stromboli.

In this novel, more than elsewhere, Verne seems to let himself go. Much of the narrative tension is sexual, but divorced from the female body and located more widely. The whole book is charged with electrical energy, both repressed and displayed: horses have a field day, and hands play an important role throughout the book. So do reinforced staves, pens, knives, telescopes, trees, giant mushrooms, thick pillars, verticality in general, tubes, pockets, purses, and goatskin bottles ("outres" from uteruses). The earth itself forms a blatant object of desire, with the twin firm white peaks, pointed waves seething with fire, gaping orifices, cavities, bays, fjords, gashes, and slits; but also the thrusting (and blocking) of the most varied penetrations, glows, eruptions, effusions, and discharges, as well as repeated falling and sinking. But Verne's real originality lies in linking these fixations with other bodily functions in the earth's bowels, including sweating, trembling, eating, digesting, excretion, and pregnancy and childbirth. The scatological episodes to his parents gloriously transmute from base matter into gold. The sex is subsumed into a general view of the world as a throbbing reflection of the observer's own consciousness—and unconscious. The novel provides a goldmine for psychoanalytically minded critics.

Verne undoubtedly wrote the novel between January and August 1864, perhaps while finishing *Captain Hatteras*. The source for the cipher was Poe's cryptogram in "The Gold-Bug" (1843) and the Runic alphabet came from an inscription in the *Univers pittoresque* (*BSJV* 135:46). That winter Verne reportedly frequented Charles Saint-Claire Deville, a schoolmate of Hetzel and specialist in seismic phenomena who had descended into Stromboli (ADF 104). With his proud multilingualism, scientific displays, and irascible passion, Professor Lidenbrock clearly parodies Pierre Verne; his name comes from Friederich Lindenbrog, also written Lindenbrocke (1573–1648),[12] bibliophile and editor of erotic Latin poetry. There are also unmistakable debts to Hoffmann, Sand, and Dumas. Cutting and pasting from Louis Figuier's *The Earth Before the Deluge* (1863) was systematic, even by the lax standards of the time.[13] It is a moot point whether the borrowing comes close to plagiarism.

One positive if wrongheaded review, based more on Hetzel's blurb than any knowledge of the text, claimed "Jules Verne is a true scientist and a delightful story-teller" (*JVEST* 14–18). The idea was absurd, of course, that Verne could be anything but a novelist, but that did not stop the idea from multiplying wildly ever after.

What the reviewers, and probably Hetzel, failed to see was what drove Verne's adventure writing. Yet the answer appears fairly obvious to modern eyes, since four works written within five years bore a strong family resemblance and exposed their workings for all to see. "Joyous Miseries," *Backwards to Britain*, *Hatteras*, and *Journey to the Center of the Earth* all featured small groups of male travelers. They all borrowed from the same exploration and travel literature, shared the same atmosphere of anguish and mystery, involved similar labyrinths, electrical storms, and volcanoes, and employed identical metaphors and writing strategies. Three of the works passed through (or under)

Liverpool and Scotland, and three, Hamburg and Denmark. All featured protagonists who structured their existence in terms of the distance they had traveled. All equated northwards progress and happiness, measuring out the monomaniacal quest toward the Nordic realms and untamed wilderness. The bare Romantic landscapes were all dazzlingly suited to admiring the patterns of nature: an obsessive phrase was "crisscrossing meanders." Linearity and networks, sensual curves and brutal straight lines, nature and artifice: this phrase, first used in describing Liverpool railways, emblemized Verne's distinctive vision of existence. His own urge to go ever further, while seeing things that didn't exist, curtailed after only one day in the Highlands, but happily renewed in Norway, generated all four works, and indeed lies at the very heart of the Extraordinary Journeys. The physical geography of Chantenay, where all routes led north, was in this way writ large over the whole globe.

Following the initial contract, covering only *Five Weeks*, Hetzel and Verne signed five other agreements, the second one on 1 January 1864, when *Hatteras* was already three-quarters finished. It offered FF 3,000 for a 10,000-copy small-format print run of *Hatteras*, 30 centimes per volume thereafter, 6 percent on illustrated editions, and 50 percent on translation and other rights. It also stipulated an advance of FF 300 per month and an option on two volumes per year, for up to eight volumes of histories of exploration. (It should be noted that "volume" meant part: *Hatteras* comprised two volumes and Verne's other books had one, two, or three volumes.)

On the surface, the second contract, especially the advance, seems better for Verne. However, it transferred ownership of the book to the publisher for ten years, including the right to publish any number of copies in serialized form;[14] and it made no mention of any further novels. Verne remained slavishly, masochistically, devoted to Hetzel; but at the age of thirty-seven, in return for some security, not only did Verne sign away his future, which Hetzel perversely saw as nonfiction, but laid the foundation for his publisher to become five times a millionaire.

What Hetzel may not have emphasized to Verne is that, in addition to his book publishing program, he planned to launch an important illustrated magazine for a young readership, combining education and "recreation," but with a pedagogic and moralistic approach. When he signed the second agreement, he had already got his team together, having contracted in April 1863 with republican educationalist Jean Macé (1815–94) to codirect the *Magasin illustré d'éducation et de récréation* (CNM 142).

Verne constituted the main plank of Hetzel's success. From April 1864 until March 1865 the *Magasin* was given away with the leading newspaper the *Temps*, a FF 200,000 loss leader that ensured a large readership from the start. The first issue opened with chapters 1 and 2 of *Hatteras* in the "children's education" section, in parallel with "Hetzel's" *Swiss Family Robinson* in the recreation section.[15] For the next 22 months Verne's gripping chiller would keep the readership on icy tenterhooks—but without him getting a centime from it.

When Jules and Honorine traveled to Chantenay in August 1864, it was their first visit since the publication of *Five Weeks*, and the whole family assembled to celebrate (RD 80).

There had been one or two changes. Paul had given up his naval career and become a stockbroker, living at 13 Rue Jean-Jacques, obliquely across the street from his parents, still at no. 6; all four siblings had started producing impressive numbers of children. Anna and Mathilde had settled near Chantenay; Marie, on the floor above her parents. Including the Châteaubourgs, the four Nantes households were thus in sight of each other, as were the four Chantenay ones (RD 62).

A homecoming reception and dance took place in the Chantenay garden, great fun for everybody—except Jules, in bed with an acute recurrence of his facial paralysis. Half his face had gone dead, conceivably due to the loss of his brilliant polar episodes.[16]

But he supposedly soon recovered enough to bellow over the church square to his former maid, butcher Mathurine Pâris, "I need your Nantes pork for lunch, otherwise Sunday won't be Sunday!"

(ADF 101). As usual in the evenings, the family recited verses, with
some ranging from the ribald to the scatological. One such doggerel
attacked Hetzel's fidelity and Verne's continence: "Take care, O novelist! For fame is far from all. / Once punctured, you plummet like a
balloon. / The prouder the flight, the greater the fall. / Will Hetzel
give you a new pantaloon?"[17] Jules's sisters also reputedly informed
him it was a mistake to have switched from theater to prose, initially
supported by Honorine and their daughters (RD 80).

Just as in the old days, the whole crowd went on excursions, pic-
nics, and visits to neighbors for frolics and card games; Mass
remained *de rigueur*. Home amusements varied as much as ever: endless conversations dominated by the menfolk as the ladies sewed;
Verne's sisters' four-handed piano; ancient romances, now yellow and
curling, sung by Pierre and Sophie; trios by Honorine, Suzanne, and
Valentine; Paul's performances of his own compositions; jokey anec-
dotes from Jules; and long sessions of billiards (RD 71).

But the author often retreated. He spent most of his time working in
his old bedroom, with the magnificent view increasingly hidden by the
now large fruit tree. Nevertheless, he would sometimes come out and
join the conversation in various states of undress, amusing the family, if
producing affectionate reproaches from Sophie (RD 82). When the children made too much noise he would suddenly open his door. Blinking
with his left eye, the right eye would level upon them a look at once fascinating, terrible, and unbearable (ADF 102). Thinking he should get
out more, Jules's mother asked Georges Allotte, her brother Auguste's
son, to take him hunting, but the hermit refused (ADF 103). He sometimes shocked the locals with his gruffness: "Yesterday I went to
Chantenay to see Verne. His son the novelist was there. I thought it
polite to compliment him on the success of his books: he was extremely
surly and disagreeable. I shall not venture again to stroke that polar
bear."[18] On one of his home breaks, the men of Indret hoped that Jules
would revisit his much-loved foundry, preparing his name in letters of
steel; Verne simply canceled (ADF 160).

From October 1864, Verne threw himself into writing _From the Earth to the Moon_ (1865). The moon novel is the most humorous and light-hearted in Verne's oeuvre, but also one of the most serious, full of daring imagery and trenchant social commentary. It carries its considerable learning lightly while exploring personalities, issues, and controversies.

In the novel, decades after the Civil War, the Baltimore Gun Club still boasts America's best artillerymen, all frustrated and crippled manic-obsessives, "with less than one pair of legs among three." The satire of militarism underscores the damage done by the war, with "cotton plants grow[ing] splendidly on the richly fertilized fields." Mixed in is a pre-Freudian simile melding the quick and the dead, sex and violence, as the men brag who has the biggest gun and who can send projectiles the furthest.

The novel features an Abraham Lincoln set in his ways. When one superannuated warmonger suggests that America should colonize Britain, the artillerymen enthusiastically agree that it would only be fair, but:

> "Go and suggest that to President Lincoln, and see what reception you'll get!"
>
> "Lincoln's getting old," murmured Bilsby through the four gritted teeth he had saved from battle.
>
> "He's been enthroned in Washington too long," concurred Tom Hunter; "we need a younger president, still keen to make a reputation for himself." (_BSJV_ 155:53).

Eventually, though, good sense prevails and it is decided to use the killing machines to fire at the moon instead. After lengthy calculations, the members construct a chain of foundries and a 1,000-foot shaft in Florida, the southernmost state. Daredevil Parisian Michel Ardan arrives, a charming, insouciant joker closely modeled on Nadar. The Frenchman announces his plan to travel inside the projectile, causing a worldwide sensation.

A conical projectile is cast, with an implausible water-filled wall to absorb the shock of the launch. It has screwed portholes, an air supply, dried food, and every home comfort. On the big day, Ardan and two Gun Clubbers climb down into the craft, resting on 200 tons of gunpowder. A titanic explosion sends them off into space, monitored by a giant telescope in the Rockies. But the target has been missed and the men end up in orbit around the moon.

Verne wrote that "of course" he would use aluminum and experiment first with animals ("the dog will eat the squirrel") [October 1864]. He established the trajectories himself, but for the equations resorted to cousin Garcet, in a café near his *lycée*. He also had them checked by astronomer Jules Janssen and Joseph Bertrand, later secretary of the Academy of Sciences, who, however, thought the story a bit thin; and perhaps sought further help from Saint-Claire Deville.[19]

 The timing seemed tight, for the Civil War was still raging when the first books rolled off the presses in the spring of 1865. Then catastrophe struck: Lincoln was murdered on April 14 and the book no longer made sense. Verne urgently deleted "Lincoln" and the relevant paragraphs, brought the action back to the present, and the presses started up again. But meanwhile, on May 26, the war had stopped.

Only in September did the book appear, in the adult review *Journal des débats politiques et littéraires*, escaping the censorship of Hetzel's *Magasin*. During the serialization, the author was meant to have received alluring fan letters (ADF 110). The Nantes newspaper *L'Union bretonne* pirated the novel in October—unless it was Hetzel who secretly authorized publication. A probably stolen chapter also appeared in the appropriately-named the *Voleur* (February 16, 1866), by successively "Vernier," Vernes," and "Vernies."[20] Given that *Hatteras* was by "Ver n" in the first printings, the jinx over the author's name remained alive and kicking, and would strike regularly over the following decades.

Surprisingly, this novel has never been properly translated into

English. The recent attempts invariably delete some of Verne's mock-learned footnotes and cut expressions that are difficult to translate or deemed un-American.[21]

In 1866, the censored *Hatteras* appeared in book form, inaugurating Verne's series of Extraordinary Journeys, a 64-work, 50-year cycle. According to Hetzel's brashly inaccurate blurb, the collected works aimed "to sum up all the geographical, geological, physical, and astronomical knowledge amassed by modern science and rewrite the story of the universe."

In the third contract, of December 11, 1865, Hetzel agreed to "take" three volumes a year, "of the same genre and for the same public" as the previous books. The publisher established absolute ownership for ten years on the unillustrated editions of the fiction and nonfiction production over the next seven years. He also owned the illustrated editions of the same works forever. Verne got in return "FF 3,000 per volume or . . . 750 per month": less if he produced less, for he was not strictly obliged to deliver any! In addition, the author ceded ownership on his four previous novels for FF 5,500. No mention was made of foreign or subsidiary rights.

Verne's income thus amounted to the dollar equivalent of $2,250 a month, or about half today's average wage in the United States. He again got nothing for the serializations. Hetzel retrospectively grabbed the illustrated editions of *Five Weeks* and *Hatteras* and all editions of *Journey to the Center of the Earth* and *From the Earth to the Moon*, not mentioned in the earlier contracts. Given that the book editions in question would sell about half a million copies in Verne's lifetime,[22] and perhaps as many again by 1965, the approximate price per copy was FF 5,500 divided by one million. Replacing the previous 25 and 30 centimes with about half a centime a copy was worse than scandalous.[23]

The new contract represented theft pure and simple, and Hetzel should have been ashamed of his behavior. If Verne had consulted

anyone who could read, he might have avoided this unmitigated
financial disaster, disinheriting himself, his son, his grandsons, and
some of his great-grandchildren. Hetzel later claimed that the change
was made "on the request of Monsieur Jules Verne, who preferred a
fixed income to a variable one"24—was the provocation deliberate?
All we know is that the third contract was signed a fortnight before
the announcement of the first illustrated edition of a Verne book.25

Soon afterward the novelist wrote "the success of my books doesn't
directly concern me" (April 24, 1866, to Pierre): presumably a reference to the fact that whether his books sold five or five hundred thousand copies made no difference to him. It did not seem surprising
that half his brain refused to function.

In 1865, Jules, Honorine, and the three children spent "nine weeks of
sea bathing" in the fishing village of Le Crotoy [September 1865] (all
such dates, it will be remembered, refer to letters to Hetzel). They
returned to Paris on about October 10, but must have appreciated the
seaside lifestyle, for in March 1866, in the midst of a storm, they moved
their summer residence to Le Crotoy. Renting a three-story house called
"La Solitude," near the port, the Vernes spent each subsequent spring
and summer there.26 Jules worked first in his second-floor office with a
view of the bay of Le Crotoy and then in the garden-shed.

Valentine and Suzanne remained at convent boarding school in
Paris, but Michel now not only attended the village school, keeping
him out of harm's way the whole day, but got extra lessons from the
teacher (May 8, 1866). Honorine and the children made frequent
visits to Amiens, and Verne to Paris for both business and pleasure,
staying of course in his apartment in Auteuil.

With 1,500 inhabitants, the "charming little hole" [July 10, 1867]
nestled on a peninsula on the Bay of the Somme, about 40 miles downstream from Amiens, Picardy (see Figure 8). The nearest doctor was 15
miles away in Abbeville. Notable only for Joan of Arc's imprisonment in
1431, Le Crotoy consisted of "nothing but sand and wild dunes"

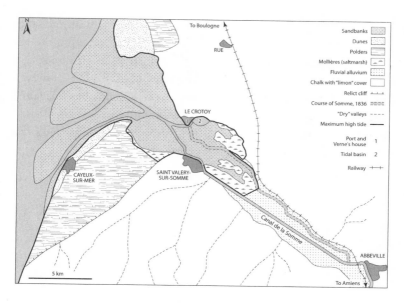

Figure 8: Le Crotoy region

[July 10, 1867]. The coast appeared rather flat and uninspiring, except when the spring and autumn tides came crashing in. Verne never tired of watching the tide gaining its three miles and 20 feet, exclaiming "Ah, the sea, what a beautiful thing, even if at Crotoy it only comes twice a day!"[27]

Marguerite poetically imagines the shrimping boats returning on the ebb tide: "One man was enough to operate each trawl, and the little boats tacked . . . around in unison, as if dancing a quadrille. Opposite Le Crotoy, Saint-Valéry projected its long dyke, bristling with wind-tormented larches and beeches as far as Le Hourdel" (ADF 114).

Why Le Crotoy? Verne liked the clean air, the opportunity to sail, and the peace and quiet for work; he appreciated the local sailors, for the Picards were "perhaps not that hard-working but very frank, honest, and intelligent."[28] His rheumatism, flu, headaches, and dizziness all disappeared when he left Paris.[29]

If Verne loved the place, and Michel had more room on the sands to let off steam, Honorine seems to have been neutral, even though it was not far from her hometown of Amiens; the girls soon got bored, longing to get back to boarding school (ADF 114). However, Honorine wrote secretly to Hetzel her concern about her husband's "discouragement," blaming it on his isolation and leaving Paris.[30] Perhaps she herself felt lonely and sad, suspecting her husband's real life took place far from the domestic hearth.

CHAPTER 11

Whole New World: 1865–67

BACK IN THE LATE 1830S, Jules had lusted after the pretty yachts skipping over the Loire. In 1846, his fantasies continued, sketching two charming lug-sails on the manuscript of *The Gunpowder Plot*. Then in about March 1862, he made a journey through Brittany; and in 1863 he had spent a fortnight in Brest, which for some reason he called the "chamber pot of France."[1] Given that he spent a fortnight sailing around Brittany in 1864 (August 12, 1864), the two earlier trips probably involved yachting as well. During his 1865 Le Crotoy stay, he went out for two extended sea trips on a friend's yacht, making him "the happiest man on earth" (September 6, 1864). No doubt as a result, but also with Paul's urging, he decided he wanted his own boat (RD 85).

Probably in 1865, Verne borrowed, rented, or bought a fishing smack from a local marine carpenter.[2] His first trip was one of his most ambitious, an 800-mile expedition from Chantenay to Bordeaux and back again to fetch Paul. With the 12 days the brothers spent in Bordeaux, the trip took three weeks [September 10?, 1866]. Verne enjoyed himself tremendously on the return leg: "I had a magnificent return by sea, an equinoctial squall, in danger of being thrown on the coast, a real storm finally . . . something to give you unforgettable memories!" [September 25?, 1866].

After a late start, Verne caught the foreign travel bug and from 1865 to 1881 left France virtually every summer, a total of more than 35 trips. (The silence of the biographers on this important question seems surprising.) In this second phase of travel, and in contrast to the Nordic urge, Hetzel and Paul seem to have provided the initial stimulus. Verne always dreamed of associating work and pleasure with the publisher who had hobnobbed with Hugo, Lamartine, Balzac, and Baudelaire. But Hetzel rarely picked up on Verne's slavish offers of hospitality, even forgetting they had been on holiday together a year or two after the event [February 27, 1967].

Three of Verne's earliest trips open up fascinating vistas. At some stage in the mid-1860s, he visited Crystal Palace, rebuilt in Sydenham in southern London, and marveled at the new cryptographic techniques (*Int.* 193). In another tantalizing snatch, he refers to "the granite rocks of Jersey" as if having been there, perhaps in 1866 [July 10, 1867]. The forgotten archipelago a stone's throw from Normandy, the last vestige of England's French empire, was inseparable in the public imagination from Hetzel's friend Hugo and his continuing exile from Napoléon III's regime.

In 1866, Verne also visited Cannes and Nice, but the relevant logbook is locked up in the city library of Amiens, which ignores requests for information.[3]

In 1865, or 1866, and probably in 1867, Hetzel and Verne holidayed together in Golfe Juan, a friendly resort squeezed in between upscale Cannes and Juan les Pins.[4] Hetzel and Verne stayed at the Hôtel du Golfe but perhaps also in nearby Villa Bruyères, the home of Edmond Adam and his wife Juliette, née Lambert. The Hôtel du Golfe stood just ten yards from the sea; the manager, Monsieur Ghien, had navigated with Dumont d'Urville.[5] Although upset by the "uncouth companions" at the hotel, Verne raved about the view from his room, sweeping across the Mediterranean and Alps (January 29, 1967).

Edmond Adam (1816–77), a Jewish journalist and politician, had collaborated with Hetzel on the *National* in about 1848. His divorcee wife (1836–1936), young enough to be his daughter, was very slim, smooth-skinned, and quite "charming," according to Sand. A prominent society hostess, Juliette wrote journalism, books about the Alps and Golfe Juan, and novels with a republican, ecological, and feminist slant. The Adams offered Hetzel and Verne several al fresco dinners; Verne also made friends with the staff of Villa Bruyères, "a nest in the rising sun" (February 11, 1868), especially "little Gibsy," possibly a chambermaid, whose pubescence delighted him [February 27, 1867].

With Hetzel, Verne visited the Alpine pass of Tende, the mountains above Nice, and the Sainte-Marguerite Islands, whose castle was made famous by Dumas's *Man in the Iron Mask*.[6] Although France had acquired Savoy in 1860, the 6,000-foot Col de Tende still lay within Italy. Possessing an age-old history, it was one of the most spectacular places in the world, with 46 horseshoe bends slicing into the incline of up to 45 degrees.

Both Golfe Juan trips went even further than Tende: "The first time we went to Italy as far as Bordighera, the second time, you yourself went as far as Genoa!" [January 18?, 1869]. From the icy peaks of Tende, a spectacular, frightening, switchback zigzagged down via isolated Italian hill villages to the sparkling sea. The famous palm trees of Bordighera sunned themselves and bathed in the Mediterranean. The train trip the seven miles back along the coast to the French border was described by Daudet as "adorable" and by the Joanne guide as "heaven on earth."

For the second trip, one or two years after the first, it is not clear where Hetzel and Verne split up, whether Golfe Juan or somewhere before Genoa. But, for several years afterwards Verne reminisced about the landscape they had enjoyed, apparently without reciprocation: "the real blue of the Mediterranean, the real blue of Provence and the Alpes Maritimes," the "Mediterranean breezes . . . the scent of the pines."[7]

In total, then, Verne made two or three trips to the Mediterranean in 1865–67, at least one including Italy, although not mentioned by biographers to date.

Verne's fifth novel for Hetzel started coming out only a year after the second, an astonishing creative outpouring. In *Captain Grant's Children* (1865), obtuse Scottish yachtsman Lord Glenarvan discovers a bottle in a shark's stomach containing a castaway's appeal for help. Although written in three languages, the message has suffered in the sea water and only the latitude, 37°S, is known. Once brilliant but absent-minded geographer Jacques Paganel has interpreted the text, the group, including Grant's son and daughter, sets off on a straight-line journey. They traverse South America, guided by the noble Patagonian Thalcave, and perilously cross the high Cordilleras. At the Pacific, Paganel is forced into a new interpretation, taking the group across New Zealand and Australia, where escaped convict Ayrton tries to hijack the yacht; adventures with floods, landslides, pirates, and cannibals alternate with entertaining geographical lessons, asides by a sardonic sailor, and even flirtations by Grant's daughter. In the end Captain Grant is discovered by chance on Tabor Island; Ayrton is abandoned there as punishment.

Verne transformed the ending after the manuscript stage, so as to maintain the suspense about the message for longer.[8] It was possible, but somehow implausible, that he based his triple-decker on a true story. In a late interview of doubtful authenticity (Klondike), he cited an episode of a tin-box containing incriminating documents thrown overboard from a slaving ship pursued by a British vessel near the West Indies. A passing ship found the box by chance in a shark's stomach, thus providing the evidence to condemn the slavers.

Verne made an effort to include a love story in the novel. However, he himself felt "very clumsy to express amorous sentiments"; and here and elsewhere invited Hetzel to add "sensitive touches": "I do the eyes, and you provide the tears if necessary."[9]

Continuing the pattern, the novel's title changed. Verne wanted *Journey Around the World*, but as usual Hetzel wanted the heroes' names, and as usual the publisher won.

From about 1867, despite four and a bit masterpieces out in four years, a boat, and a larger apartment, Verne became more taciturn and gruff. At this stage he lacked a close confidante to replace his parents, except, increasingly, Hetzel; however the relationship was one-sided from the start, with the publisher showing a certain amount of condescendence, incomprehension, and commercial greed.

Within a few years Jules and Honorine's marriage had proved problematic. Compared with the baker's dozen from his siblings by 1869, they had produced only one baby. Honorine did love Jules, and always seemed attentive to his health and patient with his moods. But she ruled the home with a rod of iron and she failed to understand him or his artistic aims. She had undoubtedly hoped he would become rich and famous much quicker, dreaming of the social opportunities this would open up (RD 60). Mme Verne also felt disappointed Jules did not take her into society; and claimed "he piles the problems produced by his discouragement onto me."[10] In sum, she probably considered him a poor husband.

Verne's attacks on marriage now appeared in his books: the coupling of the Dordogne and Garonne resembled "a long-married couple, throwing up their irritated billows"; the reply to a Mormon's earnest enquiry as to the speaker's number of wives was: "one, sir—it's quite enough!"[11]

Nevertheless, the couple maintained a façade for the outside world. Both Paul and Honorine's grandparents stayed for Suzanne's First Communion [June? 1867]. She tried to make Verne less of a lone wolf by inviting his best friends back to Auteuil: Maisonneuve, Gille, and musicians like Delibes, Delioux, Massé, and Hignard. When Hetzel was away, but apparently only then, Verne and Honorine often dined with his wife.

Michel gave his parents permanent headaches. From his inauspicious birth as his father holidayed abroad, to his diaper stage, when his screaming sent Verne mad, to first steps, Michel was not a difficult child, but a toddling disaster. The first two recorded descriptions were: "the terror of Le Crotoy"; and a "most appalling character."[12] In the boy's earliest known action, he destroyed his chamberpot (December 10, 1968). Like his father before him, he attended boarding school at a ridiculously early age (January 29, 1866).

Michel's main weapons were charm and frequent fevers, anemia, and "guts," no doubt inherited (February 5, 1869). With uncontrollable rages much of the time, he also used shouting, disobedience, and violence to get his way and escape punishment (ADF 125): he surely deserved a good spanking or a day or two on dry bread and water. But his mother alternately spoiled and neglected the boy, his father tried to ignore the problem, and his sisters, seven and nine years older, doted on him. Michel's son, the biographer, regales his readers with two stories which, when stripped of the 100 percent recall, must contain some truth. When his son's bawling brought an angry Verne out of his study, Honorine explained that Michel wanted the clock, producing the reply: "Give him the clock, then" (JJV 82). His mother was no better. While walking Michel, the boy "deliberately dropped his little walking stick down the first coal hole he saw," producing tantrums until his mother rang the bell to get it back. Told to behave himself, "he did exactly the same thing at the next hole"—causing Honorine to burst out laughing (JJV 82). Such would have not been my reaction. Even Verne, not the best child psychologist on earth, had to concede they had failed: "he's not been well brought up, I admit" [June 11?, 1869].

Was it a sign of further problems that Michel changed school so often? In January 1868, he went to the same school in Nantes as Maurice, Paul's son, for the two months his family spent there (December 10, 1868). Fifteen months later he changed again, in mid-year, entrusted "as a boarder to the strict discipline of the priests of Abbeville College" (JJV 83). Verne's most ardent desire was that he become a full boarder (5 February 1869).

When, only too soon, Michel came back for the hols, his father hastily arranged a private tutor again [June 11?, 1869].

In 1867 Verne made a transatlantic trip, his only time out of the Old World. The idea came from Paul; Jules did not even consider taking his family. He simply aimed to cross the Atlantic on the *Great Eastern* and study the "microcosm" of on-board society, seeing the United States being incidental.[13] But something was lacking; and he felt little excitement at the finest sights or most dramatic events.

The brothers shunned the direct ferry from Nantes for the London–Liverpool train. Checking in at the Adelphi, the best in town, they visited Jules's adored New Prince's Dock, the setting for virtuoso chapters in both *Backwards to Britain* and *Hatteras*.

The *Great Eastern* comprised the major attraction. While in 1859, Verne had mocked the "20,000 tons of vanity," he now marveled at the "eighth wonder of the world."[14] Built by Brunel as the *Leviathan*, it stretched 700 feet, five times longer than the next ship, and would remain the biggest for 30 years. With its three million rivets, six 200-foot masts, five chimneys, 2,600 horsepower, 500 crew, and 3,000 beds, it loomed so large that tugs sometimes disappeared under its four paddlewheels. But a single finger could steer it.

The *Great Eastern* had a checkered history. Rumors abounded that a body lay lost in the bowels. On first launch in 1857, two workers died; the ship had not left the Thames before six crewmembers perished in an engine room explosion; Brunel himself died shortly after, supposedly from the shock. Finally, the captain and ten companions drowned. When the ship was scrapped in 1887, a riveter's skeleton was indeed found trapped behind a bulkhead, explaining all the bad luck.[15]

Built to transport emigrants, the *Great Eastern* never reached Australia. It switched to laying the 2,100-mile transatlantic cable—which failed the first time. Verne was traveling on the maiden trip after a French company reconverted the ship to bring Americans over for the Paris Universal Exposition.

Verne witnessed further disasters, delaying departure a week. While men were pulling in the anchors, something in the 70-horsepower hauling engine broke, killing four crew, although nobody bothered that much. Finally setting off on 26 March, with only 123 passengers, the ship skirted North Wales. It then followed the smugglers' coast of Ireland, stopping at Queenstown (Cork) and sighting Fastnet Lighthouse and Cape Clear.

The brothers met famous people on board, including Captain Sir James Anderson [March 22, 1867]. Jules befriended Paul Du Chaillu, the African explorer, although privately mocking his "monkey literature" (August 31, 1867), and Cyrus "Transatlantic Cable" Field, the model for Cyrus Smith, the American engineer hero of *The Mysterious Island*.

Verne hated most of the on-board entertainment, like the gambling, gymnastics classes, and Anderson's photographic lectures on the Cable, preferring the talks on Mormonism and the sailors' comic turns. Both Vernes were accomplished pianists, and Paul gave a public performance, opening with two waltzes of the brothers' composition. Requested to play his National Anthem, he declined to perform the left-wing "Marseillaise" until the Northerners insisted, a sign of his died-in-the-wool conservatism.[16]

Verne derived entertainment from spying on two frustrated fiancés, who gaped at "long pistons rush[ing] towards each other, lubricat[ing] with a drop of oil on each movement."[17]

The ship came across an abandoned Spanish vessel, sailing on all alone, as well as towering icebergs. Off the Banks of Newfoundland a hurricane blew up. Anderson considered it a matter of Anglo-Saxon honor to maintain course, astonishing mariner Paul, who had never seen a worse sea. The passengers meanwhile lunched calmly. Only when parts of the ship flew away, two thousand tons of water shipped, and a sailor died did the captain finally cede. The man's burial greatly moved Jules, slipping into the water and bobbing up before finally gliding down into the clear depths. He wrote that he had had enough emotion to last a lifetime.

In perfect weather, after sighting Long and Fire Islands, the *Great Eastern* passed the Light-Boat, Sandy Hook and the verdant New Jersey heights, before finally reaching the Promised Land on April 9. The brothers stayed at Fifth Avenue Hotel, on red-light Madison Square, and enjoyed the free biscuits and cheese and the elevator, the first in a New York hotel.

Jules longed with all his heart to explore "Cooper country," meaning the Hudson Valley, the Mohawk, Lake Erie, and Niagara. But the *Great Eastern* was returning on April 17, he worried about his contractual obligations, and the return tickets were paid for. Three weeks shrank to one as the brothers decide to do New York State at a gallop.

Most of New York resembled a checkers board, but Verne appreciated the European-style southern tip and Broadway, with its marble palaces and river-like lower end, black with vehicles. After tiny stews at the Fifth Avenue they made for P. T. Barnum's New Museum at 539 Broadway, famously painted by Eugène-Alexis Girardet, to see the "educational" play *New York's Streets,* with a real fire engine putting out a real fire. Although not impressing Verne, a similar device, in an idea germinating a couple of months later, would make his fortune—and Jackie Chan's.

The following day the Vernes picked up mail at 51 Liberty Street, visited the French Consul at "2 Rowling [Bowling] Green" (xxxiv), and took a FF 20 evening cab to the Hudson River Line. There they caught the *St. John,* "one of those marvelous steamers that willingly blow up/screw" (xxxv), as Jules put it. It boasted balconies, galleries, and paddlewheels "painted with frescoes like the spandrels of St. Mark's" (xxxvi). The brothers reveled in the salon with its Corinthian columns, private gas-supply, divans, carpets, and paintings, out of bounds to the 4,000 on lower deck.

In the morning Jules found the left bank of the Hudson disappointingly flat and marshy, the right a long cemetery. The brothers had missed the early train, so visited Albany, especially its "fascinating fossil museum" (xxxvi), the New York State Museum. The talk of the town was a mastodon skeleton, dug up close by.

Verne marveled at the American trains: you walked from car to car, even bought magazines and books, which, amazingly, didn't carry a censorship stamp. Rome, Syracuse, and Palmyra impressed him less, with their omnibus-like trains running down the houseless avenues. In the Mohawk Valley he glimpsed Lake Ontario and dreamed of French trappers, the Land of the Leather Stocking, Hawkeye, and Chingachgook, and fighting the 'Ricains. In the early hours Jules and Paul changed at Rochester, crossed the Tennessee rapids, and arrived at freshly refurbished Cataract House, overlooking the Niagara Falls.

In fine morning weather, after a wooden bridge to Goat Island, the 358-foot Horse Shoe Falls on the Canadian side transfixed Jules and Paul. With the spray like virgin snow, molten silver of the irresistible current, sea-green depths, and whirlpools of liquid gold, the two-mile-wide chasm dropped into dazzling icebergs, like monsters with open jaws, every tint of aquamarine and jade. After the Three Sisters, the Irish twins fought frightening dizziness to climb Terrapin Tower, built on a speck of land on the very brink of Horse Shoe Falls, where the roar of the water, the sun's rays, and the scent of the cataract spark "never-ending ecstasy" (xxxvii). Nightfall found them still awestruck, startled by a radiance shooting across the Niagara above them, an express train. Still unable to tear themselves away from the relentless flow and all-enveloping spray, they finally experienced an indescribable vision: a "milky strip, a gossamer ribbon trembling in the shadows— a lunar rainbow" (xxxvii).

The next day, April 12, they hiked across the suspension bridge and lunched at a "British" hotel. In the visitors' book they noted Barnum, Robert Peel, Lady Franklin, Rothschild, the Count of Paris, assorted Napoléons, and Maurice Sand. Signing in turn, the Vernes made for the projecting Table Rock and admire, both Falls while trying to ignore the 300-foot chasm directly under their feet. Then they sailed back to "America" with an objectionable engineer who wanted to convert Niagara into a mill. Jules's horror appears prophetic, for an 1869 milling tunnel would go disastrously wrong, and both Falls are now over-engineered into a virtual theme park—as predicted by Verne in 1889.

Soon the brothers took the afternoon express back to Buffalo. Having broken the ice to taste Lake Erie, they caught an overnight New York Central Railway to Albany and then the Hudson Railroad. They observed "the enchanting resorts on the banks, the villages clustering appealingly around, the woods haphazardly strewn here and there like bouquets at a prima donna's feet" (*Humbug*). Jules's mood had clearly improved.

After Brooklyn on April 15, the Vernes headed for Pier 37. The *Great Eastern* sailed on the 17th with only 193 passengers, and would soon go bankrupt yet again. On the way back, Jules and especially Paul were the life and soul of the ship: dancing and flirting, dressing in drag, and generally fooling around.

On or about April 30, they were wined and dined by Anna and her family, living in Brest. And the following day, it was back to the writing grindstone.

Many questions remained about Verne's America. Did he use his freedom to womanize, or worse? Did he resent the fact that only one of his novels had come out in the United States? Did he speak to the locals? Why did he not take a later ship back?

He probably didn't really enjoy the six-week trip. Jules and Paul spoke no English, and may not have met many French-speakers. Although the novelist could write in his cabin, he still worried about his horrendous contractual obligations. Maybe Verne needed the extraverted Hignard to egg him on. Maybe he had just got older. Maybe, while loving the people, he wasn't too enamored of the country:

Members of the English-speaking races make good heroes . . . because of their coolness and go-ahead qualities (*Int.* 224).

Americans are undoubtedly the most practical, but they surely lack taste. Only look at their public buildings! Colossal, expensive, but no architecture (Int. 232).

However, Verne's six American days constituted a resounding success in terms of literary creation. Thirty novels involving Americans or America grew out of the experience. In all of them, the New World was grandiose, luxuriant, wild—and full of engineers aching to tame it.

The most obvious was *Twenty Thousand Leagues*, which opens with Captain Anderson's paddle-steamer hitting a mysterious object and limping into Liverpool Docks. The first-person French narrator arrives in New York at the end of March 1867. He takes the Fifth Avenue's screw-driven elevator and a 20-franc cab ride, visits Broadway and Brooklyn, and sails off past the New Jersey villas, Sandy Hook, and Long and Fire Islands. Nemo's pilot-house, platform, and luxurious salon strangely resemble that of a Hudson riverboat crossed with a Scottish château. Verne refers to a new sort of cannon "due to be exhibited at the Exposition" (I iv) when it has already opened—he means *he* was due to visit it.

Similarly, *Humbug*, written in about 1867 with the subtitle *The American Way of Life*, reflects Barnum's aphorism, "the American people like to be humbugged." The first-person French narrator takes a springtime steamboat upstream from New York, producing acerbic observations all the while, like on the idea "of damming the Hudson and using its water to drive a coffee-mill." The story focuses on the amazing discovery of a giant prehistoric man near Albany and satirizes modern publicity methods and the Anglo-Saxon penchant for hypocrisy—plus the extraordinary discoveries of the Extraordinary Journeys, especially *Journey to the Center of the Earth*.

Around the World, first dreamed of in 1867, also benefits directly. Even the unobservant Fogg notices New Jersey's "towns with ancient names, some with streets and trams but no houses" (xxxi).

It would take a whole book to detail Verne's fictional America. Here I can only mention *Propeller Island*, the first novel ever in the third person and present tense, about the many disasters and eventual break-up of a massive American ship touring the South Seas, or *The Will of an Eccentric* (unpublished in the United States!), where contestants chase a snakes-and-ladders inheritance across every state. Niagara haunts Verne for the next 40 years. In *Family without a Name*, the young lovers ride the Falls to their deaths; in *Master of the World*, Robur is plunging inevitably to his death on the same Falls, consoled by the same lunar rainbow—when he escapes in a flying machine.

As a matter of fact, Verne also wrote a book about his trip (my main source of information). He first mentioned his plan "to devote a whole volume to the study and description of the *Great Eastern*" in a short piece for the *Paquebot* when coming into New Jersey.[18] In 1869 François Buloz proposed that Verne contribute to the upscale *Revue des deux mondes* (January 27, 1869). Still keen to escape the genre imprisoned him, the author offered *A Floating City*, which he planned as a novel of manners, similar to *Backwards to Britain* or *Paris in the Twentieth Century*. The editor projected "a simple diary" [January 13, 1870] at the price offered to beginners—and, twelve months later, canceled the agreement. The work came out instead in both the *Journal des débats* and the Extraordinary Voyages.

A Floating City (1870) does uneasily mix three genres: the technological description and history of the *Great Eastern*; a Gothic, entirely invented plot, with an implausible Hugo-esque madwoman, a duel, and a man obsessed with shipwreck; and observation of on-board manners, American lifestyle, and land and seascapes. Falling awkwardly between travelogue and marine novel, with jarring references to "the Frenchman Paul V. . . ." (xv), the technical and melodramatic parts fall flat, while the descriptions of the ocean and the Falls read magnificently.

A Floating City appears so puzzling because Verne may not have written all of it.

I do realize that this constitutes a radical claim, which accuses many reputable publishers of misrepresentation; and that no one has made it to date. In the general case it is clear that about ten of the books still published—illegally—under Verne's name are not totally his, principally most of the posthumous production, *The Begum's Millions* (1879), *The Southern Star* (1884), *The Wreck of the "Cynthia"* (1885), and arguably *Around the World*. But in this particular instance, the strangeness of the book itself comprises my only evidence, plus, fortunately, the first-hand testimony of Raymond Ducrest. In his unpublished, confidential biography, Anna's son writes that Paul noted:

> on a daily basis, everything to enable him to produce a relation of the journey. He did it for himself, rather than his brother, so as to keep a living and durable recollection; it was nevertheless this narrative which Jules Verne revised on returning to France, and improved and published under the title *A Floating City*.[19]

Paul did collaborate on many of the novels, providing ideas and feedback; he contributed to the *Transactions of the French Alpine Club* and published two tales in the Extraordinary Journeys, "The Fortieth French Ascent of Mont Blanc" (1874) and "From Rotterdam to Copenhagen" (1880). It does not seem impossible, in sum, that Paul originally composed much of the book. The trip may even have been undertaken to allow his collaboration.

Holy Cross, the Verne parish church,
1825–about 1840

Saint-Nicolas, the Verne parish church,
about 1840–87

Second floor, 2 Quai Jean Bart, the Verne home, 1829–about 1840

Sophie Verne, Jules's mother

Caroline Tronson,
Verne's cousin and first love

Henri and Edmond Tronson,
Jules's cousins

A pyroscaph and the fish market on Feydeau Island

Verne's home at Chantenay, about 1837–48, drawn by Nagelschmit,
based on a sketch by Raymond Ducrest.

Anna, Jules's first sister (self-portrait)

Marie, Jules's third sister

Paul, Jules's brother

Third floor, 6 Rue Jean-Jacques Rousseau, the Verne home, about 1840–87

Aristide Hignard, Verne's friend
and collaborator

Alexandre Dumas *fils*, Verne's friend
and collaborator

Honorine Verne, née de Viane

Jules Hetzel, Verne's publisher

The Lyric Theater

Verne at 22

Verne at about 24

Verne at 29

Verne at 30

The extended Verne family in 1861 (From top to bottom, left to right) Jules, Pierre, Marie, Anna, Alphonsine, Honorine, Amélie, Sophie; Alphonse, Henri, and Antoinette Garcet; Grandmother Masthie Verne, Suzanne, and Valentine

Verne at about 52

Folio 140 from the manuscript of *Journey to the Center of the Earth*

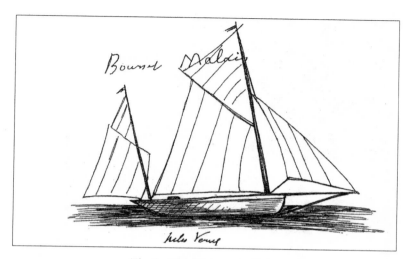

The *St. Michel I,* drawn by Verne

Part of folio 32 from the second manuscript of *Around the World*

44 Boulevard Longueville, Amiens, Verne's home, 1873–82 and 1900–05

2 Rue Charles Dubois, Verne's home, 1882–1900

Michel, Jules's son, at about 11

Adolphe d'Ennery, Verne's collaborator

Verne's study in Charles Dubois

Jules and Honorine in 1905

CHAPTER 12.

By Land and Sea: 1867–69

IN 1867 A LARGE-OCTAVO EDITION of *Journey to the Center of the Earth* came out, with an important new section. Two and one-half chapters were added (xxvii–xxix), undoubtedly because prehistory had become a major field of study in 1865. Among remains dating from the Quaternary Era, the new sections presented the perfectly preserved body of a dead white man, perhaps a previous explorer. But they also featured a living herd of mastodons, together with tantalizing glimpses of an equally alive herdsman, a twelve-foot giant carrying a giant club. Verne would rarely again stray so far into the imaginary, at least in the novels for Hetzel; the additions may have been suggested by someone else.

From January Verne was hard at work on a new project, the *Illustrated Geography of France and her Colonies*. Eminent geographer Théophile Lavallée had contracted to write it, written the introduction and thirteen of the eighty-nine sections, but fallen too ill to continue.

Verne soon realized that the thirteen installments derived from Malte-Brun's *Illustrated France*. He decided to hide the plagiarism by judicious rewriting (January 29, 1867). For his own text, he synthesized "195 kilos of dictionaries" [October 10, 1867], putting the 1866 census to good use, and getting figures from the ministry of the interior thanks to Hetzel's string-pulling.

His coverage was exhaustive. On the sensitive Alsace question, he ignored alphabetical order so as to keep the Lower and Upper Rhine together. His wife recopied the drafts at 8,000 words a day, giving her writer's cramp [end of December 1867].

The actual writing formed the least of his problems. Lavallée, reluctant to give up the project, having retained the right to "correct and revise"—but died on August 27, removing this particular difficulty. Each section listed prominent locals, and Verne had long discussions with Hetzel as to whom to leave out [February 27, 1867, May? 1867]. Fogg's pointed remark, that "(whatever he did, [he] never conferred, having realized that discussion never convinces anyone," may date from this time—although itself removed at proof stage.[1] Eventually Verne gave up, included everyone, and let Hetzel red-pencil to his heart's content. He did emphasize that he was putting his mentor in [February 1867?]; and the publisher did go easy, just this once. But the compliment was not returned.

Verne had to do the publisher's work, correcting the galley and page proofs, and supervising the illustrator, engravers, and printers [March 9, 1867]. He rudely reassured Hetzel that although Lavallée's introduction was too long, "I've stuffed [it] back in its belly" [February ? 1867]. Even when staying with relatives in Provins, the writer labored "all the time" [May? 1867]. The installments came out from late spring, unleashing a torrent of complaints. Verne doggedly refuted them, acknowledging each suggestion—only clogging his in-tray all the more.

He reached M. in November, just as well, for the 250,000-word Volume 1 came out that same month. Since Nantes closed the volume, Verne plugged his beloved Loire and Erdre, his personal train stop, and five of his colleagues. He mocked the modern architecture, however: "Holy Cross, surmounted by a heavy campanile, doubling as a belfry," "St. Nicolas . . . which, when finished, will be a fine example of thirteenth-century architecture" and his father's law courts, "with no style whatsoever."

The three million characters, seven normal volumes, really needed to be four times longer [October 10, 1867]. While Hetzel sunned himself on the Riviera, Verne signed himself "Bête de Somme": both "Stupid of Somme" and "Beast of Burden." He caught several unshakable flus.

By March 1868, it was all done. The two volumes out in June had 106 magnificent illustrations. In pride of place was Hetzel's "To the Reader," pompously sweeping across man's impending knowledge of the whole world and drawing attention to Lavallée's "so remarkable" contribution, as well as his star writer's . . . "book."

So why did Verne do the "devilish *Geography*" (December 5, 1867, to Pierre)? When his father criticized its dryness, the slogger riposted: "it's not designed to be read, but looked up, if need be. It's a dictionary." Furthermore, it might bring in "FF 15,000 to 20,000 [$45,000 to $60,000] and it's 15 months gained on my agreement that I was wrong to make so long" (December 5, 1867, to Pierre).

The publisher again behaved dishonestly, probably paying in fact just FF 18,000.[2] If he had calculated by length, even at the slave-driving 200,000 words a year, the half-million words would have counted for two and one-half years, or nearly two times longer. As it was, Jules had committed to a horrific eleven more volumes in the next three and one-half years.

Verne perhaps wished to escape the fictional straitjacket and achieve fame, if not fortune, in a more respectable writing field. But he may above all have doubted the wellsprings of his creative imagination. He could sustain purple climaxes for the closing chapters of his novels by first indulging in lots of feints and fables, detours, documentary, and dialogue. He had to alternate the paroxysmal achievement of the long-desired goals with less tiring ways of keeping up his readers' excitement. As he entered his fifth decade he surely wondered how many more climactic masterpieces he could tease out of his exhausted brain.

On the rebound from the arid *Geography*, Verne immediately switched to creating his most ambitious novel, *Twenty Thousand Leagues under the Seas* (to give the correct title). However, this novel in which, along with *Hatteras*, he most revealed his soul was not appreciated by the publisher, and one of the great masterpieces of western literature only saw the light of day in hacked-about and censored form.

Twenty Thousand Leagues recounts a circumnavigation by submarine, with many spectacular episodes, such as the passage under the Antarctic icecap, the planting of a black flag on the South Pole, and the discovery of the ruins of Atlantis. But much of the interest comes from the relationship between Captain Nemo ("nobody" in Latin) and his guest, Dr. Aronnax. We see everything through this aging academic's interpretations—or lack of them, for he misunderstands most things, but especially the captain's exile from society. Nemo exhibits an unhealthy interest in vessels in distress, although this seems difficult to connect with his portraits of a woman and two children. He locates the wreck of the *Vengeur* on the Atlantic seabed, of great significance, and is then attacked by an unidentified warship, before sinking it. On the closing page Aronnax suggests that the submarine may not have survived the terrible Maelstrom, but that, if it has, Nemo must improve his attitude: "may the lawmaker disappear and hate die down in that wild heart."

Many English commentaries have concentrated on the *Nautilus*, but Verne's technology was emphatically not innovative. So crowded, indeed, were the deeps that Verne feared being sued for plagiarism.

Much of *Twenty Thousand Leagues* came from Verne's own experience. In addition to his childhood experiences of Feydeau and the Loire, he picked the brains of mariners in Le Crotoy and Nantes, especially his brother Paul. In 1865, the George Sand suggested to Verne that the sea was the one area where he had not yet harnessed his "knowledge and imagination" (*Int.* 138). We saw, above all, that in that same year Verne acquired a fishing-boat.

For two dramatic scenes, Nemo's surveying of the ruins of Atlantis and claiming of the Antarctic continent, some of the inspiration may have come from his Scottish visit. Nemo's name and character must derive from the prickly Scottish motto, "*Nemo me lacessit impune*" (No one attacks me scot-free). His domestic arrangements in the heart of the raging depths may similarly come from the rain-swept but luxurious Inzievar House in Fife. Verne indeed acknowledged a debt when Nemo played only on "the black keys, giving his melodies an essentially Scottish tonality": his Amelia Bain similarly "us[ed] only the black keys."[3]

For the preparation, Verne read scores of volumes and hundreds of articles. As well as the Bible, Homer, Plato, Hugo, Michelet, Scott, Melville, and Poe, he referred to the scientists and popularizers Maury, Cuvier, Figuier, Mangin, Larousse, Agassiz, and Renard. Although the novel cited one nineteenth-century encounter with a giant squid, an unquoted source, Denys de Montfort, surely constituted the main origin of the captain's epic battle. The model for Nemo himself was Gustave Flourens, a scientist and international freedom-fighter praised in *Paris in the Twentieth Century*.[4]

As research, Verne also visited the Universal Exposition on the Champ-de-Mars [June 1867 to Pierre]. He observed such important inspirations as the Rouquayrol-Denayrouze diving apparatus; Hallet's submarine *Nautilus* (1857) with its riveted sheet metal, side tanks, and magnifying panes; and models of Bourgeois and Brun's *Plongeur*, a 146-foot, 80-horsepower submarine (1863 and 1867).

The more he researched, the more excited Verne got:

I'm also preparing our *Journey under the Waters*, and my brother and I are arranging all the mechanics needed for the expedition. I think we'll use electricity (August 10, 1866).

After 15 months abstinence, my brain greatly needs to burst: so much the better for the *Journey under the Waters*, there'll be overabundance, and I promise I'll give myself a good time [July 29, 1867].

From March to August 1868, his excitement mounted further as he looked forward to the actual writing: he believed the idea would give meaning to his whole life:

I've had a brainwave that perfectly fits the subject. This unknown man must no longer have any contact with humanity . . . He's not on earth any more . . . the sea must provide him with everything, clothing and food . . . if I don't pull this book off, I'll be inconsolable. I've never held a better thing in my hands [March 28, 1868].

How many good things I've found in the sea while sailing on the *St. Michel* [June 14, 1868]. Oh the perfect subject, my dear Hetzel, the perfect subject! [August 11, 1868]. I'm moored off Gravesend . . . finishing the first volume of *Twenty Thousand Leagues under the Seas* . . . How beautiful it all is and what fuel for the imagination! [August 19, 1868].

We may wonder what Verne heatedly held in his hands, given the "overabundance" on the point of bursting out. After he had submitted both volumes in March 1869, however, his world turned upside down. The publisher didn't like the book. And he wanted the best parts removing.

It would seem important to study (a) what Hetzel disliked and (b) what Verne did about it, a question no one, unbelievably, has considered to date.

The title usually provided a bone of contention, and the underwater epic was no exception, being successively called *Twenty-Five Thousand Leagues under the Waters*, *Twenty-Five Thousand Leagues under the Seas*, and *Twenty Thousand Leagues under the Oceans*.

Another irritation was that, with everything finished, Hetzel casually suggested increasing the length by half by adding a new volume, like a butcher measuring out sausage. To achieve this, he said, Verne could "easily" add episodes, such as the escape, capture, and reconciliation of one of the guests; the involvement of John Brown, the famous abolitionist murdered in 1856; or the particularly unhinged idea of saving Chinese boys from Chinese pirates and keeping one on board, "to cheer things up"! [April 25, 1869].

But the novelist's stomach really churned at Hetzel's ideas on the closing chapters and Nemo's mission. In rapid summary, the publisher vetoed Verne's cherished ideas, first of having Nemo fight the whole of humanity and then of making him a Pole whose country had been wiped out by the Russians—because the idea would displease the Russian government. Furthermore, the publisher considered the captain's attacking of ships intolerably violent and morally reprehensible.

the
much
out

Verne protested in a whole series of letters from April to June. For the breadth of the changes, the extent of his indignation, and the strength of his logic, his letters best tell the story:

What you say about backing the *Nautilus* into a cul-de-sac from which [Nemo] cannot escape except by sinking the ship . . . is good . . . [but] impossible.

I agree . . . the end of the voyage through the English Channel between Calais, Boulogne, and Dover is crowded out. It needs redoing. You mustn't know where you are. It would be dreadful and the bombshell of the Maelstrom even more dreadful.

As for a slaver, corsair, or pirate vessel, you know full well that these ships don't exist any more . . .

There was the battle of the outlaw against those who had made him an outlaw, a Pole against Russia. That was forthright. We rejected it for purely commercial reasons.

But if it is now just a battle by Nemo against an implausible enemy as mysterious as him, it's not a duel between two individuals any more. It singularly reduces the whole thing.

No, as you say, we need to keep it vague, and we'll manage to.

I can see full well that you're picturing a very different fellow from mine . . . We have agreed on two main points: 1) to change the horror that the captain inspires after his great execution, in the character's interest; 2) to speed up the action after the sinking of the double-decker. This will be done, but, for the rest, all I need do is justify the captain's terrible action in terms of the provocation he undergoes. Nemo doesn't run after ships and sink them every five minutes, he responds to attacks. Nowhere, whatever your letter says, have I made him a man who kills for killing's sake. He has a generous nature and his feelings are sometimes brought into play in the environment he inhabits. His hatred of humanity is sufficiently explained by what he has suffered, both he and his family . . . I'm sure I've followed a very natural crescendo. There *are* generous sentiments, especially in the second volume and only the force of events makes our hero a somber lawmaker . . . But vis-à-vis Captain Nemo it's not the same, and when you explain him in a different way you change him to the point where I can't recognize him.

What I mean is that if he was a fellow to be done again— which I feel perfectly incapable of, for I've been living with him for two years . . . it wouldn't be a day that needed spending in Paris, but a month . . . In sum, your letter has tortured me.

I refuse to write the letter in question concerning Captain Nemo if I cannot explain his hatred, or I will remain silent about the reason for the hero's hatred and life, his nationality, etc. Or, if necessary, I will change the ending . . . You say: but he performs an evil act! I reply no; imagine again—this was the original idea for the book—a Polish nobleman whose daughters have been raped, wife killed with an axe, father killed with a scourge, a Pole whose friends all die in Siberia and whose nationality will soon disappear from Europe under the Russian tyranny. If that man doesn't have the right to sink Russian frigates wherever he finds them, then revenge is but an empty word. In such a situation, I would sink without hesitation. In order not to feel as I do on this matter, you'd need never to have hated.[5]

One must have considerable sympathy with the author. The captain is completely misunderstood by the publisher, who falls into the elementary trap of judging his violent actions without looking at the reasons for them. The climax follows on so much from the previous 40 chapters that Hetzel's memory-dead quick-fix changes do seem of a nature to "torture" his author. In his letters Verne perfectly expresses the coherence of Nemo's actions and Old Testament moral system. He is scathing about Hetzel's no-brain suggestions that the *Nautilus* be trapped by a surface vessel in a cul-de-sac or that the captain be attacking slave-transporting ships in the late 1860s. Even telling Verne to write to the press "explaining" Nemo's behavior after 600 pages of justification seems crazy.

But if we read the published book, which had already started coming out in March, we see that Verne does keep his word. The author seems to make the best of a bad job, by accepting nearly all the publisher's ideas, but simultaneously subverting some of them—so subtly as to have taken in many readers.

Thus Verne spirits the submarine past his beloved Brittany and Picardy and out of the Channel without a single mention. He does not allow Nemo to be French, or Polish, or any nationality at all. He does not permit his rebellion to strike at any particular governmental authority, but drops a mishmash of evasive hints at Confederate, Russian, British, French, and even Turkish ships. While this does lend the captain a modern aura in our extraterritorial century, it also creates a distinct problem as to why he sails the oceans sinking ships. It is not surprising, in sum, that he has an identity crisis and goes around looking for anonymous enemies to defend himself against.

Hetzel's censorship of both Nemo's agenda and the meaning of the novel was catastrophic, for it resulted in an incoherent plot. All was not irremediably lost, however, for Verne kept the evidence in case posterity was interested. The novelist may have overestimated posterity, for no one to date has read the manuscripts. Here we will explore these two earlier drafts, on an exclusive basis, and hence search for what Verne really intended when he wrote his masterpiece.

In the manuscripts, a debt to Dumas *fils* is acknowledged and the location of the captain's home port, which he takes such pains to hide, is given away as near "Tenerife." The hero is called "Juan Nemo," perhaps an allusion to his Spanish grandiloquence or anti-Don Juan lifestyle. Aronnax is Nemo's "prisoner" rather than "guest," and has to formally undertake never to escape; however, at the end the doctor throws in his jailer's face his moral right to leave, and Nemo throws back: Well, leave then!

We see, above all, a different Nemo, more independent and more intransigent. In addition to being an engineer, naturalist, collector, writer, and freedom-fighter, the original Nemo is a composer, preferring his own music to "all the ancient and modern." Da Vinci's "Virgin" is here "a half-dressed woman" and the incongruous Christian element is absent, especially Nemo's anguished cry of "God almighty! Enough!" When scores of Papuans invade his ship, the captain simply electrocutes them, deliberately and without remorse.

The climax has not yet undergone its harrowing political cleansing. Thus Nemo is allowed to identify the sunken wreck as *Le Vengeur du peuple*—*The People's Avenger*—calling it a patriotic ship, lying in a "grand heroic tomb," an essential part of "the Republican legend." He supports, then, the underdog, the French Revolution, and socialism.

When Aronnax says that sinking the mysterious warship "would be the act of a barbarian," Nemo responds, "in an irritated tone," that he is only responding to attacks, rather than initiating them. In the manuscript the warship is "of the Solférino class"—or French—and "darkens the depth of the sky," indicating Verne's loathing of Napoléon III's regime.

Then, after the submarine has passed clean through the ship, a horror-stricken but fascinated Aronnax observes the underwater death-throes of its occupants, especially "a poor little cabin boy, as if chained in the pale flame, twisting in a last convulsion."

As if to balance this, several scenes of peace and harmony occur as the submarine approaches Le Crotoy. Verne cannot resist taking his submarine past his birthplace and into the "flat . . . sandy valley . . . between Britain and France." After keeping "quite close to the coast of north-west France," it enters the Le Havre area and the bay on which Verne was writing:

> By evening, we had covered the whole of the Channel between Brest and the mouth of the Seine . . . the lights of La Hève sent us their electric brilliance. I recognized the magnificent cliffs of Cape Antifer, which took on a fantastic appearance as night fell: the limestone strata, dotted with clumps of grass, produced an interminable procession of strange figures, queens of the middle ages arranged with the roughness of the old painters, a Cimabue or a Mantegna . . . At about midnight, we passed near the Bay of the Somme, whose 10,000 hectares of sand are covered by the rising tide (MS2 127).

After this visit to Verne's home patch, the submarine finally forms part of a scene of happy dawn and sunny tranquility, whose existence has never been suspected:

> The *Nautilus* was floating a few miles from land, to starboard. A hot day was in store. The sky was white, the air calm. Not a breath of wind. On the sea small regular ripples created crisscrossing diamond shapes. The sun picked them out in sparkling points. The water, like liquid emerald, heaved in broad waves that the *Nautilus* did not even feel. In the quivering haze, a few far-off fishing boats and two or three coastal luggers with flaccid sails faded indistinctly away. The smoke from a steamer traced a motionless cloud on the backdrop of the sky (MS2 128–29).

In both scenes, Verne reveals his powerful visual imagination, stimulated by the natural complexities and the artists he mentions. The impression is given that he wishes to bring the *Nautilus* surging up in front of his garden-shed. What seems incredible is that these two descriptions are the only ones of his native land in his first 30 novels. In sum, we can greatly regret the fine visions of a *Nautilus* moving under and over a tranquil and harmonious sea, if only because we know how important the English Channel was for Verne.

The *Nautilus* then sights the lights of North Foreland, at the tip of Kent, and Great Yarmouth, in East Anglia. As it moves up the North Sea, Aronnax plans to "land in Scotland." It's not really on their route, but as in several other novels, Verne cannot resist the idea of heading back to his beloved Caledonia.

The closing words of the manuscript confirm Nemo to be still alive and praises him as the "impregnable . . . Man of the Waters, entirely free." The difference with the book version forms the key to resolving the profound misunderstandings about the message of the novel. Many naiver readers, especially in America, have taken the captain to be a villain. But this is a narrative trap. Aronnax's opinions and interpretations are nearly always wrongheaded, sometimes based on Hetzel's weirder suggestions. Verne does not share the good academic's criticism of Nemo, and we should sympathize with his freedom-fighter side, as convincingly demonstrated by the earlier, superior draft. The final description of the captain's unassailable freedom constitutes an ultimate defiance thrown at Hetzel and all conformists.

At the end of our journey to the center of the text, then, we have rescued the true Nemo and the conceptual core of *Twenty Thousand Leagues under the Seas*. We have belatedly vanquished Aronnax's moralizing and Hetzel's evisceration. The way we should remember Nemo is not the Hollywood version, distorted from a truncated mistranslation of a tragically censored text. We should think of Nemo instead as a creative artist playing his own compositions in his self-constructed submarine. We must allow him the politically incorrect liberty to exercise self-defense in line with his Scottish motto; to

[handwritten annotation at top of page: "✗ impossible no matter how desirable. After all, JV did sign the proofs for the book a we know at"]

imprison the egregious, invasive Aronnax; to execute the savages assailing him; to unhesitatingly sink his enemies' ships. We must permit him the consolation of the Channel seabed, of medieval visions at Le Havre, of Le Crotoy's broad sands, and of one last sunny, peaceful dawn.

The rescue has taken 138 years. In a never-visited file in the National Library, Nemo still freely rides the seas. Let's hope that a publisher will, one day, be bold enough to let him out.

In spring 1868, the novelist had a new smack built by "one of the best captains of Le Havre," Charles-Paul Bos (b. 1826), weighing "5½ tons for the customs, 12 in reality."[6] Le Crotoy-born Bos, who often stayed with his brother, a minute's stroll from Verne's, had been a naval officer. He would often tell the writer about a giant squid he had seen, at that time unrecognized by science: "he came across one such colossal monster in the Indian Ocean . . . in 1861."[7] Bos took responsibility for Verne's navigation expenses, duly noted in the writer's logbooks, and may be one of the two mysterious sea-captains added to the crew that same year.[8]

Former fisherman Alexander (Sandre) Delong (1831–1900) was charge of Verne's boat, "the best skipper of the bay" [June? 1668]. Renowned for his self-control and experience, he had fought in the Crimea and Italy, finishing up as cannon quartermaster. The weathered sea-salt eventually became "my old friend Alexander," with Verne sending him eight signed and dedicated books (*BSJV* 151:16). In the crew was a Michel Bulot, soon replaced by young Alfred Bulot (1834–1932), fisherman in the winter and Verne's cook/sailor in the summer; he had spent two years in New Caledonia and cracked jokes about cannibalism.[9]

Verne now had to wait for the consummation: "The boat is making progress! She's going to be fantastic. I'm in love with this assembly of nails and planks as one is of a mistress at twenty. And I'll be even more faithful to her!" [March 28, 1868]. Two months later he took possession: "I'm writing to you on board the *St. Michel*, *forecastle astern ?*

where I'm all set up for my work" [May 30, 1868]. With a forecastle astern for the crew, the cabin at the back contained two bunk beds with kelp mattresses in a space of six by five feet and four and one-half feet headroom. One climbed down via a ladder, behind which were books on the tides, a few hydrographic charts, and three or four large dictionaries and travel volumes. On deck stood an ancient, dangerous-looking cannon that would later blow up in Sandre's face (*Int.* 23).

Verne wore a waterproof fisherman's smock or knitted striped cardigan and oiled leather hat or beret. Sometimes he took the helm or operated the sails, but if it got choppy he handed command back to the skipper. Sandre and Alfred joked they could never catch a single fish while Verne was on board. Even when they netted a fine mackerel and placed it on deck, it managed to bounce itself back into the water (*Int.* 23).

From 1868, as a result, Verne's foreign travels changed. After Italy and America, he switched to the English Channel on the upgraded *St. Michel*. Each spring he was off like a shot.

His first trip on the refurbished craft, now a "perfect boat" with enhanced sails, took him an ambitious 160 miles in five days, pre-sumably for the Le Havre Maritime Expostion: "I arrive from Le Havre after a journey full of problems, a rather rough sea, which allowed the *St. Michel* to display all her nautical qualities."[10]

Soon Verne was leaving Le Crotoy almost as soon as he arrived, com-posing several works in the peace and quiet of his "floating study," but causing his wife and daughters to worry.[11] He would supposedly write either on the mattress or face down on deck, causing Honorine to exclaim, at least according to Marguerite: "How can you write such fine things, my poor boy, when you only look at the sky with your arse!"[12]

Jules's excitement rose as the storm glass fell: "very shaken, very shaken! But without that where would be the fun?" [May 31?, 1869]. At first his trips were along the coast: Le Havre again, Saint-Valéry en Caux, Le Tréport, Berville, and Dieppe probably in early August 1868, and Boulogne and Calais a fortnight later.[13] Under the wake of the *St. Michel* an imaginative eye could just make out the shadow of a rebel submarine. Although apparently never able to entice his publisher out on his beloved yacht, Verne took the publisher's son out for a two- or three-day trip, with young Jules Hetzel then coming back for a much longer stay.[14] The marine novelist possibly sailed up the Loire to Chantenay in January 1869 (RD 93). He visited Calais and Boulogne again the same year, Le Havre again in July, with his wife for once, Cherbourg, probably in August, and Boulogne, Calais, Gravelines, and Dunkirk in July 1870, despite the threat of war.[15] It was on these trips that he last sighted the Man of the Waters.

The British Isles were the nearest destination after exhausting the French coast, and Verne went there at least twice a year, perhaps as a substitute for the transatlantic neighbor, since "England . . . is a bit of a European America" (August 22, 1852, to Pierre). Particular trips included Dover in June 1868, Gravesend and London two months later probably with his brother, the south coast of England in mid-June 1869, and London again in August, possibly returning via Ostend in Belgium.[16]

From 1867 until 1870, Verne led a triple existence. In addition to Paris and Le Crotoy, he escaped from his seaside hideaway for about half the time on his boat, with a few foreign trips overland as bonus evasion.

In 1866, the Vernes moved their Paris residence to Place de la Croix Rouge, in the Sixth, presumably the same as the Carrefour de la Croix Rouge.[17] By February 1867, they had moved to 2 Rue de Sèvres, staying until April 1869 and paying "FF 2,000 rental."[18] Rue de Sèvres lay between Boulevards Saint-Germain and Raspail, an area redolent with two thousand years of history. It provided an idyllic combination of peace and activity, a return to Verne's early days in Ancienne Comédie: not as posh as Auteuil, where it is awfully chic to feign a British accent, but much nicer. The Vernes' apartment overlooked Rue du Four, with Boulevard Saint-Germain in the distance. Curiously enough, the home addresses of 1863–69 have not been provided by a single biographer to date. And yet it was at these three locations that the Verne family kept its furniture, had its official residence, and spent two-thirds of those six years. They were also where the most famous books of the nineteenth century were written.

In addition Verne made many shorter-trips, whether on the boat, back to Paris in the summer (e.g., August 6–10 and September 10–27, 1867), or to "my daughter's grandfather's at Doullens, from there to Amiens, and thence to Paris to take Valentine and Suzanne back to their convent" [October 3, 1867]. The Vernes traveled to Amiens for much of November and December 1869, and twice again in early 1870. Another excursion with Hetzel was for three or four days in October 1868, when they visited the "mountains and forests" of Baden-Baden, ten miles from the French border [September 18, 1865]. He only did it to please his publisher: "Hetzel kept on so much I decided to go with him" (September 30, 1868, to Pierre).

Jules also went to see his parents, notably in August 1864 and 1866, November 1867, mid-December 1868 to February 1869, and for the first week of September 1870. The slightly reduced frequency was probably because he hoped, in vain, that his parents would come and see him in Le Crotoy. In summer 1867, Verne also had a short stay with his mother at a Breton bathing resort, writing huffily at his father's nonappearance: "I spent as much time as I could with Mother. Unfortunately you decided not to come" [August ? 1867].

During the 1867 visit, the assembled family put on a play at Chantenay called "A Bourgeois Rendezvous." Stage debuts were made by assorted neighbors, Jules as his namesake Caesar, Honorine, and the two Maries, sister and cousin. The play was billed as an "operetta, libretto by Victor Hugo, music by famous German composer Rossini. But since Rossini was Italian and Hugo did not compose comic operas—although Hoffmann wrote one called "A Bourgeois Rendezvous"—the words and music may have been by Paul and Jules.[19]

The long visit at the beginning of 1869 may have been because Aunt Châteaubourg was dying (February 17, 1869). Verne stayed with brother Paul and the four neighboring households made complex arrangements to meet each evening, often shouting across the street or sending one of the young nephews over (RD 65). As before, there were playlets, word games, charades, improvisations, and piano recitals. Jules would recite songs and poems, often a little salacious, to educate the children, he said. He made efforts with his nephews, asking them questions and explaining things in simple terms. However, the children were not allowed to interrupt at the table and had to show proper manners. Uncle Jules would act as discipline master by half-closing his left eye or producing a caustic utterance, amusing the grandparents but embarrassing the miscreant (RD 69).

Aunt Châteaubourg, to whom Jules had written his first letter, hung on for a long time. But she died after Verne went back to Paris (April 2, 1869).

CHAPTER 13

Gathering Clouds: 1868–71

JULES VERNE WAS GLIDING OUT of the Bay of the Somme.[1] Luckily it was the turn of the tide, not yet draining the sands as fast as a galloping horse. As the tiny *St. Michel* hit the Channel and gamely mounted the waves, he tacked to port—he always preferred desert shores. He jubilantly breathed in the salt air. A spring storm was blowing up, giving him frissons of excitement. He buttoned up his blue pilot-coat and pulled his sou'wester lower. Why the hell hadn't he bought a boat a decade ago?

Paris was the reason. How his life had changed in six years! Before that, he'd slogged on because of the success of his early plays, but had never made much, he could now admit. He'd needed to find an office job to support Honorine and his ready-made family. Nadar had helped him make new friends; and that magical trip to Edinburgh and the glorious Highlands opened his eyes, changing him forever—for a start, the idea of switching to prose.

And then he met Hetzel! *Sit lux* in the heavens! His fantastic success, surpassing his wildest dreams, came when he'd been wondering, for the umpteenth time, why he was wasting his life on things nobody wanted. Since then he'd written a dozen volumes, more than a million words, every syllable mulled over and polished until it wouldn't shine any more. Where had he got all those ideas from? And would he be able to do it again?

All had not been plain sailing though. For *Paris in the Twentieth Century* he'd dreamed of an inland sea lapping at the city walls. Now he'd recovered, more or less, from Hetzel's response, he must remember to keep the manuscript in a safe place, away from Michel's destructive habits. He still couldn't understand why the publisher laid into it so devastatingly: was it his ideas on society that upset him?

In those days, when he'd just dreamed of being a real writer, he used to fantasize about the lifestyle. No boss, no clocking in, no gossiping colleagues, no limits at all! To know that your thoughts might change human beings as much as anyone's can. To have a chance, however small, of echoing down through posterity. And to tell everyone "I'm a writer," especially all those adoring brunettes . . .

So why hadn't it turned out like that? His timidity didn't help. Also he didn't really like women's company, he'd be the first to say. So changeable, so affected by their humors, so unrealistic, so talkative. They didn't appreciate music, travel, the sea, just followed the crowd. Perhaps women could see in his eyes that he didn't play their games, which was why scores of women didn't kneel before him. Still he hadn't done that badly, after a slow start. His woman in Paris still gave him the shivers, and there was one girl in the theater district who just turned him around . . .

Also, his success wasn't as broad as he'd hoped, and he'd been hurt not to find his books in New York or London. With one exception, no translations, no stage adaptations, no comic operas. Even in France he was ostracized. No serializations in the fashionable weeklies. No reviews in the qualities. No recognition from the universities. No mentions in the histories of literature. Why, some of his nephews didn't even know he wrote books, perhaps because their parents made fun of his "inventions," as they half-mockingly called them.

At least he'd crawled out of poverty. At least he now lived from his pen: how many people could say that? Although the inheritances hadn't done any harm either. He'd barely got by on his efforts as a stockbroker. He was now one notch above the schoolteachers, though still below the doctors. No room for luxuries or extravagances—even though Honorine managed quite a few. They couldn't save anything, and his dream of becoming a property owner after all these years was just a fantasy.

A zigzag of purple lightning and a deafening clap straight afterwards. Perhaps it would strike the fishing boat, and he could at last observe ball lightning and St. Elmo's fire! But spotting foaming rocks closer than he thought, he reluctantly decided to run before the storm, all sails furled. Who knows, perhaps London for dinner!

His mind wandered again. He'd already started planning a new book. His first inkling was the Reform Club—so English, so stuck up! He'd visited it of course, but most of the ideas came from Wey, an absolute lifesaver. He might set some of it in the late '50s, since that was the London he knew. Funny how your mind worked, his own experience all mixed up with Dickens and Nadar's and Cham's caricatures. That might do for the setting. He'd need a hero and his hero would need a name. London, peasoupers . . . yes, Fog, got it! Age, forty, a good age to be. Profession, member of Parliament. Setting, at home. Character, snobbish but outspoken, highly sexed, yes, the sort of man who'd joke about what "his organ" was expressing today.[2] That would do, always better not to force things, let the mind wander where it would. The English, how do their minds work? Aha, they don't, that's the point! Fog remains blissfully ignorant of his own thoughts; his behavior will surprise even himself, two people inside his head. All good stuff, must jot it down.

No title yet. How he hated them! But there was something about the word "Journey" that gave him a warm feeling, well . . . between the thighs. Even if Hetzel always seemed to hate his ideas, coming up with utter banalities, and somehow always getting his way.

But then Verne's thoughts ranged wider. Why didn't he feel the same joy at small incidents as that snowy November, all those years ago, when he'd been a free man in Paris? And what did he have to look forward to? More of the same. Until a year or two ago, he'd been a young, well youngish, man. But now, at forty, already gray and receding, forehead and upper cheeks furrowed, he'd slipped into uncomfortable middle age. His life was ordered to a fault, his clothes meticulously classified, his environment regulated, his routine well oiled. Why, that might do for his new hero, the rigid, priapic Englishman, cocooned in his domestic comforts. He must get it on paper, just climb down to the tiny cabin. He often slipped things into his books, places visited, friends' names, lovers, aspersions on his wife's virtue, but nobody ever seemed to notice. Now where was he? Ah yes, the future. He needed to get out more, that was sure. The girls were noisy, but nothing compared with Michel, completely out of control—at the age of seven! Why couldn't he be more like his cousin Gaston, so hardworking and serious? Did children catch only their parents' bad habits? But really, he needed to get on with his books quickly. Two more to finish in twelve months. What made it worthwhile was that things would suddenly take on a life of their own. You'd be there vaguely dreaming, when out of the blue yonder thoughts would come rushing, faster than you could get them down. Each new revelation would generate others, the hairs on your thighs and neck tingling slightly, and you just had to hang on for grim life until the pulsations stopped and the abundance stopped flowing. For Nemo it had been the underwater burial, and the ruins of Atlantis, and the pirate flag on the South Pole, and the hordes of giant squid, and the terrifying Maelstrom. What a shame Hetzel had been so bloody-minded about the slightest political allusion. Did his Russian mistress put him up to it?

When he had a moment, he wanted to do more work on the book closest to his heart, the desert-island story he'd been working on for years, dreaming about since his first shipwreck. It went back to *The Swiss Family Robinson*, but made fun of Defoe, who had no common sense. A single footprint in the sand, I ask you—did he fly there? The whole globe was explored, you might as well head for the South Pacific and found a colony; everybody else was . . .

As we leave Verne, halfway through his life and happily ruminating on his masterpieces to come, we should take stock. If he had had a crystal ball to visualize the future—his own, since scientific ideas bored him stiff—he might have had some inkling of the futility of his best-laid plans, the disappointments and tragedies lying in wait around the next bend.

His publisher would vitriolically reject his desert-island book. Everyday life would become impossible when the French attacked the Prussians and were rapidly crushed into humiliating defeat, leading to a tragic invasion, occupation, and civil war. He would be enlisted, his cousin would die among the general starvation of Paris, and Hetzel would cease activity. Verne's finances would reach such a nadir as to make him go back to stockbroking. He would move to Amiens, losing both Paris stimulation and access to his boat. His parents would die, perhaps predictably but a jolting shock all the same. He would be sued for plagiarism—but plagiarized by Offenbach. His desert-island story, rewritten from scratch, would be savaged once more, with Hetzel deleting the ideological core of the novel and imposing his own absurd ideas on the plot. His son would go half-insane and be imprisoned. Honorine would fall critically ill and the doctors would give up hope. Verne would have two illegitimate grandchildren. His beloved nephew Gaston would try to murder him, handicapping him for life. His health would fail, causing him to feel out of sorts nearly all the time. And his books would crash, with the last thirty selling atrociously.

The year 1868 represented, then, a peak. Those last moments on the English Channel, with peace, health, financial security, and masterpieces pouring out by the bucketload, would seem in retrospect very heaven. The maelstroms and tsunamis about to be unleashed would make his present billows seem mere ripples in comparison. The next chapters will cover the few consolations Verne had but above all his repeated catastrophes, some insidiously seeping up and some breaking with much pomp and majesty.

The fourth contract, of May 8, 1868, started by recapitulating the terms for the first four books, just in case it wasn't clear, namely nothing on the illustrated editions, ever. While at it, Hetzel extended the abusive purchase idea to future books. Payment went up to "FF 833.33 per month," but was now conditional on delivery of the three volumes a year; in other words, the volumes were bought outright for FF 3,300 each. Put yet another way, Verne committed to writing two million words over the next ten years. From 1873 until 1878 he would admittedly have "half the profits" after any *un*illustrated printing of the earlier works sold out. The *Geography* was—erroneously— deemed included in the previous outright purchase, and so apparently paid according to the time to do it, thus cleverly cutting payment by nearly 50 percent. In sum, the publisher was rolling in it while Verne had barely enough to support his family, negligible savings, and no hope of ever buying a property.

What is astonishing is that Verne knew the publisher was raking in "at least a hundred thousand francs a year": he knew because with the contract safely signed, the cheeky publisher asked him to invest in the company [June 1868, to Pierre]. In 1875, Hetzel boasted his pub- lishing house was rich (*BSJV* 144:12)—not surprising when it took such outrageous profits off poor Verne's back, now beginning to break under the unbearable load it was carrying.

An insight into Hetzel's outrageous greed appears in his accounts of late 1870.[3] This crucial document, kept secret from the author, details retailing of the two editions of the first five novels and of small-format editions of the next two.[4] Small-format sales totaled 45,000, versus 106,000 illustrated copies. The publisher's net profit (not income) on the first seven novels amounted to FF 182,788, and the author's, 25,666.[5] In other words, Hetzel put into the bank more than seven times as much as poor Verne did.[6] Such a disparity leaves one speechless.

Throughout the 1860s, Verne's health problems came and went much as before. Escaping Paris, he said, made for the best cure: "My sailor's blouse, galoshes, sea air, boat, and Le Crotoy keep me in good health" [May 4, 1870].

As well as bouts of flu that laid him low for a month at a time, making him "cough like a hanged man" (March 10, 1868), rheumatism invaded his back and arms (March 1868). The "dizziness and buzzing, stronger than ever" in his head [November ? 1869] surely corresponded to the jointly physical and existential anguish in his brain. Such familiar complaints as facial paralysis and "guts" resurfaced, or rather the opposite: "I've stomatitis, general inflammation in the mouth, mouth ulcers, etc. The whole North Pole is affected, and even *my South*!" [June 30, 1869]. The metaphor is illuminating for it links Verne's life and work, spatial and bodily notions, opposing the noble upper regions, icy and calm, to the boiling maelstrom of "down there," unmentionable locus of uncontrollable spasms.

It is tempting to look for early signs of the diabetes that would eventually kill Verne: the most obvious being his bulimia, the worry of locating the next meal, the compulsion to wolf down food, to fill the void inside him with scant attention to taste. In his works, critics have had a field day cataloging the obsessive variety of world food his travelers ingest, from sea-slugs to human brains, as if wanting to swallow the whole world. But it would be a bold scholar who attempted to swim upstream from such rich oceanic pickings to spawn offspring carrying genes from both the life and the works, for she would have to leap over the uncharted dams of what Verne ate in his daily life.

ugh!

Verne's reading was voracious but discriminating, sampling most of the classics and contemporaries, especially English-language writers and books for young people.

He regularly studied geographical and scientific periodicals, especially *Tour du monde*, an important source for his writings, for some of his manuscripts even bear cross-references to it. His newspaper was the *Figaro*, plus the short-lived, ferociously anti-government *Lanterne* (1868–69).[7]

Verne kept Dickens's complete works in his bedroom, devouring them several times, but especially *Mr. Pickwick, Martin Chuzzlewit, The Old Curiosity Shop, Nicholas Nickleby, David Copperfield,* and *The Cricket on the Hearth* (*Int.* 106). "The master of them all" possessed "pathos, humour, incident, plot . . . dwarfing all others by [his] amazing power and facility of expression" (*Int.* 106; 218–19). He perhaps planned at some stage to complete Dickens's unfinished detective novel, *The Mystery of Edwin Drood.*[8]

Other reading included Shakespeare, of course; Laurence Sterne's *A Sentimental Journey* and *Tristram Shandy*; Jean de Lafontaine's *Fables* illustrated by Gustave Doré; Stendhal, Chateaubriand, Hugo, and Hoffmann; and Zola, whom he read and reread: "disgusting, malodorous . . . repugnant, stomach-churning, and . . . prodigious."[9]

Cooper's complete works in thirty volumes hugely influenced Verne, who cited the American to bolster his claim that novels do not have to have identifiable heroes to generate interest (*Int.* 206). His prediction that Cooper would "be remembered long after the so-called literary giants of later ages" showed his dislike of many in the public eye, perhaps Zola or Joris Karl Huysmans, given his derogatory comments on the conventional "psychological novel" (*Int.* 105).

But the single most important influence must be Poe's *Tales of the Grotesque and Arabesque* (1848) and *The Narrative of Arthur Gordon Pym* (1838), which he annotated intensively. Baudelaire translated Poe's approximately forty tales in popular periodicals over the period 1852–60, with collections in 1856, 1857, and 1864. In the French tradition, his versions were more recreations than translations, with poetic expression prevailing over fidelity and a huge number of errors—for instance the famous "human figure" at the end of *Pym* translated as "face." The copy of Poe reinvented by Baudelaire that Verne owned was dated 1862; and indeed in 1864 he published the only literary study of his career, "Edgar Allan Poe and his Works." That essay, which is mostly just plot summary, focuses on *Pym*, "The Facts in the Case of Monsieur Valdemar," "The Gold-Bug," 'The Purloined Letter," "Three Sundays in a Week," and the two balloon stories. What fascinated Verne was Baudelaire-and-Poe's pseudo-science, for instance hypnotism as a means to suspend death, while abhorring the lack of verisimilitude, the "inadequate physical means" (August 9, 1867).

Probably the most important influences on Verne were thus both American. Neither, of course, belonged to the mainstream novel, then thought to consist only of stories conveying the innermost thoughts of a small group of characters, using authorial omniscience. The main thrust of Verne's own fiction was to overcome this fundamental implausibility by sticking, as far as possible, to observables, while making ironical forays into psychology as it was conventionally conceived. This innovative technique—designed to revolutionize narrative focus and point of view in the European novel—has hardly been investigated to date.

Another obvious but surprising feature of Verne's favorites was that they were foreign. It is hard to think of any other major nineteenth-century writer who rejected his roots to the extent of attempting to think in another culture. Even within English literature, Cooper and Poe remained low in the pecking order. For a start, they hailed from the United States, still struggling to establish a linguistic and literary identity. And to clinch it, they wrote mere adventure and mystery stories. The literary establishment preferred novels that dealt with safer subjects like love and modern life, works that have usually sunk without trace. Verne's models, in sum, were a hundred miles from official recognition, but then so was the writer himself: the literary canon at least showed consistency.

Like *Hatteras*, which first appeared as two works under separate titles, the moon novels had an uneasy status, for the second volume was both a completion and a sequel. Although *From the Earth to the Moon* was subtitled *Nonstop in 97 Hours 20 Minutes*, it ground to a frustrating halt after the launch; readers had to wait five years to do the journey itself, in *Around the Moon* (1869). As always, Verne threw himself heart and soul into his composition, "living in the projectile"

[January 18?, 1869]. For the algebraic parts, he again enlisted "my cousin the mathematician".[10] Relatively accurate solutions were found to the problems of airlessness, weightlessness (universally believed to occur only at the equilibrium points between the earth and the moon), and the navigation of the projectile (by expulsion of hot gases). However, the book was weighed down by excessive technical detail and contains much less political and social reference than the first.

As if the 200,000–400,000 signed words per year were not enough, Hetzel dumped time-consuming drudge work on his most creative writer. One example among several was an abridgement of James Greenwood's *The Three Old Sailors*. Hetzel had published it once already; after Verne put a lot of work into it [May 31?, 1869], it was simply placed in the files at Rue Jacob. Verne probably got not a centime for his work.

On March 20, 1869, Verne changed his mind about where his heart lay, after more than twenty years. He finally left "that horrible Paris," with "its heavy climate and ammoniacal atmosphere," giving up the lease on Rue de Sèvres.[11] The family moved its furniture to Le Crotoy: they now occupied a huge mansion overlooking the harbor, built in 1860 on the ruins of the castle and previously owned by the mayor (PV 81). Jules got "a locksmith's hand [due to the] excess of moving out, moving in, workmen, masons, carpenters, hammering, trunks to empty, books to arrange, etc." [March 30, 1869]. However, he soon rushed back to Paris, creating the suspicion he was simply trying to get Honorine out of the capital so as to make his own sojourns there more rewarding.

Honorine's own social relationships remained focused on the Amiens region, including her first husband's parents, family, and even friends. However, in 1870, a series of disasters struck: a major smallpox epidemic hit France, killing about 70,000 or 80,000 people within a year. First her brother Ferdinand, Verne's student and stockbroker friend whose wedding had led to his own and who made him a broker, caught the disease and died, on May 23, 1870, aged 42. The tragedy so upset Honorine that she in turn sickened, apparently fearing she had caught it herself. Her parents also fell "very seriously ill"; but Jules felt unable to tell his wife for fear of making her worse [May 30, 1870]. Then her first husband's sister in Amiens caught smallpox in turn and died [June 9, 1870]. Verne reported "Honorine is very upset indeed" [July 1870, to Pierrre], as her health took another turn for the worse. However, her problems may have been connected with his philandering.

Verne seems to have had at least one mistress, although most of the evidence remains circumstantial, based on family stories or close reading of the works. Like most of his century, his tastes tended to the full-blown: he took pity on the shapely and attractive Nellie Bly, exclaiming: "My God, what a shame to see such a clever woman treated so badly by nature . . . as thin as a match, neither bottom nor bosom!" (*Int.* 34).

In May 1870, the author decided to sail to Paris. Honorine disapproved, rationalizing that with the drought they were having he was bound to run aground, which would serve him jolly well right (ADF 125). On his first attempt, he did indeed get no further than Le Havre before hearing of Ferdinand de Viane's death in Amiens, meaning he had to rush off to the funeral [May 27, 1870]. He accordingly sent the *St. Michel* ahead, then rejoined it in Paris, mooring for ten days in the Latin Quarter, "a little above the Pont des Arts" [May 30, 1870]. Verne was "madly in love" with a mistress (if, that is, the liaison was heterosexual), as evidenced by the correspondence, however fragmentary the information:

> My wife is upset at the idea you want to keep me [in Paris] a fortnight! We'll arrange that when I get there.

> When you reply to this letter, lead me to understand that my presence is required at the end of the month . . . Which is true in any case.

I cannot think of anything else [than my Robinson]. *Crusoe*

Except in Paris, where I always arrive *furens amore*, and leave in the same state! Oh nature![12]

Honorine felt so upset at Jules's behavior that she secretly wrote Hetzel an anguished letter, asking for news of his wanderings and concluding: "Forgive and pity me, my husband is slipping from my hands, help me to hold on to him" (August 15?, 1870 in CNM 182).

The great-niece drops heavy hints about a single "siren" of Verne's over several years, a literary handmaiden and a prosperous widow with a suburban villa, while begging Hetzel *fils*, still alive in 1927, for information about a "widow Jules Verne ran into at Le Crotoy in about 1870."[13] To counter accusations of the writer's homosexuality, the grandson biographer cites presumably the same rich widow, a "Mme Duchesne" (a Nantes name) of Asnières, near Paris, with whom Verne held literary discussions (JJV 96–97, 264). In addition, "nearly every week" over a period of years the novelist would stay "three or four days" in Paris, often with a secret friend, very probably female (JJV 157). Only twenty years afterwards did Honorine discover the existence of the woman friend, who may have possibly have been Herminie, but simply laughed (JJV 97); the woman friend died in about 1885, leading Verne to write *Carpathian Castle* (1889), focused on dead singer La Stilla (JJV 177). Another biographer names "Estelle Hénin, Mme Duchesnes [*sic*]," who "died aged 29 . . . in 1865," and assumes that the name La Stilla comes from Estelle.[14]

All the information, in sum, remains unreferenced and so unverifiable and inconclusive. Although it is far from clear how many different women are being talked about, it is probable that Verne did have some sort of liaison or liaisons, although it would be hard to prove that it was not platonic.

Two other names have been suggested. It has been speculated that in February–March or April 1870 Verne was in Sion, Switzerland, with a "Polish or Russian woman," with "lovely smoky-gray eyes," possibly Maria Alexandrovna Markovich, née Countess de Velinskaya

(1834–1907); in 1878, Verne did say he had visited Switzerland.[15] A Ukrainian-Russian who also published in French, she lived in Paris (1860–67) under the pseudonym Marko Vovchok. She seems to have been Hetzel's mistress, translated several titles of Verne's into Russian, and wrote *Maroussia*, which Hetzel published, falsely ascribing it to himself.[16] A purported relic of Verne's stay at the "Haenni house, Rue de l'Eglise [Sion] in 1870" still survives, but, there seems little substance to this story.

More plausible is Luise or Louise Teutsch (b. 1845) from Homorod, Brasov District, Transylvania, who arrived in Amiens in 1878, and the same year married Swiss chef Gustav MÅller, her third husband. MÅller was related to Louise Berton, a friend of Valentine and especially of Suzanne who worked as a primary school teacher, as did Luise Teutsch.[17] The couple went back to Bucharest in 1881, where, shortly after, Luise had a baby with a strangely French name, Eugénie Jeannette Marie-Rose. Eugénie Maller traveled to Amiens in about 1896, aged approximately fifteen, to train as a primary school teacher, and lived there for two or three years, often meeting the Vernes. Her direct descendants claim she was Verne's daughter.[18] A DNA test would presumably settle the question, one way or another.

In February 1870, Hetzel, probably with Suez Canal builder Ferdinand de Lesseps, a keen reader of Verne, requested the Legion of Honor for the author.[19] Consent was given and it just needed to be signed by the emperor—when on July 19 war broke out against a Prussian-led coalition, the first conflict on French soil for two generations. Three days before losing office the minister signed the decree and had it countersigned by the Empress; it was awarded on 9 August.

Verne, essentially a pacifist, expressed no opinion as to the justness of the Franco-Prussian War, but thought France had a good chance of winning even as late as December (December 17, 1870, to Pierre). He laid into the flag-wavers, especially his father:

really your last letter was a little chauvinistic. I don't that much want to give the Prussians a good hiding . . . Let's not be stupid or boastful and admit that the Prussians are as strong as the French, now that everyone's fighting with long-range weapons [July 28, 1870 in *BSJV* 144:10?].

While the French lost battle after battle, Verne was blissfully out sailing [August 6, 1870]. When the Third Republic was proclaimed, two days after the surrender at Sedan (September 2), he was traveling to Nantes to see his parents [August 31, 1870]. Jules took nearly four days to get back to Le Crotoy via Le Mans, Rouen, and Dieppe, since the Prussians had besieged Paris and occupied much of northern and eastern France (September 21, 1870). At forty-two, he was not called up for active duty, although buying "a chassepot rifle and 150 cartridges just in case," but served in the local National Guard (November? 1870 to Pierre).[20] Verne sent his family to Amiens, believing they would be safer there, and abandoned his post to go and see them five or six times.[21] Hetzel mailed Verne two letters by balloon from Paris, perhaps using Nadar's postal service.[22] By December, with northern France overrun, Jules again visited his family for three days. Four "gentle, peaceful" Prussians had been billeted on the house, which "they appreciate—I'm not surprised! They don't eat like that at home. We're giving them rice so they're as constricted as possible. It's less messy that way" (December 17, 1870, to Pierre).

During the Paris Commune (March 18–May 28, 1871) and its aftermath, Verne probably visited the capital three times, the last time being at the beginning of June when he stayed with Paul in his apartment on Rue Tronchet, in the Eighth (JJV 99; ADF 134). Cousin Henri, who had stuck to his post at the *lycée*, had died from the privations of the siege (ADF 133). With his brother Jules visited the devastated areas of Paris (JJV 100).

Hetzel had left Paris for health reasons in spring and publishing had come to a halt, with most of the typesetters called up and then taking part in the Commune (ADF 133). However, the publisher continued to read Verne's manuscripts, and even negotiated a new contract, with payments to start from November [September 25, 1870]. Although peace was signed in May, Hetzel probably paid Verne nothing for much of 1870–71, whether temporarily or not is not clear. He came back to Paris only in November—but without seeing the novelist, called away by bad news from home. However, he resumed publication, with two Verne volumes out in the second half of 1871.

Already in 1868, Verne had found his father gouty, rheumatic, and unable to "think of anything except his family and his God" [December 26, 1868]. In August 1870, he had seemed much older than 72, but still delighted to see his son.[24] In mid-1871, Verne sent his family to Chantenay, either to save money or to help look after Pierre, who had suffered a great deal from difficult conditions during the war.[24]

Jules took the overnight train, and on the morning of November 3rd found his father gravely ill and paralyzed.[25] Pierre "died at three o'clock in the afternoon, an admirable and kind death with all his children around him."[26] Verne was moved to tears, writing "he was a veritable saint" [November 4, 1871]. A week later, Monsieur Verne was buried at the St. Nicholas's which he had helped build [November 7, 1871]. The funeral address revealed that just weeks before, Pierre had said he was happy that Jules had devoted himself to literature (ADF 136).

CHAPTER 14

End of Exploration: 1871–72

IN THE AFTERMATH OF THE WAR, with no sign of the publisher coming back to Paris, Verne was in dire financial straits.

Part of Verne's financial problems stemmed from Hetzel's inefficiency. The writer apparently used the publisher as a sort of bank account, having entered into byzantine three-way arrangements with him and a banker to guarantee a substantial loan on the basis of future earnings (April 22, 1871). But Hetzel took months to transfer sums, causing Verne to owe first "FF 700 just in interest," then "FF 6,000, plus about 1,000 in interest for lateness."[1]

As outlays, the Vernes paid FF 2,000 rental on the Rue de Sèvres property [August? 1868], meaning that the combined rent on their two properties must have been about 3,000 or 4,000 per year. On the income side, Verne had 10,000 a year from his writing, enough for a single man but inadequate for a family. As expected, Honorine had inherited from the "rich uncle": Verne had estimated 80,000 in 1856, but the sum seems in fact to have been merely 12,500 as capital, with the interest going to Honorine's sister.[2] The income from the 80,000 marriage settlements should have produced about four to five thousand a year, if invested properly. Occasional windfalls came, like FF 2,500 from the French Academy in June 1872.

The net result of expenditure exceeding income was, per Mr.

Micawber, unhappiness—or rather desperation. Verne had continued working as a jobber for a year or two after his first publishing success, despite detesting his clientele (September 4, 1863). But by 1866 he was "rarely going to the office at Eggly's, and . . . to the stock exchange never, thank God."[3] However, he never severed all contact, continuing to deal with his father's investments, still having a financial interest in Eggly in 1873, and maintaining an account for depositing his writing income and using the letterhead indefinitely.[4]

By July 1871, it had all come to a head, and, despite the volatile market, Verne returned to stockbroking, hoping to write one volume a year instead of the usual three: "here I am back at the stock exchange . . . I'm trying to deal only with the best Parisian banks" [Jul.? 71]. This was to be his last letter to his father, surely making him turn faster in his grave. In fact the jobbing proved just a stopgap until early November. The resumption of payments from Hetzel, the end of Verne's broking, his final departure from Paris, and Pierre's death happened within days of each other.

One possible reason Verne had to scrimp and save was the money he wasted maintaining homes in different towns, in addition to his boats. Within months of giving up the Paris pied-à-terre, he went back to his old habits, no doubt a sign of another tug-of-war with Honorine. The decision would determine the rest of his life.

His wife had always missed Amiens, where her roots lay and her family lived. Verne could write anywhere, the obvious choice being Nantes, the home of dozens of close relatives. Even if the city itself retained unpleasant memories, any number of unspoiled fishing villages beckoned; even Le Crotoy might have been preferable. But Amiens it was, to please Honorine (Lemire 42).

A first chalet was rented in November 1869, at 3 Boulevard Saint-Charles, then 23 Boulevard Guyencourt from February 1870 onwards. Guyencourt, just south of the center, ran along the railroad, with Verne's study overlooking the tracks; it faced Honorine's parents' place (Lottman 160). Nevertheless, for most of 1869–71, Verne lived apart from his family, rejoining them only in November 1871 (*BSJV* 136:23). His National Guard and broking duties kept him away from Amiens, but the habit had been adopted a good twelve months before the start of the war; and so the marriage must have been in trouble.

Verne fitted in quickly, coming to like Amiens's gray skies and civic responsibility after the Parisian arrogance and egotism. Very soon he felt "a fully fledged local citizen. It's as if I were born here . . . Amiens is . . . near enough to Paris to get the reflections, but without the noise and intolerable agitation" (*BSJV* 132:45).

Although it seemed only yesterday that the daughters had been small, they soon became engaged: Valentine to wounded war veteran Captain Henri de la Rue de Francy, Suzanne to local burgher Georges Lefebvre (JJV 104). They married in 1872 and 1873 (CNM 196).

In March 1873, the three remaining Vernes moved down the street into 44 Boulevard Longueville, which they bought. Two damning insights showed the problems of the household: when Verne took Michel to Chantenay, it was so he could be in a family, "the family he's never known"; Hetzel thought the Verne couple should go out even less into society, as otherwise Honorine's "illiterate blunders" would embarrass Verne.[5]

The purchase, and the receptions and high living that ensued, must have been due to the social ambition of Honorine and the daughters, as Verne disdained luxury (RD 101). Indeed, when they had their Wednesdays Honorine had to beg Jules to come down, for he said he killed conversations, which was probably true; he would courteously listen to the musical or literary performances, but disappear on the stroke of ten.[6]

Inevitably, the writer transmogrified his writing environment, where he spent most of his waking existence, into his heroes' domestic arrangements. Before heading for the center of the earth, for instance, we see charming medieval Hamburg, where aged elm and house form a mutually supportive couple, with the spring buds probing the leaded windows. Fogg has innovations such as electricity, gas, and a speaking-tube to guarantee his anal-retentive punctuality. Nemo sleeps in a Spartan cell but writes in a magnificent library containing all the best humanity has written, albeit with just one French novelist, a woman.

Like Verne on his boats, the characters had the best of both worlds since they took their homes with them. A basket over the African savannas, an igloo in the polar wastes, a padded capsule in lunar orbit, or an Indian steam caravan allowed observation of natives or monsters from a safe distance. Verne's narrators invariably avoided direct action, as did, increasingly, the author himself.

The slave-driving three volumes each year, every year, had begun to exhaust Verne. From the sunny Riviera, Hetzel consented to reduce the three volumes to two, for the same monthly payment. In his reply, Verne thanked him profusely, but argued that 10,000 a year was still not enough to support a family. "I'm very confused, very perturbed, very distressed by all that, for the revenue from my books is absolutely inadequate" (April 22, 1871).

The fifth contract, of September 25, 1871, duly stipulated two volumes a year. It was swings and roundabouts, though, for the contract extended both the duration of the agreement and the license to sell *un*illustrated editions without extra payment to the author. The elusive half-share of profits on the most successful books, due to come into effect in 1873, receded three further years, meaning that Verne perhaps lost on the deal.

As time went on, the fatal date of 1876 crept nearer when Hetzel would have to split part of the income on the books of the early 1860s. He would also need to make sense of the "not very clear" series of partial recapitulations and amendments (the phrase is his, in a secret letter to his son (January 15, 1875), that never quite indicated which works were covered. He might even have to admit that Verne had the right to publish his bestsellers with—horror!—another publisher.

Hetzel decided to tear up the previous agreements. The sixth contract, of May 17, 1875, again put off the date when Verne would get a cent more than his derisory 1,000, if only on the unillustrated editions, to 1882! The publisher's unabashed cheek and greed were hard to credit. While ignoring the running sore of the gouging of the illustrated editions (which would fester for another thirty years), it claimed to clear up the repeatedly opened wound of the amputation of the *un*illustrated ones—by enlarging the wound by six years! If I had been Verne, my reply would not have been printable. Hetzel again added insult to injury by writing into the contract the claim that the idea was Verne's.

Admittedly, on new books, Verne would get 50 centimes per unillustrated volume and 5 percent on the first 20,000 illustrated copies (10 percent thereafter), plus, at long last, 50 percent of income on translation and serialization.[7] The changes may have been prompted by new laws to prevent exploitation of authors, mentioned for the first time in the contract. Even these various concessions would only come into effect two years later, that being the time the editor needed to get his accounts in order! (article 10). In a final twist, the books of the hugely profitable plays could be published only by Hetzel, even when the plays were coauthored. In other words, the editor laid claim to the dramatic production of the rest of the world!

When Verne, while expressing his gratitude and apologizing for raising the question, dared to inquire whether the illustrated copies could not go up to from 5 to 15 percent, Hetzel replied, in a non sequitur, "your observations [are] totally false" since the illustrated editions had to have a print run of 20,000![8] The information came as a revelation to Verne, completely in the dark about the large-format copies of "his" works. For about the only time, Hetzel patronizingly called Verne a "friend," said "let's work together," and swore his conscience was clear in the matter. He was careful, however, not to let out any information about actual print runs, profit margins, or indeed anything that might bother his golden goose's pretty little head.

If any confirmation of the theft were required, it came after Verne's death. On examining the 1875 contract, Michel felt horrified. On the basis of much smaller sales, the son obtained 10 percent of the cover price on all editions, compared with his father's average across all editions of less than 2 percent. Hetzel would have given Verne a minimum of 10 percent had he had a drop of justice or friendship in his grasping heart.

From 1870, Verne composed the extraordinary *The "Chancellor."* The theme of cannibalism, which had occurred obsessively but episodically in the previous novels, here received full and systematic treatment. The book stemmed from the horrifying events on the Raft of the *Méduse*, which killed over three-quarters of those abandoning ship in shallow waters off the west coast of Africa.

Clearly also echoing the Franco-Prussian War, Verne's novel relates a voyage from Charleston to Liverpool that turns to tragedy as the cotton cargo starts to spontaneously combust. After a hurricane, the heroic second-in-command decides to abandon ship. On the improvised raft, the starving sailors eat a dead body, then draw lots to see who will be sacrificed for the common good, with the shapely limbs of the young miss a prime target. The novel ends up as a horrific story of man's inhumanity to man, with murder and fifty-seven varieties of flesh-eating. It contains no science whatsoever; and precious little optimism. It in fact forms a landmark in the history of Western literature, being the first narrative novel to be written in the present tense.

Adventures of Three Russians and Three Britons (1871) features the measuring of a meridian through South Africa. The geodesic work is demonstrated by means of a diagram from Garcet's *New Lessons in Cosmography* (1853). The two nationalities of the title work harmoniously until the Crimean War breaks out, whereupon dangerous animals and natural disasters reinforce their enmity. However, they reunite to repulse natives, and part the best of friends. This little-known novel lacks the excitement of the earlier works, with their exploration of virgin areas of the globe in search of some transcendent point. On reading it and *The Chancellor* Hetzel surely worried that his golden years might be less long than he had imagined.

Now that Verne had left Paris, he still spent one week out of four in the capital, partly to stay in touch with the literary milieu.[9] But he and Hetzel also sent each other up to three letters a day. From the beginning a fundamental asymmetry reigned over the exchanges. Nearly everything the novelist suggested had little effect; nearly everything the publisher wanted, he got. In terms of style, the disparity seemed even greater, with Verne invariably respectful, but Hetzel oscillating from the distantly dismissive to the downright derogatory. Whether it was missing proofs or the nationality of Nemo, the Franco-Prussian War or the financial arrangements, Verne argued his side logically, patient point by cogent point; whereas the publisher appeared not to understand the books very well, never admitted the slightest error, and resorted to bluff or bluster as and when needed. Sometimes Verne would get invitations to contribute to, for instance, the *Gaulois* (*BSJV* 130:31). The publisher's normal response was that he had no right to publish elsewhere (e.g., [February 27, 1873]).

Their styles, in sum, could not have been more different. On the one hand a conscientious and hardworking individual, who spent hours answering the least fan letter. On the other a forgetful businessman, with a brief attention span.

To date no one has explored the manuscripts of France's best-known works, a commentary on both Verne's status in the academic world and the methodology used by the commentators.[10] However, on the basis of my experience of the question, a few clear conclusions stand out. In many cases, the publisher transformed the ideology and meaning of the most important works, deleting sections with social commentary and inserting his own happy endings in place of Verne's duels, suicides, and disasters. In most cases, the passages that did not see the light of day hold at least as much intrinsic interest as the published works. In a few cases, they represent the very peak of Verne's writing. In all cases they help to understand the plots of works that have captivated generations.

One detail in the manuscripts appears emblematic. Occasionally, Verne made innocent remarks about contemporary France, but these rarely survived his publisher's vetting.[11] Amazingly, the books were not allowed to visit France—which creates considerable distortion when going from London to Switzerland (*Around the World*) or from Sicily to Belgium (*Twenty Thousand Leagues*). The paradox, then, visible across the entire Extraordinary Voyages, is the absence of Verne's country of residence and predominant readership.[12] Even "The Flight to France" (1887) stops short at the frontier.

Hetzel of course had had the perspicacity to discover the author in the first place. But his two main effects on Verne seem to have been deleterious. He emphasized his own commercial conceptions, using rules-of-thumb like, do not kill off your hero in case you need him again later (May 14, 1876)—think what Shakespeare or Dickens would have become under Hetzel. And he restricted Verne to just one genre, the geographical novel, which he had admittedly virtually invented, but whose limitations he chafed against and which he bitterly regretted not being able to leave (*Int.* 207).

Around the World in Eighty Days (1872) describes the journey undertaken for a bet by eccentric Englishman Phileas Fogg. The mood is humorous and the pace fast-moving; but there are also serious points to the work, such as the shrinking of the world caused by the end of exploration and the building of the railways.

Practically nothing is known about Fogg except his self-control. Having appointed a new servant, acrobat Passepartout, he heads for the Reform Club, where the conversation turns to the size of the globe. Fogg claims it can now be circumnavigated in 80 days; and to prove it, he and Passepartout set off via Calais and Suez. While crossing the Indian jungle, the travelers stumble upon the preparations for a suttee. Having rescued the beautiful Princess Aouda, they reach Hong Kong, where Inspector Fix, thinking Fogg a bank robber, separates Passepartout from his employer. But Fogg, the young widow, and Passepartout meet up again, cross the Pacific, and catch the transcontinental railroad. After an attack by Indians, when Fogg rescues Passepartout, they take a land yacht to Omaha. Missing a ship in New York, Fogg hires a boat and, when it runs out of fuel, burns it down to the hull for fuel. But when he gets home, he is still five minutes late. He falls into despair and thinks of suicide; Aouda proposes to him; we cut to the Reform Club; and Fogg marches calmly in to win his bet. The imperturbable gentleman had gained a day in the Pacific, taking only seventy-nine days, and the book closes with Phileas and Aouda happily married.

By a miracle, the very first lines where Verne thought of the novel are extant—although I am the only person to have deciphered them. After doodles, the novel opens:[13]

The reform club, Pall mall, 1858 . . . Burgh
60 clubs in London reform club . . .
1 October 1872, a 40-year-old man,
—Face isn't the only expressive organ, rem. gentleman.
—Fog's foot never rxxx—accordingly, given Article 29 . . .
Fog at home.

where "deciphered"

The fragment shows that the Reform Club and "Fog" are central from the beginning. But it is the year indicated, "1858," which is a revelation, for this fourteen-year gap perhaps implies a radically different conception of the book, raising the question whether Verne planned to describe a circumnavigation before the railroads existed. The date also hints at the first trip to Britain, a vital influence on the following production.

The clearly legible "Face isn't the only expressive organ," with its laconic form prefiguring Fogg's elliptical style, also revolutionizes understanding of the novel. Its sexual reference declares that the mind's composition is not in the face, that Fogg's imperturbability conceals the strongest impulses, that his fate will ultimately be determined by his libido.

The basic idea of circumnavigation had clear origins in the opening of the Suez Canal and the railroads across America and India (1869–70). Verne drew from his own travels, especially for New York, the Atlantic crossing, Liverpool, and London. About half a dozen main written sources seem plausible for the idea of circling the globe, including Thomas Cook, Poe, magazine articles, and books by a W. P. Fogg and a G. F. Train. But the idea had in fact become a commonplace, as indicated by the very subtitles of *Captain Grant's Children*: *A Voyage Around the World* and *Twenty Thousand Leagues under the Seas: A Submarine Trip Around the World*.

As we shall see in the next section, the novel originated from a play. It does not therefore seem surprising that it has a cipher for a hero and an acrobat as his sidekick, with a lack of conventional psychology. However, and ahead of Zola or Maupassant, Verne introduces new psychological conceptions in place of the traditionally introspective ideas so much in fashion at that time. His objection to accepted views of the novel is its subjectivity and arbitrariness, for the movements of the soul are invisible. With his simultaneously skeptical and romantic imagination, Verne seeks tangible signs of the workings of the mind— nothing new one might say. But from the pseudo-scientific vocabulary of electricity and engineering, he generates a new vocabulary for motivations hidden from the protagonists themselves: "hypnotized," "instinctively," "mechanically," "automatically," "secretly," and "involuntarily." This culminates in the first use of the word "unconsciously," in the dazzling climax of "the day unconsciously gained." French dictionaries claim the first use of the term as 1876; but as if to prove it was not a fluke Verne repeated the feat in *The Mysterious Island* (1874). Phileas Fogg is thus the first person in the world to have his unconscious investigated: who better than that paragon of rationality, all superego and therefore all the more vulnerable to surprises from the depths of his soul? Freud famously said that writers have most of the ideas before the scientists; *Around the World* certainly contains remarkable pre-Freudian views on the unconscious mind. If Fogg seems inscrutable, this does not mean that he is an automaton. The fact that his face expresses should not prevent us from interpreting the behavior of other parts of his body.

Verne reportedly read his novel out to daughter Valentine and her new husband in November 1872 (ADF 140). Then as it came out in

the *Temps*, the newspaper's circulation soared and the Paris corre-
spondents of American dailies are meant to have cabled excerpts to
New York (although no one has ever given dates or names). Apparently, some readers believed that the journey was actually taking
place, bets were placed, and international liner and railway companies
made lucrative offers to be allowed to bring Fogg back to Europe.[14]

Ever since *Five Weeks*, Verne had playfully interwoven fact and fiction, using the most up-to-date sources and inserting topical material
during the serialization. Here he managed things so well that the closing
date of the novel, December 22, 1872, was also that of its serialization.

Reviews were very good, for instance "[its] marvels outdo Sinbad
the Sailor's" or "tour de force."[15] However, a number of the real-life
Reform Club sent a letter of complaint, saying the conservative *Daily
Telegraph* was barred there; and Verne reportedly deleted the mention
for the next edition.[16]

Following Towle and d'Anvers's English translation (1873), hundreds of publicity seekers, including Nellie Bly and Jean Cocteau,
sought to improve on Fogg's time. Even today journalists short of
good copy often use Verne's idea. Recently Michael Palin made a hit
television series—and novelization—purloining Verne's title,
although seemingly not having read the book.

The inevitable Hollywood version came out in 1956, starring
David Niven, Noël Coward, John Gielgud, Marlene Dietrich, Frank
Sinatra, and 70,000 other extras. Perhaps intended as a spoof, it
replaced the brainwave of the self-consuming transatlantic vessel with
a balloon ride. Verne had the last word, however, for he commented
ironically that a balloon crossing "would have been dangerous, and
impossible anyway" (xxii).

All but one of Verne's novels appeared in English only in the 1870s,
long after he had written much of his best work. It must have been
galling for the part-British author of *The British at the North Pole*
(*Hatteras*'s first title) to see the book unavailable on his first dozen
visits to that country. But fate was perhaps being kind to him after all.

Belatedly, and well after other languages, English-language publishers discovered Verne's works and hastily translated them en masse,
usually both in authorized versions, where at least the woodcuts were
paid for, and pirated ones, often in the United States.[17] The "translations" often came out truncated by up to half with the rest in gob-
bledygook, like "with a lentil, he lighted a fire" (*lentille*), "the passage
of the North Sea" (*Nord-Ouest*), or "each square ? of an inch" (*cen-
timeter*), to quote but three.[18] Although virtually all of the Extraordinary Journeys appeared in English, most of the hundreds of attempts
must be considered failures. From the beginning, the English Verne
stemmed from, but also contributed massively to, the masking of the
creative artist of the first order. The Extraordinary Journeys indis-
putably constituted literary works with textual "thickness" and a sense
of overall belonging—except in English. There was no equivalent
here to Scott Moncrieff's Proust or Beckett's Beckett.

As one example, *Journey to the Center of the Earth* was translated
more than ten times, but most versions betrayed the text. The best-
known text, an anonymous one of 1872, rebaptized Axel as Harry
and Lidenbrock as Hardwigg, made them both Scottish, finished
each paragraph with an invented sentence, and inserted whole chapters (see Appendix D for further information). As another, *The Ice
Sphinx* (1897) is more than 100,000 words long in French; in the
1982 version sold by one of the very biggest English paperback publishers, it had fewer than 20,000 words.[19]

Because Verne's novels were twice mangled, by the French and the
English publishers, the translated texts were, more often than not,
travesties of what Verne had actually written. It was perhaps fortunate
that he could not read a line of English.

CHAPTER 15

Last Paradise: 1872–79

DID VERNE SAIL TO GET AWAY from his problems? Certainly the frequency and distance increased with time.

In early June 1872, he went back to London once more, visiting Woolwich with his wife and brother and staying at a hotel on the Strand (June 8. 1872). That summer he sailed to Saint-Malo, then caught the train to Nantes to see his mother for a week, and later took Michel out on a four- or five-day sea trip.[1]

Possibly the same year, he made an ambitious trip along "the English coast and up the Ocean to Scotland," which must mean the west coast, although probably not getting as far as the Hebrides (*JVEST* 43). It must have been on this voyage that, with Hetzel *fils* and friend of Hetzel's, Edgar Raoul-Duval (1832–87), Verne revisited Ireland (if his stop at Queenstown on the *Great Eastern* counts as a visit).[2] Given that he would write a third Scottish book in 1876–77, and later a volume set in Ireland, the navigation was one of his most crucial, despite the frustrating lack of information.

Most probably in September of that same 1872, the writer returned to Jersey, with the slight possibility he went to see Hugo, back in Guernsey for some of that month.[3] Hetzel also invited him to Jersey, Guernsey, and Sark by steamship for about August 14–24 the following year, an invitation he seems to have accepted.[4]

So as to write the second script of *Around the World*, Verne spent
the winter of 1873–74 on the Riviera, staying with d'Ennery in
"Chênes verts." Designed and built with the proceeds from previous adaptations, this magnificent villa stood astride the verdant
isthmus of Cap d'Antibes—"the finest place in the world."[5] It had
a lake right beside the house and sea views extending 270 degrees:
to the east the eye ranged enticingly past Monaco as far as beloved
Bordighera, with the snowy Alps rearing up behind. Verne's west-
ward-facing bedroom gave breathtakingly onto the Mediterranean
and the green coast of Golfe Juan (November 21, 1873). The four-
story mansion, more like a rose-covered museum, had sweeping
entrances on opposing sides, and balconies, terraces, and verandas
sprouting everywhere.

When Honorine came down later (since she and Verne had just
become grandparents), the couple headed for Monaco to see Hetzel.[6]
Verne returned to Amiens at the beginning of April, probably stopping off at Marseille (*BSJV* 147:13).

On a second visit in January 1875, Verne and Honorine felt less
cheerful. Not only did d'Ennery live with his girlfriend, an "excited
tart" according to Hetzel, but "[Louis] Cantin's coming for a few days
with his mistress, a real slut. It's extremely embarrassing for my wife,
and really most unpleasant."[7] Things then went from bad to worse:
"it's dire here," "I'm leaving as soon as the scenario's finished."[8] In fact
things became pure "hell," since d'Ennery was completely worn out
and Verne had to do and redo the script ten times.[9] As revenge, Verne
destroyed the "vile" villa in a cataclysm in *Hector Servadac* (1877).
From February 22nd to about the 26th, the Vernes again stayed in a
hotel on the heights of Monaco (February 20, 1875).

Two biographers claim that Verne sailed back to Norway on his
yacht in the 1870s but this seems improbable.[10]

The Mysterious Island (1874) represented the culmination, and cul-
de-sac, of many long-maturing Vernian ideas. It centered on the
desert-island dream, closely associated in Verne's mind with the ideal

community, but simultaneously mocked the facile manipulation of the plot in *Robinson Crusoe*.

In 1865, a violent storm sweeps a balloon and five Unionist prisoners-of-war across the Pacific and onto an island. After satisfying basic needs, engineer Cyrus Smith, reporter Spilett, sailor Pencroff, adolescent Harbert, and Neb the Black find a single match and one grain of wheat, and proceed to rebuild much of modern civilization. They also construct a boat, sail to the neighboring island of Tabor, and rescue Ayrton, abandoned there in *Grant* and now an animal. However, a series of puzzling discoveries convinces the colonists they are not alone, including a lead bullet, a dog catapulted from a pond, and a washed-up chest. At long last they realize that Captain Nemo, escapee from *Twenty Thousand Leagues*, has been helping them all along. Nemo reveals his true name to be Prince Dakkar, then dies, and is entombed in his *Nautilus*. Following a volcanic eruption, the island disintegrates, leaving just a small rock, from which the settlers are rescued by one of Captain Grant's children.

This novel represents Verne's best attempt at depicting individual Americans. Smith is intelligent, analytic, encyclopedic, and pedantic: eminently practical but lacking spark. He resembles Frenchman Aronnax who has a good logical mind but not much else, and surely reflecting one side of Verne's own character. Pencroff must be modeled on sailors the novelist knew, perhaps including his crew on the successive boats. Like the other earthy, irreverent working-class men, Pencroff is out of his depth on intellectual issues. But his practical philosophy beats that of his social superiors hands down, as do his communication skills, all epigrammatic humor and pithy concision.

What should not be glossed over is the systematic racism of the novel. Verne and the colonists' prejudice remains blind and unrelenting, shared with much of the century. While sympathetic, Neb the Black's physical appearance and behavior are described in unacceptable terms (close to animals, lack of intelligence and perseverance, etc.). Worst of all, persistent unfavorable comparisons are made by all and sundry with Top the dog and Jup the orangutan.

While the publisher atrociously mauled *Twenty Thousand Leagues*, *The Mysterious Island* suffered a worse fate, through four distinct manuscripts over more than ten years. At least since meeting Hetzel, Verne had been "dreaming of a magnificent Robinson" [September 18, 1865]. But the publisher hated what emerged, claiming it was just a draft, that the clay was too soft and too grey, that the characters "are not at present interesting . . . your people get out of situations worse than the simplest robinsons [*sic*] of the past" [July 21, 1870]. His comments knocked Verne for six, causing him to suspend writing [February 15, 1871].

Despite the author's valiant resistance, the third and fourth manuscripts underwent a similarly harrowing series of cuts, additions, and changes, totally changing the conclusion. In the published version, but not in the manuscripts, we read of Nemo's deathbed remorse and Smith's pompous and presumptuous assessment of his life as an "error." In the book, Nemo, or rather Hetzel, gives the settlers jewelry, but in the manuscript, the giant pearl the captain had so carefully nurtured in *Twenty Thousand Leagues*. In Verne's original idea, the destruction of the island marked the end of the novel; in the "Hetzelized" version, the settlers have to laboriously start again in Iowa. The published book contained the captain's dying words, the absurd "God and my country!" The manuscript read "Independence!"

An exploration of *The Mysterious Island*, in sum, throws up several major problems with accepting the work as published. Because Nemo is not what Verne wanted him to be, this falsifies his destiny and that of the settlers, and in turn the whole meaning of the novel. To the ambivalence and irony beginning to take over Verne's works in the 1870s, then, we must add our own skepticism as to every sentiment and deed in *The Mysterious Island*, especially the pious or noble ones. Behind each episode and phrase lurk a line of darker copies, like Macbeth's ghosts, running back through the correspondence with Hetzel and the four manuscripts but even into *Twenty Thousand Leagues* and *its* multiple manuscripts and protracted correspondence.

The novel is disappointing if judged purely as a sequel, for it contradicts and undermines the magnificent conclusions of the previous work, its heroic defiance of human society and its magical exploration of the ocean depths. However, as an independent work, and on condition it is read at a second level, *The Mysterious Island* remains a resounding success.

Verne did not in fact write *Around the World* unaided; "with the Assistance of Édouard Cadol" should arguably appear on the title page.

After the war Verne had had the idea of making a play out of *Hatteras*, writing enthusiastically of "northern lights, whales, storms, shipwrecks . . . I'd replace the American . . . with a Frenchman so as to unfurl the tricolor at the Pole!" [February 1872]. In his script a dog occupied center stage in the tragic climax (*BSJV* 57:37). Verne discussed the play with part-time bachelor and neighbor Henri Larochelle (1827–84), director of several theaters, who reacted enthusiastically [Febuary 1872]. However, the idea never quite made it to the stage.

At roughly the same time, Cadol and Verne began work on a play called *Around the World in 80 Days*. Following a synopsis at the beginning of 1872, with Verne creating some of the characters and plot, Cadol wrote a 150-page script. On March 29, Verne started a novel of the same name, importing dialogues from the play. From June Cadol submitted the play to directors, but could not place it, and undertook to produce a condensed version. Even after Verne completed the novel and published it (November and December), the revised play had still not found a home. So Verne enlisted prolific playwright Adolphe d'Ennery (1811–99) and together they wrote a new script. For a fortnight in 1874 the two stayed together in the thermal resort of Uriage-les-Bains near Grenoble, reputed for its laxative qualities (August 31, 1892).

Cadol, understandably, blew up. First, the novel signed Verne was based on the first play, where Cadol did the bulk of the work, before the novel was begun. And Verne's collaboration with d'Ennery seems both hypocritical and dishonest, canceling out all Cadol's work, undertaken in good faith, with the additional suspicion that the second play drew from the first one. Quite justifiably, Cadol wrote two letters of complaint to the *Figaro*; and as a result, he established his right to half of Verne's receipts from the d'Ennery play, or 25 percent. However, the book continued, for whatever reason, to be deemed entirely Verne's, including the royalties, or at least the crumbs Hetzel left (*BSJV* 125:15).

Colonnader Duquesnel staged the second play at the Porte Saint-Martin Theater on November 7, 1874, in a no-expenses-spared production that included an elephant shipped over from London. The show received very good reviews from journalist Albert Wolff (*BSJV* 130:31) and the London *Times* (November 12, 1874), which praised it as one of the year's best plays in Paris. The public went absolutely wild. The play ran for 414 straight nights in the first production alone, grossing nearly FF 3 million, of which Verne got 2.5 percent, or about FF 70,000 [April 11, 1875]. In 1879, the Châtelet Theater revived the show with 11 elephants and several baskets of live snakes, and ran it, on and off, for 50 years. Verne probably got about FF 400,000 out of the ten million total: a fortune, more than he had gotten to date from his three million words for Hetzel. The iniquitous contracts not having had the foresight to cover nonbook rights, the publisher, I hope, got nothing on the play itself.

Zola madly coveted his senior's success, belatedly describing the play as "an uninterrupted procession of banalities . . . [in an] idiotic genre . . . nearly all the plot is of a rare triteness."[11] Verne must have been laughing all the way to the bank.

In 1876, Verne was already the most successful novelist in France and on the way to becoming the most popular novelist of the century, without even mentioning his triumph in the theater (*BSJV* 154:10). His runaway successes had made him a household name from Honolulu to Hong Kong and Toronto to Tierra del Fuego. But his works continued to be shunned by the journalistic and literary establishment. Perhaps influenced by the success of the plays, a few timid studies of his novels did finally begin to come out (*BSJV* 147:31), with, however, much mere paraphrase and plot summary and virtually no real analysis. Verne's name remained absent from all the encyclopedias.

Furthermore, he failed to place many of his short stories, plays, and reference works. Since a complete listing appears in the bibliography, only a few salient works can be studied here. ⟩ LOG

In 1873, while working on *The Mysterious Island*, Verne went for his first balloon ascent. The excursion from Place Longueville in Amiens, just beside the author's residence, was made with balloonist Eugène Godard, a friend of Nadar's who distinguished himself during the Siege of Paris. It was described in Verne's first-person "Ascent of the *Météore*," translated only in 2002, in Hong Kong.[12]

In 1874, Hetzel finally consented to publish a collection of Verne's short pieces, as *Dr. Ox's Experiment and Other Stories*. "A Drama in the Airs," "Master Zacharius," and "Wintering in the Ice" had been published in the 1850s; but Hetzel now censored them, cutting out many of the most interesting parts. In the only new story, "Dr. Ox," a mad scientist secretly radicalizes and sexualizes the behavior of a sleepy Flemish town by oxygenating the atmosphere. Like "Master Zacharius," the comedy explores the mind-body problem and reductionism, with mankind's highest endeavors controlled by base corporeal factors. Also included in the collection was Paul Verne's "Fortieth French Ascent of Mont Blanc," whose dullness was matched only by its title.

In the fascinating Hoffmannesque short story "Dr. Trifulgas" (1884), an egotistical doctor, who refuses to treat anyone who cannot pay, is dying, only to discover *in extremis* that the patient is himself. He has split into two personae, patient and doctor, payer and payee, but enters a sort of time loop and self-destructs. The tale is thus a study in self-absorption, but also an exploration of the logical contradictions of the Cretan Liar Paradox.

An allegorical fairy tale, "The Adventures of the Rat Family" (1891), features a "gouty rat" no longer tempted by adventure but philosophical and calm, an idealized self-portrait, following the catastrophic events of 1886, but also a recreation of the author's childhood, including the sweet shop near Holy Cross, The Gouty Rat.

Often translated as *Child of the Cavern* or *The Underground City*, *The Black Indies* (1877)—a reference to England's other Empire, under the Scottish soil—largely follows Verne's 1859 route and borrows from his experiences, with much cutting and pasting from *Backwards to Britain*.

A letter from his former supervisor Simon Ford tells engineer James Starr about the discovery of a new seam in the long-dead colliery of Aberfoyle, central Scotland. Ignoring mysterious goings-on, Starr blasts into an immense underground cavern, finding endless amounts of coal. Mining starts up again and a community of miners settles in the cavern. However, after much dangerous but mysterious sabotage, Ford's son Harry discovers a beautiful girl lying unconscious, who has never been above ground and speaks only Gaelic (!). As Harry educates her, Nell marvels at her first dawn from the peak of Arthur's Seat. As the wedding preparations get underway, they are suspended by the appearance of a dark malevolent figure, the same one haunting the tunnels. But he is revealed to be Nell's great-grandfather, previously sacked from the mine, and all ends well.

The book was originally very different. The following summary, based on a painstaking deciphering of the earliest surviving version, is exclusive to this volume.[13]

In the manuscript Verne dreamed of an industrialized "parallel world" stretching under the whole of Britain. In chapters 13–14 we discover an entire subterranean county, appropriately called "Underland," with a Coal City and surrounding settlements that are startlingly different from the "Flemish village" of the Hetzelized version. Verne indeed shows a bustling commercial metropolis and a complex network of railways reaching as far as Glasgow, plus tramway, steamboat, and telegraph systems. Underland has a thriving commercial life, with Verne providing very detailed descriptions of brand-names and institutions. Nowhere else in his 200 works does Verne demonstrate such accurate knowledge of his favorite country, presumably drawn from both personal experience and up-to-date reading of periodicals.

However, Hetzel disliked the whole idea, preferring to develop instead the love story between Harry and Nell, resulting in fraught discussions. The publisher even resorted to writing his own version of the ending, all cloying sentimentality and hackneyed cliché; having the whip hand, he won as usual.

Despite increasing age and work pressure, Verne's friendships prospered, both old and new. Some of his friends had fallen by the wayside: Béchenec had been driven mad and killed by the events of the Franco-Prussian War; Adolphe Bonamy, probably the brother of the prizewinning Nonboarder and law student, came to beg FF 50 in charity, dressed in rags and homeless, convincing Verne he would end up a common thief.[14] The author remained in touch with Wallut, Gille, Dumas, and Nadar for many decades, and even saw Caroline occasionally, perhaps because she had been widowed the same year that he had married. Many of his more recent friends were colleagues from publishing, including his illustrators, but almost never fellow authors. Although Hetzel often gave him the cold shoulder, his son, often working with him and increasingly taking responsibility in the firm, visited frequently.

Verne struck up a number of new friendships with men of note in Amiens: industrialist Édouard Gand, founder of the Industrial Society, applied mathematician Albert Badoureau, and Albert Deberly, lawyer and deputy for Amiens.[15] The Vernes' most faithful friend, Robert Godefroy, a relative of Honorine's through her first husband, was a successful lawyer and local civil servant, later deputy mayor of Amiens and prefect of the Doubs. Another was Paul Poiré (b. 1832), fellow member of the Industrial Society and, like Godefroy, a regular passenger on Verne's boat.

From about 1878 Verne rubbed shoulders with royalty. Mooring at Le Tréport he bumped into Henri d'Orléans, Count of Paris, pretender to the French throne, and great reader of his works. He and the Countess invited the author back to their place, which he enjoyed a great deal, giving them one of the manuscripts of *Twenty Thousand Leagues* in return (RD 108). Through Henri he made friends with his first cousin Gaston, Count of Eu, next-in-line for the imperial throne of Brazil. Invited to the inauguration of the Château of Eu, a few miles from Le Crotoy, Verne reportedly shoved the card in his pocket—where Honorine found it three days too late (ADF 161).

In the English manner, much of Verne's social life revolved around his clubs and societies. After his brief flirtation in the 1860s, he never rejoined a purely scientific society, but from 1864 attended the sessions of the Society of Geography, at least when in Paris, delivering lectures there on May 3, 1867 and March 20, 1868.[16]

He often dreamed of being elected to the prestigious French Academy. It had previously honored the *Magasin*, and incidentally two and one-half of Verne's novels (1867), and then all those published by August 1872, with a further award in 1874.[17] Verne attended the 1872 ceremony: when the proceedings reached his works, the audience apparently applauded so energetically that the age-old dust flew up and suffocated the author, discreetly hidden in the corner (ADF 138).

Verne's dream continued for many years. For every vacancy from 1877 to 1885 he discussed his chances with his publisher, supported by Dumas and Ernest Legouvé, feverishly calculating which amongst his and Hetzel's contacts might add their weight. However, he never actually plucked up courage to apply. In about 1880, Hetzel also thought of applying: Verne was more encouraging to his publisher than vice versa. But the Academy, while appointing several score nonentities, never came near to considering the Frenchman who perhaps contributed the most to the century's cultural activities.

As if to compensate for the coldness of the Paris institution, Verne enlisted as an active member of the Amiens Academy of Sciences, Letters, and Arts (1872). Attending nearly all the sessions, he invariably showing himself courteous in interchanges and a good listener. He read extracts from his forthcoming works and was twice elected director (1875 and 1881) (Lemire 117).

He also joined an impressive number of other local societies: the Industrial Society, the Horticultural Society, where he chaired the annual general meeting and made speeches, the Caisse d'Epargne, the Alliance Française, the Picardy Artistic and Literary Society, the Amiens Dickens Society, and a succession of clubs with well-stocked libraries (OD 188).

People continued to produce divergent appreciations of Verne's character. Physically, his boat and his success had made him more confident, even as his Demosthenes-like beard grayed, his hair thinned, and his waist thickened.[18] At five feet five, average for the time, he presented "a powerful, almost swarthy figure": "a fine type of a sailor, economical with words, a man used to commanding."[19] With his "frank expression and affable manners, but almost feminine timidity with strangers," a few interpreted his modesty and simplicity as quality of soul, as simply showing a "good man."[20] His bluntness shocked some (RD 103), but others detected refinement and sensibility, disguised under the speed with which he did everything, especially walking: "a mocking gentleness contrasting with a certain brisk brusqueness of movement. Lips a little thick, relatively sensual, but so frank . . . flared nostrils, the nose of a sleuth" (*BSJV* 130:40).

Two succinct judgments stood out: "a Breton, a Catholic, and a sailor"; and "Uncle Jules had only three passions: freedom, music, and the sea."[21] Two terms in the pronouncements differ, and only one converges.

The man did surprise those who knew only some of his facets. Verne's love of music went back to his childhood but emerged in his ability to compose music and in Nemo's "distant chords from the organ, the sad harmony of an indefinable tune, the veritable complaint of a soul wishing to break all earthly ties."[22] Other surprising facets included his at drawing and his noble status. He was in fact a talented artist, filling notebooks and manuscripts with rapid but charming sketches. He himself never seems to have referred to his (remote) aristocratic ascendance—or the title (and seal) he inherited from his father. The paradoxes in fact abounded: intelligent, skeptical, naive, internationalist, ecological, not good with children, catastrophic with women, shy, uninterested in sport, nature-loving, not very club-bable but devoted to his successive societies.

Verne took ascetism to a fault, drinking wine only occasionally, smoking only episodically, and writing in a cubbyhole. Many of his traits came from his professional activity—or had produced it—including the independence of mind, attention to detail, intellectual curiosity, low boredom threshold, capacity to throw himself entirely into his creation but forget it thereafter: "As soon as I've finished a work I'm unhappy and I think about the next one; not doing any-thing is torture" (Lemire 91).

In his practical life, Verne lacked know-how, both the suave charm to gain friends and influence people, and the street fighter's ability to battle fast-talking property agents, rapacious banks, greedy pub-lishers, and two-faced lawyers. The places he lived in, the deals he got on his boats, the extent to which he reached his planned sailing des-tinations, the problems generated by his son—all showed that he took little control of his life, that he lacked the singleness of purpose and energy of his best heroes. In contrast, his professional organiza-tion was impeccable, with clear and timely communication with the publisher, efficient filing system, successful use of available informa-tion systems, attention to detail, and timely delivery of impossible numbers of quality books. He lived to write and wrote to live.

Another trait was his changeability. From provincial to Parisian and then provincial again; the first thirty years firmly rooted on French soil, then a couple of decades spending more time offshore than on, then two further decades of Gallic isolation; campaigning against marriage and ogling anything in a skirt, then desperately seeking wedded bliss, then renouncing of both; living in, by, and for his Nantes family, then not seeing them for years on end, failing to bring Michel up properly, then arguing for decades with him, then making up again; loving the dynamism, openness, and stoicism of the Anglo-Saxons, then attacking British colonialism and American capitalism, then opening up to almost exclusively English-language journalists; seminary schoolboy, apologist for the Pope and believer that Catholics had priority for heaven, then nonattender at church for fifty years, then papal devotee and deathbed confessor; political campaigner, then ideological agnostic, then half-time politician.

It is not as if we could appeal to the works, since severe contradictions have tripped up all those seeking coherent philosophies in Verne's works. Socialists have often found Verne to be left-leaning; nationalists, pro-French; Americans, naïve, optimistic, and science oriented; Canadians, confused as to identity; Swiss, stay-at-home; and British, unintellectual and insular. Only the wisest of scholars have concluded on an essential inconclusiveness in the works. It would be unwise, in sum, to look for general tendencies as to Verne's character in his books, partly because most of the works he wrote have never been read in their original form, but mainly because the views expressed are so inconsistent as to cause total confusion.

CHAPTER 16

Freedom, Music, and the Sea:
1876–80

IN APRIL 1876, HONORINE fell critically ill with uterine hemorrhaging. Losing large amounts of blood over a fortnight, she suffered total anemia and the worst was feared for a week. On the 21st she confessed and took extreme unction, before receiving a transfusion of blood from her son-in-law, "a unique event in the history of humanity," as Verne wryly noted (RD 103). However, she got even worse. "The doctors . . . have abandoned her, giving her 48 hours to live" (April 23, 1876). By some miracle, though, she pulled through, and struggled back to health over the following months.

In order for Honorine and their daughters to be received more often in society, the family planned a magnificent all-night masked ball, the first in town for 35 years. It cost FF 4,000, which Verne would have preferred to spend on travel [April 13, 1877]. When the 350 guests arrived at the Salons Saint-Denis, mostly disguised as Verne characters, including Nadar as himself, Honorine was not there to greet them. The gynecological problem had returned (April 4, 1877)—destroying the point of the ball.

Hetzel did not come either. Verne wrote angrily "if you had, you'd have come disguised as an *imbecile,* and nobody would have recognized you" [March 11, 1877].

Three years later, Honorine again fell so gravely ill with peritonitis that the doctors once more declared her lost [March 1, 1879]. She remained very sick with pneumonia over most of the summer, undergoing repeated emetics [August 23, 1879].

On May 1, 1876, Verne took delivery of a new yacht built in Le Havre. Baptized the *St. Michel II*, the 40-foot, 19-ton, FF 13,000 sailboat boasted a crew room, dining room, cabin, and a toilet.[1]

The novelist tested its qualities on two more trips across his beloved English Channel. In June he took Suzanne's husband to Boulogne and Dover, refusing an invitation to a regatta reception by the Royal Yacht Club and the Prince of Wales.[2] In July he sailed for Cherbourg, picked up a pilot, and made for Southampton, where his lifeboat was stolen. After visiting Cowes he landed at Ryde (Isle of Wight), and took the ferry to Portsmouth to admire the warships there (PV 104). It may have been on this occasion that he traveled on to London and Brighton (*Int.* 216).

In August Verne took Michel from Saint-Valéry-sur-Somme to Dieppe, probably where Michel accidentally allowed the yacht to drift off. Jules angrily wanted to throw the fifteen-year-old into the sea, but was stopped by Delong and the crew; so he beat Michel instead (PV 106). From father and son sailed back to Le Tréport, to meet a convalescing Honorine; henceforth the Verne couple would sometimes stay in the local Hôtel de la Plage, before renting a holiday villa (PV 106).

The same year, Hetzel, for once, consented to holiday on Verne's home ground at Le Tréport. Drinking and eating too much, he seems to have had a reasonably good time, although disliking Honorine's histrionics (September 19, 1876). In November, Verne enjoyed visiting the colliery of Anzin with Hetzel's son, researching *The Black Indies* (November 11, 1876).

The years 1877–88 involved a bewildering cat's cradle of land and sea journeys, as Verne juggled with the demands of Michel, his mother, d'Ennery, and Honorine. On about May 15, 1877, he traveled to Paris to work with d'Ennery; on June 5 he went up again, and then to Mettray, near Tours, to decide about Michel's future; then to

Chantenay with his son for a couple of days; then to Amiens via Tours, Le Mans, and Rouen; and then immediately off for four or five days' sailing.[3] On July 23, he sailed from Le Havre with Michel, sacrificing nearly three weeks' work to put in at Caen, Courseulles-sur-Mer, Cherbourg, Guernsey, Perros-Guirec, Brest, and Le Croisic, before taking a carriage to his mother's.[4] He felt very disappointed at his crew's refusal to take the vessel all the way to Nantes.[5]

why?

During that stay, he and Paul visited an extravagant yacht in the shipyard on Quai de la Fosse: originally costing 100,000, it was now on sale at 55,000. He offered 40,000 but allowed himself to be browbeaten back up to 55,000 (November 1, 1877). The 100-foot, 38-ton, 100-horsepower *St. Michel III*, as it was inevitably called, had a chimney and masts, all leaning stylishly backwards. Forward was Verne's single bedroom, in light oak; aft, a mahogany living room with two sofa-bunks, two-berth bedroom, dining room, the captain's room, galley, kitchen, and crew room. Too big to enter Le Crotoy Harbor, the vessel needed ten crewmen: the sometimes overcautious captain, Charles-Frédéric Ollive (b. 1825) from Trentemoult, near Chantenay, with 25 years' experience (JJV 122); and his son as first officer, two sailors, a manservant, a cabin boy, a cook, engineer Joly, and two stokers (May 18, 1878). However, Joly was killed by a boiler explosion in Nantes just after leaving the *St. Michel* that November (November 7, 1878).

Paul came on many cruises; the two brothers, in nautical rig, gleefully helped with the maneuvers. Other regulars were Hetzel *fils*, Raoul-Duval, Verne's brothers-in-law, and assorted nephews. Jules enjoyed resting on the deck in the evenings, chatting to his companions; given the choice, he would have lived on the yacht permanently.[6] When Honorine accused him of just wanting to escape his home environment, and Hetzel disapproved for some reason, Verne defended himself by claiming to work better on board, using his portable writing-desk.

Verne stayed in Paris in the first half of April 1878, perhaps to work with Duquesnel, then fetched his new vessel from its winter port in Nantes. He headed off for Brest, then on a week's tests to Lorient and Brest again, with Paul, Gaston, and Maurice—although his wife had lain ill in bed for a month with a recurrence of the hemorrhaging problem.[7] He and Paul returned to Brest yet again on about May 20 [May 7, 1878]; and then embarked on a major navigation to, they hoped, a dozen countries in three continents.

Leaving on May 25 with Hetzel *fils* and Raoul-Duval, they headed down the Loire from Nantes, up the coast to Carnac, then southward to Vigo, Spain (June 3), arriving at the same time as a French warship (see Figure 9).

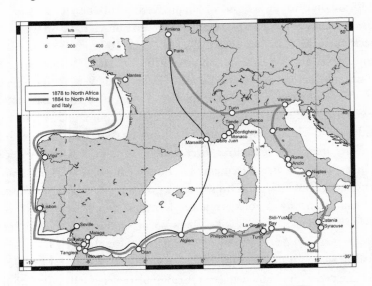

Figure 9: The Mediterranean, showing the journeys to North Africa in 1878 and to North Africa and Italy in 1884

After lunch with the captain, Hetzel borrowed a diving suit to explore the depths of Vigo Bay, where Nemo had salvaged sunken French gold pillaged from the Incas; Verne, at 50, was too old to join in.[8]

Then they turned toward Lisbon, Cadiz, Seville, and Tangiers, Morocco, including a boar hunt (June 10); and the Strait of Gibraltar, the Columns of Hercules, Gibraltar itself, Malaga, Tétouan (Morocco), and Oran. The group may have visited Mostaganem

(Algeria), shown around by Verne's cousin Captain Georges Allotte (ADF 158), as well as Algiers, with a sumptuous on-board dinner (June 24–26).[9] Verne had dreamed of reaching Rome and Constantinople but had his hopes dashed; while Paul took the *St. Michel* back to Nantes, the other three took a commercial steamer to Marseille, arriving there on July 4.[10]

With Honorine and Suzanne Verne made an excursion from Rouen down the Seine to Cherbourg and Jersey, including Hugo's house at Marine Terrace (about August 12–21); then one further sea trip.[11] He and Honorine stayed two days at Hetzel's in Rue Jacob while the publisher was away; then from September 17 the restless soul stayed a fortnight in Le Tréport.[12]

During the 1870s and '80s, Verne went back to Chantenay for brief summer visits, more often than not without his family (RD 99). During a picnic on one stay he entertained Caroline's grandchildren by exchanging the cake on his plate, deadpan, for a superb cowpat, which he then proceeded to slice up for all present. In a similar vein, if Caroline's beautiful daughter was absent when he dropped in, he would leave a chamber pot (in French a "*jules*") on the dining room table, thinking they'd know "Jules passed by, as he left his visiting card."[13] In 1879, Uncle Châteaubourg, the oldest in the extended family, died. Jules and Honorine attended the funeral: they had to, because not only was his fortune considerable, but also the various Verne branches inherited virtually everything and Jules was the oldest surviving male. Although the will was considered fair and looked after everybody's interests, long discussions were held in Sophie's apartment. To split up Châteaubourg's personal possessions and documents, lots were drawn by Anna's son, Raymond Ducrest (RD 104).

More than a dozen of the works that the Library of Congress still lists as entirely Jules Verne's, perhaps a million words, are no such thing. Verne purloined considerable parts of his published works, and was twice sued for breach of copyright and libel, escaping conviction only by twisting the truth. In some cases, he perpetrated fraud with his publisher's active connivance; but in some Hetzel probably suspected nothing.

Nineteenth-century attitudes and behavior with respect to intellectual property were different: the basic principles remained the same, but implementation difficulties meant that there was considerable leeway in practice. However, the considerably fewer works were published, increasing the probability of detection.

Around the World, where nearly everyone concerned, even modern commentators, treated the original playwright badly, should warn us that the winners write history: Verne surely trampled on the rights of many other contemporaries, sometimes dragged into it by Hetzel's commercialism but often of his own accord.

In Verne's case it worked both ways. His million words of nonfiction—as much as most writers in a lifetime—contained only three or four footnotes, although entirely dependent on written sources. But one paradox is that he used as many as 60 or 70 notes in some novels, although very few acknowledged sources, with most serving to didactically explicate his own text. For the preparation, conversely, he acted as if the novels were reference books, reading exhaustively, copiously taking notes, and inserting entire essays into the opening chapters: often a concise and informative survey of contemporary knowledge on the subject. Unfortunately this question of Verne's "internal" borrowing has hardly been scratched to date. In most cases, there is no record of the infringed authors protesting.

But fortunately the evidence lies before our eyes, for Verne often cites or mis-cites the name of the author, or else cuts and pastes so directly that Google takes you directly to it. In some works, in other

words, many plagiarism detection programs will take you more or less directly to the origin of his writing.

Four main subcategories may be identified: "internal" borrowing, where Verne recycled published sources; sections where Hetzel put his back to the plow; cases where Verne signed works he did not originate; and the works published after his death.

For the first category, as we saw, *Hatteras* simply cut and pasted entire pages from a previously published text, and *Journey to the Center of the Earth* closely followed Figuier. The London parts of *Around the World in Eighty Days* borrowed from Francis Wey, although Verne may not have realized it, because he was reusing passages from *Backwards to Britain*, and so probably forgot the original debt.

Secondly, Hetzel wrote passages for his author for *The Underground City*, *The Begum's Heritage*, and *Michel Strogoff*, inserting most of the appeals to divine providence in the latter case (CNM 204). However, the publisher's style lacked distinction, as can be seen from the following extract from his writing, never cited before: "Among the prisoners was an old woman whose very taciturnity seemed to set her apart from those sharing her fate. No complaint emerged from her lips. She resembled a statue of suffering. This woman was, however, the most closely kept and supervised, although she apparently did not notice it" (*Strogoff* II ii).

But Hetzel's ghostwriting, which may of course have been based on original drafts by Verne, paled in significance beside the third category, partial or complete ghostwriting. We saw above that *A Floating City* may conceivably have been mostly Paul Verne's work. The first documented instances occurred in 1879, when the author signed *The Begum's Heritage*, originally written by ex-Communard and escapee from New Caledonia journalist André Laurie (1844–1909), and "Mutineers of the *Bounty*," written by Gabriel Marcel then revised by Verne (*BSJV* 153:2). *The Southern Star* (1884), signed just Verne, was written by Laurie as *The Blue Diamond*, with Verne's contribution minimal. *The Wreck of the "Cynthia"* (1885) was signed by both Verne and Laurie, although Verne simply did a surface revision at proof stage. The opening chapters of "Verne's" *Geography* and nearly all of "his" *Great Navigators of the Eighteenth Century* (1879) and *Voyagers of the Nineteenth Century* (1880) owed little to the novelist.

In nearly every case the initial idea came from the publisher. In a few cases Verne did pass the text sufficiently through his own imagination for them to have at least an authentic flavor. In some instances the public was not fooled, protesting that the texts differed from previous ones; but in many cases the critics were taken in, producing extensive commentary on what are now considered mediocre texts.

From 1889, the final category, Verne aided and abetted Michel, by first signing his name to the science fiction short story "In the Year 2889," although entirely by his son, and then by giving him the idea for a novel (October 12, 1895 to Paul), probably *The Thompson Travel Agency* (1907), although the author subsequently listed it as his own work.[14] All of the production of the years 1905–14 (see Epilogue below) was, to varying degrees, by Michel. But before condemning the son's subterfuge, we must take into account the fact that the father initiated the passing-off process himself.

Inevitably, the shoe switched to the other foot. Verne was sued for plagiarism by a Léon Delmas. Under the pseudonym René de Pont-Jest, he had published a short story called ">La Tête de Mimers" in the *Revue contemporaine* of September 1863. The hero is German; he finds the document that causes the journey in an old book; it is written in runic characters; a shadow indicates where to look; and the journey takes place underground—all as in *Journey to the Center of the Earth*. The affair dragged on more than a decade until a court case in 1877, which Verne won: even though the similarities are not very extensive, Verne perhaps did read the short story, although categorically denying it (*BSJV* 135:13).

The most public pilfering of both Verne's reputation and text was performed by Offenbach, or rather by the three librettists of the four-act opera *Journey to the Moon* (1875), for which the composer did the music. Not only did the opening borrow from *From the Earth to the Moon* but also the conclusion from *Journey to the Center of the Earth* (November 2, 1875). Did it make it worse that one of the authors was Verne's friend Philippe Gille? In any case the author felt understandably upset, both on principle and because it stopped him attempting a similar adaptation, with even the publisher agreeing it was plagiarism (November 3, 1875). But Hetzel did nothing—unless he reached secret accommodation, since the same Offenbach, again with Gille as the main collaborator, soon composed music for an opera of Verne's "Dr. Ox" (1877), this time with approval. The 6 percent of the FF 120,000 receipts was split three ways, with Verne getting FF 2,400.

An affectionate homage and spoof of Verne, Albert Robida's *The Most Extraordinary Journeys of Saturnin Farandoul*, appeared in 1879. Again the novelist was aghast, citing the legal principle that you couldn't borrow famous characters just like that. But again nothing was done about it.

While his father was busy writing and sailing, Michel had grown from a turbulent toddler into a tumultuous teenager. Verne expressed permanently shock at his attitude: "infinitely vain," "absolute lack of respect," "intractable," "this child, who is 25 at 16, has a precocious perversity," "evil nature, a braggart of vice . . . absolutely devoid of common sense," the "doctors agree he has no degree of responsibility for his acts."[15] So aggressive did Michel's behavior become as to turn the whole family upside down: "several times" he "moved to attack" someone in authority.[16] Ducrest states that he behaved violently towards his female cousins; later Michel's half-sisters refused to see him; and one of his books graphically depicts an assault and rape of a half-sister, avoided by a whisker.[17] The violence, in other words, may have involved him forcing his attentions on a close relative.

At the end of his tether, Verne had Michel imprisoned for eight months in the detention center of Mettray, near Tours, under the general supervision of famous psychiatrist Dr. Blanchard. Harshness having failed, and seriously afraid of "madness or suicide," the novelist tried gentler means, which simply made matters worse: "I've just received from Michel the most *horrible* letter a father has ever received!"[18] As a result of his unbearable anguish, he broke down: "poor Verne is suffering horribly. He threw himself on my couch sobbing."[19]

The father tried taking Michel to Chantenay for a stable home environment [June 16, 1877]. Given the initial success of the experiment, he took the radical decision in August of 1877 to transfer his household to Nantes and send Michel, conceivably after St. Stanislas, to the Collège Royal, now the Lycée de Nantes.[20] The Verne family moved into a rented apartment at 1 Rue Suffren, on the corner of Jean-Jacques Rousseau, directly opposite Paul's at no. 13.[21] The convalescing Honorine had reportedly to make her way alone to Nantes (JJV 128).

However, Michel fell into bad company and got into debt. In desperation, Verne had him brought before a judge and again imprisoned (January 20, 1878). Then the young man was taken by force to Bordeaux, entrusted to a merchant marine captain acquaintance of Paul's with Verne anxiously looking on, and on February 4 packed off to the East Indies for 15 months. His behavior continued on the ship, for he raised his fist against a superior officer.[22]

Only in September 1878, strangely, did the Vernes move back to Amiens (September 1, 1878). When Michel returned, his father took him on nealy all his boat trips, including the Scottish epic. Michel, still a minor, soon fell in love with an actress three years his senior, Thérèse Tâton. However, he generally behaved as badly as ever, "to the extent that his family feared to leave him alone with cousins of either sex" (RD 104). Verne listed "dissipations, crazy debts, horrifying theories . . . desire to grab money by every possible means, threats, etc."; Dr. Blanchard, "a small dose of indisputable madness and a frightening perversity" (October 4, 1879). That same autumn, Michel unsuccessfully requested permission to marry Thérèse.

Things finally reached such a head that Verne decided to expel his son: "He's got his room in town, eats in lodgings, and does nothing" (December 9, 1879). In fact Michel, now a "slender, elegant, blonde young man," was piling up huge IOUs, which Verne had to explain to the police chief and eventually pay back, FF 20,000 ($60,000) in 1880 alone.[23] Possibly to Verne's secret relief, Michel then eloped and cohabited with Thérèse [April 6, 1880]. Although the son made an honest woman of her in 1884, Verne still disapproved—and skipped the wedding. The same year Michel ran away with 17-year-old Jeanne Reboul, not telling her he was married, and soon had two illegitimate babies with her (June 4, 1885). The distraught new grandmother wanted to sue the son for corruption of a minor, but Verne received her visit rather coldly [October 17, 1885]. As the novelist grew fonder of Thérèse, and took her in (June 4, 1885), Michel divorced her and married Jeanne.

Verne's exasperation no doubt consisted of equal parts of apprehension and jealousy.

CHAPTER 17

Salvation through Work: 1879–83

VERNE MADE ALL HIS EFFORTS on the *Geography* in vain. He did not even prepare the revised edition of 1876, farmed out to the professional geographer Edmond-Yvon Dubail. Hetzel must have profited, however, for in the following years he made the novelist work on other encyclopedic projects. The trilogy *Discovery of the Earth* (1870), *The Great Navigators of the Eighteenth Century* (1879), and *The Voyagers of the Nineteenth Century* (1880) attempted to cover the history of exploration from the origins to the 1830s. In the end, although signing the finished product, Verne paid Gabriel Marcel to do volumes 2 and 3 for him (CNM 183). The opening chapter, "Celebrated Travelers before Homer: Moses (1645 B.C.), Ulysses (1270), Jason (1263)," was one of the most interesting, as it attempted to apply textual methods to the Bible. However, this chapter was cut, perhaps because Verne argued that much of the scriptures was not historical fact (*BSJV* 142:56).

As Hetzel grew older, his comments on Verne's novels grew more critical and his meddling worse. For *Michel Strogoff*, he worried tremendously about sales . . . in Russian. Although the fourth contract had split translation rights 50–50, the fifth placed them back in limbo, and logically therefore 100 percent Verne's. But that still did not prevent Hetzel from grabbing some of the derisory income (*Int.*

86). The publisher's sudden interest in Russia probably stemmed from his ex-mistress, Marko Vovchok, Verne's Russian translator, whom we met as a contender for mistress status in Switzerland. With Hetzel's interfering ways, he showed the manuscript of *Strogoff* to three different people: novelist Turgenev, Prince Orlov, and a mysterious "Count de ***" ([September 16, 1875], September 2, 1875). Most of the resulting comments were unconstructive, concerning geographical implausibility or political sensibility, especially regarding the Tsar of All the Russias. Although objecting to most of them, Verne accepted the political ones.[1] He needn't have bothered, though, as Hetzel just redlined anyway and, over Verne's formal objection, added a note saying the novel was mere fiction (in the *Magasin*). Also, despite a last-minute change of title that Verne opposed, from *Courier of the Tsar*, the Russian translation was banned in any case,[2] proving the publisher right to have worried but wrong to have demanded all the cuts.

Verne never gave up his belief he could make a successful playwright. The runaway success of *Around the World* vindicated him after three decades and over the following years he devoted considerable energy to a variety of projects.

His *Nephew from America*, written with Wallut a dozen years before, opened in April 1873 to a modest success, praised notably by Zola (OD 56). Since some of the money went to Cadol, he may have had a part in revising it.

Perhaps to compensate for the failure of the *Hatteras* play, Verne planned a work in 1875 that would "summarize the Extraordinary Journeys" and "embark all our chaps—Fergusson, Aronnax, Fogg, Clawbonny, etc.—and . . . sail them across the world on a 'heavier-than-air' " [August 4, 1875]. It sounded like an "insanity," as Hetzel *fils* kindly said (February 11, 1880) to his father, an attempt by a past-it writer to squeeze one last drop out of his aging heroes, while at the same time capitalizing on his (false) reputation for scientific prophecy.

D'Ennery, the architect of the previous triumph, had proved

difficult to work with, so for the following plays the two often collaborated at distance. Although Hetzel pressed Verne to travel down to Cap d'Antibes to work on *Captain Grant's Children*, he felt reluctant to do so, saying the play bored him; somehow, however, he and d'Ennery reached a *modus operandi* to complete a rather insipid play, little to do with the novel (1878).[3] Most of the reviewers panned it (JD 328).

The idea of a *Strogoff* play may have antedated the novel.[4] In any case, Verne mentioned the idea to Duquesnel, who obtained requested exclusivity on the stage production (Lemire 136). Accordingly, in February 1880, despite his earlier refusal, Verne spent a few weeks in Cap d'Antibes collaborating on both *Strogoff*, perhaps following a scenario by Duquesnel, and his crazy 1875 idea, under the title *Journey through the Impossible*.[5]

Strogoff was put on at the Châtelet in November the same year with 30 horses on stage. It was a huge triumph. With revivals running for decades, total French-language receipts amounted to FF 7 million (*Int.* 86). In 1881 four different stage productions ran in New York.[6] Verne perhaps made about a hundred thousand francs.

The fantasy drama *Journey through the Impossible* (1882) did turn out catastrophic. Four of the greatest early heroes came back to life in unrecognizable form—Nemo had already been done to death in *The Mysterious Island*. The critics, quite justifiably, lambasted it.

Forty years after writing "the instinct for the theater is pushing me," Verne still felt at heart a dramatist: "I adored the stage and all connected with it, and the work that I have enjoyed the most has been my wirting for the stage."[7] However, the fantastic successes of *Around the World* and *Strogoff* would be the last, despite further attempts with *Keraban the Inflexible* (1883), *Mathias Sandorf* (1887),[8] and *Tribulations of a Chinese in China* (1888–90). *Keraban* in particular got atrocious reviews: the hero was "an incredible cretin," "unbearable," his creator just "as obstinate."[9]

Due to the greater media attention, myths began to sprout about Verne at this time. With inappropriate presentations from his publisher but no backing from the literary establishment, he was forced

[handwritten annotation: × the term will not be invented]

[handwritten annotation: ?]

[handwritten annotation: forced]

into the role of technology fanatic. But in no case could Verne be considered a science fiction writer. One good reason was that few of the Extraordinary Journeys involved any science; and another, that the events nearly always happened just before the present. A significant number of the works did depend on transport, whether underground, underwater, or in the air. But Verne preferred low-tech. His first four vehicles were balloon, raft-power, sailing-ship, and dog-sled. *Around the World in Eighty Days* went out of its way to avoid any technological extrapolation, reverting to elephants or wind-sled each time the railway failed. Science fiction, above all, was an absurd label, since . . . it would not be invented for another 60 years.

[handwritten annotation: × /]

The real thrust of Verne's works, their raison d'être, was to explore the globe. If a genre classification really was necessary, he fell into that of travel or adventure. All the Extraordinary Journeys in the Known and Unknown Worlds (as Hetzel baptized them in 1866) dealt with an "elsewhere." Even his first completed book-length narrative, *Backwards into Britain*, had been a voyage of discovery: Verne described his excitement at the idea of a myth-laden Caledonia, with every hill and street redolent with memories: an excitement specifically historical and literary.

Although some of Verne's books after the age of 50 dealt with conventional historical or geographic themes, once in a while he produced a surprising gem, apparently from nowhere—perhaps from his own life. In *Tribulations of a Chinese in China* (1879) Verne's vision was rich and detailed. Unlike most European writers of the period, he was actively Sinocentric, with a Chinese hero, or rather antihero, living a Chinese life in China. His cultural, historical, political, sociological, and linguistic information and commentary foregrounded a humorous novel of travel and adventure.

The novel centers on Kin-Fo, young, westernized, and bored with life in spite of good advice from his elderly philosophy teacher, former *[handwritten annotation: ?]* Taiping Wang. Kin-Fo has announced his marriage to young widow Lé-Ou, but when the stock exchange crashes, he insures himself heavily and decides to end his life. Wang promises to kill him before the insurance policy runs out. However, Kin-Fo discovers his fortune is not lost after all: he flees but gets a letter from Wang explaining that he has entrusted the suicide note to a ruthless Taiping. Kin-Fo immediately sets out to buy off the thug, who instead captures him. Packed in a box for an endless voyage, he experiences every torment of a man about to die. Blindfold, he bravely asks to be put out of his misery—only to find himself at home, surrounded by his friends. Wang engineered the whole implausible plot to add excitement to Kin-Fo's life. Healed from his lethargy, with charming Lé-Ou at his side, he faces a new life.

The novelist emphasized his wide reading on China, adding, obscenely: "I've plunged into the Celestial Empire to the very tip of my tail. It has grown nine spots or buttons like a mandarin of the first class" (October 13, 1878). In fact as early as 1863, Verne had published "A Chinese Song," featuring a Tanka boat girl. It was writer Théophile Gautier who almost single-handedly introduced French intellectuals to Chinese language and culture. Given that Gautier had known Verne since at least 1853, written the first full-length review of a Verne work, and gone yachting with Hetzel, he may have been the source of Verne's interest for the Middle Kingdom.

"The Voluntary Assassinee," as Verne called the book, was originally set in the United States, with American characters (April 12, 1878). Hetzel baldly rejected the title: "suicided, assassinated are only labels, titles not to be kept" (September 11, 1878). The ending, where Kin-Fo is brought back home without realizing and returns to a life of marriage and hard work, was written by Hetzel. The publisher omitted to tell Verne that the ideas came from his son.

V's or H's ?

Verne's sexuality constituted one of the great enigmas of his life. From his adolescence, when he made eyes at every girl he met, through the repeated rebuffs by well-brought-up young women, to the burning desire to get married "eyes closed," heterosexual desire clearly governed much of his life. Confirmation was provided by the repeated visits to accommodating madams, the whirlwind romance with Honorine, and the tantalizing hints at mistresses in Paris, Amiens, or Switzerland.

But at the same time, an inescapable undercurrent emerges, with a remarkable number of hints, none conclusive in itself but significant when laid end to end. The all-male boarding schools, Paul as "a mademoiselle" (July 15, 1859, to Pierre), the affectionate childless uncles as "unmarried husbands," Genevois's rumored preference, the mixing of fresh adolescents and mature adults in the Nonboarders Club, Eleven Bachelors, and Colonnaders, the mincing parody of the Lyric diva, Verne's resemblance to his "pretty, pretty, pretty" sister, the idea of suckling the prince imperial, the transvestite longings—"How I'd have loved to be a woman!"[10]—the mixing up of "Mlle" and "M. de Viane," or the romantic poems dedicated to members of the same sex—all indicated at least a bisexual undercurrent.

In Verne's artistic milieu, homosexuality remained an accepted fact of life. Even the introduction of a friend to prostitution and the Bachelor dwelling on the unsavory aspects of female anatomy may have bisexual connotation. One more substantial trope was Hignard, rumored to be a homosexual: the shared boarding school, the common British and Scandinavian hotel rooms, the joint composition of a half-dozen works; the all-male skinny-dipping in icy Portobello; Hignard's habit of insisting on "walking behind me" ("Joyous Miseries"); and the give-away habit of using "we," without needing to name names.

Verne consciously camped up homosexuality, for his letters vibrated with innuendo: the hose stretching out, the nozzle standing up, the flexible tube extending, the need to close his mouth and open his . . . ; "I hug your [behind] for you"; "we'll mutually electrify each other"; "at the end of month I'll fall into your arms and we'll chat"; "I feel a burning desire to embrace you, my dear Hetzel, it's ages since we rubbed our skins together, and it's making me itch."[11] On one occasion, Verne walked off with his publisher's tie: "it's almost as funny as if I'd walked off in your underpants!" (April 23, 1869). Hetzel engendered systematic similes of "marriage"; in Verne's style, the very metaphors would multiply like tomcats, all openly revealing their networks of desire—here the link between getting hitched and finding "the richest of partners."

Did the writer compensate for his frustrations by channeling the sensuality back into his writing? Certainly the rampant desire, evident also in his letters, forms part of a generalized and throbbing pansexuality. A third tendency, then, which subsumes and transcends the first two, is a repressed desire, localized nowhere or everywhere, attached incongruously to throbbing earth-mothers or ancient pianos or aged aunts or orally fixated double-entendres.

Three biographical bestsellers derived their interest from a homosexual Verne, but without a shred of evidence, apart from the authors', admittedly homosexual, intuition. One desperate biographer fantasized a one-night stand with a ravishing Spanish Jewess wherein Verne simultaneously lost his virginity and proved her greatest lover ever.[12] Among Vernians controversy has raged from Caroline to Herminie as the epicenter of his frustrated longings and then back to Caroline again—surely Marie is due to have her day soon?

The works do provide, it is true, a treasure trove of sly sexual hints, humming as they are with desire, innuendo, and imagery, from the "good boy's . . . exercise of the fourth finger" while "compromising one of his most charming students,"[13] to the climax of *The Green Ray*, in Fingal's cave, where each successive stage of sex between Oliver Sinclair and Helena Campbell is simulated. Chevalier and Hetzel allowed surprisingly open allusion to bestiality and masturbation to slip in, like coyotes mating with women or the man who "felt a sort of itch in his right hand. / Instinctively, his fingers closed and took hold of a slightly knobbly cylindrical body of reasonable size, that they were certainly in the habit of manipulating."[14] *Journey to the Center of the Earth* focuses on the penetration of the orifices of an explicitly female earth, and abounds with daggers, pillars, geysers, burning eruptions, etc., mixed with much digestive and excretory

imagery. What the fiancée does for the novel's young hero is quite
explicit. Again, the elephant in *Around the World* is in "musth," an
uncontrollable paroxysm of sexuality, which Passepartout deliberately
provokes.

Verne, in sum, greatly enjoyed ambiguously bisexual flirting; and
his sexuality was not fully heterosexual, diverted here, there, and
everywhere. The Pope, the great-niece, and Disney's sanitized,
neutered Verne are therefore a travesty. But it would be a foolhardy
biographer that leaped upstream from the books to the life. Although
Verne expressed strong urges, their exact nature remains unclear.
However strong the urge, we cannot observe, with a conveniently
angled lens, what went on in his 40 successive home bedrooms and
hundreds of hotel rooms.

Given the excitement of Verne's 1859 journey to Scotland, it seems
inevitable that he would go back for a third time. 1879 was another
crucial trip, for Verne headed to quasi-sacred places that had inspired
the whole Romantic movement. Setting out with Godefroy, Gaston,
and Michel on 1 July, the *St. Michel III* fled from a storm in the port
of Boulogne (July 1–6). The expedition put in at Yarmouth, meeting
more stormy weather, before reaching Leith, the port of Edinburgh,
on July 13. The ship arrived in a torrential downpour, with three
inches of rain in a day and the rivers reaching their highest point for
decades. Hetzel *fils* now joined them for a fortnight. Catching the
train for Glasgow, the five men set off on the "Royal Route" that
Queen Victoria had traced in 1847, the itinerary also followed in *The
Green Ray* (see Figure 10).

First they took the fast steamship *Columba* in perfect weather,
seeing Helensburgh and Rothesay [February 26, 1882], although
much of the ship swarmed with rowdy Glasgow holidaymakers. To
pass through the 15-lock Crinan Canal, crowded with fishing smacks,
they must have switched to the 270-passenger track-boat *Linnet*,
where top-deck passengers had a 360-degree view of the desolate,
treeless mountains. Probably taking the SS *Glengarry* from Ballanoch,

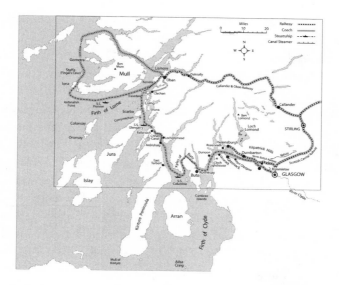

Figure 10: The West Coast of Scotland, showing the route followed in *The Green Ray* and Verne's near-identical 1879 journey.

Verne and his companions gaped at the awe-inspiring Corryvrekan Whirlpool off Jura. This was the second biggest in the world, with a roar audible from six miles and standing waves of up to fifteen feet, the site of a famous wreck. In the village of Oban they presumably stayed at the Caledonian Hotel, a luxurious Georgian pile on the harbor front, marveling at the lilting, elven Gaelic all around.[15] They may have taken a carriage to the island of Seil to admire the famed sunset.

From Oban they steamed, presumably on the SS *Pioneer*, to "world-forgotten Iona" (*Int.* 105). Then to Staffa, possibly visiting the cave near Clamshell Bay, with Ben More soaring to more than 3,000 feet behind. But the highlight of the visit was a boat trip to nearby Fingal's Cave, a world-famous magnet for artists, including Mendelssohn: "This vast cavern, with its mysterious shadows, dark, weed-covered chambers and marvellous basaltic pillars, produced upon me a most striking impression" (*Int.* 216). After a stop on Mull, the party headed around the island, the furthest point north, and back down the Sound of Mull (July 29, 1879), admiring the suddenly calm waters in the golden sunshine and heavenly blue sky.

For the return, they journeyed by coach from Oban through the west Highlands to Dalmally railhead, passing the nearly complete Callander and Oban railroad and the Falls of Cruachan; then by the new train through spectacular landscape to Callander and Stirling, and back to Edinburgh (July 20–23). But the sea was so bad that they twice had to return to port, before worked their way down to Yarmouth (July 24), Dover, Le Tréport, and finally Le Havre.[16] Despite the awesome scenery, perhaps the wildest in Europe, the whole journey to Scotland, Verne confessed, created "a series of worries and problems" [August 7, 1879]. His anxiety probably stemmed from the boat or the atrocious east-coast weather, but perhaps also Gaston or Michel.

On July 29, apparently without bothering to go home, Verne and Michel sailed off again to Brest, where they lost the ship's cannon but admired the Fleet's maneuvers, and thence to Chantenay (*St. M.*) Ten days later the writer took his mother and lots of young relatives sailing (PV 132); two days after that, he, Paul, and Michel headed out once more, seeing friend Lorois at Brest and reaching Lorient for the launching of the *Dévastation*, France's most formidable ironclad.[17] From his mother's, Verne steamed away yet again on August 26, carrying off his former flame Caroline. The *St. Michel* was rammed in Saint-Nazaire Harbor, causing Verne, Paul, Michel, presumably Caroline—and perhaps her pretty daughter—to rush on deck in their nightshirts: the novelist's 100-ton vessel had lost its bowsprit, bow, and anchors, and tacked dangerously around the harbor all night.[18] Saint-Nazaire was unrecognizable from the fishing village where Jules had first seen and tasted the sea 39 years previously. In between, he had featured the port in the opening chapter of *Twenty Thousand Leagues*, though it was cut by the editor.

A fortnight later, Verne left Nantes one last time, heading for Brest yet again. After a final sea trip, he rented a holiday home near Le Tré-port with Honorine for the first week of October; then traveled to Paris on about the 10th, where he often stayed at Hetzel's place.[19]

In 1881, Verne navigated to Saint-Malo, and later to Ramsgate with a mysterious male passenger. But the main event of the year was another mammoth cruise, with regulars Paul, Gaston, and Godefroy, this time to England, Belgium, Holland, Germany, Denmark, and Sweden. Sailing on June 1st, they visited Deal, where Verne drank a curious combination of beer, sherry, and whiskey, and Yarmouth, where Verne took a tram to Gorleston (PV 130). After staying in Rotterdam (June 5–9), sailing around Denmark was too risky, hence "to cross Holstein by canal we removed the bowsprit" so the vessel could squeeze into the locks (June 18, 1881). The four sailed up the Eider to, successively, Hamburg, Kiel (in Denmark last time, but now German), and Copenhagen, where they spent nearly a week, plus a day-trip to Helsinborg. They had longed to reach Stockholm and Christiania, but now simply headed back to Antwerp (June 20), Deal, Ryde, Portsmouth, Cherbourg, and Saint-Malo (July 4).[20]

That same month, for about the first time, Hetzel consented to sail, heading with Verne along the Normandy coast to Saint-Malo. It may have been during that trip that the *May Fly* rammed the *St. Michel*, dragging it off its anchors. The same year even Honorine agreed to a trip to Ramsgate and Dover, with a large number of friends (PV 143).

In 1883–85, Verne went to Paris at least five times, partly to see Dumas and pursue his dream of entering the French Academy and partly to keep an eye on a revival of *Around the World*. He stayed in the Hôtel d'Angleterre, in the same street as Hetzel's press, bookshop, and town house, often dining with Massé, d'Ennery, or Larochelle (JD 342). Slipping out early to avoid hangers-on, he would climb on the top deck of a bus and head to rehearsals of his plays or the Librairie Nouvelle bookstore.[21] Verne repeatedly asked his publisher to write that his presence in Paris was "absolutely necessary," but not to send his letter to Amiens—at the very least a sign of chafing against Honorine's tight leash.[22] Since Hetzel now spent much time on the Riviera, there may have been an illicit reason for the visits.

All the while the indefatigable author continued to produce his contractual two volumes per year. Indeed, in the 1880s he began to move ahead of the game, creating a backlog.

A few of the works written, or at least begun, have not been located to date. In 1873, Verne was "preparing *The Marvels of Science*, a 'grand mechanism' . . . with staging helped not only by painting, velvet, silk, and the ballet, but the dynamic agents of physics, chemistry, and mechanics."[23] At some juncture he published a short work about the Picard peasantry, full of local color and religion, entitled "Confitebor," "corrected" by an Amiens editor to "Confiteor" (Lemire 145).

In *The Green Ray* (1882), set partly in the Hebrides, the brothers Melvil, virtual Siamese twins, are bachelors "with no regrets" and with a strong homosexual flavor, being indeed called "Papa Sam and Mamma Sib."[24] Their character came from Ossian; to supplement his memories of his three trips, Verne ordered photographs of the main scenes.[25]

Verne had started off as an ardent Anglophile and Scotophile. His first novel kicked off in London, his second one initially appeared as *The British at the North Pole*, and a score of others had British heroes. Postcolonial critics have gleefully extracted Verne's occasional later critical remarks on British colonial policy; but have rarely gone to the end of their logic. His attacks on U.S. expansionism and Americans abroad seemed equally trenchant and probably more extensive. Two book-length examples involving nefarious American capital were *Propeller Island*, where a pseudo-colony sails the South Pacific, and *Topsy-Turvy*, where greedy financiers attempt to melt the North Pole.

In addition, the evolution in Verne's attitude focused on national policy, rather than individuals, and on Britain as a whole, rather than its northern part in particular. Scotland remained in fact exempt from the change, with invariably sympathetic descriptions of both the country and the people.26

While it is true that Verne occasionally noted the negative effects of late nineteenth-century colonialism, he also ascribed benefits to the French, British, and American presence abroad. Very rarely did he suggest as a solution the independence of a third-world colony. With the general exception of "the only God-given country," his mocking attacks on overbearing or ridiculous individuals encompassed all nationalities.27

As the years went by, Verne continued to produce his novels with exemplary regularity. *The Archipelago on Fire* (1884), about Greece's fight for independence, originally had a radically different ending from the published one.28 *Mathias Sandorf* (1885), set on the Adriatic, describes a dramatic near-shipwreck off Malta, drawing on Verne's own experience.29

Robur-the-Conqueror (1886) centers on the still-vigorous struggle between the "lighter-than-air" and "heavier-than-air." Ever since 1863, Verne had believed powered aircraft would win out, since only they could be steered, while adopting balloons as tried and trusted technology in three of his works. But here he goes further, in one of his first novels set in the future, by having a propeller-driven aircraft fight a balloon (in the manuscript—in the Hetzelized version it has to save it (4 Jun. *85*)). His craft remains memorable for its ship-like characteristics and 37 mast-mounted propellers, which leave the passengers' late-Victorian headgear unruffled. Robur is a rebel, a spiritual descendant of Nemo, a man whose aeronautical ideas in the end prove too innovative for his own good. The concluding hope that posterity would recuperate and vindicate the failure of all his dreams was, however, inserted by Hetzel.30

As Jules Verne approached sixty, his life seemed to be on cruise control. His income soared heavenwards, mainly due to the *Around the World* and *Strogoff* stage productions. Even his income from

Hetzel had tripled, reaching FF 40,000 a year.[31] His literary output stayed at an enviable level, with novels that would remain in print for centuries. Nevertheless, he felt the strain:

> Obviously, I'll still keep as much as possible to the geographical and scientific, since that's the aim of the complete works; but . . . I'll give maximum body to the novels I still need to do by using everything my imagination gives me, within the rather restricted milieu where I'm forced to have my being [December 2, 1883].

In addition, and as his school reports no doubt concluded, his personal life left much room for improvement.

CHAPTER 18

Home Front: 1882–90

FROM OCTOBER 1882, the Vernes rented 2 Rue Charles Dubois, at the intersection with Boulevard Longueville and one block further up the railroad line. However, the writer continued to receive his mail in Longueville for the rest of his life and Hetzel referred to a New Year gift for "Mme Verne's new house."[1] On this slender evidence it has been suggested Jules may have lived apart from Honorine for the 1880s and '90s.

We in fact know little about the dynamics of the couple. Although the sole surviving letter from Honorine to Jules seems relatively affectionate, ending "goodbye, I kiss you as I love you," it is signed with a frigid "H. Verne."[2] They had in fact gone through considerable travails, including everything to do with Michel, the death of their four-year-old grandson Tony, and the loss of many nephews.[3] Smaller matters they were no doubt able to laugh off, like the newspaper articles which appeared from 1875 making Jules Verne a Polish Jew naturalized as Julius de Verne—without realizing that the legend would run for a good sixty years, almost as ineradicable as bird flu.

Certainly their characters contrasted, the husband controlled and withdrawn, the wife carrying things to extremes, not hiding her feelings, even frequently bursting into tears (September 19, 1876). Also, Jules had admitted that "life in Paris with my wife, such as you know her, was impossible" (April 4, 1877). In addition, his wife showed remarkably little understanding of his literary aims, committing blunders in the increasing numbers of interviews with journalists, for instance describing the novelist as a predictor of technological marvels or women as absent from his works. In sum, the couple showed considerable dissent, but seems to have struggled to at least keep up appearances. While Honorine's view of the situation has not survived, Verne later concluded that marriage in general, and his own in particular, constituted "an immense and irreparable folly," which had blighted his entire life (August 14, 1893, to Paul).

The new house was a spacious combination of elegance and comfort in countrified surroundings. Protected by a mossy wall, the sandy courtyard led to a garden with impeccable lawns on the left, the central kitchen and two-story servants' quarters in the middle, and on the right the two-, three-, and four-story house, approximately 2,000 square feet. Via four curved steps leading to a glass-plated hall filled with palms and flowering shrubs, one entered the living and dining rooms, rarely used since most meals were taken in the servants' quarters (JJV ix). The opulently carpeted living room, on the corner of Dubois and Longueville, boasted a wood fire, chandeliers, great clocks and mirrors, oils of Jules and Honorine, and an oriental vase (JJV ix). On the right were a billiards room, a smoking room, and an office. A gaslit spiral staircase in a circular tower took one up, past Honorine's second-floor domain, to the library, running along Dubois. With portraits of explorers and a large table usually piled with periodicals, books covered three walls to the ceiling (*Int.* 45). Here there were also housed cardboard pigeon-holes containing more than 20,000 index cards culled from Verne's reading, including the 20-odd periodicals he subscribed to: "all the documents accumulated since his youth," including information sent by Paul and other relatives.[4]

The contents of the library provided insight into Verne's reading. In addition to Poe, Cooper, Scott, Dickens, and other favorites, it gave pride of place to Homer, Virgil, and Montaigne, Arago's seventeen volumes, two of Garcet's books, two or three works by science journalist Figuier, atlases, Malte-Brun's *Universal Geography*, a complete run of the *Tour du monde* and *Bulletin de la Société de Géographie*, and all of geographer Élisée Reclus's works, as well as a book dedicated to Verne by Maupassant, "the greatest psychologist the world has ever known."[5] The writer also delighted in Stendhal, rereading *The Charterhouse of Parma* "for the 20th time," *Sapho* by Daudet, and Maupassant's short stories—"but don't let your wife read them!" (August 14, 1884).

From the fifth floor room at the top of the tower a ladder led to a belvedere roof: Verne tried working there in a lean-to, surveying all of Amiens, but found it too hot (*BSJV* 65–66:53). In contrast with the library the adjoining study was small and monastic. A single two-paned window with lace curtains and external shutters looked north over Longueville and onto the mature trees of the public garden, the main Paris–London railroad, and the cathedral spire in the distance. Above Verne's hearth small statues of Molière and Shakespeare kept watch, with a gaslight, a bright blue watercolor showing the *St. Michel III* in the Bay of Naples, and further portraits of explorers. The carpeted, trapezoidal room was maniacally tidy, with only one padded armchair, a broad low metal bed in the corner, and later an electric lamp on a side table. The L-shaped table, made of deal and sometimes covered with green baize, held just Verne's ink-bottle, pen holder, and current manuscript.[6] Since the Paris Meridian passed through Amiens, the author would argue, half-seriously, that it cut through his house and even his desk.[7] Verne lived day and night in this 150-square foot room, with hardly space to push back the chair and not a patch on his 1851 eighth-floor apartment. To tell the truth, he felt lost in the rest of the house (JJV 199).

In the long, deathly quiet evenings, did Verne dream of his care-free 1850s existence? His present metronomic, monastic life certainly contrasted with the overlapping networks of his youth: the Non-boarders, Bachelors, and Colonnaders, Dumas, Arago, and Nadar, musicians, writers, and artists, Bretons, reactionaries, and homosexuals. Somehow the gay student had become a tired recluse.

This leads in turn to the question of Verne's hometown. Amiens and Nantes have long trumpeted the novelist as theirs, with the paradoxical result that Verne's Paris decades have been neglected. And yet the capital was the center of the world, the heart of the Old Continent, the place where Lucien de Rastignac issued his famous challenge "*A nous deux!*," the literary and scientific focus of every nation's intellectuals. Verne was an undergraduate there, twice a stockbroker, almost a lawyer, a playwright, and then a prolific novelist. He may have lost his virginity in the cold-hearted city, had married, had his only child, and written his greatest masterpieces there. Verne's Paris: the phrase sounds incongruous, presumptuous even. The city belongs to Balzac, Baudelaire, even Beckett. Yet *Paris in the Twentieth Century* never left that city and the author was described as "a Parisian to his finger-ends" (*Int.* 95). The most successful books ever published in Paris were *Twenty Thousand Leagues* and *Around the World*. Although of course born in Nantes, and spending longest in Amiens, Verne wrote little about those cities: for me, he will always be a Parisian deep down, despite his love-hate relationship and despite the city's ignoring of its most famous son.

The 1884 trip to the Mediterranean formed Verne's travel swan song. If he had visited many of the places in 1879, only this time did he see Italy, a special place to him since his early sojourn(s). Whatever his religious fervor, he had a soft spot for Rome and the Vatican, focus of "The Siege of Rome" and *Alexander VI* and favorite destination of his devout relatives. Only this time did his wife come, ignoring her customary seasickness. And only this time did Verne "come out," exposing himself to the full glare of publicity and exploitation by the diplomatic machinery.

Verne had bought his massive yacht to visit "Constantinople, St. Petersburg, Norway, and Iceland" (November 1, 1877), but reached none of these on it. The Mediterranean represented a bourgeois compromise: "a lazy little lake" you could almost see across, much less interesting than "the Northern Ocean" (*Int.* 19). To tell the truth, he found steam navigation too easy—and expensive. The whole idea of the *St. Michel III*, he eventually concluded, was perhaps a mistake, and indeed he planned shortly to buy a sailboat instead. Only on a smaller vessel could he indulge his passion for storms and danger, and have close contact with the crew (*BSJV* 145:14).

Leaving Nantes on May 13, Jules, Maurice, and Paul (who set off on all four major cruises, although he had to leave the Scottish one while still in France) moored for a night at Vigo, Spain, where the French Consul's daughters were reportedly all over Jules.[8] In Lisbon Jules had dinner with the minister for the navy (May 23). In Gibraltar Verne observed the apes, and was made so drunk by the British mess he couldn't stand up: in a vengeful story published in 1887, he found the garrison to be indistinguishable from the apes.

Then Morocco and Oran, Algeria, where they collected Honorine, visiting her widowed sister, Mme Auguste Lelarge, and the local Society of Geography held a special session in Verne's honor.[9] In the capital city of Algiers, they not only picked up Michel and Godefroy, but greeted Valentine, her husband, and cousins Maurice and Georges Allotte. Verne may conceivably have attended a punch (about June 3), and listened as the eminent geographer Élisée Reclus proposed a toast to revolutionary Louise Michel and upset local society (*BSJV* 145:17). After a week, mostly wasted on official visits, the group sailed as far as Philippeville (Skikda), where, on a stormy sea, they passed the wreck of the *Immaculate Conception*, sunk only hours before (*BSJV* 145:23). Taking fright, Honorine insisted on traveling to Tunis overland. Accordingly, while Captain Ollive took the ship to La Goulette, the party visited Bône (Annaba), without interest, and Souk Ahras—where the railway stopped. The party hired an ancient carriage along rocky tracks to Oued-Mougras, provoking a rare and un-Fogg-like outburst by Jules at "vile *terra firma*" and at Honorine for refusing the comfort of the *St. Michel* (*JJV* 124). After jolting on mules and fording rivers, they caught a train along a line not yet officially opened, ending up at Ghardimaou, Tunisia, where the flea-ridden lodging made Verne ill (PV 150). Fortunately, early the following day, the Bey of Tunis put his personal flower-strewn Pullman car at their disposition. They were thus able to get to the capital for lunch, greeted by royal red carpets and exotic dancing girls, with a sumptuous banquet to follow.[10]

After a reception in Carthage, they sailed from La Goulette for Malta, but the sea was so rough they had to take refuge in Sidi-Yussuf Bay behind Cape Bon (Tunisia) (June 18). In Marguerite's probably embroidered account, a delighted Verne contemplated the arid dunes, imagined shipwreck, and danced around a make-believe totem pole. Michel, still on board, fired a gun to get attention, and the locals responded with defensive shots (ADF 168).

The following day the *St. Michel* again tried to reach Malta. First, Paul and Maurice were put ashore on the west coast, to go and fetch a pilot; however, without quarantine clearance, they were arrested.[11] Then a fierce storm blew up, surrounding the vessel with lightning bolts. Ollive raised a distress signal off the island of Gozo but it was so bad all the pilots supposedly refused to come out and help (ADF 165). As the night storm worsened to a gale and the ship drifted towards rocks, the vessel remained on the brink of destruction for hours, with Verne invoking St. Michael of Peril at Sea. But a pilot appeared; and soon they were relaxing in the military port of La Valette.[12]

Once he had recovered, Verne was shown around by the Governor-General. After Syracuse and Catania (Sicily), with an excursion up snowy Etna, the ship headed north to Messina. They now had to decide their route. Jules longed to visit Greece and the Adriatic, but Honorine objected (JJV 125). Accordingly, after a bumpy crossing, they sailed for Capri and the Bay of Naples, the spitting image of the bay of Christiania.[13] After a train ride from Naples to Pompeii, the group ascended Vesuvius by horseback and palanquin (PV 153). At the railhead of Anzio (July 3) the party landed and headed for Rome.

The novelist had no clean clothing in the Hôtel d'Angleterre, his baggage still in customs at Anzio, so a local official offered his own

(*BSJV* 145:25). Visits and receptions followed, with the novelist notably telling the Prefect of Rome things about the layout of his city he did not know.

Verne requested a private audience with Pope Leo XIII (1810–1903), a conservative but energetic leader. The morning appointment was canceled and the afternoon one delayed, but eventually the writer spent nearly an hour in enclave with the Holy Father from 5 P.M. on July 7, together with Honorine, Paul, and Michel.[14] The two chatted about "the situation in Italy, divorce, freemasonry, and the Verne family."[15] The novelist received an encouragement to continue writing and a blessing for his works' moral values—showing the Pope can't have read them, but been impressed by their number.[16] According to Marguerite, the writer came out "in tears"; according to Verne himself, Leo was "a large old white man with closed eyes."[17]

Jules wanted to go home, but Honorine longed to see northern Italy (RD 111). Jules preferred to sail to Genoa but Honorine felt safer on a train—so Ollive took the yacht back to Nantes.[18] Jules's attempt to make up for not seeing Genoa with Hetzel again therefore produced disappointment.

The party managed to stay in Florence incognito; in Venice, after a gondola ride and a meal on St. Mark's Square, Verne signed in as "Prudent Allotte" in memory of his uncle, but Honorine divulged their name, resulting in fireworks, a crown of laurels, and "Giulio Verne" in lights over the hotel.[19] While Honorine and the young men felt delighted, Verne retired early. After passing though Turin, the party was home again on July 18.

For a couple in their mid-50s, cruising seemed an ideal way to combine hot baths and home cooking with reasonably ambitious travel: Honorine should have been happy at for once accompanying her illustrious husband. But holidays form a notoriously stressful time, and this cruise culminated in a catastrophic rupture in Verne's life, for he stepped off his magnificent steam yacht for the last time at Anzio. Breaking the pattern of the past 20 years, he would never again feel the spray on his face as he rounded yet another sunny headland.

In 1880 and 1882, Verne had not navigated, needing to work with d'Ennery, nor in 1883, either to save money or because Ollive wasn't up to scratch and he often had to stay on deck at night.[20] How he must have regretted the simple fishing smack he could just leave on the mudflats and the leaky single-master that sank off Mabon in 1840! The first cracks in the steam-yachting dream may in fact have begun as early as autumn 1879, when the novelist was seconds away from sinking to the bottom of Saint-Nazaire Harbor.

Perhaps Verne had simply traveled enough for a lifetime—he had toured the British Isles a remarkable, albeit universally unremarked, 20 times. His seafaring dreams ended, then, probably due to a combination of fear at his narrow escape, a desire for change, his wife's hostility, the unwieldiness of setting sail with a crew of ten, and, astonishingly, financial problems due to paying off Michel's huge debts.

It is difficult to establish the truth about Verne's finances since his expenditure remains a mystery. How much he paid for his house, whether he took out a mortgage, and exactly how large Michel's debts were, are merely some of the unanswered questions about where it all went. On the income side, more information is available, thanks to meticulous researchers.[21] Two items were the stockbroking income and the inheritances from both Jules's and Honorine's families. In July 1885 the *St. Michel III* was sold to the Prince of Montenegro for 55,000, via Nantes shipowner Martial Noë, with another manuscript of *Twenty Thousand Leagues* thrown in for free (PV 156). In addition, Verne's lifetime writing income probably amounted to about two-and-one-third million francs.[22] While this was less than many contemporaries—Dumas *père* had made "300,000 a year . . . Scribe is four time a millionaire" (March 1851 to Pierre)—most people could have lived on it for half-a-dozen lifetimes. If the reason Verne could not get by on seven million U.S. dollars was really Michel's debts, the son must have robbed the bank at Monte Carlo or run several score mistresses.

In 1885, the couple threw a second ball, in their house this time, which they called The Inn of Around the World. Verne dressed as a headwaiter, his wife as a chef stirring an immense stewpot, and their two granddaughters as milkmaids.[23] Although he had initially recoiled from the idea, once it got going Verne enjoyed himself.[24]

At 5:15 one wintry Tuesday in 1886, a down-in-the-dumps Verne was heading home. As he turned right into Dubois and approached the reassuringly solid entrance, his nephew Gaston attempted to murder him, aiming for the genital region and abdomen; one shot missed, but one lodged in his ankle. The apparently simple operation to remove the bullet actually made things worse, merely perforating the tibia.[25] The wound suppurated and bled for many years after, and Verne took the slug with him to his grave.[26]

Certainly Gaston was not compos mentis, and his family had its share of dramas, both before and after; but the way the whole thing was hushed up inevitably led to speculation as to motive. Verne and the entire family in fact conspired to lie barefacedly about the order of events, insisting that the novelist's renunciation of sailing, and indeed traveling, stemmed from his lameness. In fact he had made the decision to sell the yacht in 1882 (March 17, 1882 to Michel).

Gaston's role remained enigmatic. Although indicted with attempted murder,[27] he never went to trial, transferring instead to a nursing home chosen by Verne. After 1897, he sometimes even traveled to Amiens, calmly visiting the novelist with his brother Maurice (JJV 160).

And that's about as far as one can reasonably go, until the descendants divulge the family papers. My own guess, based on the Sherlock Freud principle of looking for missing links, is that either Michel or Gaston's father Paul, with their own meshes of tensions and passions, were the main witnesses to question. The circumstantial evidence indeed adumbrates a whole nexus of seething jealousies and resentments, especially around Michel, the focus of so many nightmares. Money or sex were likely to be involved, to judge from the part of the body aimed for and if the attack followed the pattern of most home-brewed killing attempts.

Over the years that followed Verne was badly affected by the attack, as well as by the death of Hetzel, only a week later. He became "less Parisian" (*JVEST* 186); and he could not sleep, despite a morphine prescription. In his fevers, he returned to the habits of his youth, writing a sonnet about the drug, 80 years before Mick Jagger's attempt. He also composed 4,000 crosswords and word puzzles.[28] The novelist in fact lay immobilized for several months, with "only one leg, like a heron" in August, then tried a wheelchair or crawling around the garden on his bottom.[29] He had "entered the black series of my life . . . if I couldn't take refuge in my stubborn slogging . . . I'd be very much to be pitied" (December 21, 1886, to Hetzel *fils*).

Jules's mother had to be told about the attack; and she too died in 1887, at the age of 86, without her eldest son attending either her deathbed or the funeral. Did he skip it because he disliked ceremonies? From one angle he owed Sophie one last visit, since she had perhaps the greatest influence on his character, reputedly transmitting her imagination to him. She had discreetly coordinated the whole extended family over most of the century, including her sisters Châteaubourg and Tronson and her 97 descendants (*Int.* 87). She had acted as behind-the-scenes impresario of the grand spectacle of Chantenay's natural delights and pastoral peccadilloes. She had supported Jules through the difficult decades, secretly sending him cash and fruit from the lower garden. She had done her level best to set him up with a whole series of luscious young ladies. For a decade in Paris he had reserved for her his most intimate written thoughts. She had preserved like saint's relics his vulgar similes, still believing, like all mothers, in the exceptional destiny of the fruit of her womb.

Jules did rouse himself sufficiently to travel for the settling of her affairs (RD 113)—and perhaps to take one last look at Chantenay. He presumably inherited a sum of the order of FF 50,000.[30] The oil portrait of his father as a fastidious desk-bound notary had been left to Anna; in a fit of generous meanness, she lent it to him . . . until his death (ADF 175).

The Chantenay of 1887 was unrecognizable from the pastoral paradise of the 1840s. For a start Pierre had built ugly three-story annexes, ruining the rustic balance of the ancient master's house. But more tragically, industrialization and progress had caught up with the island beyond time. Black smoke replaced the scents of the trees and a smutty railway ran below the back garden: every time a slow clanking monster passed, the hoi polloi would stare at the back-garden activities. Roads covered the towpath where Caroline had flaunted shapely ankles and swelling bodice, probably as well as the track where a stocking had lasciviously been stripped off; factories replaced the welcoming inns, grubby proles the forelock-tugging countryfolk, black water the leaping fish. The house where Jules had grown up, dreamed of the ocean, got his school-leaving results, studied law, and written much of *Hatteras* and *From the Earth to the Moon* was sold without hesitation (RD 113).

With the energy that constituted his heroes' cardinal virtue, Verne attempted to overcome the outrageous blows of cruel fate. In November 1887, he went on an 11-day speaking tour to Brussels, Antwerp, Liège, and Amsterdam, probably meeting King Leopold II.[31] However, he uninspiringly read a strange fairy tale, "The Rat Family," about a hermit with a cane, to audiences brought up on Nemo and Fogg. Although he feigned not to notice, many walked out, reviewers were unhappy, and he never went abroad again.

Out of the blue, Verne decided to stand as an Amiens city councilor, on a left-wing list, shocking Honorine to the core.[32] His political views now tended to the reactionary, with however a surviving anarchistic streak; the choice of ticket was opportunistic, for his many interventions remained resolutely apolitical. As councilor he worked very hard at attending meetings, listening to debates, sitting on commissions, and studying all the necessary questions, especially fine-arts education, charity, and the theater (Lemire 61). Among his endeavors ranked building a circus (it still stands, a fine circular structure) and an attempt to stop that daring new invention, the bicycle, from going up one-way streets (*BSJV* 131:47). He worked tirelessly for decades, *?* promoting both progressive and reactionary causes: for setting up a School of Medicine, building a phallic central tower on a church, publicly displaying the city's artwork, naming streets after clerics or archangels, allocating extra space in case the theater was later enlarged, and enabling firm police action; but against building barracks, including women in the vote on artistic questions, allowing locomotive smoke to pollute the town, or permitting trolleybuses' overhead wires on public squares.[33] Verne was eventually promoted officer of the Legion of Honor, not, irony of ironies, for helping to form the minds of young Tolkien, Proust, or Sartre, but for his composition of long tedious reports and metronomic attendance at committee meetings.[34]

The one constant in Verne's political views remained an opposition to socialism: "Who can tell if it will prove a success—for the poor man?" (*Int.* 224). He opposed every revolution and insurrection before 1851, viscerally hated the Paris Commune ("I really hope . . . they shoot the socialists like dogs"), and lived in constant dread of left-wing revolution, which, "even if beaten down again this time, will one day devour us."[35]

But he simultaneously opposed capitalism, fearing both the effect of industrial pressures on the environment and the Disneyfication of cultural life from commercial publicity à la Barnum: "If I were young enough I would be tempted to [wirte a novel about the remorselessness of American big business]" (*Int.* 224). His anarchistic streak appeared as a long tirade against private property in "Ten Hours' Hunting" (1882), but was mostly social, in his rejection of modern society in favor of a utopian, agrarian ideal as far away from modern civilization as possible.

Although expressing sympathy for the two or three kings-without-a-throne among his friends, he detested Napoléon III and was realistic enough to recognize that "the Republic . . . is the only just and legitimate government" (November? 1870 to Pierre). Never especially keen on democracy and anti-Dreyfusard in the 1896 Affair, he had become a conservative and a Conservative by late middle age.[36] Later he adhered to the right-wing League of the French Fatherland, joining Charles Maurras, later founder of the Action Française (*BSJV* 31–32:189). Whole books have been written making Verne a covert radical, an underground revolutionary, an anti-colonialist; but for every criticism of the Indian Empire or native subjugation, you can find an opposing support of the same ideas. It all depends what one looks for.

Like his politics, Verne's religion showed much continuity but without (him) coming out with a clear declaration on the question. Resisting extremism and dogmatism since his early days at the seminaries, with a keen eye for hypocrisy and humbug, he nonetheless never came close to suggesting God might not exist. "More Catholic than Voltaire," as he teasingly put it, a deist[37] but not really a Christian, he made no attempt to put Jesus's precepts into practice; and indeed Christ is remarkable by his absence from both his works and his life. In the 1850s and '60s, he debated the tenets of orthodox Catholicism, questioning the Pope's infallibility but accepting the dogma of original sin and its corollary that unbaptized babies went into limbo (December 27, 1869). To his bigoted father he said that the afterlife was bunkum and that even if it did exist, it made no difference; but to his atheist publisher, that Catholics pressing the intercom of the pearly gates would go to the head of the line.[38] "A believer but hardly a faithful practitioner" in fact a "rather wishywashy" one, imbued only with "a sort of Catholic mentality," his ambivalence came to a head on one key issue, the extent to which God acted in this world.[39] On the one hand, he invariably attacked "positivism," which must come as a surprise to those who know him only through his science fiction reputation. By this he meant scientism and explanations in purely rational terms, his major criticism of

Poe. Occasionally he took the side of Catholicism against reason: "science and positivism work hand-in-hand against religion and it is a bad thing" (*BSJV* 153:36–38).

But on the other hand, he mocked the idea that God ever perceptibly intervened in human affairs. The irony was perfectly encapsulated in the word Providence, for it implied an intelligent design in human events, but was always twinned with chance, with the net result a force with a mischievous sense of humor and perfect timing, that did its utmost to both play a divine role and reduce to entirely natural causes. Ultimately, then, Verne opposed both atheism and religion as explanations of human affairs—as in other matters remaining a skeptic.

In 1868, Monsignor Dupanloup, a leading educationalist, criticized the *Magasin* for being insufficiently Christian; in parallel, the influential Catholic journalist Louis Veuillot complained about God's absence from Verne's works.[40] Proving that educationalists often failed to educate and journalists to read, an eight-year-old could have checked that the word "God" in fact occurred thousands of times in Verne's novels. What no doubt went beyond the understanding of the two obscurantists was a first paradox that Verne, vaguely Catholic, was forced by atheist Hetzel to write pious sentiments so as to sell more copies. Another was that the required insertions seethed with subtle irony. If they had bothered to open Verne, the two leaders would have discovered that the, admittedly rather revolutionary, teachings of the New Testament were replaced by racism and anti-Semitism, as well as mockery of the Church—but that God was ubiquitous.

CHAPTER 19

Heading for the Hundredth: 1890–1905

VERNE'S NOVELS AFTER 1887 showed a drop in quality, perhaps due to failing inspiration or insufficient revision. Sales fell to less than 30,000 but never remotely approached a point where publication became problematic. Most of the books did have some interest, whether an original plot or further reflection on a theme already covered.

North against South (1887), set in Florida 1862, dealt with the issue of slavery and an unjust accusation because of identical twins, with a tragic ending. *Topsy-Turvy* (1889), formally a sequel to the earlier moon novels, showed an eminently fallible scientist and satirized "Americans who, for the sake of speculation, make an attempt to change the axis of the earth so as to convert the polar regions into fertile gardens" (*Int.* 51). *Carpathian Castle* (1892) focused on a nobleman's obsession with the audiovisual image of a dead singer. In *Claudius Bombarnac* (1892), the eponymous journalist journeyed along the newly opened, but fictional, railway from Paris to Peking.

Propeller Island (1895) featured an American millionaires' "*Great Eastern* magnified 10,000 times" (*Int.* 108), which toured the South Seas but broke up due to tensions between two rival factions.

In *For the Flag* (1896) Verne depicted a forty-five-year-old scientist and his "autopropulsive" invention, capable of delivering phenomenal explosive charges. His ideas were rejected by all nations,

causing him to end up in a mental asylum. However, a patriotic
Frenchman kidnapped he was in an attempt to get the formula.
Verne mentioned the inventory "Turpin" twice in the novel, even
calling the novel "the Turpin" (August 26, 1894, to Paul). Chantenay
sharpshooter Paul Perret warmly reviewed it as "a wonderful story"
(*BSJV* 150:5), but the 45-year-old scientist, who had also written of
an "autopropulsive" device, quite reasonably considered himself
libeled (*BSJV* 129:16). In the ensuing court case, Verne was defended
by Raymond Poincaré, future president and a great admirer of his
works. He had to go to Paris for the case (November 1896)—and for
the appeal (February–March 1897). But he saw almost nobody, just
Hetzel *fils*, his brother, and one or two old friends (RD 118). Thanks
to his lawyer's eloquence, he won both. But the fact that Verne never
conceded any wrongdoing should not blind us to the conclusive evidence. He lied between his teeth and clearly libeled poor Turpin,
even by the lax standards of the time.

The Mighty Orinoco (1898), about a search for the river's source,
really just rewrote a true-life tale of exploration by Jean Chaffanjon,
who was related to Caroline Tronson's husband and hence by marriage to Verne. *Will of an Eccentric* (1899) consisted of a board-game
across the United States, still unpublished there today, and grew from
Jules and Paul's games of snakes and ladders with Uncle Prudent
(letter to Paul in ADF 201). While planning it, Verne dreamed that
"the American colossus will collapse and three or four great nations
will rise from its ruins," including a Germanic one in the Mississippi
Valley and possibly a Gallic one in the north-west of the continent.[1]
Prophecy was never one of his strong points.

The disorder in Verne's practical life formed a mirror image of his
writing, with each stage planned like a military operation.

After a one-liner he often shared with Hetzel *fils*, he would gather
material. Some of it came from conversations or his own experience
(*Int.* 260)—he witnessed, for instance, a public execution in August
1872, going so far as to share the twenty-two-year-old's last hours,

including his waking at 2:30 A.M. and the drop of the blade [August 7, 1872]. But observation seemed to him, paradoxically, "much less accurate than what I saw in books."[2]

Then a synopsis—"he claimed he started a story without knowing how it would finish"—"a chapter plan,"[3] and a paragraph-by-paragraph summary in point form, if *Around the World* is typical. If at this stage inspiration didn't come, he gave up the idea (*Int.* 106). Then extensive reading of all conceivable documentation—perhaps skimming "500 books" for *Robur-the-Conqueror* (*Int.* 232). At some stage, his 20,000 index cards would be brought into play; after use, he destroyed the relevant notes to avoid repetition [end 96].

Each new story featured a different country, ultimately planning to cover the whole globe in 100 volumes; Verne kept track using flags on a map, but eventually he gave up because there were too many (*Int.* 138).

Next a "first rough copy in pencil, leaving a half-page margin for corrections and emendations; I then read the whole, and go over all I have already done in ink," with usually six or more ink versions, each carefully recopied (Hetzel gave him a typewriter but he never learned to type).[4] Although he claimed never to use a secretary, occasionally his wife, and later his granddaughters, would copy his manuscripts, or possibly even Michel.[5] At the end of the revision process more than two-thirds of the first draft had disappeared, with much of the rest also vanishing at later stages (*Int.* 63).

Up until 1886 the result was sent to Hetzel *père* and the comments incorporated. Often the publisher's comments were both casually expressed and brutal: "why not switch around the chapters?"; "The poem is terrible, find a better one" (November 12, 1876). With Hetzel *fils* the relationship was less confrontational but also less productive of new ideas.

Then the genuine work started: "I consider that my real labour begins with my first set of proofs, for I not only correct something in every sentence, but I rewrite whole chapters. I do not seem to have a grip of my subject till I see my work in print" (*Int.* 106). "He was worse than Balzac. Never in 37 years of professional life have I seen an author . . . count on the revision of so many proofs to complete his novels" (Hetzel *fils* in *BSJV* 104:4). His main aim, from the beginning, was to have as lucid and flowing a style as possible (*Int.* 89).

From the 1890s, a flood of interviewers, nearly all British or American, visited Verne at home, providing an invaluable record of both his ideas and domestic environment. Even on the beach, he invariably wore a loose dark gray suit, white shirt, bow-tie, black leather shoes, and the tiny red lapel button of the officer of the Legion of Honor. Around town he would present the perfect picture of an elderly gentleman, with his rolled-up umbrella, bowler hat, and waistcoated paunch; later he wore a cloth cap at home because of his rheumatism. With his longish, snow-white hair and off-white beard—both slightly unkempt—good complexion, bright eyes, and lively manner, he could still convey energy and enthusiasm, although something ineffable, or at least elusive, still hung around him.[6]

Most interviewers agreed on his paradoxical combinations, presenting him as Parisian in his wit but cosmopolitan in his imagination; a gay conversationalist but an inexhaustible inventor, and a man about town but a loner (*Int.* 87). Others found him unremarkable, more like a "retired army general, professor of physics, or civil servant" (*Int.* 112). Many expressed surprise at the difference between the affable and friendly man and his heroes' laconic wanderlust. In fact he hated to talk about his own persona—"the story of my life would not be interesting"—and writing formed his only reality: "If I don't work I feel I'm not living."[7]

When, inevitably, interviewers accused him of misogyny, he sometimes agreed, sometimes rationalized: "I am not a good hand at female characters"; "they'd talk all the time, not allowing a word in edgeways"; and "they would often have distracted his characters from their goals."[8] But previously he had been franker about the limitations Hetzel had imposed on him: "If only I could slip in a few adulteries, how much easier it would be!" (JJV 76).

Even about his works, he remained relatively unforthcoming,

constrained by language and cultural barriers, and by the fact that most of the interviewers had not read his books and showed little sympathy for his literary aims. As a result, he was reduced to talking about the "sources" of his novels, oversimplistically, since modern critical editions have identified many thousands of cultural references in the works.9 To communicate with young reporters dimly aware of only one or two titles, he sometimes parodied their own style, talking of his total production as "at least three yards" (*Int.* 200).

In interview after interview, decade after decade, Verne patiently explained that, despite what his wife and most of humanity thought (*Int.* 199), he was not a writer of "anticipation" (the nineteenth-century term for science fiction). He kept repeating that he was in fact rather anti-innovation, that he knew little about science and liked it even less, that he was not a technofreak, just a novelist, a mere storyteller. Sometimes he tried subtlety, sometimes he just hammered it in. In many cases the answers revealed as much about the interviewers' prejudices as the interviewee:

> . . . the submarine existed before I wrote *Twenty Thousand Leagues*"; "Verne . . . has little sympathy with automobilism"; "[its main effect will be that] the rich will certainly take more and more to country life"; "I don't think we'll ever communicate with Mars"' "You must not reagrd me as . . . an engineer or chemist"; ["I don't really believe in progress, except that of the Japanese in war.]"10

Since the message still did not strike home, Verne tried variations on a theme:

> "understand, above all, that I do not claim to be a scientist or inventor"; . . . "I would not allow myself to play the role of prophet, since the time of prophets has passed"; "human nature [is] the greatest science of all"; "there will not perhaps

always be scientists, but there will always be poets"; "do not dive too deeply into science, that sublime void . . . where humanity sometimes loses itself"; "my main subjects of study are geography and humanity"; "I'm a novelist"; "I'm an artist"; "I'm the most unknown of men."[11]

But it made little difference, since inevitably a new reporter would keenly ask the same old questions about his "predictions" the following month. As a result of the misunderstandings about the books and an obscuring of the man behind them, ignorance was general. For the public, indeed, he had no definable traits: it was denied that the one writer whose works were universally known had any personality or even existed (*Int.* 112). One interviewer claimed not to be able to find him:

> I asked for the celebrated author Jules Verne; yet nobody at the station seemed to know such a person. The cab driver took me to a Monsieur Verne who sells the comic weeklies, next to Monsieur Verne of a stationery store and to a third Monsieur Verne, an employee of the paper mills.

He finally realized his mistake: "you should have asked for Verne the alderman."[12]

After his Low Countries speaking tour, Verne traveled all the way down to Cap d'Antibes to work with d'Ennery, spending about six weeks from December 1888 on a scenario of *Tribulations of a Chinese in China*, because d'Ennery could only work an hour a day.[13]

Verne gave up his dream of going back to America for a lecture tour (*Int.* 56). From July 15 to August 15, 1890, he again stayed at d'Ennery's, this time in the beach resort of Villers-sur-Mer, near Deauville, working on *Tribulations of a Chinese in China*. From August 16 he holidayed with Michel and his family at Petites Dalles, a tiny hamlet near Fécamp, again in Normandy, beside a striking sea cliff painted by Claude Monet and Camille Pissarro.[14] In August

1893, the Verne couple stayed for a month at "Le Grondin," a villa rented by Michel's family near Dinard, just yards from a deserted beach (JJV 182). In September he took Honorine on a trip to Le Havre, Caen, and Saint-Malo, presumably trying not to think about his never-to-return sailing days (JJV 183).

Verne skipped his brother's funeral in 1897. His family repeatedly invited him to Nantes and Chantenay: for the launch by his shipowner nephews of a yacht called the *Jules Verne*, for the wedding of his nephew Maxime, for the family council after Paul's death—but to no avail each time.[15]

His daily routine varied little. Up before dawn, he wrote from five till eleven, producing 300 words each day.[16] After lunch, over by noon, a limping constitutional on Rue des Trois Cailloux and Rue des Corps Nuds sans Têtes, using a cane sent by his British fans in the Boy's Empire League and resting in Square Saint-Denis (ADF 203). Following a tram ride to municipal business at City Hall, a cake and a glass of milk in Sibert's pastry shop; from there to the reading room of the Industrial Society, to shake hands wordlessly with the other regular readers and scour the newspapers and reviews for ideas for his works. Then a look in at the City Hall again, the University Circle, or the Circle of the Union, and finally a stroll along the boulevards, to get home at five or six. At least twice a week he would make for his box at the theater, sometimes taking Honorine out to dinner at the Continental Hotel on the way, but often leaving before the last act, although at times taking supper in a café.[17] And then to bed at eight. Among his favorite reading, or rather rereading, at this time were Chateaubriand's *Itinerary from Paris to Jerusalem* (1811) and Émile Erckmann and Alexandre Chatrian's *Story of a Conscript in 1813* (1864), *Waterloo* (1865), and *The Blockade* (1879) (March 21, 1881).

As the years went by, Verne's life underwent withdrawals and retreats in the most varied of domains. He wrote an aggressive poem about the new mayor (OD 190). When, after ten years, his coat began to look a little worn, he simply had it turned (JJV 200). If he felt exhausted while out for a stroll, he would just sit down on the nearest doorstep (JJV 200). He forgot much of the contents of his earlier works.[18] Instead of going to see Hetzel *fils*, he often had the publisher come and see him. For the first time, he noted a slight decline in his yearly income from Hetzel, from FF 25,000 in 1889 to 24,000 in 1890 (April 28, 1891, to Hetzel *fils*). When Americans wrote to "Jules Verne, France," he never read beyond the first page, while still answering them all personally (JJV 200). He bitterly noted the betrayal of his works under the guise of translations, but without being able to do anything about it (November 5, 1897, to Turiello). His 80,000 investment in Michel's stove business disappeared without trace; altogether he wasted 200,000 on his son, not counting his three grandsons' education.[19] He insisted Michel sign IOUs, and sent him sharp reminders when he inevitably forgot. He stopped his grandson being punished for calling his father "Pig!"[20] Michel and his "charming" wife and children stayed for a month, but Suzanne persuaded nearly all of Verne's friends to send them to Coventry (JJV 181). On this and other occasions, Suzanne showed her dislike for Verne, because he was not her biological father, supported by Valentine's husband (JJV 182). He now had little contact with his Nantes family, whose names his daughters did not even know.[21] He saw Paris on one last visit in 1898 for his grandson's First Communion.[22] Honorine's affectionate white Angora cat died (*Int.* 41). His contemporaries were lost one by one: brother Paul in 1897; traveling companion Hignard in 1898; his cheerful old family maid in 1900; his first love, cousin Caroline Tronson in 1901. In the end it was if he "were no longer of this world" (June 1, 1896, to Turiello).

Verne last traveled in 1899, again staying with Michel and his family at Petites Dalles, in an adjoining house called "Tour Pelletier" (JJV 199). He resigned from the Paris Society of Geography (1898) and skipped the Universal Exposition (1900), including the first Metro. In October 1900, he and his wife moved out of rented Rue Charles Dubois and back into their own ill-lit and cramped 44 Boulevard de Longueville. The furniture huddled forlornly in the dining and living rooms, the tiny garden was invaded by sparrows, and the needed repairs took forever.[23] On the second floor, Verne's recreated his ascetic bed-sitter: just "two tables, a padded armchair, a camp bed," and a pipe-rack, still with the *St. Michel* before Vesuvius, but now with a Corot, whom he had liked since at least 1857.[24]

In 1894, Hetzel *fils* telephoned him at the Circle of the Union, but Verne did not recognize his voice or understand much of what he said (JD 401). He broke off relations with Michel, again, over his son's support for Captain Dreyfus, the Jewish officer convicted of treason on forged evidence. In 1898, he burned most of his personal papers, including hundreds of letters, account books, and even unpublished manuscripts—worth a nabob's fortune today. He also gave away his personal items as widely as possible, to impede future researchers' work his great-niece surmises (ADF 211). Michel came for a visit in a newfangled motor-car.

The novelist's health deteriorated. To his swollen stomach were added writer's cramp, bronchitis, and rheumatism: "I'm living off milk and eggs and my legs are useless."[25] So severe did the ringing in his ears and dizziness become as to make him almost fall out of his carriage, meaning he no longer dared go out alone.[26] With increasing pangs from diabetes, he could not wait for meals, but ate alone, sitting on a stool so as to go faster (JJV x). He was meant to have eaten six huge artichokes each day for years—and one day a whole leg of lamb, leaving none for his family.[27] To the cataract in his left eye was added one in his right. Canceling the needed operation in 1900 made him "very distressed": "I can scarcely see what I'm writing."[28] In March 1901 a nasty flu kept him in his room for two months making him "very, very ill" (*Int.* 146). In 1903 he acquired spectacles but lost one ear, "so risking hearing only half the stupidities and mischief . . . a great consolation" (ADF 212). His diabetes suddenly got worse in the fall of 1904, but he did little about his health, apart from joking to Hetzel: "If you find a new stomach to replace mine . . . do send it."[29]

His presence, taking refuge in silence, "more aged than really old," terrified his future biographer, aged nine, except when he animatedly talked about his books with Michel (JJV x). From 1902 his health worsened, his "words run[ning] away and ideas no longer com[ing]," making journalists depart disappointed. His second great-grandchild was born and he sent Michel another FF 40,000 ($120,000).[30] In 1903, "the only time he went out was for his short constitutional."[31] That year came shocking news about Gaston's brother, Marcel Verne, who followed through a suicide pact with a lady friend in a Swiss lake, unless it was just an insurance scam.[32]

Yet Verne struggled on through the growing gloom. He appreciated Pontet-Canet, an intensely rich dark vintage (*Int.* 67). He sarcastically endorsed coca-based Mariani Wine, guaranteed to cure both flu and impotence.[33] He took malicious pleasure in pointing out Wells's implausibilities (*Int.* 199). Honorine, who still loved him deeply if a little uncomprehendingly, maintained her affectionate care. He had been triumphantly reelected in the Amiens municipal elections of 1900, although now nodding off in meetings and speaking less and less. In 1902, he was still rising at four o'clock (*JVEST* 243). Not only did he compose the first draft of *Lighthouse at the End of the World* between March and May 1901, but on occasion he could still appear "upright, like the master he is . . . his eyes [showing] . . . a singular vivacity" (*Int.* 146). In about 1904 he was heartened by a letter from the White House, claiming that President Roosevelt—clearly a fine linguist—had read "all" of Verne's novels with great pleasure (Lemire 133).

And still the books kept pouring out: the anti-desert island story *Second Homeland* (1900); *Traveling Scholarships* (1903), about touring the West Indies; *A Drama in Livonia* (1904), featuring German-Slav rivalry; *Master of the World* (1904), where a megalomaniac Robur-the-Conqueror returns in a car-plane-sub.; *Invasion of the Sea* (1905), about flooding the Sahara.

The Yarns of Jean-Marie Cabidoulin (1901) provided a vivid portrait of the eponymous sailor, whose stories possibly delighted the eleven-year-old Jules. Indeed the novel, about a hunt for sea-monsters, featured a whole range of names from Verne's distant past: Lieutenant

Coquebert, whose family we last met in the 1830s, a Lieutenant Allotte, a bosun Ollive, and a harpooner Ducrest.

In *Treetop Village* (1901), "I'm trying to reconstitute the intermediate race between the most perfect of monkeys and the most imperfect of men"; Verne was resolutely anti-evolutionist: "did man have monkeys for ancestors? It . . . is not proven."[34] In *The Brothers Kip* (1902), perhaps in honor of Paul and about a judicial error, Verne attacked both the intelligence of the Tasmanians, "stupid, wild Negroes situated on the lowest rung of humanity," and their disappearance, like those of all first Australians, "under Britain's powerful hand."

Yet other books were composed, adding to the backlog, for only one or two came out each year: *The Beautiful Yellow Danube* (written in 1896–97), sailing through central Europe; *Magellania* (1896–99), where the solitude-seeking hero must govern castaways; *The Golden Volcano* (1899–1900), about the Klondike gold rush and depicting treacherous and rapacious first Canadians; *The Secret of Wilhelm Storitz* (1901), about an invisible man; *Meteor Hunt* (1901), with a gold-bearing asteroid; and four and one-half chapters of "Study Trip" (1903–04), set in French colonial Africa.

All in all, Verne had written about ten million words for Hetzel and five to eight million other words.[35] For sixty years' work he had gotten perhaps FF 800,000 from his plays and FF 1.35 million from the publisher:[36] on average about thirteen centimes a word or FF 3,600 a month.

Amid the sometimes slow-moving stories, one surprising gem shone bright, proving Verne could still write outstanding action stories. *Lighthouse at the End of the World* (1905), although not taken to proofs by the novelist, packs a surprising narrative punch. In 1859 the sloop *Santa Fe* leaves Vasquez, Felipe, and Moriz on subpolar Staten Island, claimed by Argentina, to tend the new lighthouse at Elgor Bay. But a gang of wreckers, led by diabolical Kongre, have long been stranded there, and soon hoist a false light to lure the schooner *Maule* onto the reefs, killing all hands. They kill the trusting Felipe and Moriz, forcing Vasquez to flee. The pirates draw in an American ship, killing all on board except First Officer John Davis. Vasquez and Davis, swearing revenge, delay the refurbished *Maule* using a salvaged cannon. The pirates are finally leaving—when the *Santa Fe* looms back into view. The wreckers retreat ashore and attempt to storm the lighthouse. In the dramatic climax the pirates die and Kongre proudly commits clifftop suicide.

With cold perseverance and great resourcefulness on both sides, *Lighthouse* resembles a game of chess played by Chinese businessmen, endlessly guessing what the opponent might know and doing multi-variate probabilistic analysis on the labyrinthine possible courses of action. In this suspense thriller crossed with a sea novel, against all the bloodshed and evil, darkness, death, and despair, the lighthouse shines only a little light: positive action in a fallen world can at best hold back the dark forces.

Lighthouse thus forms one possible conclusion to the writer's career. The greatness of Jules Verne, unparalleled master of the adventure story, radiates in his simplest work.

On Thursday, March 16, 1905, the only universal Frenchman fell ill with a serious attack of diabetes. He left his third-floor study for the last time and moved into his wife's bed on the second floor. On Sunday paralysis crept up his right side. On Tuesday morning sister Marie came for a few hours, just in time to hear Jules's "I'm very happy to see you, you did well to come," his last clear words.[37] Michel, Valentine, and Suzanne, arrived, plus Michel's wife and three sons—Mathilde and Anna were too old to travel. On Wednesday Verne slowly lost his voice; that night he beckoned Honorine and Michel over and embraced them, then turned to face the wall (JJV ix). On Thursday morning Hetzel came but was not recognized. Starting from 10 P.M. Verne underwent terrible suffering for several hours, trying to move his arm, which was getting stiffer and stiffer; at about 2 A.M. he fell into a coma and received the last rites; death throes began at 11. By about 3 P.M. on Friday, March 24 it was all over (*BSJV* 154:7).

As newspapers worldwide reported his death, tributes poured in from politicians, explorers, scientists, and writers—but not from a single academic (ADF 219).

Present at the funeral on March 28 were sisters, wife, Michel, grandsons, daughters, granddaughters, and four nephews, not including Gaston. Official representatives included Hetzel, a junior schoolteacher, and a representative from the Society of Geography, plus 5,000 members of the public. No one came from the government or the Academy.

Honorine burned the IOUs and other documents.[38] It took the city of Amiens several years to find the funds to build a statue. After a storm and a falling tree decapitated the monument, Verne's severed head reportedly lay unclaimed in the grass for a year (ADF 220).

Communing with the Dead

AFTER VERNE'S DEATH, eight novels and three short stories were published in the series of Extraordinary Journeys. These works differed from the previous ones. *The Survivors of the "Jonathan"* (1909), for example, went much deeper than before in its analysis of anarchism, socialism, and communism, seeming to conclude that solitude was the only satisfactory social or political solution. *The Barsac Mission* (1914) presented an authoritarian anti-Utopia in darkest Africa, complete with robots and self-correcting aircraft. Michel publicly declared that he had prepared some of the works for publication but denied doing anything more, and the posthumous works were generally accepted as authentic by generations of publishers and readers worldwide.

Only in 1978 did Count Piero Gondolo della Riva prove, with a dramatic flourish, that many parts of the post-1905 works were not by Jules Verne at all, but by Michel. This discovery, which is now indisputable, leads to some tricky choices as to which versions of the works to consider authentic.

The son's participation in the collected works was far from a crass bolt-on job, and his contribution must be considered an important literary oeuvre in its own right. It was an excellent imitation of his father's style; but it also furnished an extraordinary commentary on the Extraordinary Journeys as a whole—including the posthumous production itself.

In his will Verne reportedly left his manuscripts and projects to his son with a wish they be published (*Int.* 248). Previously he had encouraged Michel's considerable writing talent, and, as we saw, signed his name on two of his son's works. Given the amount of work needed on the manuscripts, and given Verne's reputation as a mere entertainer, Michel's action in revising the works would seem justified by the standards of the time. After all, he was faced with a pile of unfinished manuscripts, with large numbers of errors and inconsistencies, most of which would not otherwise have been published.

Since then, however, the situation has evolved. With the recognition of Jules Verne's literary value and with the modern tendency to seek authenticity, even over and above coherence, we need to respect the original works. In sum, we cannot, unfortunately, correct the manuscripts the novelist left in 1905, except in incidentals like the proper names; and so we are stuck with the flawed versions. It is a frustrating paradox, only partly resolved by critical editions where the reader can be informed of the problems. But unfortunately French publishers have shunned scholarly editions of the Extraordinary Journeys, with not a single one published to date.

However, none of the above can apply to one exceptional story, a posthumously published work whose brilliance overshadows the often dull writing of both late Jules and Michel. So outstanding is the story as to force itself upon us as a keystone to the entire Extraordinary Journeys. The purists who have vehemently condemned Michel's literary contribution steer well clear of taking on this work, for it would be manifestly absurd to exclude it from the works on the basis of its shared authorship.

The short story in question, "Edom," was published in the collection *Yesterday and Tomorrow* (1910, under the title "The Eternal Adam"). Set 20,000 years hence it ranges back to the very beginnings of human existence. On the way, it observes the Flood, Atlantis, and a total destruction of modern civilization. The story opens with Sofr, an eminent Land-of-the-Four-Seas scholar who firmly believes in scientific progress. He remains convinced that no advanced humanity has existed before his, although legends go back to the mists of time, with even the name of the first man and woman dimly remembered. But one day Sofr discovers underground a roll of manuscript. He finally deciphers the unknown script and reads a "tale from beyond the grave," written by a twenty-first century Frenchman.

One evening the Frenchman is receiving friends and discussing humanity's conquest of nature and plans for immortal life—when a formidable quake shakes the earth, causing the ocean to wash in and cover every continent. After months the handful of survivors finds a new land risen from the waves where Atlantis once stretched. They disembark and found a colony; at the end of his life, the Frenchman decides to write a diary and bury it for future generations.

Overcome by his reading, Sofr realizes that these beings scrabbling for their lives were his own ancestors. His naive optimism gives way to a painful recognition that all man's "efforts throughout the infinity of time" have been fruitless, that we must resign ourselves to "the eternal recommencement of all things."

There is no reference in the contemporary documentation to the dazzling short story, at best a reference by Hetzel to a work called "In Two Thousand Years' Time."[1] I have seen a photocopy of part of the manuscript, in Michel's hand, with many stylistic corrections. The son's revisions, while not altering the structure, are considerable, and the moving philosophical conclusion may be his. The son must therefore be credited at least as coauthor. It seems clear, in sum, that the work must represent collaboration between Jules and Michel from beyond the grave.

"Edom" thus constitutes a fascinating and thought-provoking piece of literature; but also an unparalleled commentary, occasional pastiche, and brilliant apex to the whole sixty-year series.

It seems emblematic that Verne's most moving masterpiece should never have appeared in a mainstream publication in English.

APPENDIX A: HOME ADDRESS

Move-In Date	Address
8 February 1828	Fourth Floor, 4 Rue de Clisson, Nantes
Probably late 1828	Second floor, 2 Quai Jean Bart
October 1834	Mme Sambin's pension, 5 Place du Bouffay
About 1837	Place de l'Église, Chantenay
3 October 1837 or October 1836	St. Stanislas School
About 1840	Third floor, 6 Rue Jean-Jacques Rousseau
October 1840	St. Donatien Junior Seminary
October 1844 or 1843	Collège Royal
11 July 1848 (until 3 August)	Probably near Henri Garcet's, Fifth Arrondissement, Paris
12 November 1848	About sixth floor, 24 Rue de l'Ancienne Comédie, Sixth
March 1849	Third floor, 24 Rue de l'Ancienne Comédie, Sixth
Possibly late 1850	Possibly first floor, Rue Louis le Grand, Second
About February 1851	A furnished room in a hotel
9 April 1851	Eighth floor, 18 Boulevard Bonne Nouvelle, Second
8 March 1855	A hotel, possibly at 47 Rue des Martyrs, Ninth
15 March 1855	Sixth floor, 18 Boulevard Poissonnière, Second
End of April 1857	Rue Saint-Martin, Third
1858	54 Rue du Faubourg Montmartre, Ninth
1858	Upper floor, probably 18 Boulevard Montmartre, Second
First half of 1861	45 Boulevard de Magenta, Ninth
Mid-1862	18 Passage Saulnier, Ninth
By 10 September 1863	39 Rue La Fontaine, 16th (Auteuil)
Spring 1866	"La Solitude," Rue Lefèvre (modern 9 Rue Jules Verne), Le Crotoy
1866	Place de la Croix Rouge, Sixth (presumably the same as Carrefour de la Croix Rouge, Sixth)
February 1867	2 Rue de Sèvres, Sixth
March 1869	On the site of the former castle, Le Crotoy
November 1869	3 Boulevard Saint-Charles, Amiens
February 1870	23 Boulevard Guyencourt
March 1873	44 Boulevard Longueville (now Boulevard Jules Verne)
August 1877	1 Rue Suffren, Nantes
September 1878	44 Boulevard Longueville
October 1882	2 Rue Charles Dubois
October 1900	44 Boulevard Longueville

Verne made more than 30 journeys to 15 countries and half a dozen dependent territories, the majority of them to the British Isles.

Date	Places	Companions
Early November 1849	Presumably Belgium, Switzerland, or Germany	None
28 July–6 September 1859	Bordeaux, Liverpool, Edinburgh, Highlands, London	Hignard
Possibly 1859 and 1860 (winters)	Montreux (Switzerland)	"Mme Witz"
2 July–8 August 1861	Belgium, Germany, Sweden, Norway, Denmark, Germany	Hignard, Lorois
Mid-1860s	Sydenham	
1865 or 1866	Tende and Bordighera, Italy	Hetzel
1866?	Jersey	
1867	Britain, United States, Canada	Paul
Probably the second week of January 1868	Italian coast, but not as far as Genoa	Hetzel
June 1868	Dover	
19 August 1868	Gravesend, London	Probably Paul
Three or four days in October 1868	Baden-Baden	Hetzel
Mid-June 1869	South coast of England	
August 1869	London, possibly also Ostend	
About 8–15 June 1872	London, Woolwich	Honorine, Paul
Possibly 1872	"The English coast and up the ocean to Scotland," probably via Ireland	Hetzel *fils* and Raoul-Duval
1872, most probably in September	Jersey	
About 14–24 August 1873	Very probably Jersey, Guernsey, Sark	Hetzel
2–3 March 1874	Monaco	Honorine
22–about 26 February 1875	Monaco	Honorine
About 21–27 June 1876	Dover	Suzanne's husband
18–23 July 1876	Southampton, Isle of Wight, Portsmouth	

30 July 1877	Guernsey	Michel, Louis Thuillier, and Monsieur Brasseur
1878	Spain, Portugal, Gibraltar, Morocco, Algeria	Paul, Raoul-Duval, Hetzel *fils*
About 20 August 1878	Jersey	
1–29 July 1879	England, Edinburgh, and Hebrides	Paul (as far as Boulogne), Godefroy, Gaston, Michel, and Hetzel *fils* (Scottish part)
1 June–about 2 July 1881	England, Belgium, Holland, Germany, Denmark, Sweden	Paul, Gaston, Godefroy
6–9 August 1881	Ramsgate	Probably one male passenger
Late August or early September 1881	Ramsgate and Dover	Honorine and many friends
13 May–18 July 1884	Spain, Portugal, Gibraltar, Morocco, Algeria, Tunisia, Malta, Italy, the Vatican	Paul, Maurice, Honorine (from Oran), Godefroy, and Michel (from Algiers)
21 November–1 December 1887	Belgium, Holland	
?	Brighton	
Before 1878	Switzerland	

Appendix C: Journeys
on St. Michel II and III

An important document in Verne's hand (in Paumier 23), apparently untitled, reads:

2nd St. Michel

1877 23 July	[Le] Havre, Caen, Courseulles[-sur-mer], Cherbourg, Guernsey, Perros[-Guirec], Brest, [Le] Croisic, Nantes Pornic, lunch at [Jules-Arsène?] Arnaud's 16 August

3rd St. Michel

1878	Various journeys, and navigation to Algiers. Paul, Duval, Hetzel, me.
1879 1 July	Paul, Godefroy, Gaston, Michel. Boulogne, Scotland, [Le] Havre back 29 July, Michel with xx Nantes pilot, picked up [Alfred Dubois de] Jancigny, went to Brest, lost cannon (1 Aug.), and Michel left for xx alone? xx, we got there 3 August.
1879 16 Aug.	Left from Nantes?, Paul, Michel, and me—(Quiberon by sail-power) —and at? Lorois' in Brest. Lorient, launching of the *Dévastation*.
1879 26 Aug.	Left from Nantes, the Dezaunays [Caroline and her grown-up children]. Collision in harbor of the *St. Michel* [Saint-] Nazaire and broke the boom. Back to Nantes.
1879 16 Sept.	Michel and me. Left from Nantes, Brest, put in at xx cove, sent boat back early.
20 [Sept.]	arrival in Le Tréport. Sea excursion on the 22nd. Ill. [Ernest] Obry, his daughter. Honorine—rented house and sent ship back to Nantes.
1880	no sailing.
1881 1 June	Navigation North Sea and Belgium, Paul, Gaston, Godefroy, and me, back 17 July.
6 August	Journey to Ramsgate and passenger? Back 9 August.
1882	no sailing.
1883	no sailing. Rented boat to [Donatien] Levesque.
1884	Left from Nantes Tuesday, 13 May. Paul, me, Maurice, to Oran, then Honorine xx to Algiers then Godefroy and Michel. 3 July, boat left at Porto d'Anzio, and left again for Nantes. In Rome, 3 July evening.

APPENDIX D: PUBLISHING MALPRACTICE

American and British publishers, including the most prestigious ones, still illegally pass off editions that are travesties. *Journey to the Center of the Earth* is just one example.

The anonymous translation starring "Von Hardwigg," "Harry," and "Gretchen" was the first (*The Boy's Journal* in 12 installments in 1870) and remains the most widely available edition today. As a translation it is, unfortunately, an utter failure.

Hardwigg's creator shows a fine Victorian turn of phrase, but errors also abound. Thus we read "manometer" for "chronometer," an added footnote reading "*(?) Nasal." [*sic*], "sight" for "sigh," and so on. More curious are the changes of names and nationalities, and the translator's habit of inserting one or more invented sentences at the end of each paragraph. Thus extraneous growths appear like "This day, as on other Sundays, we observed as a day of rest and pious meditation," or "The whole state in which we existed was a mystery —and it was impossible to know whether or not I was in earnest." The entire opening paragraphs of the book form a Hardwiggian tumor, as can be seen in the following table:

The Boy's Journal	*French Text* *(Paris: Hetzel, 1867)*	*My Translation*
Looking back to all that has occurred to me since that eventful day, I am scarcely able to believe in the reality of my adventures. They were truly so wonderful that even now I am bewildered when I think of them.	Le 24 mai 1863, un dimanche, mon oncle, le professeur Lidenbrock, revint précipitamment vers sa petite maison située au numéro 19 de Königstrasse, l'une des plus anciennes rues du vieux quartier de Hambourg.	On May 24, 1863, a Sunday, my uncle, Porfesssor Lidenbrock, came rushing back towards his lttle house at no. 19 königstrasse, one of the oldest streets in the historic part of Hmaburg.
My uncle was a German, having married my mother's sister, an Englishwoman. Being very much attached to his fatherless nephew, he invited me to study under him in his home in the fatherland. This home was in a large town, and my uncle a professor of philosophy, chemistry, geology, mineralogy, and many other ologies.	La bonne Marthe dut se croire fort en retard, car le dîner commençait à peine à chanter sur le fourneau de la cuisine.	Martha the maid must have thought she was running very late, for dinner had hardly begun to simmer on the kitchen range.

With time our man gets bolder. He invents every word of chapter 41, describing "Harry's" bird-nesting in the age-old crags of a Scottish castle. About 30 percent of the text bears no relation to the French original.

APPENDIX E: OVERVIEW OF THE WORKS

The Extraordinary Journeys are characterized by simplicity, most evidently in their language, where clarity of thought and a fluent style produce ease of comprehension. Like the Parables or Aesop's Fables, though, layers of implicit meanings often work against the surface level. Again, the subject matter ostensibly avoids what many have thought to be the primary aim of the novel, namely an account of psychological processes, especially relationships between men and women. In the best-known works, the depiction of society at large in its sociological, political, and historical aspects is not very much in evidence either; neither is the transmission of pure ideas. Verne's works, at least in their published form, are concerned with physical, material existence or, more simply, the interaction between people and things. Virtually all of them are situated in a definite time and place, often far away, with the journey a central element.

Verne's imagination works on an unusual sensitivity to the physical world, with the dimensions of space representing a constant interest (rarely "outer space," but frequently "inner"). Modern criticism has found a huge variety of innovative literary techniques in his novels. Reading Verne nearly a century after his death, the abiding impression is that of a distinctive voice and a personal vision: of literary works that remain (or have become?) startlingly modern.

In a chronological course on literature, Verne's first few novels fall between Stendhal's *Scarlet and Black* and Gustave Flaubert's *Sentimental Education*, between Herman Melville and Mark Twain, and yet somehow appear closer to our own era than these works. In purely literary terms, Verne must be considered modern because of his anticipation of the twentieth century's use of self-awareness or "self-consciousness" at all levels: the creation of self-reflecting structures, devices turned back on themselves, symbols that symbolize their own existence, a text that exposes itself to lay bare its own innards.

Despite the "objectivity" of the style, then, the Vernian vision of the world is an intensely personal one. The political, historical, scientific, and geographical themes act principally as vehicles for a profound angst. Nihilism, or at least systematic skepticism, is one of the few common threads running through all the Extraordinary Journeys.

BIBLIOGRAPHY

More than 200 books have been published on Verne, of which perhaps half contain some biographical elements. Biographies in English have, however, been mediocre, devoting considerable space to plot summary. Despite the score in print in France alone, there is no life of Verne available in English.

This bibliography attempts to list all book-length biographies and studies of Verne in French and English, excluding university theses and dissertations; however, space is lacking to indicate the estimated 3,000 articles.

Hachette, Michel de l'Ormeraie, and Rencontre (reprinted by Edito-Service) represent the only complete editions of the Extraordinary Journeys since the original Hetzel publication, but 44 of the books have been issued in Livre de Poche.

Although most English translations of Verne hardly merit that name, with many mistakes, systematic deletion of real-world information, and up to five-sixths of the text cut, a number of reliable ones have appeared recently.

Critical editions of Verne have been notable by their absence. However, in recent years a dozen works have appeared in English with introductions, notes, and other explanatory material (see below: Critical Editions).

The only scholarly books on Verne in English are: Arthur Evans, *Jules Verne Rediscovered: Didacticism and the Scientific Novel* (Westport, CT: Greenwood Press, 1988); William Butcher, *Verne's Journey to the Centre of the Self: Space and Time in the "Voyages extraordinaires"* (London: Macmillan and New York: St. Martin's, 1990); Andrew Martin, *The Mask of the Prophet: The Extraordinary Fictions of Jules Verne* (Oxford: Clarendon Press, 1990); Edmund J. Smyth (ed.), *Jules Verne: Narratives of Modernity* (Liverpool: Liverpool University Press, 2000); and Timothy Unwin, *Jules Verne: Journeys in Writing* (Liverpool: Liverpool University Press, 2005). Mention should also be made of the issue of *Science Fiction Studies* on Verne (vol. 32, part 1 (March 2005)).

The main secondary bibliographies are Jean-Michel Margot, *Bibliographie documentaire sur Jules Verne* (Amiens: Centre de Documentation Jules Verne, 1989); William Butcher, "Jules and Michel Verne," in David Baguley (ed.), *Critical Bibliography of French Literature: The Nineteenth Century* (Syracuse: Syracuse University Press, 1994), 923–40; Volker Dehs's excellent *Guide bibliographique à travers la critique vernienne* (Wetzlar: Phantastische Bibliothek, 2002); and Jean-Michel Margot's outstanding listing of all 10,000 known studies (unpublished).

Thinking about Verne has been transformed recently by the publication of primary material in the *Bulletin de la Société Jules Verne* (*BSJV*); Olivier Dumas, Piero Gondolo della Riva, and Volker Dehs (eds.), *Correspondance inédite de Jules Verne et de Pierre-Jules Hetzel (1863–1886)*, volumes 1, 2, and 3 (1999, 2001, and 2002); Daniel Compère and Jean-Michel Margot (eds.), *Entretiens avec Jules Verne* (1998); and Jean-Michel Margot (ed.), *Jules Verne en son temps* (2004).

Biographical Books

Allott, Kenneth, *Jules Verne*. London: Crescent Press [1940]. Useful for setting Verne in the Romantic context.[1]

Allotte de la Fuÿe, M[arguerite]. *Jules Verne*. Paris: Simon Kra, 1928. (Trans. Erik de Mauny. London: Staples Press, 1954). The great-niece-by-marriage's biography, used in most subsequent studies and English-language encyclopedias, is frequently erroneous or adulterated.

Anderson, K. J., *Captain Nemo*. New York: Pocket Books, 2002. Hypothesizes that Nemo was a real person, and that Verne, while transcribing his adventures, felt jealous of his active life. While containing many inaccuracies and unconvincing as biography, its readability and historical context bring Verne's life to a wider audience.

Annales de Nantes et du Pays nantais. Nantes, Nos. 187–88, 1978.

Avrane, Patrick. *Jules Verne*. Paris: Stock, 1997. Superb illustrations but lacking a clear focus.

Becker, Beril. *Jules Verne*. New York: G. P. Putnam's, 1966. Derivative and for young people.

Boia, Lucian. *Jules Verne: Les paradoxes d'un mythe*. Paris: Belles Lettres, 2005. Lacking a clear focus.

Born, Franz. *The Man who Invented the Future: Jules Verne*. New York: Prentice-Hall, 1963. Derivative.

Chesneaux, Jean. *Une Lecture politique de Jules Verne*. Paris: Maspéro, 1971. Fine analysis, but overambitious in its attempt to synthesize Verne's political philosophy.

Claretie, Jules. *Jules Verne*. Paris: A. Quantin, 1883.

Compère, Cécile (ed.). *Visions nouvelles sur Jules Verne*. Amiens: Centre de documentation Jules Verne, 1978.

Compère, Daniel. *La Vie amiénoise de Jules Verne*. Amiens: Annales du centre régional de recherche et de documentation pédagogiques d'Amiens, 1974.

Compère, Daniel, and Jean-Michel Margot (eds.). *Entretiens avec Jules Verne*. Geneva: Slatkine, 1998. Esp.: Adrien Marx, "Jules Verne" (1873, 17–22); Charles Raymond, "Jules Verne" (1875, 23–29); Nellie Bly, chapter 4 of *Around the World in 72 Days* (1890) (39–47); Robert H. Sherard, "Verne's Bravo" (1890, 65–72); Robert H. Sherard, "Jules Verne at home" (1894, 83–97); Marie A. Belloc, "Jules Verne at home" (1895, 99–109); Edmondo de Amicis, "Une Visite chez Jules Verne" (1896, 111–20); Adolphe Brisson,

"Jules Verne" (1897, 133–39); Robert H. Sherard, "Jules Verne Revisited" (1903, 196–201); Gordon Jones, "Jules Verne at home" (1904, 213–20). All interviews, even those published in English, are cited in this biography following their page numbers in this authoritative volume. With the correspondence the most important source of knowledge about Verne.

Costello, Peter. *Jules Verne, Inventor of Science Fiction.* London: Hodder and Stoughton, 1978. Although illuminating about English-language sources and the scientific context, unfortunately based on Métral's invented biography and other apocrypha.

Dehs, Volker. *Guide bibliographique à travers la critique vernienne.* Wetzlar: Förderkreis Phantastik in Wetzlar, 2002. Invaluable.

Dehs, Volker. *Jules Verne.* Hamburg: Rowohlt, 1986. Excellent minibiography in German, using the correspondence and dealing with the works through their inception.

Dehs, Volker. *Jules Verne.* Dusseldorf: Artemis and Winkler, 2005. The only fully researched and trustworthy biography.

Dekiss, Jean-Paul. *Jules Verne l'enchanteur.* Kiron: Editions du Félin, 1999. Useful biography setting the philosophical, historic, social, and educational contexts but adding little that is new and spending too long on an arbitrary choice of works.

Dekiss, Jean-Paul. *Jules Verne: Le Rêve du progress.* Paris: Gallimard, 1991. Entertaining if unambitious biography, with some errors but fine illustrations.

Dekiss, Jean-Paul (ed.). *Jules Verne: Le Poète de la science.* [Paris]: Timée, 2005. Nicely illustrated collection of about 30 mini-essays on individual aspects of Verne's life, useful but insufficiently critical.

Ducrest de Villeneuve, Raymond. Unpublished, untitled illustrated typescript [1930] by Verne's nephew, partly brought up in his home. Crucial information about the early environment, although some of the information is erroneous. The only copy cataloged is in the Jules Verne International Center in Amiens.

Dumas, Olivier. *Jules Verne: Avec la publication de la correspondance inédite de Jules Verne à sa famille.* Lyon: La Manufacture, 1988. 191 letters (1842–98) to Pierre, Sophie, Paul, Marie, and Maurice Verne, the most important source of information on Verne's life. Withdrawn from sale after a court case and two appeals.

Dumas, Olivier. *Voyage à travers Jules Verne.* Montreal: Stanké, 2000. Update of banned 1988 book, without the family correspondence. This thematically arranged biography, with an accurate chronology of the works, is one of the best, argued with passion and knowledge, although going too far in interpreting Verne's names and unfair on Michel.

Dumas, Olivier, Piero Gondolo della Riva, and Volker Dehs (eds.) *Correspondance inédite de Jules et Michel Verne avec l'éditeur Louis-Jules Hetzel (1886–1914).* Vol. 1 (1886–96), vol. 2 (1886–1914). Geneva: Slatkine, 2004, 2006. About 700 letters ([Jan. 86]–1914).

Dumas, Olivier, Piero Gondolo della Riva, and Volker Dehs (eds.) *Correspondance inédite de Jules Verne et Pierre-Jules Hetzel (1863–1886)*. Vol. 1 (1863–74), vol. 2 (1875–78), vol. 3 (1879–86). Geneva: Slatkine, 1999, 2001, 2003. The second-most important source of information on Verne, with 700 annotated letters, an index, a useful chronology of the works, and appendixes.

Dusseau, Joëlle. *Jules Verne*. Paris: Perrin, 2005. Although largely deriving from published documents, the most complete biography available in French.

Evans, I. O. *Jules Verne and His Work*. New York: Twayne, 1966. Covers the ground, albeit with little originality and many mistakes.

Frank, Bernard. *Jules Verne et ses voyages*. Paris: Flammarion, 1941. Follows Allotte de la Fuÿe but invents additional episodes.

Freedman, Russell. *Jules Verne: Portrait of a Prophet*. New York: Holiday House, 1965. Derivative and for young people.

Gallagher, Edward J., Judith A. Mistichelli, and John A. Van Eerde. *Jules Verne: A Primary and Secondary Bibliography*. Boston: G. K. Hall, 1980.

Gondolo della Riva, Piero. *Bibliographie analytique de toutes les oeuvres de Jules Verne*. Vols. 1 and 2. Paris: Société Jules Verne, 1977, 1985.

Grandmaison, Henri de. *Jules Verne: De Nantes à Amiens*. Montreuil: CMD, 1999. Proficient and finely illustrated.

Harold, Peter. *Jules Verne* (in Swedish). Forthcoming. Lively but derivative and unresearched.

Jules-Verne, Jean. *Jules Verne*. Paris: Hachette, 1973. (Trans. and adapted by Roger Greaves. *Jules Verne: A Biography*. New York: Taplinger 1976.) Grandson's biography is invaluable, especially on relations between the writer and his son, but misquotes the correspondence, has overlong plot summaries, and is selective; the translation has new material and reads better. (While page numbers refer to the English edition, translations of the French text are sometimes my own.)

Lemire, Charles. *Jules Verne, 1828–1905: L'Homme, l'écrivain*. Paris: Berger-Levrault, 1908. Fine work by Amiens friend of Verne's.

Lottman, Herbert R. *Jules Verne: An Exploratory Biography*. New York, St. Martin's Press, 1996. Efficiently uses recent research, but fails to synthesize and produces unconvincing evaluations of the novels. Catastrophically reviewed.

Lynch, Lawrence. *Jules Verne*. New York: Twayne, 1992. Thin and uncritical.

Marcetteau, Agnès, Annie Ollivier, and Claudine Sainlot. *Catalogue des manuscrits de Jules Verne*. Nantes: Bibliothèque Municipale, 1988.

Margot, Jean-Michel (ed.) *Jules Verne en son temps* (Paris: Encrage, 2004). An important collection of contemporary accounts and reviews of Verne.

Martin, Charles-Noël. *Jules Verne: Sa vie et son oeuvre*. Lausanne: Rencontre, 1971. Intelligent and perceptive: at the time the only reliable account, and still important today.

Martin, Charles-Noël. "Recherches sur la nature, les origines et le traitement de la science dans l'oeuvre de Jules Verne" (Ph. D. Thesis, Paris, Sorbonne (Université Paris 7), 23 June 1980). Unfocused and tendentious, but containing important original research.

Martin, Charles-Noël. *La Vie et l'oeuvre de Jules Verne.* Paris: Michel de l'Ormeraie, 1978. With many unpublished documents, outstanding on the early years and the publishing contracts, but partly superseded by the publication of the correspondence.

Maudhuy, Roger. *Jules Verne: La Face cachée.* Paris: France Empire, 2005. Little awareness of the correspondence or unpublished sources, but intelligent and readable summary, with one or two vital contemporary documents.

Moré, Marcel. *Le Très curieux Jules Verne.* Paris: Gallimard, 1960. Huge impact at the time, but now useless.

Moré, Marcel. *Nouvelles explorations de Jules Verne.* Paris: Gallimard, 1963. Huge impact at the time, but now worthless.

Paumier, Jean-Yves. *Jules Verne.* Grenoble: Glénat, 2005. Competent but adding little that is new.

Peare, Catherine Owens. *Jules Verne.* New York: Henry Holt, 1956. Derivative and for young people.

Peare, Catherine Owens. *Jules Verne: His Life.* New York: Henry Holt and Company, 1956. Paraphrase of Marguerite for 12-year-olds.

Poivre d'Arvor, Olivier, and Patrick Poivre d'Arvor, *Le Monde selon Jules Verne.* Paris: Mengès, 2005. Incoherently written in the first person.

Prouteau, Gilbert. *Le Grand roman de Jules Verne: Sa Vie.* Paris: Stock, 1979. Despite its fine style, vitiated by failure to distinguish between invention and the new primary documents cited.

Rivière, François. *Jules Verne, images d'un mythe.* Paris: Henri Veyrier, 1978. Derivative and dated but with good pictures.

Robien, Gilles de. *Jules Verne: Le rêveur incompris.* Neuilly-sur-Seine: Lafon, 2000. Readable volume partly ghost-written for the senior minister in the Chirac government, but adds nothing new, concentrating on Verne's life in Amiens.

Robin, Christian. *Un Monde connu et inconnu.* Nantes: Centre universitaire de recherches verniennes, 1978. Good on the Nantes sections, and with useful reproduction of illustrations.

Schoell, William. *Remarkable Journeys: The Story of Jules Verne,* 2002. Derivative and for young people.

Soriano, Marc. *Jules Verne (le cas Verne).* Paris: Julliard, 1978. Fluently written and adequately researched, but much too speculative.

Streissguth, Thomas. *Science Fiction Pioneer: A Story about Jules Verne.* New York: Carolrhoda, 2000. Derivative and for young people.

Teeters, Peggy. *Jules Verne: The Man Who Invented Tomorrow.* New York: Walker and Co., 1992. Adequate but derivative and for young people.

Valetoux, Philippe. *Jules Verne: En mer et contre tous* (Paris: Magellan, 2005). Rather general and showing little awareness of published sources, apart from the invaluable description of the *St. Michel* voyages, perhaps drawn from the unpublished logbooks.

Waltz, George H. *Jules Verne: The Biography of an Imagination.* New York: Henry

Holt, 1943. Nicely written and insightful, but fails through excluding French sources.

Weissenberg, Eric. *Jules Verne: Un Univers fabuleux*. Lausanne, Favre, 2004. Usefully dispels the science fiction myth, with fine illustrations and a few new claims, but over-long and general.

Critical Editions of Verne's Novels

Adventures of Captain Hatteras, The. Trans. with an introduction and notes by William Butcher. Oxford: Oxford University Press, 2005.

Around the World in Eighty Days. Trans. with an introduction and notes by William Butcher. Oxford: Oxford University Press, 1995.

Backwards to Britain. Trans. Janice Valls-Russel, introduction by William Butcher, consultant editor William Butcher. Edinburgh: Chambers, <u>1992.</u>

Begum's Millions, The. Trans. Stanford L. Luce, ed. Arthur B. Evans, introduction and notes by Peter Schulman. Middletown, CT: Wesleyan University Press, 2005.

From the Earth to the Moon. Walter James Miller (ed.). New York: Crowell, 1978.

Humbug. Trans. with an introduction and notes by William Butcher. Acadian: Edinburgh and Hong Kong, 1992.

Invasion of the Sea. Trans. Edward Baxter, ed. Arthur B. Evans, introduction and other material by Arthur B. Evans. Middletown, CT: Wesleyan University Press, 2001.

Journey to the Centre of the Earth. Trans. with an introduction and notes by William Butcher. Oxford: Oxford University Press, 1992; revised edition with new material, 1998.

Lighthouse at the End of the World. Trans. with an introduction and notes by William Butcher. Nebraska: Nebraska University Press, forthcoming 2006.

Meteor Hunt. Trans. with an introduction and notes by Frederick Paul Walter and Walter James Miller. Nebraska: Nebraska University Press, forthcoming 2006.

Mighty Orinoco, The. Trans. Stanford L. Luce, ed. Arthur B. Evans, introduction and notes by Walter James Miller. Middletown, CT: Wesleyan University Press, 2002.

Mysterious Island, The. Trans. Sidney Kravitz, ed. Arthur B. Evans, introduction, appendices, notes, and other material by William Butcher. Middletown, CT: Wesleyan University Press, 2001.

Twenty Thousand Leagues under the Sea. Trans. and annotated by Walter James Miller and Frederick Paul Walter. Annapolis, Maryland: Naval Institute Press, 1993.

Twenty Thousand Leagues under the Sea. Walter James Miller (ed.) New York: Crowell, 1976.

Twenty Thousand Leagues under the Seas. Trans. with an introduction and notes by William Butcher. Oxford: Oxford University Press, 1998.

trans!?

Novels Published during Verne's Lifetime

English Title (with short title) Verne's First Title, if Different French Title	Written [2] First Published [3] Print Run (000s) [4]
Five Weeks in a Balloon (Five Weeks) *Journey in the Air* *Cinq semaines en ballon*	1862 1863 (Hetzel) 76
The Adventures of Captain Hatteras (Hatteras) *Journey to the North Pole* *Voyages et aventures du capitaine Hatteras*	1863–64 1864–65 37
Journey to the Center of the Earth *Voyage au centre de la Terre*	1864 1864 (Hetzel) 48
From the Earth to the Moon *Journey to the Moon* *De la Terre à la Lune*	1864–65 1865 (*Débats*) 37
Captain Grant's Children (Grant) *Journey around the World in Search of Captain Grant* *Les Enfants du capitaine Grant*	1865–66 1865–67 38
Twenty Thousand Leagues under the Seas *(Twenty Thousand Leagues)* *Journey under the Waters* *Vingt mille lieues sous les mers*	1866–69 1869–70 48
Around the Moon *Return from the Moon* *Autour de la Lune*	1868–69 1869 (*Débats*) 31
A Floating City *The "Great Eastern"* *Une Ville flottante*	1869 1870 (*Débats*) 30
Adventures of Three Russians and Three Britons *Adventures of Half a Dozen Savants* *Aventures de trois Russes et de trois Anglais dans* *l'Afrique australe*	1870 1871–72 36
The "Chancellor" *Survivors of the "Chancellor"* *Le Chancellor*	1870–74 1874–75 (*Le Temps*) 27

Around the World in Eighty Days[5]	1872
The Journey in 80 Days	1872 (*Le Temps*)
Le Tour du monde en quatre-vingts jours	121
The Fur Country	1871–72
Journey to the Fur Country	1872–73
Le Pays des fourrures	25
The Mysterious Island	1873–74
Uncle Robinson	1874–75
L'Île mystérieuse	45
Michel Strogoff (Strogoff)[6]	1874–75
Courier of the Tzar	1876
Michel Strogoff	54
Hector Servadac	1874–76
The Comet	1877
Hector Servadac	17
The Black Indies (also known as *The Underground City* and *Child of the Cavern*)[7]	1876–77
A Corner of the Black Indies	1877
Les Indes noires	31
The Boy Captain	1877–78
A 15-Year-Old Hero	1878
Un Capitaine de quinze ans	31
Tribulations of a Chinese in China	1878
The Voluntary Murderee	1879 (*Le Temps*)
Les Tribulations d'un Chinois en Chine	28
The Bégum's Millions[8]	1878
The Heritage of the Langevol	1879
Les Cinq cents millions de la Bégum	18
The Steam House	1879
The House on Wheels	1879–80
Maison à vapeur	17
The Giant Raft	1880
The Amazon	1881
La Jangada	14
School for Robinsons	1881
The Fake Robinson	1882
L'École des Robinsons	10

The Green Ray	1881
Le Rayon vert	1882 (*Le Temps*)
	15
Keraban the Inflexible	1882
Around the Black Sea	1883
Kéraban-le-têtu	13
The Archipelago on Fire	1883
	1884
L'Archipel en feu	12
The Southern Star[9]	1883
The Northern Star	1884
L'Étoile du Sud	11
Mathias Sandorf	1883–84
	1885
Mathias Sandorf	11
Wreck of the "Cynthia"[10]	1884
The Mediterranean	1885
L'Épave du "Cynthia"	6[11]
Clipper of the Clouds	1885
Conquest of the Air	1886 (*Débats*)
Robur-le-conquérant	12
Lottery Ticket	1885
No. 9672	1886
Un Billet de loterie	10
North against South	1885–86
Two Brothers	1887
Nord contre Sud	9
Two Years' Holiday	1886–87
A Boarding School for Robinsons	1888
Deux ans de vacances	8
Family without a Name	1887–88
Canada	1889
Famille-sans-nom	7
Topsy-Turvy	1888
Righting the Axis	1889 (Hetzel)
Sans dessus dessous	8

César Cascabel	1889	
Backwards Journey	1890	
César Cascabel	9	
Carpathian Castle	1889	
	1892	
Le Château des Carpathes	9	
	20[12]	
Mistress Branican	1890	
Mistress Branikan	1891	
Mistress Branican	7	
Claudius Bombarnac	1891	
Notes of a Reporter	1892	(*Le Soleil*)
Claudius Bombarnac	8	
	20	
Little Fellow	1891	
	1893	
P'tit-Bonhomme	6	
	16	
Adventures of Captain Antifer	1892	
	1894	
Mirifiques aventures de Maître Antifer	6	
	14	
Propeller Island	1893	
	1895	
L'Île à hélice	7	
	14	
Drama in Livonia	1893	
	1904	
Un Drame en Livonie	5	
For the Flag	1894	
Ker Karraje	1896	
Face au drapeau	12	
	17	
The Mighty Orinoco[13]	1894	
Orinoco	1898	
Le Superbe Orénoque	5	
	12	

Clovis Dardentor	1895
Dardentor	1896
Clovis Dardentor	6
	16
The Ice Sphinx	1895
Antarctic Sphinx	1897
Le Sphinx des glaces	5
	14
Treetop Village	1896
The Great Forest	1901
Le Village aérien	6
	12
Second Homeland	1896
New Switzerland	1900
Seconde patrie	4
	11
Will of an Eccentric	1897
	1899
Le Testament d'un excentrique	5
	12
The Kip Brothers	1898
The Norik Brothers	1902
Les Frères Kip	4
	11
Tales of Jean-Marie Cabidoulin	1899
A Marine Monster	1901
Les Histoires de Jean-Marie Cabidoulin	5
	12
Traveling Scholarships	1899
	1903
Bourses de voyage	4
	10
Invasion of the Sea	1902
The Saharan Sea	1905
L'Invasion de la mer	4
	9

Master of the World	1902–3
Master after God	1904
Maître du monde	5
	9

Published Short Stories

Five of Jules Verne's short stories underwent major changes when reprinted as part of the Extraordinary Voyages: "The First Ships of the Mexican Navy," renamed "A Drama in Mexico"; "A Balloon Journey," renamed "A Drama in the Air"; "Martin Paz," "Master Zacharius," and "Dr. Ox." "In the Year 2889" (*The Forum*, Feb. 1889) was signed Jules Verne but written by Michel.

Title in English Title in French	Approximate Year Written Date and Place of Publication
"The First Ships of the Mexican Navy" "Les Premiers navires de la Marine Mexicaine"	1850 1851, *Musée*
"A Balloon Journey" "Un Voyage en ballon	1851 1851, *Musée*
"Martin Paz" "Martin Paz"	1852 1852, *Musée*
"Master Zacharius" "Maître Zacharius"	1853 1854, *Musée*
"Winter amid the Ice" "Un Hivernage dans les glaces"	1853 1855, *Musée*
"The Count of Chanteleine" "Le Comte de Chanteleine"	? 1864, *Musée*
"Blockade Runners" "Les Forceurs de blocus"	1865 1865, *Musée*
"Dr. Ox" "Le Docteur Ox"	1871 1871, *Musée*
"Mutineers of the *Bounty*" (based on a manuscript by Gabriel Marcel) "Les Révoltés de la *Bounty*"	 1879 1879, Hetzel
"Frritt-Flacc" "Frritt-Flacc"	1884 1884, *Figaro illustré*

"Gil Braltar"	1886
"Gil Braltar"	1886, *Petit Journal*
"Flight to France"	1860s?
"Le Chemin de France"	1887, *Le Temps*

| "In the Year 2889" (by Michel Verne) | 1888 |
| "In the Year 2889" | 1889, *The Forum* |

| "The Rat Family" | 1886 |
| "La Famille Raton" | 1891, *Figaro illustré* |

| "Mr. Ray Sharp and Miss Me Flat" | 1892 |
| "Monsieur Ré-dièze et Mlle Mi-bémol" | 1893, *Figaro illustré* |

Novels and Short Stories Not Published during Verne's Lifetime

Title in English Title in French	Written Publication
A Priest in 1835 *Un Prêtre en 1835*	1846–47 1992
"Jedediah Jamet" "Jédédias Jamet"	1847 1993 (in *SC*)[14]
"Pierre-Jean" "Pierre-Jean"	ca.1852 1988
"The Marriage of Monsieur Anselme des Tilleuls" "Le Mariage de Monsieur Anselme des Tilleuls"	ca.1855 1991
"San Carlos" "San Carlos"	ca.1856 1993 (in *SC*)
"The Siege of Rome" "Le Siège de Rome"	ca.1859 1993 (in *SC*)
Backwards to Britain *Voyage à reculons en Angleterre et en Ecosse*	1859–60 1989
Paris in the Twentieth Century *Paris au XXe siècle*	1860, 1863 1994
Humbug[15] "Le Humbug"	ca.1867 1910

Uncle Robinson[16]	1870–71
L'Oncle Robinson	1991
The Beautiful Yellow Danube[17]	1896–97
Le Beau Danube jaune	1988
Magellania[18]	1896–99
En Magellanie	1987
The Golden Volcano	1899–1900
Le Volcan d'or	1989
Meteor Hunt	1901
La Chasse au météore	1986
The Secret of Wilhelm Storitz	1901
Le Secret de Wilhelm Storitz	1985
Lighthouse at the End of the World[19]	1903
Le Phare du bout du monde	1905
"Study Trip"[20]	1903–4
"Voyage d'études"	1993
"Edom"[21]	?
"Edom"	1910

Plays and Libretti

The first publication of most of the plays was in *Manuscrits Nantais* (Nantes: Bibliothèque Municipale, 1991), published in a very small number of copies. Nearly all the plays were reprinted in Christian Robin (ed.), *Théâtre inédit* (Paris: Cherche Midi, 2005) (*TI*).[22]

English Title **French Title** **Form**	**Written** **Collaborator(s)** **Performances 1851–1905 / Published**
No known title	Rejected by the Riquiqui Puppet Theater (Nantes)
Tragedy in verse	The text is lost, mentioned only in ADF 23
No known title	1845
Vaudeville	*TI* 1004–1030 (only Act 2 survives)

The Gunpowder Plot *La Conspiration des poudres* Five-act tragedy in verse	1846 *TI* 23–110
A Drama under Louis XV *Un Drame sous Louis XV*[23] Five-act tragedy in verse	1846 *TI* 211–88
Alexander VI *Alexandre VI*[24] Five-act drama in verse	1846–47 *TI* 124–97
Rabelais's Quarter-Hour *Le Quart d'heure de Rabelais* One-act comedy in verse	1847 *TI* 312–33
Sea Outing *Une Promenade en mer* One-act vaudeville	1847 *TI* 341–78
"Don Galaor" "Don Galaor" Synopsis of one-act comedy	1847 *TI* 298–307

Broken Straws
Les Pailles rompues
One-act comedy in verse
	1849
	Dumas *fils*
	Historic Theatre, 12–25 June 1850,
	    12 or 15 performances[25] /
	    Beck, 1850; *Revue Jules Verne*, 11, 2001, 33–94

The Grouse *Le Coq de bruyère* Synopsis	1849 *TI* 382–87
Abdullah *Abd'allah* Vaudeville in two acts	1849 *TI* 402–39
Sometimes You Need Someone Smaller *On a souvent besoin d'un plus petit que soi* Synopsis	1849 *TI* 448–54
Thousand and Second Night *La Mille et deuxième nuit* One-act play in verse	1850 Music by Aristide Hignard *TI* 463–92

Who Laughs Dines	1850
Quiridine et Quiridinerit	
Three-act comedy in verse	*TI* 499–566
The Guimard	1850
La Guimard	
Two-act comedy	*TI* 574–635
"The Savants"	1851, 1867
"Les Savants"	
Three-act comedy	The text is lost
"The Breton Fiancés"	1851
"Les Fiancés Bretons"	The text is lost
From Charybdis to Scylla	1851
De Charybde en Scylla	
One-act comedy in verse	*TI* 642–69
Mona Lisa	1851–55
Monna Lisa [*sic*]	
One-act comedy in verse	Cahiers de l'Heme, Paris: L'Herne, 1974
Castles in Caifornia, or A Rolling Stone Gathers no Moss	1851
Les Châteaux en Californie, ou Pierre qui roule n'amasse pas mousse	Pierre Chevalier
One-act comedy	*Musée des familles*, June 1852
The Tower of Montlhéry	1852
La Tour de Montlhéry	Charles Wallut
Five-act drama	*TI* 680–782
Blind Man's Bluff	1852
Le Colin-Maillard	Michel Carré; music by Hignard
One-act comic opera	Lyric Theater, 28 April 1853, 45 performances / Levy, 1853; *BSJV* 120
The Adopted Son	1853
Un Fils adoptif	Wallut
Comedy	*BSJV* 143
The Knights of the Daffodil	1852
Les Compagnons de la marjolaine	Carré; music by Hignard

One-act comic opera	Lyric Theater, 6 June 1855, 24 performances / Levy, 1855; *BSJV* 143
Happy for One Day *Les Heureux du jour* Five-act comedy in verse	1855–56 *TI* 799–882
War on Tyrants *Guerre aux tyrans* One-act comedy in verse	1854 *TI* 886–921
Beside the Adour *Au bord de l'Adour* One-act comedy in verse	1855 *TI* 926–52
Mr. Chimpanzee *Monsieur de Chimpanzé* One-act operetta	1857 Perhaps with Carré; music by Hignard Bouffes-Parisiens, 17 February 1858, several performances / *BSJV* 57
The Ardennes Inn *L'Auberge des Ardennes* One-act comic opera	1859 Carré; music by Hignard Lyric Theater, 1 September 1860,
Eleven-Day Siege *Onze jours de siège* Three-act comedy	1854–60 Wallut Vaudeville Theater, 1 June 1861 /
An American Nephew, or The Two Frontignacs *Un Neveu d'Amérique, ou Les Deux Frontignac* Three-act comedy	1860 Wallut; very probably revised by Édouard Cadol Cluny Theater, 17 April 1873, for two months / Hetzel, 1873; published with *Clovis Dardentor*, Paris: Union Générale d'Éditions, 1979
"The Sabines" "Les Sabines" Comic opera or operetta in two or three acts	1867 Wallut *TI* 963–90 (only the first act has survived)

"The North Pole" "Le Pôle Nord" Synopsis	1871 *TI* 993– 97 (the play itself is lost)
Around the World in 80 Days *Le Tour du monde en 80 jours* Four-act play	1872 Cadol and Verne *BSJV* 152:5–80

Around the World in 80 Days
Le Tour du monde en 80 jours
 	
Play in five acts and one prologue
	1873–4
	Adolphe d'Ennery; music by
	   J. J. Debillemont
	Porte Saint-Martin Theater, 7
	   November 1874, 415
	   performances and thousands
	   more in subsequent
	   years / Hetzel, 1879

Captain Grant's Children
Les Enfants du capitaine Grant
Play in five acts and one prologue
	1875
	d'Ennery; music by Debillemont
	Porte Saint-Martin Theater, 26
	   December 1878, 113
	   performances / Hetzel, 1881

"Dr. Ox"
"Le Docteur Ox"
 	
Three-act comic opera
	1877
	Philippe Gille and Arnold Mortier;
	   music by Jacques Offenbach
	Variétés Theater, 42 performances /
	   Choudens, 1877

Michel Strogoff
Michel Strogoff
Five-act play
1880,
	1878
	d'Ennery
	Châtelet Theater, 17 November
	
	386 performances and thousands
	   more in subsequent years /
	   Hetzel, 1881

Journey through the Impossible
Voyage à travers l'impossible
 	
Three-act play
	1882
	d'Ennery; music by
	   Oscar de Lagoanère
	Porte Saint-Martin Theater,
	   November 25, 1882,
	   43 performances [26] / Paris,
	   Pauvert, 1981

Keraban the Inflexible *Kéraban-le-Têtu* Five-act play	1883 Gaffe Lyrique Theater, 3 September 1883, 49 performances / *BSJV* 85–86, 27–134
Mathias Sandorf *Mathias Sandorf* Five-act play	1887 William Busnach and Georges Maurens Théâtre de l'Ambigu, 27 November, 1887, 85 performances / Paris, Société Jules Verne, 1992
Tribulations of a Chinese in China" "Les Tribulations d'un Chinois en Chine" Play	1888–90 Text is lost

Other Works Published
English Title
French Title
Published

"Is There a Moral Obligation for France to Intervene in the Affairs of Poland?"
"Y a-t-il obligation morale pour la France d'intervenir dans les affaires de la Pologne?"
Cahiers Jules Verne, 8:1–16

The Salon of 1857
Le Salon de 1857
Revue des beaux-arts: Tribune des artistes, 27th Year, Vol. 8, 1857 *(Beaux-arts)*[27]

Backwards to Britain (BB)
Voyage en Angleterre et en Ecosse
Cherche-Midi, 1989

"Joyous Miseries of Three Travelers in Scandinavia" ("Joyous Miseries")
"Joyeuses misères de trois voyageurs en Scandinavie"
Géo, Special Issue [2003], xvii–xxii

"Concerning the *Géant*"
"A propos du *Géant*"
Musée des familles, December 1863

"Edgar Allan Poe and his Works"
"Edgard Poë [sic] et ses oeuvres"
Musée, April 1864

"The Meridians and the Calendar"
"Les Méridiens et le Calendrier"
Journal d'Amiens, no. 4968, 14–15 April 1873, 3

"Ascent of the *Météore*"
"Ascension du *Météore*"
Journal d'Amiens, 29–30 September 1873

llustrated Geography of France and its Colonies (*Geography*)[28]
Géographie illustrée de la France et de ses colonies
Hetzel, 1867

"An Ideal City"
"Une Ville idéale"
Mémoires de l'Académie des sciences, belles-lettres, et arts d'Amiens (vol. XXII, 1874–75)

Discovery of the Earth
Découverte de la Terre
1870

The Great Navigators of the Eighteenth Century
Les Grands Navigateurs du XVIIIème siècle
1879

The Voyagers of the Nineteenth Century
Les Voyageurs du XIXème siècle
1880

"Ten Hours' Hunting"
"Dix heures de chasse"
Hetzel, 1882

"Memories of Childhood and Youth" (MCY)
"Souvenirs d'enfance et de jeunesse"
The Youth's Companion (9 April 1891), as "The Story of My Boyhood"

"Future of the Submarine"

Popular Mechanics, 6 (June 1904)

"The Solution of Mind Problems by the Imagination"

Heart's International Cosmopolitan (New York), vol. 85, no. 508, October 1928

Letters to and from Jules Verne

191 letters (12 Dec. 42–15 Oct. 98) in Olivier Dumas,
Jules Verne: Avec la publication de la correspondance inédite de Jules Verne à sa famille
About 700 letters (26 Jun. 63–[19 Mar. 86]) in Dumas, Olivier, Piero Gondolo della Riva, and Volker Dehs (eds.)
Correspondance inédite de Jules Verne et Pierre-Jules Hetzel (1863–1886). Vol. 1 (1863–74), vol. 2 (1875–78), vol. 3 (1879–86).

About 700 letters ([Jan. 86]–1914) in Dumas, Olivier, Piero Gondolo della Riva, and Volker Dehs (eds.) *Correspondance inédite de Jules et Michel Verne avec l'éditeur Louis-Jules Hetzel (1886–1914)*. Vol. 1 (1886–96), vol. 2 (1886–1914) (Geneva: Slatkine, 2004, 2006).
About 200 letters to Dumas *fils*, Ferdinand de Viane, Théophile Gautier, Nadar, Mario Turiello, and others: references in Dehs, *Guide.*

Poems and Songs

Eighty-eight poems in *Poésies inédites*, Christian Robin (ed.), (Paris: Cherche Midi, 1989) and *Textes oubliés*, Francis Lacassin (ed.), Paris, Union Générale d'Éditions, 1979).
About 30 other songs and poems, listed on http://jv.gilead.org.il/biblio/poems.html; seven were published in Aristide Hignard, *Rimes et mélodies* (Paris: Heu, 1857) and three in Aristide Hignard, *Rimes et mélodies* (Paris: Heu, 1863).

Speeches

16 reports on the operation of the Municipal Theater, published in *Bulletin municipal de la Ville d'Amiens* (1891–1900), listed on http://jv.gilead.org.il/biblio/speech.html.
About 20 speeches, mostly made to the Academy of Amiens and local civic organizations (1875–98), listed on http://jv.gilead.org.il/biblio/speech.html.
About 60 interventions at the Municipal Council (1888–1903), listed by Volker Dehs in *BSJV* 112:56.

Manuscripts and Unpublished Works

Nantes owns the manuscripts of more than 130 works (about 13,000 folios), including the overwhelming majority of novels, short stories, and plays. The Web page at www.arkhenum.fr/bm_nantes/jules_verne provides a complete listing and description, with two or three high-quality color folios from each and plans to add the remainder.
The French National Library (Department of Manuscripts, NAF 16932–7152 and Vols. 67–80) keeps the two known manuscripts of *Twenty Thousand Leagues*, the second manuscript of *Around the World*, those of "The New World" and "The Old Continents" (unpublished full-length geographical works revised by Verne on the basis of a draft by Gabriel Marcel), and various other unpublished materials. The manuscript of *Journey to the Center of the Earth* is in private hands in the United States. That of "Edom" is held by Verne's descendants in France, with

photocopies of the first and last folios, in Michel's hand with large numbers of corrections, circulating among specialists.

The city of Amiens recently bought the legendary FF 25 million, 30,000-piece Gondolo della Riva collection, but has kept its contents secret to date and refuses requests for information. It is reported to contain the following documents: travel notes of the 1861 Scandinavian and 1867 American journeys; logbooks of the 1879 Scottish and 1884 Mediterranean trips (all the trips of 1875–84, according to OD 274); an itinerary of the 1859 Scotland visit; the research card index, with more than 20,000 unused items, both factual and commentary, covering principally Verne's reading, but also with biographical information;[29] 29 volumes of press cuttings (1862–1914), including 600 pages of newspaper obituaries; 300 letters from Verne to Michel; and many other documents.

Resources Online

The two main sites with specialized resources on Verne are http://jv.gilead.org.il/ and http://home.netvigator.com/~wbutcher/.

An up-to-date list of corrections for future editions of *Jules Verne: The Definitive Biography* appears on http://home.netvigator.com/~wbutcher/books/jvdb.

PERMISSIONS

Many of the photographs and illustrations have been cropped for the present publication. Acknowledgment is made for kind permission to reproduce the following photographs and illustrations: Société Jules Verne nos. 11, 18, 21, 22; Société Académique de Nantes et de la Loire-Atlantique 3, 8, 9, 10; and Daniel Compère, 27.

The following photographs and illustrations are reprinted from the sources indicated: 1, 2 (lithographies by Ph. Benoist in *La Bretagne contemporaine* (1865)), 3 (*Annales 36*), 4 (ADF 33), 5 (ADF 17), 6 (Avrane 24), 7 (lithography by Asselineau, in *France de nos jours* (Paris: Sinett, 1853–56)), 8 (*Annales de Nantes,* no. 100 (1955), 12), 9 (*Annales,* 1978, 10), 10 (*Annales,* 1978, 12), 11 (*BSJV* 69:49), 12 (author's collection), 13 (Grandmaison 22), 14 ("Alexandre Dumas II," unsigned engraving (Paris: Chardon [ca.1850])), 15 (ADF 48), 16 (author's collection), 17 (Avrane 30), 18 (BSJV 150:10), 19 (*Revue Jules Verne,* no. 18 (2004), 129), 20 (ADF 49), 21 (*BSJV* 140:14), 22 (BSJV 70:73), 23 (*Le Monde illustré,* 4 Dec. 1880), 24 (reproduced by kind permission of the owner), 25 (*Around the World in Eighty Days* (Boston: Osgood, 1873)), 26 (in the French National Library), 27 (Daniel Compère, *Vie amiénoise,* 24), 28 (Charles Lemire, Jules Verne (Paris: Berger-Levrault, 1908), 32), 29 (JJV 38), 30 (*Le Monde illustré,* 4 Dec. 1880), 31 (Lemire 33), 32 (*L'Illustration,* 1 April 1905).

The maps on pages 33, 39, 135, 167, and 263, drawn by Mike Shand, are reproduced with the generous permission of Ian Thompson and Mike Shand.

NOTES

Introduction (pp. xix–xxvi)

1 Verne is "the most read, the most published, and the most translated among all world literature" (Martin, Ph. D., 70).

2 Dates of works are those of beginning of first publication, usually in serial form; where works did not come out in Verne's lifetime, the date of composition will be indicated instead.

3 The science fiction sections of this story are probably not by Jules Verne, but by his son Michel. The definition of science fiction employed here is "a genre of fiction based on imagined future technological or scientific advances, major environmental or social changes, etc., and frequently portraying time travel and life on other planets" (*Oxford English Reference Dictionary* (Oxford: Oxford University Press, 2003)).

4 Abbreviated titles of the most frequently cited works will be used, as indicated in the Bibliography. References to Verne's works will be by chapter (as roman numerals, with part number if any (e.g., II xxxix)) to allow use of any edition.

5 Cited by Walter James Miller, "Jules Verne in America," in *Twenty Thousand Leagues under the Sea*, Walter James Miller (ed.) (New York: Crowell, 1976); vii–xxii; detected by myself at proof stage of *Backwards to Britain*.

6 *Verne's Journey to the Centre of the Self* (New York: St Martin's Press, 1990) and the eight critical editions listed in the Bibliography.

7 Raymond Ducrest de Villeneuve, unpublished, untitled illustrated typescript [1930], the only cataloged copy of which is in the Jules Verne International Center in Amiens, the original being in the City Library of Nantes (MJV B 233). Dehs lists the biography in his *Guide* (79). The works mentioned briefly in this introduction are fully referenced in the Bibliography.

8 Jean-Michel Margot has generously sent me a copy of his unpublished catalog, an impeccable work of scholarship analyzing and thematically classifying all 10,000 known documents about Verne. Dehs's 2005 biography was also based on exhaustive knowledge of material published to date.

9 If only the book *The Salon of 1857* (1857), discovered in 2006.

10 *Michel Strogoff* (1876) was not published in Russia until the twentieth century; *Tribulations of a Chinese in China* (1879) appeared in China only in 2003 (with the political parts removed); *Humbug* appeared in English in 1992.

Prologue (xxvii–xxxii)

1 In a letter to Paul of 20 June 1894.

2 "In the Year 2889"; the story was in fact written by his son Michel.

3   This account derives from a large number of sources, including: Verne's own recollections as reported by interviewers (*Int.* 117, 179); [9 Mar. 86] and [10 Mar. 86] to Hetzel *Fils*; Volker Dehs, "En 1886," *BSJV* 118:32–37; Norbert Percereau, "Le Destin de Gaston Verne," *BSJV* 155:4–52; and the contemporary newspapers, especially *L'Univers illustré* of 20 March 1886, London *Times* of 11 March 1886, and *Journal d'Amiens*. (The system of abbreviated references to letters by date is explained in note 13 to chapter 2 below.)

Throughout these notes, references separated by semicolons refer to distinct ideas in the text, those by commas to the same idea.

1: Island Adrift: 1828–35 (pp. 1–18)

1   Régis de Véron de La Combe, "En Remontant la Loire," BSJV 150:36–37.

2   Reported on http://www.nantesmetropole.fr/.

3   In a letter to Verne's publisher of 4 November 1871.

4   Marguerite Pichelin (1875–1959) was the daughter-in-law of Maurice Allotte, Sophie's nephew.

5   Dekiss, *Jules Verne l'enchanteur,* 11.

6   As recorded in the birth certificate (CNM 265–66).

7   Verne's 1842 poem to his mother (in CNM 24) implies both he and his sister were breastfed.

8   Given that he did so for Jules's sister ([3 May 37] from Sophie to Pierre's mother, reproduced by Volker Dehs in *J.V.* (Amiens), 31 (1994):20–21).

9   At least according to Verne's 1842 poem.

10   "L'Origine des Allotte de la Fuÿe," BSJV 11:55–56. The "droit de fuye" also involved jurisdiction over surrounding land, loosely the concept of a domain, including three levels of dispensation of justice, with the power to clap in irons (Roger de la Fuÿe 52). Prouteau (59) indicates the name as Baron "Norbert Allott."

11   Additional, albeit allusive, support is given by Jules himself: "we must have an ancestor who got those rheumatisms from robbing in the woods and stopping stagecoaches on the main roads in the thirteenth century when British reiters roamed the countryside" [Mar.? 68].

12   According to an important article, unknown to researchers, Sieur Allott was related to fishmonger Sir John Allot (ca. 1548–91), famous Lord Mayor of London (1590–91); the family of the Franco-Scottish "Sir Allott" went back to 1390. The family acquired the title of Count before 1696 (*Armorial de tours*, folio 1172) (Dr. Roger de la Fuÿe (1890–1961), "Jules Verne inconnu: Mon oncle," *Connaissance du monde*, no. 3 (Feb. 1959), 51–60).

13   Robert Taussat, "Rêverie sur un vieil almanach," *BSJV* 16:160–63.

14   Given his work as a Nantes sea captain to South America at a period when nearly all the transatlantic trade dealt in slaves.

15   Luce Courville, "Jules Verne, La Famille Raton et le 'Rat-Goutteux' de Nantes," in *Jules Verne—Histoires inattendues* (Paris: Union Générale d'Éditions, 1978), 439–42.

16   Jean Chesneaux, *Jules Verne: Un Regard sur le monde* (Paris: Bayard, 2001), 166.

17   Yves Guillon, "Jules Verne et sa famille," *Bulletin de la Société archéologique d'Ille-et-Vilaine*, Vol. 78 (1974), 121–38.

18   Lassée 56, Dumas 34.

19   JJV states that "according to my father he practised self-flagellation," additional evidence being Pierre's surviving notes praising the role of "material and corporal penance" (2—although the word "corporal" is missing from the first edition of the biography in French (1973)).

2. Chantenay Castaway: 1836–39 (pp. 19–35)

1   30 Mar. 36 in CNM 20.

2   Taussat 161.

3   Francis Lefeuvren, *L'Education des garçons* (Nantes: Forest, 1886), 14.

4   Lefeuvre 13.

5   Georges Bastard, "Jules Verne, sa vie, son oeuvre," *Revue de Bretagne*, April–May 1906, 337–59.

6   JJV 9; 15 Sep. 45.

7   Yves Lostanlet, "La Guerche en Brains et Jules Verne," *Bulletin du Pays de Retz*, 13:9–12.

8   At 2 Rue Suffren (Taussat 163).

9   Guillon 132–33.

10   "Memories of Childhood and Youth" (MCY) first appeared in *The Youth's Companion*, in English translation; first French publication was in *L'Herne*, no. 25, 14 Oct. 1974, 57–62.

11   Added then deleted from the first manuscript of MCY, reproduced in *Cahiers du Musée Jules Verne*, no. 10 (1990), 7–21.

12   Nephew Maurice Verne, cited by ADF 122.

13   In greater detail: references to letters generally quote either the exact date (here 14 August 1850) or the month and year (Aug. 50), as given by Verne himself. Where dating is incomplete, the missing part of the reference will be in italics; where it is absent, [14 Aug. 50] will be used. All letters not included in the following are fully referenced: Dumas, *Jules Verne*; *Correspondance inédite de Jules Verne et Pierre-Jules Hetzel*; and *Correspondance inédite de Jules et Michel Verne avec l'éditeur Louis-Jules Hetzel*.

14   30 Mar. 36 in CNM 20.

15   *Jules Verne écrivain* (Nantes: Municipal Library, 2000), 164.

16   RD (33) is adamant that it was copied from miniatures of Henri and Edmond painted by Châteaubourg on Empire vases kept in Pierre and Sophie's bedroom.

17   Roger Maudhuy, *Jules Verne*, 66. Cécile Compère places the drowning at nearby Doulon ("Jules Verne de Nantes," *Revue Jules Verne*, 4:11–24).

18   Unpublished documents at Nantes, RD 9, and Compère 20.

19   Despite what is invariably claimed, Pierre did not purchase the house until 1846, as shown by the land records.

20   The description of the house at Chantenay derives from RD (20–26), including his sketch maps and drawings.

21   Bastard 351.

22   RD 33; Bastard 337.

23   The one for 1836–37 is missing from the archives. OD (23) says Jules also did third and fourth grade at St. Stanislas. Paul transferred with him, into the grade below (Compère 14).

24   Alain Chantreau, "Jules Verne à Saint-Stanislas," *Annales de Nantes*, no. 187 (Jan.–June 1978), 25–27.

25   At least according to a later headmaster, Chantreau (26).

26   In the first term of fifth grade, Jules came fifth out of an estimated 25 in his cohort in "examination" and fourth in singing; in the second term, fifth in "examination" and geography, fourth in recitation from memory, and apparently first in singing. For the first term of sixth grade, he got a fifth in singing, but in the second, a sixth in

geography and fourth in translation to and from Greek. The following year, he came fifth in singing and fourth in Latin unseen.

27 ADF 21–22. Marguerite changed some of the information in a preface in 1928 (cited in OD 25): Jules grows from 11 to 13, no longer buys out the cabin-boy but exchanges clothes with him, is caught and handed over by the captain himself, and so on. However, the episode remained unchanged in the revised 1953 edition.

28 E.g., a letter from Jean Jules-Verne in 1978 (in JD 44).

29 Maurice d'Ocagne, "Jules Verne raconté par le fils d'un de ses amis," *La Revue Hebdomadaire*, vol. 37, no. 9 (Sept. 1928), 35–54.

30 Volker Dehs, "Fait ou légende?," *Revue Jules Verne*, nos. 19–20:169–74, citing Paul Eudel, *Figures nantaises* (1e partie) (Rennes: Imprimerie de *L'Ouest-Eclair*, 1909), 197.

31 Roger de la Fuÿe 54.

3. Schoolboy Writer: 1840–46 (pp. 37–51)

1 [3 May 37] from Sophie to Pierre's mother, reproduced by Volker Dehs in *JV*, 31 (1994), 20–21.

2 Ducrest astonishingly says that "Pierre moved into Quai Jean Bart, near his practice, and a little later into Rue Kervégan . . . but the family moved out after a few years. So Jules spent his earliest years on Feydeau" (14). The biographer may have been thinking of the boy's birthplace on Rue de Clisson, since the building was on the corner of Kervégan, or Pierre may simply have had an office there. In any case, the Vernes must have spent much time with Dame Sophie.

3 RD 21; [Feb. 55]; "Impromptu Verses," *Annales de Nantes*, no. 187 (Jan.–June 1978), 16–18.

4 "Together" in Ducrest's phrase (16).

5 The whole tour is again courtesy of Ducrest (17–19), who lived there for much of his childhood.

6 "Jules and Paul lived in this study; the father himself initiated them to all these curiosities with conversations and explanations" (RD 19).

7 RD 18. However, this testimony dates from the 1860s at the very earliest, and may be affected by the distorted views of Jules Verne prevailing in 1930.

8 Preface published only in the first illustrated edition of *Second Homeland* (1900). Instead of "Mallès," Verne wrote "Mollar."

9 Preface in the first illustrated edition of *Second Homeland*. Woillez and Desnoyers are mentioned only in the draft of the preface.

10 OD 23, citing Robin 27; however, this citation does not appear on that page.

11 E.g., Costello 102.

12 Compère 35.

13 Maudhuy 80.

14 Ducrest confirms that "from his earliest childhood [Paul] showed a very strong predilection for a naval career and everything to do with it. Everything drew him to it: his mind, more scientific than his brother's, more directed towards new discoveries in navigation, his very strong taste for travel, and his reading."

15 Maudhuy 82.

16 [12 Dec. 42] in CNM 23. There is a P.S.: "Many things to Father, sisters, Auntie, and Grandma who, I hope, is well. I was pleased to learn Uncle no longer had sore eyes," probably referring to Sophie's brother, Auguste Allotte. The romance "Adieu mon

beau navire" has not been traced, although the words occur in the poem "Matelots," in Tristan Corbière's *Les Amours jaunes* (1873), dedicated "To the author of the *Négrier [Slaver]*."

17 Robin 250.

18 D'Ocagne 280.

19 Paul transferred in 1844, but entered the two-year special preparatory class for the Naval, Military, and Forestry Schools; he did well in mathematics, history and geography, translation into Latin, and general performance.

20 Compère 20.

21 Jean-Louis Liters, "Jules Verne au Collège Royal de Nantes," *Cahiers du Musée Jules Verne*, no. 12 (1992), 28–39, although the source for this information is not indicated; Vallès, *Les Souvenirs d'un étudiant pauvre* (Paris: Gallimard, 1930).

22 Vallès, *Souvenirs d'un étudiant pauvre*; Paul Eudel, *Centenial Yearbook* (1909), 287.

23 Eudel (197), nine years his junior at the school, reported that "he did good Classical studies, but nothing more," claiming in addition that he had "a marked taste for mathematics."

24 ADF 22–23, who further reports that Jules, Couëtoux du Tertre, Genevois, and Maisonneuve passed the baccalaureate together.

25 Genevois's father, Ange, was a businessman and president of the Nantes Chamber of Commerce in the 1830s. Serpette must have been related to the West African oil and soap and shipowning business Serpette and Co. (active in Nantes 1840–80) and to Nantes musician Gaston Serpette (1846–1904).

26 Liters, "Jules Verne au Collège Royal de Nantes," 28–39.

27 In a private communication, Dehs reports evidence that Schwob was brought up in Rouen rather than Nantes.

28 Norbert Percereau, " 'Marie se marie,' mais le marié n'est pas Marie," *BSJV* 149:21.

29 When Pitfold died in 1853, Verne wrote "I was his oldest companion and his death caused me great sadness" (14 Mar. 53).

30 JJV 24; Liters 28.

31 Poupart-Davyl printed *Journey to the Center of the Earth* and *From the Earth to the Moon*, although later going bankrupt. In 1856 he fought a duel with Vallez.

32 Volker Dehs, "Emergence d'un ami d'enfance: Paul Perret," *BSJV* 150:5.

33 ADF 19; RD 15.

34 *The Green Ray* (xiii).

4. What Use are Girls?: 1846–48 (pp. 53–69)

1 Guillon 127.

2 Guillon 132.

3 Reprinted in *BSJV* 123:11–13 (it is in fact another version of the poem quoted above (*Poems* 15)).

4 [Apr.? 53]; 15 Jun. 56.

5 Daniel Compère, *Jules Verne: Parcours d'une oeuvre* (Amiens: Encrage, 1996), 11.

6 21 Sep. 53 in *Dix lettres inédites* (Nantes: Société des Amis de la Bibliothèque Municipale de Nantes, 1982); ADF 26.

7 "An Ideal City."

8 Kenneth Allott, *Jules Verne* (London: Crescent Press [1940]), 12, citing Mmes Levesque and Le Breton of Nantes, apparently in 1848.

9 Letter from Robert Godefroy to Frédéric Petit (31 Jan. 88), in *L'Herne*, 119–30.

10   Costello 33.
11   All arrondissements indicated are the modern ones.
12   Marcel Moré, *Le Très curieux Jules Verne* (Paris: Gallimard, 1960) and *Nouvelles explo-
      rations de Jules Verne* (Paris: Gallimard, 1963).
13   Eudel 194.
14   *Int.* 89; Lemire 7.
15   Letter to Hignard in ADF 28.

5. Law Student in the Literary Salons: 1848–51 (pp. 71–85)

1   Robien claims that Maisonneuve, Hignard, and Verne's rooms were "adjacent" (40).
2   2 Apr. 49.
3   6 Dec. 48, 21 Nov. 48.
4   RD 39, d'Ocagne 281.
5   3 Dec. 89 to Abraham Dreyfus (extract in Piero Gondolo della Riva, *Jules Verne et
     le spectacle* (Campredon: L'Isle-sur-la-Sorgue, n.d.), 8–9); *Int.* 90.
6   Dumas published at this time *Dr. Servans* (1849), *Césarine* (1849), *Diane de Lys*
     (1851), and *Regent Mustel* (1852).
7   *Nouvelles littéraires*, 24 March 1966.
8   28 Jun. 50; ADF 39.
9   Reputed to have had a dissolute youth, he wished to marry only to get rich; he
     showed interest in Anna Verne, but Jules advised his father against pursuing the
     matter (23 Mar. 55).
10   Lottman 8; Martin, Ph. D., 574.
11   However, the surface plausibility of some of Verne's information is misleading, for he
     was served by poor copyediting, perpetuated worldwide over hundreds of millions of
     copies. Here "Aguijan" is Guajan; and the *Constanzia* should logically be the *Con-
     stancia*; henceforth I will silently correct spelling (but not factual) mistakes by Verne
     and others.
12   Jacques Noiray, *Le Romancier et la machine* (Paris: Corti, 1982), 20.

6. Plays and Poverty: 1851–54 (pp. 87–101)

1   19 Sep. 96 to Perret in *BSJV* 150:6.
2   19 Sep. 96 to Perret in *BSJV* 150:6.
3   Mar. 51. Later, Verne says it is going to be "*11* Boulevard Bonne-Nouvelle" (4 Mar.
     53), but this may be a slip.
4   *3 Apr. 51*; [6 Apr. 51].
5   JJV 22; ADF 53.
6   21 Sep. 53 in *Dix lettres inédites*.
7   21 Jun. 55; 14 Dec. 54.
8   Bastard 339–40.
9   Bastard 339.
10   4 Dec. 51; [6 Dec. 51].
11   Nevertheless, Verne wrote "I'm actively looking for a place, I'm going to see Ferdinand
     Favre" (mid–Oct. 51). Favre was a pro-Louis-Philippe politician, mayor of Nantes
     (1832–48 and 1852–57), and sugar-refining and shipping businessman. Verne was
     presumably seeking a business or law job.
12   22 Aug. 52; 8 Dec. 52; ADF 64.
13   In Rue Amsterdam. Martin, *Jules Verne*, 27; Allott 17.

14   22 Aug. 52; RD 45.

15   Verne staged Donizetti's operetta *Elisabeth* at the Lyric on 4 January 1854 in a double bill with *Blind Man's Bluff* (JD 278).

16   [Jul. 52], cf. [29 Apr. 53].

17   If the careers of two later secretaries of the Lyric are any guide, the job carried long-term financial rewards, for both became owner-managers (JJV 22).

18   Volker Dehs, "Nous boirons, nous rirons," *BSJV* 143:14.

19   8 Dec. 52, cf. 2 Dec. 52.

20   Allott 24–25, reporting the contemporary but untraced "Haucilly."

21   Dehs, "Nous boirons," 14; [end 54].

22   Extrapolated from figures provided by Volker Dehs, "Une 'Bonne nuit' compromise," *BSJV* 156:7–8.

23   JD 102; *Int* 20.

24   ADF 38–39, JJV 24.

25   23 Apr. [51?]; [10? Dec. 53]; 21 Jun. 55; [19 Feb. 56].

26   In Soriano 68–69.

27   "Impromptu Verses" 17; 14 Mar. 53.

28   [25 Mar. 53], extract in *Jules Verne à Dinard* (Dinard: Mairie, [2000]), 77.

29   Lottman 55; ADF 61.

30   Charles-Noël Martin, "Les Amours de jeunesse de Jules Verne," *BSJV* 29–30:103–20; ADF 61.

31   7 Apr. 54; 29 Apr. 54.

32   [Jun. 55]; 21 Jun. 55.

33   Mlle Pauline Méry of Nantes (1835–71) married a . . . Chéguillaume, Joseph-Paul-Auguste (1825–97), in Nantes in 1854.

34   "Impromptu Verses" 17.

35   5 Nov. 54 in *BSJV* 151:10; Alain Genevois, *Annales*, 15.

36   Gilbert Doukan, "Un Auteur à succès malheureux en amour," *BSJV* 48:237–46.

37   J. Dillon, *Les Bordels de Paris* (Paris, 1790).

38   21 Sep. 53 in *Dix lettres inédites*.

39   [Mar. 56]; [27 Mar. 56]; [18 May 56] in ADF 69.

7. Tribulations of a Frenchman in France: 1854–57 (pp. 103–19)

1   Not only was the captain "Juan Nemo" in an early draft, but the *Nautilus*'s home base is in the Canary Islands.

2   The cover of *Beside the Adour* (1855) has "47 Rue des Martyrs," although confusingly crossed out and replaced by "18 Boulevard Bonne Nouvelle."

3   12 Dec. 48; 15 Nov. 52.

4   [Oct. 54?]; 20 Jun. 55; 5 Nov. 53; 22 Mar. *52*; 7 Sep. 56; 5 Sep. 56.

5   [Feb. 51]; 23 Apr. *51?*.

6   16 Nov. 49; 2 Apr. 49.

7   31 May *52*; 12 Dec. 48.

8   Nov. 55; 8 Aug. 64.

9   [Oct.? 55]; 6 May 54.

10   31 Dec. 52; 25 Nov. 54; letter of 1854–55 in *to* Generovois in *BSJV 100:7*; *27 Feb. 49* to Genevois in *BSJV* 100:12.

11   "Impromptu Verses" 17.

12   A list of plays appears in the Bibliography.

13   *The Knights of the Daffodil* was also staged at the Graslin Theater in Nantes.

14   CNM 86; [29 Apr. 53]; 4 May 53; Dekiss, *L'Enchanteur*, 40.

15   Dehs, "Nous boirons," 20–22.

16   In a dedication on the title page of a copy of *Journey to the Center of the Earth* (*BSJV* 155:56).

17   Dehs, *Jules Verne* (2005), Appendix 2 calculates Verne's total official earnings from his plays and operas in 1861 as FF 2,650; 4 Jul. 56.

18   Allott 31.

19   31 May 52; 22 Jan. 51.

20   Mar. 51; [20 Nov. 55].

21   15 Nov. 52; 17 Jan. 52.

22   In *Paris in the Twentieth Century*.

23   Her new brother-in-law, Auguste Lelarge, was also brother-in-law to Henri, Verne's cousin.

24   *Int.* 42; photograph in ADF 48–49; picture in *Ouest France*, special issue [2005], 18.

25   7 Sep. 56; 22 Nov. 56.

26   Cited by Dusseau 117 without reference.

27   4 Jul. 56; 7 Sep. 56.

28   [summer (Aug.?) 56].

29   10 Sep. 56; 29 May 56.

30   1 Nov. 56 in *Dix lettres.*

31   Cited in *BSJV* 109:8–11.

32   16 Nov. 56 in *BSJV* 109:8–11.

33   29 Nov. 56; [3 Dec. 56]; 29 Dec. 56.

34   22 Nov. 56; [end Nov. 56].

35   [mid-Dec. 56]; 22 Nov. 56; Cécile Compère, "Le Contrat de mariage des époux Verne," *Revue Jules Verne*, 2:76–81.

36   Compère, "Le Contrat," 77.

37   G. Dumas, *Mémoires* (Laon: Fédération des Sociétés, 1977), 22, says Honorine's possessions were worth 3K; Compère ("Le Contrat" 77), 30K.

38   Compère, "Le Contrat," 77.

39   5 Nov. 54 in *BSJV* 151:10.

40   *Textes oubliés* (ed. Francis Lacassin; Paris, Union Générale d'Éditions, 1979), 49.

8. Married, with Portfolio: 1857–59 (pp. 121–36)

1   17 Dec. 56; ADF 77.

2   RD 54–55; [mid-Dec. 56].

3   Cited without reference by ADF 78.

4   7 Dec. 56 to Uncle Châteaubourg in ADF 78.

5   JD 118–19; *Textes oubliés, par Jules Verne* (Paris: Union Générale d'Éditions, 1979), 44.

6   ADF 78; JD 119.

7   7 Dec. 56; ADF 78.

8   Elisabeth Léger de Viane, "L'Entourage familial de Jules Verne," in *Visions nouvelles sur Jules Verne* (Amiens: Centre de Documentation Jules Verne, 1978), 20–27.

9   13 Apr. 86 to Léon Guillon in *Dix lettres.*

10 Guillon 130.

11 Dehs, *Jules Verne* (2005). It is possible the daughters continued to live with their grandparents (Dehs, private communication).

12 Dehs, *Jules Verne* (2005), Lemire 14.

13 *BSJV* 136:23; contract between Hetzel and Verne of 23 Oct. 1862.

14 ADF 85; "Joyous Miseries."

15 16 Nov. 56 in *BSJV* 109:8–11.

16 [Mar. 57]; ADF 82.

17 Verne says 1859, but he was in Britain at that time.

18 Cited without reference in ADF 75–76.

19 The three refusals and fourth attempt are mentioned in 16 Nov. 56 in *BSJV* 109:8–11.

20 De Viane was too busy to write much, but Verne thanked him nevertheless, in 22 Nov. 56 (in *BSJV* 109:8–11), summarizing his response to his father (22 Nov. 56). Dekiss (ed.), *Le Poète*, 37, says that Verne did work for both Ferdinand de Viane and his associate in Paris, but without making it clear what this means.

21 JJV 47; Charles-Noël Martin, "Le Mariage de Jules Verne," *BSJV* 65–66:62.

22 ADF 80; CNM 114; [26 May 56].

23 Félix Duquesnel, cited by ADF 80.

24 Taken from the description of Joe in *Five Weeks* (vi), for whom Duquesnel was the model (Félix Duquesnel, *Le Gaulois*, 23 March 1905 (in *BSJV* 132:37)).

25 Duquesnel, cited by ADF 80; cf. Bastard 340.

26 RD 55; Félix Duqesnel, *Le Gaulois*, 22 April 1909 (in *BSJV* 132:43).

27 Duquesnel, reported by ADF 80.

28 [10? Jan. 54]; [20 Nov. 55]; 20 Jun. 55.

29 [26 May 56]; 4 Jul. 56.

30 Copies are kept in the Municipal Library of Nantes, so the find may originally have been made by Luce Courville, Colette Galois, or other staff of the library.

31 The title implies that 17 previous articles had appeared, possibly by Verne or his professional associates.

32 CNM 114; Robien 85.

33 Volker Dehs, "Jules Verne correspondant de Victorien Sardou," *BSJV* 150:19.

34 According to *BB*, approximate dates were as follows: travel to Nantes 27–28 July, Nantes 28–30, Bordeaux 2–22 August, Liverpool 26–27, Edinburgh 27–30, Oakley 31, Balloch, Loch Lomond, Loch Katrine, Callander, and Stirling 1 September, Edinburgh 2, London 3–4, and Dieppe 6 September.

35 ADF 83; *BB* iv.

36 Much of the information for the Scottish visit comes from Ian Thompson, "Jules Verne, Geography and Nineteenth Century Scotland," *La Géographie: Acta Géographica*, Dec. 2003, 48–71. "Amelia's" reall name was Margaret Bain.

37 *BB* xxxviii; xxxiv; xxxiii.

9. Destiny Draws up her Skirts: 1860–63 (pp. 137–52)

1 ADF 87 and RD 58 say he traveled for free on a cargo boat again arranged by Alfred Hignard, setting off luxuriously installed with a cargo of coal, and accompanying pine planks on the return journey. According to these accounts, the three put in at various points on the Norwegian coast, visiting the fjords and "sad northern seas and islands,"

with Verne imagining he caught a glimpse of Iceland and the vision leaving a deep impression on him.

2   ADF 87 and JJV 54 say 15 June, but may have adjusted the date to fit with the return date of about 3 August, apparently an embellishment to enable Verne get back for the birth of his son.

3   Volker Dehs, "Impressions d'Hambourg," *BSJV* 149:55; Scandinavian Notebook kept in Amiens Library.

4   *Wreck of the "Cynthia"* iv.

5   *Lottery Ticket* xvii.

6   Henri Pons, "Jules Verne en Norvège," *BSJV* 28:75. Dal no longer exists, but was near the modern town of Rjukan.

7   *Lottery Ticket* ii.

8   *Lottery Ticket* ii.

9   Claude Pétel, *Le Tour du monde en quarante ans* (Villecresnes: Villecresnes reprographie, 1998), vol. I, 58.

10 *Journey to the Center of the Earth* ix.

11 ADF 87; JJV 54; CNM 120.

12 *Journey to the Center of the Earth* vii.

13 *Journey to the Center of the Earth* viii.

14 "Joyous Miseries."

15 Dehs, "Impressions," 56, and Scandinavian Notebook.

16 Duquesnel (1909), 43; cf. Bastard 352.

17 RD 56; Véron 17; Duquesnel (1909), 43; Georges Bastard, "Célébrité contemporaine," *Gazette illustrée*, 8 Sept. 1883 (in *L'Herne*, 88–92) .

18 According to Tolstoy, reported by Alexander Zinger, "Récit d'une visite a Tolstoï," in *BSJV* 41:12, cited by OD 18.

19 RD 51–54; d'Ocagne 291; *Int.* 84.

20 ADF 89. Verne must be referring to "Le Canard au ballon" (The Duck in a Balloon/Balloon Hoax), Baudelaire's punning translation (1856) of Poe's "The Balloon Hoax" (1844).

21 RD ADF 90.

22 Daniel Compère, "Renversants, ces débutants!," *BSJV* 10:40, citing an unnamed journalist in about 1872. However, this may simply be a misreading of a reference to the editor of the *Revue* (in 27 Jan. 69 to Hetzel).

23 ADF 88, RD 60.

24 Maurice Crosland, *BJHS* (2001), 34: 301–22. The periodical had six volumes (1860–65), then two volumes in a new series as *Presse scientifique* and *Industrielle des deux mondes* (1865–67).

25 Jean Prinet and Antoinette Dilasser, *Nadar* (Paris: Armand Colin, 1966), 255.

26 JJV 58, RD 59.

27 D'Ocagne 286.

28 *Int.* 135. "Verne showed his manuscript to Dumas who liked it enough to put Verne in touch with the novelist Bréhat. And Bréhat introduced him to Hetzel" (JJV 54).

29 ADF 91–92, RD 77.

30 *Int.* 101, Bastard 352; RD 75, 78.

31 RD 75, 78; ADF 91.

32 RD 77, ADF 92.

33   ADF 92. Cf. "his meeting with Hetzel . . . almost did not work out" (RD 75).

34   ADF 92, cf. JJV 56 Antoine Parménie and C. Bonnier de la Chapelle, *Histoire d'un éditeur et de ses auteurs* (Paris: Albin Michel, 1853), provides an unreferenced and extremely general account of the revision process: Hetzel told the author that "the novel" was "poorly constructed and the style less than perfect"; he asked him to change the order of the episodes and "indicated the chapters to expand and reduce . . . the characters to reinforce . . . the weakness and the clumsiness of expression: 'Revise quickly your novel and bring it back to me, I'll publish it without delay' " (428).

35   ADF 93; *Int.* 27.

36   Jacques Noiray, *Le Romancier et la machine* (Paris: José Corti, 1982), 45.

37   Noiray 46.

38   *Int.* 91; *Int.* 101.

39   Reproduced in Martin, *Jules Verne*, 306–07.

40   Duquesnel (1905), 39.

41   Chapter 33, as evidenced by the draft blurb. In the only surviving part of the manuscript, nearly all of chapter 36 is stuck onto the sheets Verne used for the first manuscript of *Twenty Thousand Leagues* (Marcel Destombes, "Le Manuscrit de *Vingt mille lieues sous les mers* de la Société de Géographie," *BSJV* 35–6:59–70); cf. JJV 56.

42   French National Library, Department of Manuscripts, NAF 16932–17152 and Vols 67–80. The published version of the blurb appears in CNM 132.

43   *Figaro*, 8 February; *Moniteur universel*, 18 February; *La Presse*, 3 March; *Le Temps*, cited by JD 164.

44   Jean-Marie Embs, "Une Caution scientifique aux débuts de Jules Verne," *BSJV* 142:53; F. de Gramont, "Oeuvres de Jules Verne," *BSJV* 144:56.

45   Dehs, *Jules Verne* (2005), Appendix 2.

46   Virtually all Verne's books came out in three formats: serialized with accompanying illustrations; unillustrated small format; and illustrated large format (octavo). Overall sales figures are available only for the small-format editions and for the 17 worst-selling large-format novels (in Volker Dehs, "Les Tirages des éditions Hetzel," *Revue Jules Verne*, no. 5. (1998), 89–94); here it will be estimated, conservatively, that the small-format sales were half those of the large-format ones.

47   Jan Feith, "Le Globe-trotter chez lui," *BSJV* 145:10.

48   Cofounders were Baron Taylor, Gabriel de La Landelle, and Gustave de Ponton d'Amécourt; the Society for the Encouragement of Aviation or Aerial Locomotion by means of the Heavier-Than-Air was based at Nadar's residence (25 Boulevard des Capucines) and remained active until at least 1866.

49   At least according to one of the men in the balloon, Robert Mitchell ("Souvenirs," in *Le Gaulois* (1902), cited by JD 164). The *Figaro* of 4 October also listed Verne among the passengers. However Nadar wrote "absolutely false" in the margin of Mitchell's memoirs.

50   Dehs, *Jules Verne* (2005), Appendix 2.

10. Golden Years: 1863–66 (pp. 153–68)

1   Verne in 1863, cited without reference by Dekiss http://www.adpf.asso.fr/adpf-publi/folio/julesverne/.

2   *Int.* 136, cf. *JVEST* 226.

3   In the sense that the American rights set an absolute record (*Publishers Weekly*, 1

Jan. 1996, no. 1, 28). The total rights seem to have been at least a million francs (*Revue Jules Verne*, no. 15 (2003), 133).

4   *BB* carries the address of Verne's probable residence from 1863, implying that Verne worked on it after the Hetzel contract.

5   Commentators have often blandly asserted that in his books Verne always opposed the idea of slavery and was pro-Abolitionist in the Civil War. However, such views are based on a partial reading.

6   Further details are provided in the "Introduction" to *The Adventures of Captain Hatteras*, trans. with an introduction and notes by William Butcher (Oxford: Oxford University Press, 2005).

7   E.g., Charcot, cited by JJV 59, or Finn Ronne, "Introduction," in *The Adventures of Captain Hatteras* (New York: Didier, 1951), 5–6.

8   *Int.* 138; Émile Zola, *Le Salut public*, 23 July 1866; Théophile Gautier, "Les Voyages imaginaires de M. Jules Verne," *Moniteur Universel*, no. 197 (16 July 1866), 4.

9   Agnès Pierron (ed.), *Dictionnaire de citations et jugements* (Paris: Les Usuels du Robert, 1991), 1220.

10   René Escaich, "A propos des *Aventures du capitaine Hatteras*," *BSJV* 28:88; OD 90.

11   *The Adventures of Captain Hatteras*, xvii–xx, 350–54, and notes (*passim*). Previous to my discovery Daniel Compère pointed out that the last two pages of the manuscript were different (*Un Voyage imaginaire de Jules Verne* (Paris: Lettres Modernes, 1977), 21–24).

12   Dehs, "Impressions," 55.

13   John Breyer and William Butcher, "Nothing New under the Earth," *Earth Sciences History*, vol. 22 (2003), 36–54.

14   While none of the contracts before 1875 made any mention of payment for serialization, Hetzel's general practice was to pay his authors "25 centimes a line (35 centimes from 1885)" (private communication from Volker Dehs). Verne may easily have gotten this sum, then, which amounts to 4 centimes a word or FF 2,500 per volume.

15   The phrase "children's education" was Hetzel's (Parménie and Bonnier de la Chapelle 491). From this point on, virtually all Verne's novels will appear first in serialized form in the *Magasin* or occasionally other journals, and then in two different book forms by Hetzel. The title indicated here is the final one, and the year, that of the beginning of serialization.

16   ADF 100, 8 Aug. 64, 12 Aug. 84.

17   ADF 101, citing "Verses Found in a Hat," in a private collection.

18   ADF 104, citing artist and local historian Anthime Ménard in September 1864.

19   ADF 108; [18? Jan. 69]; RD 85.

20   O. Dumas and E. Weissenberg, "Verne avant la gloire," *BSJV* 135:4.

21   For instance, most translators omit "reverse-ricochet shots" ("des feux . . . de revers") on the first page of the novel, presumably because it is difficult to translate.

Lowell Bair, the translator of the bestselling Bantam edition, is notorious for a *Mysterious Island* which manages to mislay more than 100,000 words. On the first page Bair deletes a comment on gigantic American artillery, "far less useful than sewing machines, but just as surprising and much more admired." Harold Salemson, translator for the Heritage Press, claims to provide "the complete text," but simply copies Lewis Mercier's bowdlerized and abridged 1870 version.

The most scholarly looking version is the Gramercy one by Walter James Miller (1995); it is generally of a reasonable standard, but mistranslates words and gratuitously adds or deletes material (in the first chapters alone, "boulets" as "bullets" rather than "cannonballs," "grenades" as "shells," and "savannas" as "swamps"; the addition of the Gun Club "library" or a "fender" on the fireplace; and the deletion of the italic phrases in: "they mastered 'the art of war' *as well as their Old World colleagues*" and "*an international incident* to allow us to declare war *on some transatlantic power*" (i)).

22   Sales figures appear in the Bibliography.

23   In the 37 years following his entry into the public domain, Verne sold 8.8 million copies in one French edition alone (*Magazine littéraire*, 3 May 2005), implying total French sales of about 20 million by 1978 (*Elle*, 6 Feb. 1978) and about 30 million by the turn of the century. World sales would total perhaps ten times that number.

24   Contract of 17 May 1875.

25   Although the book came out before the announcement, the draft contracts probably preceded that publication.

26   Most of July–November 1867, April–September 1868, April–October 1869, and May–August 1870.

27   6 Sep. 65; [28 Mar. 68].

28   [3 Oct. 67]; *Geography*, Somme, 666.

29   [17 Jul. 67]; 6 Nov. 67.

30   [Aug. 15? 70]; in CNM 182.

11. Whole New World: 1865–67 (pp. 169–82)

1   Dehs, "Impressions," 56, and Scandinavian Notebook; [24 Aug. 78]; 4 Sep. 63.

2   Jacques Béal, "Jules Verne en Somme," *Revue Jules Verne*, no. 4 (1997), 55–60; d'Ocagne 290 states he bought "a former fishing smack."

3   Dehs cites the Scandinavian notebook in "Impressions" 56.

4   29 Jan. *67*, [18? Jan. 69].

5   Modern address: 81 Boulevard des Frères Roustan, 06220 Vallauris; 29 Jan. *67*.

6   [Feb.? 67]; [10 Jul. 67].

7   [27 Feb. 67]; [9 Mar. 67].

8   Private communication from Masataka Ishibashi.

9   [First three months? 66]; [14 Aug. 68].

10   [Aug. 15? 70] to Hetzel in CNM 182.

11   *BB* vii; *Around the World* xxvii.

12   [18 Sep. 65], 24 Apr. 66 to Pierre.

13   *A Floating City* i.

14   *BB* xliv; [9 Apr. 67].

15   Robert Taussat, "Le Malheureux destin du *Great Eastern*," BSJV 15:138–41.

16   Most of the information in this and the following paragraphs is taken from Verne, *A Floating City* (1870).

17   *A Floating City* xv.

18   "Letter to the Editor" dated 9 April, published 4 May.

19   RD 87. Ducrest does not mention Jules's logbook; so it is possible he simply mistakes Paul's notes for his brother's.

12. By Land and Sea: 1867–69 (pp. 183–99)

1   "Introduction," *Around the World in Eighty Days*, translated with an introduction and notes by William Butcher (Oxford: Oxford University Press, 1995).

2   The estimate in Dehs, *Jules Verne* (2005), Appendix 2.

3   II xxii; *BB* xxiv.

4   This account summarizes the findings in my critical edition of *Twenty Thousand Leagues* (Oxford: Oxford University Press, 1998), where more detailed references are provided.

5   [29? Apr. 69]; 15 May *69*; [17 May 69]; [11? Jun. 69].

6   [Jun.? 68], undated letter in *BSJV* 61:170.

7   *Twenty Thousand Leagues* II xviii.

8   [Jun.? 68]; Tarrieu 16.

9   A. Tarrieu, "Sur les traces des hommes du *Saint-Michel*," *BSJV* 151:16.

10   [Aug.? 68] to Pierre; [11 Aug. 68]; [Jun.? 68] to Pierre; [3 Jun. 68].

11   *22* Jul. 69, *Int.* 18; Ducrest 85.

12   ADF 127; ADF 116, citing Wallut.

13   [Aug.? 68] to Pierre; [Aug.? 68] to Pierre.

14   [16 Aug. 68]; 23 Jul. 68.

15   [31? May 69]; [14 Jul. 69]; [28? Jul. 70] in *BSJV* 144:10.

16   ADF 124; [19 Aug. 68], [Aug.? 68] to Pierre; [11? Jun. 69]; [14 Jul. 69].

17   *BSJV* 136:23; JJV 46.

18   [Feb.? 67]; [Aug.? 68] to Pierre.

19   The poster is reproduced in CNM 152.

13. Gathering Clouds: 1868–71 (pp. 201–15)

1   This section does not benefit from a contemporary brainwave scan, but simply attempts to assemble ideas attributable to Verne at this time, including those in unpublished documents.

2   This sketch of the scene where Verne invents Fogg is based on the unpublished manuscript of *Around the World*.

3   Cited and intelligently commented in Martin, *Jules Verne*, 319–21, although encountering an astonishing silence among most commentators since then.

4   As follows (in rounded-down 000s, averaged across the one, two, or three volumes of each novel): *Five Weeks*: 15 (small format), 22 (large format); *Hatteras*: 7, 28; *Journey to the Center of the Earth*: 9, 22; *From the Earth to the Moon*: 8, 15; *Grant*: 6, 19; *Twenty Thousand Leagues*: 4, n/a; *Around the Moon*: 4, n/a. Confirmation that the tendency continued over the subsequent works is provided in a 1906 document (detailed in the Bibliography below), which indicates total small-format sales for the 17 worst selling novels as 101,000, and the large-format sales, 229,000, a ratio of 2.3.

5   The profit for the publisher on the first seven small-format novels was FF 64,429, for the author, 7,666. For the five large-format editions, the figures were respectively 118,358 and a suspiciously round 18,000.

6   For the foreign rights, all or most of the income came from the illustrations rather than the text: here, Hetzel apparently kept all the profit.

7   23 Jul. 68; 30 Sep. 68 to Pierre

8   Compère, *La Vie amiénoise*, 59.

9   7 May *67* to Pierre; [9 or 16 Feb. 77].

10   [8 Jun. 69].

11   [17 Jul. 67]; *BB* ii.

12   [1 May 68]; [4 May 70]; [17? Feb. 70].

13   ADF 186; Volker Dehs, "Les Belles soirées de Claudius B.," *BSJV* 140:64.

14   Charles-Noël Martin, "Recherches sur les maîtresses de Jules Verne," *BSJV* 56:292.

15   Lottman 146; Ion Hobana, cited by Martin, "Recherches," 292; Jean-Michel Margot, "Jules Verne et le Portugal," *BSJV* 61:176. However, the Swiss visit(s) may have been in about 1859–60, since a "Mme Witz," probable author of *Un Roman à Montreux* (Geneva: Georg, 1877), writes: "22 January 1876 / My Dear Verne / It's now 15 years since I left Montreux. Both of us spent two happy winters there [together]. . . / With your health improved, you returned to Paris" (in *JVEST* 125).

16   Hobana cited by Martin 292.

17   Hobana cited by Martin 295.

18   Hobana cited by Martin 295.

19   [14 Aug. 70]; Lemire 127.

20   The great-niece claimed he was in the Coastguard, defending Le Crotoy with the *St. Michel*, 12 Crimean War veterans, three flintlock guns, and his rusty signaling cannon and bravely patrolling far out to sea (ADF 131).

21   [Nov.?] 70 to Pierre, 13 Jan. *71*.

22   13 Jan. *71*, JJV 108.

23   [6 Aug. 70], [31 Aug. 70].

24   [Jul.? 71] to Pierre, ADF 133, RD 97.

25   [4 Nov. 71], ADF 135.

26   RD 97, [4 Nov. 71].

14. End of Exploration: 1871–72 (pp. 217–28)

1   22 *Apr. 71*; [Feb. 72].

2   Cécile Compère, "Extrapolations autour d'un acte de mariage," *BSJV* 62:214.

3   29 Jan. *66* to Pierre.

4   20 Sep. 70 to Pierre, *JVEST* 45.

5   [16 Jun. 77]; [16 or 17 Apr. 77] to Hetzel *fils*.

6   ADF 152; Compère, *La Vie amiénoise*, 34.

7   This clause is difficult to reconcile with the approximately FF 2,500 per volume for the serialization rights noted above. The contract clearly says all serializations in "journals and reviews": perhaps magazines were not deemed included, or perhaps Hetzel thought the clause did not apply to in-house deals.

8   [14 May 75]; [15 May 75].

9   D'Ocagne 291.

10   I list the handful of studies of the manuscripts on the nonposthumous Extraordinary Voyages in "Verne en version originale," in Jean-Pierre Picot and Christian Robin (eds.), *Jules Verne cent ans après* (Nantes: Terre de Brume, 2005), 35–51.

11   Butcher, "Introduction," *Twenty Thousand Leagues*.

12   Among the handful of exceptions are some of the short stories, *Clovis Dardentor*, with just one embarkation in Sète, and *Robur-the-Conqueror*, where the hero flies over Paris but without stopping.

13   The 32nd folio of the first manuscript contains a vital early sketch of chapter 1, upside-down in the left margin. The first two lines are lightly crossed out, not indicated in my transcription.

14   ADF 140, *Int.* 148.

15   *Le Moniteur*, 27 Dec. 1873; *Le Constitutionnel*, 20 Dec. 1873.

16   *JVEST* 43–44.

17   For this reason Verne reportedly expressed "enmity for American publishers" in about 1896 (visit by Edward Bok, reported by David McAllister, *Extraordinary Voyages* (1996), 6).

18   Mercier Lewis's translation of *Twenty Thousand Leagues* (London: Sampson Low, 1872); some howlers are cited by Miller, "Jules Verne in America," in *Twenty Thousand Leagues under the Sea* (1966), vii-xxii.

19   I've promised my publisher not to name any names. The incriminating book can easily be found, however, in any good online bookstore (keywords "Verne," "Antarctic Mystery," "Beaver").

15. Last Paradise: 1872–79 (pp. 229–41)

1   [2? Jul. 72]; [17 Aug. 72].

2   *JVEST* 44, *Int.* 216, RD 109, ADF 162.

3   *JVEST* 43, [*BSJV* 130:36].

4   28 July 73; 3 Sep. 73.

5   *Hector Servadac* I xvi.

6   [26 Feb. 74], [1 Mar. 74].

7   15 Sep. 77; [26 Jan. 75].

8   [3 Feb. 75]; [10 Feb. 75].

9   16 Feb. 75 in *BSJV* 140:59.

10   ADF 162, CNM 218.

11   *Le Bien public*, 29 Oct. 1877.

12   In the *Journal d'Amiens*, 29–30 Sept. 1873; the translation appeared on http://home.netvigator.com/~wbutcher/articles/24m.htm.

13   An online article, reproducing the cut chapters, appears on http://home.netvigator.com/~wbutcher/articles/IN%20Manuscript.doc.

14   Lemire 11; 24 Apr. 66 to Pierre.

15   ADF 138, CNM 196.

16   *Int.* 43; 28 Mar. 68.

17   22 Jun. 72; JD 275.

18   *Int.* 18; *Int.* 26.

19   *Int.* 42; ADF 100; *Le Figaro*, 8 Nov. 74, cited by ADF 141.

20   *Int.* 18; Hector Malot, cited by Lemire 29.

21   *JVEST* 46; Maurice Verne, cited by ADF 121.

22   In 1858 Jules composed the music for a song written by Pierre (*Annales* 18). But his love also had a utilitarian streak, for ten of the twelve musicians cited in *Twenty Thousand Leagues* were opera composers put on at the Lyric Theater, mostly by himself (*BSJV* 125:22).

16. Freedom, Music, and the Sea: 1876–80 (pp. 243–53)

1   13K was Verne's asking price when he sold it, but he dropped to 8K (12 Oct. 76 to Abel Le Marchand in PV 113); PV 113.

2   [27 Jun. 76]; PV 103.

3   17 *Apr.* 77; [4 Jun. 77]; [18 Jun. 77]; [18 Jun. 77].

4   *St. M.*, 5 Aug. 77.

5   5 Oct. 77 to Abel Le Marchand in PV 111.

6   RD 107–09, cf. CNM 218.
7   St. M, [12 Apr. 78]; [25 Apr. 78]; [12 Apr. 78].
8   28 Sep. 01 to Hetzel *fils* in *BSJV* 58:54.
9   *BSJV* 58:53, CNM 218.
10   *Le Phare de la Loire*, 8–9 July 1878.
11   *BSJV* 58:53; PV 128; [24 Aug. 78]; 8 Sep. 78.
12   11 Sep. 78; *BSJV* 58:53, 13 Oct. 78.
13   Guillon 136.
14   29 Jan. 89; Dumas 225, arguing from "Michel's just spent a week here after working on the novel for which I gave him the idea and which will be an extension of the ones I do. He certainly has remarkable writing ability" (12 Oct. 95).
15   [mid-Aug. 77]; [13 May 77]; 5 Aug. *77*; [mid-Aug. 77]; 31 *Aug. 77*; 11 Jan. 78.
16   24 Jan. 79 to Captain Eymery.
17   *The Barsac Mission* (1914) II xi-xii.
18   [13 May 77]; [2 Jun. 77].
19   6 Jun. 77 to Hetzel *fils* in *BSJV* 137:44.
20   [18 Jun. 77]; RD 103.
21   1 Nov. 77. Two biographers claim that the apartment had been rented since 1873/74 (CNM 194, JJV 128).
22   24 Jan. 79 to Captain Eymery.
23   ADF 163; 31 Dec. 79; *BSJV* 154:42.

17. Salvation through Work: 1879–83 (pp. 255–68)

1   23 Nov. 75; 26 Nov. 75.
2   *Michel Strogoff*, critical edition by Louis Bilodeau (Exeter: Exeter UP, 1994), xxi. The play was also banned.
3   27 Mar. 76; 23 Oct. 76.
4   *BSJV* 130:46; *JVEST* 155.
5   Lemire 136; 9 Feb. 80.
6   Bilodeau xliii.
7   22 Aug. 52; to Pierre *Int.* 101; *Int.* 90.
8   With friend and honorary Colonnader William Busnach, an experienced adapter, and Georges Maurens (*BSJV* 130:3)
9   *Le XIX ͤ siècle*, 11 Sept. 1883; *Le Soleil*, 10 Sept. 1883; *La Presse*, 10 Sept. 1883.
10   Cited by Compère, *La Vie amiénoise*, 58.
11   *BSJV* 100:7; *22* Jul. 69; [25? Feb. 70]; [3 Oct. 67].
12   Costello 41.
13   "Ten Hours Hunting" x-xi.
14   "The First Ships of the Mexican Navy"; *Tribulations of a Chinese in China* iv.
15   Ian Thompson, in private correspondence, has confirmed the similarity between Verne's own journey and that described in *The Green Ray* (where the ship from Glasgow was spelled *Columbia*.)
16   PV 131; 29 Jul. 79.
17   [23 Aug. 79], *St. M.*
18   2 Sep. *79*; PV 132.
19   26 *Sep. 79*; [2 May 80].
20   PV 142. However, *St. M* says "17 July."

21 Bastard 350.
22 26 *Sep. 79*; 30 Dec. 84.
23 *JVEST* 46.
24 *The Green Ray* i.
25 6 Mar. *82*; [26 Feb. 82].
26 Boia, *Jules Verne*, 238.
27 *Topsy-Turvy* ii.
28 Private communication from Masataka Ishibashi.
29 The hero's name was taken from Jules Claretie's Hungarian *Prince Zilah*, full name "Prince Zilah Sandor" (2 Mar. 85 in Lemire 96).
30 29 May 85 to Verne.
31 Martin, *Jules Verne*, 321.

18. Home Front: 1882–90 (pp. 269–82)

1 *BSJV* 155:59; 24 Dec. 82.
2 [Jan. 79] in *BSJV* 103:20.
3 [14 Mar. 78]; RD 114.
4 Bastard 352; RD 83–84.
5 *BSJV* 114:49–55 and 118:44–45; *Int.* 172.
6 *Int.* 104, *Int.*116, Lemire 31, *Int.* 43–45.
7 Maurice Garet, "Jules Verne, amiénois," *BSJV* (first series), vol. 1, no. 3 (May 1936), 115–35.
8 Maurice's notebook of the trip cited by ADF 166.
9 Ducrest states that the party visited the Balearic Islands before Oran (RD 110), but this seems implausible.
10 *BSJV* 145:23, JJV 124.
11 Ian Thompson, "New Light on the Visit to Malta by Jules Verne in June 1884," *Extraordinary Voyages*, vol. 12, no. 2 (December 2005), 10–12.
12 ADF 168, *BSJV* 145:23, PV 150.
13 *Lottery Ticket* xvii.
14 Volker Dehs, *Jules Verne* (Dusseldorf: Artemis and Winkler, 2005), JD 350; Dehs, *Jules Verne*, citing Ange Galdemar, "Un Après-midi chez M. Jules Verne," *Le Gaulois*, 28 Oct. 1895; PV 154.
15 Christian Robin, "Verne tous azimuts," *Cahiers de l'Académie de Bretagne et des Pays de la Loire*, vol. 25 (1998), 139–50.
16 JJV 125, Lemire 48, RD 110.
17 ADF 169; JD 350, citing Verne's logbook.
18 ADF 169; *BSJV* 145:25.
19 JJV 125; *Int.* 118.
20 *St. M.*, [7 Aug. *79*].
21 Principally Martin's and Dehs's various publications.
22 Martin, *Jules Verne*, 321; Dehs, *Jules Verne* (2005), Appendix 2.
23 Lemire 54, CNM 227.
24 RD 111; ADF 172
25 24 Aug. 86 to Dumas *fils.*
26 JD 356, *Int.* 56. The bullet must presumably still be underground in Amiens, conceivably detectable to keen researchers with metal-detectors.

27   Norbert Percereau, "Les Disparus d'Yverdon-les-Bains ou le tragique destin de Marcel Verne," *BSJV* 151:21.
28   Lemire 56, JJV 200.
29   Dusseau 356; *20* Apr. *86* to Hetzel *fils*; [early Jun. 86] to Hetzel *fils*.
30   The parents' net worth when Pierre died was FF 438,000.
31   Garmt de Vries and Kees Waij, "Les Deux voyages faits par Jules Verne en Belgique et aux Pays Bas," *Revue Jules Verne*, nos. 19–20, 138–47.
32   11 May 88 to a friend called Charles, in ADF 181.
33   Compère, *La Vie amiénoise*, 67–71.
34   He was honored (1892) only on the insistence of Frédéric Petit, mayor of Amiens; his sponsor was Robert Godefroy (Lemire 127).
35   [6 Dec. 51] to Pierre; *Nov.?* 70 to Pierre; letter of 71 to Pierre.
36   Lemire 61; 30 Oct. 98 to Turiello; Compère, *La Vie amiénoise*, 62.
37   [9? Jul. 56] to Pierre; JJV 63.
38   *7* Apr. 51; 6 Nov. 67.
39   RD 82; Nadar in *BSJV* 131:48; Duquesnel (1909), 45.
40   "I have not yet read the Extraordinary Journeys of M. Verne. Our friend [Léon] Aubineau tells me they are charming, except for one absence . . . which leaves the marvels of the world an enigma. All is beautiful but inanimate. Someone is missing" (in OD 214).

19. Heading for the Hundredth: 1890–1905 (pp. 283–95)

1   12 Feb. 96 to Étienne Richet in *BSJV* 55:248–49.
2   Cited by Duquesnel (1909), 45.
3   *Int.* 222; Lemire 38.
4   *Int.* 106; *Int.* 61; *Int.* 223.
5   *Int.* 183; *Int.* 156, Lemire 38; *Int.* 187.
6   *Int.* 41; Dr. Fournier, cited by Lemire 24.
7   Turiello 1901; Amicis 702.
8   *Int.* 68; *Int.* 20; *Int.* 225.
9   The 2,000 endnotes to my critical editions of *Journey to the Centre of the Earth* (219–31), *Around the World* (213–47), *Twenty Thousand Leagues* (385–445), and *Hatteras* (367–402).
10   *Int.* 205; 207; 224; 223; 203; 224.
11   *Int.* 192 *BSJV* 125:8; *Int.* 188; Fergusson, in *BSJV* 154; *Int.* 223; 203; 224; 192; 188; JD 401; *Int.* 187; 263; 2 Mar. 95 to Turiello.
12   "Jules Verne's Hundredth" 5–8.
13   Text cited by Dehs, "Les Belles soirées," 60.
14   17 Aug. 90 to Dr. Félix in *BSJV* 88:15.
15   21 Aug. 94 to Paul; 7 Dec. 97 to Maurice Verne in *BSJV* 155:60.
16   *Int.* 130; *Int.* 61, given his output of two novels a year.
17   *Int.* 96, Lemire 41, ADF 183, JJV 200.
18   10 Sep. 94 to Mario Turiello (*Europe*, May 1980, 108–38).
19   13 Feb. 91 to Hetzel *fils*; 8 Aug. 94.
20   Jean Jules-Verne, "Souvenir de mon grand-père," *L'Herne*, 112–16.
21   [23 Mar. 05] from Marie Verne to a family member, in CNM 250.
22   Compère, *La Vie amiénoise*, 44.

23   JJV x; JJV 199.

24   JJV x; *Int.* 222.

25   17 Aug. 90 to Dr. Félix in *BSJV* 88:15; 15 Oct. 98.

26   JJV 178; JJV 193.

27   Jean Jules-Verne, "Souvenirs de mon grand-*père*," *L'Herne*, 112–15.

28   20 Dec. 00 and 6 Jan. 01 to Turiello, in *Europe*, 58 (May 1980), 128. That summer his eyesight was no better: "he can no longer read, no longer write" (*Int.* 156).

29   ADF 212; 15 Oct. 04.

30   O. Dumas, "Quand Michel Verne fait flèche de tout bois," *BSJV* 154:42

31   Jan Feith, "Le Globe-trotter chez lui," *BSJV* 145:10.

32   Percereau, "Les Disparus," 19.

33   *L'Album Mariani*, vol. 3 (Paris: Henry Floury, 1897), 76.

34   *Int.* 148; VA viii.

35   Martin, Ph. D., 232, estimates 20 million.

36   Martin, *Jules Verne*, 321; Dehs, *Jules Verne* (2005), Appendix 2.

37   [23 Mar. 05] from Marie Verne to a family member, in CNM 250.

38   Elisabeth Léger de Viane, "L'Entourage familial de Jules Verne," in *Visions nouvelles sur Jules Verne* (Amiens: Centre de documentation Jules Verne, 1978), 20–7.

Epilogue: Communing with the Dead (pp. 297–99)

1   The letter by Michel in April 1905 mentioning "six short stories of which two are completely unpublished," probably referred to "Pierre-Jean" and "Humbug," although "Edom" cannot be excluded (*BSJV* 142:58). In the context of the complete underground nation in Scotland, as described in *The Black Indies*, Hetzel wrote: "the pleasure of rediscovering your hypothesis of 'In Two Thousand Years' Time' misled you" (2 Jan. 77).

Bibliography (pp. 307–29)

1   This section benefits from Dehs, *Guide*, 80–85, especially for some of the comments on the books.

2   With acknowledgment to OD. Where based on a manuscript by someone else, the year refers to Verne's work, rather than the original composition.

3   All in both the *Magasin* and the series of Extraordinary Journeys, except where marked. "(Hetzel)" means that the novel was not serialized; "(*Débats*)," that it appeared in the *Journal des débats politiques et littéraires*.

4   In Hetzel unillustrated editions by 31 March 1905. The multi-volume works have been averaged across the volumes. The total French nonserial print run was more than three times as great (see ch. 13 above).

5   Based on a script cowritten with Cadol.

6   A few pages were written by Hetzel.

7   A few pages were written by Hetzel.

8   Based on a manuscript by Laurie, with some pages written by Hetzel.

9   Based on a manuscript by Laurie.

10   Based on a manuscript by Laurie, but published as by "Jules Verne and André Laurie."

11   Not published in the Extraordinary Journeys.

12   The second row shows large-format sales of less than 20,000. Where the fourth line is absent, sales exceeded 20,000 (Dehs, "Les Tirages," 91).

13   Based on a manuscript by Jean Chaffanjon.

14   *San Carlos et autres récits inédits* (Paris: Cherche Midi, 1993).

15   Edited by Michel Verne.

16   Original manuscript of *The Mysterious Island.*

17   Original manuscript of *Le Pilote du Danube* (1908, *The Pilot of the Danube*).

18   Original manuscript of *Les Naufragés du "Jonathan"* (1909, *The Survivors of the "Jonathan"*).

19   Published in a version edited by Michel Verne.

20   Unfinished manuscript, added to and published by Michel Verne as *L'Étonnante aventure de la mission Barsac,* (1914, *The Barsac Mission*).

21   Published as "L'Éternel Adam" ("The Eternal Adam"), added to and revised by Michel Verne.

22   The table appears with acknowledgment to Jean-Michel Margot, "Jules Verne: The Successful, Wealthy Playwright," *Extraordinary Voyages*, Oct. 2005, 10–16.

23   Other title *Un Drame sous la Régence* (*A Drama During the Regency*).

24   Other title *Cesar Borgia.*

25   Revivals: Nantes, 7 November 1850; Théâtre du Gymnase, 1853 (45 performances); Théâtre du Gymnase, 1871 (40 performances).

26   54 performances in 1883.

27   The book was published as eight individual articles: "Artists' Portraits: XVIII" ("Portraits d'artistes:XVIII"), 115–16, "The 1857 Salon: Introductory Articel" ("Salon de 1857: Article préliminaire"), 231–34, "The 1857 Salon: First Article" ("Salon de 1857: Premier article"), 2491–54, "The 1857 Salon: Second Article" ("Salon de 1857: Article Deuxi´me article"), 269–75, "The 1857 Salon: Third Article" ("Salon de 1857: Troisiéme article"), 285–91, "The 1857 Salon: Fourth Article" ("Salon de 1857: Quatiriéme article"), 305–13, "The 1857 Salon: Fifth Article" ("Salon de 1857: Cinquiéme article"), 325–30, "The 1857 Salon: Sixth Article" ("Salon de 1857: Sixiéme article"), 345–49,

28   Théophile Lavallée wrote the introduction and the first draft of chapters 1–13.

29   Extracts are cited in Piero Gondolo della Riva, "Un patrimoine à découvrir," *Revue Jules Verne*, No. 16 (2003), 43–64.

INDEX

References to WSM: 331, 343, 346, 312

---

255 - derisory?   258 - "...in no case could
Verne be considered a s – f – writer." !!
The term wld not be invented for another 60 yrs

Arthur Evans' "Early Classics of S-F-" ? used
260 - TROPE ?   to call it fiction abt sci
266 - But WB pictures TV as non-science (fiction)
   ditto 267 268   271 BELVEDERE

280-282 BELIEFS   284- vague on Turpin, as
tho rdr knows the case
286 - excellent on journalist interviewers

that it was
called "horseless
carriage" did no
deny fact that
it was an
automobile

111 ff - good estimate of JV at -28?

130 - V's art crit reflects 19th C. rel betw art
    + lit - teamwork of illustrator + author

131 - incredibly long time "stuck" in wrong medium

CH 8 - very good   142 - ditto   DOWDY 143

155 - a surprise for those of us who've been
    insisting he was an <u>adult</u> author — Was the
    limit put on all Hetzel writers? Is it fair
    now to insist he was not <s>just</s> a children's
    writer but rather a <s>family</s> author?
    "partly juvenile"? a <u>YA</u> writer?!

the mutiny theme - oedipal base?   [161 - pronoun
158 - 160 excellent analysis   case]

343 - ugm ed of <u>FTETTM</u> - ignores intro of
annotated ed

171 - AL FRESCO dinners   172 - eyes + tears

182 - extreme guesses, for effect

188 ff — the big problem - we have to accept
    the book that JV signed w his by-line. It's
    different w a posthumous work like <u>TMM</u>.

203 - a nice experiment in biog

209 - def of 19th C novel

222 - an innovation in W Lit -

237 - fraught

250 - JV intimated "passing off" process himself - i.e.,
    letting Michel use JV's name as sole author?

xxvi — a mass of tentative charges, paradoxes, and revelations, any small sampling of which would have reduced the reader, becomes instead a massive confusion — overdone, self-defeating

9 — mother-in-law's intrusions vaguely handled

11 — ditto on "bedrooms lashed off the back"

12 — "muscadin" 13 WB good on SLAVE TRADE, his own exposé making rdr wonder re relation to JV's racism

15 — a typical missing source, rarely missed

16 — good on Pierre's self-flagellation & effect on JV

17 — WB wonders whether corporal punishment by Pierre would have affected JV's sense of justice (altho he admits it was the time's way) + his lifelong timidity

60 — ".thyphallic"

84 — From the first short story — "The First Ships of the Mexican Navy" — to his latest work, The Key Brothers — JV is interested in "getting rid of the captain." This is a clear oedipal trend, getting rid of Pierre.

Ch. 5 — WB at last is thinking & wtg well, putting facts together into good original interpretation

93 — bore the brunt

Ch 6 — really rolling now

112 — guanxi